PERU AND THE UNITED STATES, 1960–1975

RICHARD J. WALTER

PERU AND THE UNITED STATES, 1960– 1975

HOW THEIR AMBASSADORS MANAGED FOREIGN RELATIONS IN A TURBULENT ERA

THE
PENNSYLVANIA
STATE
UNIVERSITY
PRESS
UNIVERSITY
PARK,
PENNSYLVANIA

Library of Congress Cataloging-in-Publication Data

Walter, Richard J.
Peru and the United States, 1960–1975 : how their ambassadors managed foreign relations in a turbulent era / Richard J. Walter.
   p.   cm.
Includes bibliographical references and index.
Summary: "Examines relations between Peru and the United States for the period 1960–1975. Focuses on the roles of both nations' ambassadors in trying to deal with the difficult foreign policy issues that arose in these years"—Provided by publisher.
ISBN 978-0-271-03631-1 (cloth : alk. paper)
ISBN 978-0-271-03632-8 (pbk. : alk. paper)
1. United States—Foreign relations—Peru.
2. Peru—Foreign relations—United States.
3. Ambassadors—United States—History—20th century.
4. Ambassadors—Peru—History—20th century.
I. Title.

E183.8.P4W35 2010
327.73085090'04—dc22
                              2009036196

Copyright © 2010 The Pennsylvania State University
All rights reserved
Printed in the United States of America
Published by The Pennsylvania State University Press,
University Park, PA 16802–1003

The Pennsylvania State University Press is a member of the Association of American University Presses.

It is the policy of The Pennsylvania State University Press to use acid-free paper. Publications on uncoated stock satisfy the minimum requirements of American National Standard for Information Sciences—Permanence of Paper for Printed Library Material, ANSI Z39.48–1992.

for GUS AND LUKE

CONTENTS

List of Illustrations   viii
Acknowledgments   x

Introduction   1
1 Peru and JFK   6
2 Belaúnde, LBJ, and the "Mann Doctrine"   38
3 Belaúnde, the Counterguerrilla Campaign, and the Role of the United States   62
4 Belaúnde's Position Begins to Crumble   87
5 The End of the Belaúnde Administration   114
6 The Coup and Its Aftermath   142
7 Velasco and the Nixon Administration   168
8 Public and Private Negotiations   205
9 Continuity and Some Change   224
10 Change, Crisis, and Continuity   249
11 Nixon and Velasco Exit the Scene   279
Conclusion   310

Bibliography   321
Index   328

ILLUSTRATIONS

1. President Lyndon B. Johnson and Assistant Secretary of State for Inter-American Affairs Thomas Mann. (Courtesy of the LBJ Presidential Library.)
2. President Johnson with Latin American ambassadors. (Courtesy of the LBJ Presidential Library.)
3. President Johnson with his Latin American foreign policy team. (Courtesy of the LBJ Presidential Library.)
4. President Johnson and Jack Hood Vaughn, director of the Peace Corps. (Courtesy of the LBJ Presidential Library.)
5. President Johnson meeting with U.S. Ambassador John Wesley Jones and Covey T. Oliver. (Courtesy of the LBJ Presidential Library.)
6. President Johnson and Assistant Secretary Oliver. (Courtesy of the LBJ Presidential Library.)
7. President Johnson and Ambassador Jones. (Courtesy of the LBJ Presidential Library.)
8. Fernando Berckemeyer, Peruvian ambassador to the United States. (Reprinted with permission of *El Comercio*.)
9. Fernando Belaúnde Terry, president of Peru. (Reprinted with permission of *El Comercio*.)
10. General Edgardo Mercado Jarrín, foreign minister of Peru. (Reprinted with permission of *El Comercio*.)
11. Celso Pastor de la Torre, Peruvian ambassador to the United States. (Reprinted with permission of *El Comercio*.)
12. General Miguel Angel De la Flor, foreign minister of Peru. (Reprinted with permission of *El Comercio*.)
13. General Juan Velasco Alvarado, president of Peru. (Reprinted with permission of *El Comercio*.)

14. President Richard M. Nixon speaking to the Organization of American States. (Courtesy of the Nixon Presidential Library, National Archives and Records Administration.)
15. President Nixon (center front) with his cabinet. (Courtesy of the Nixon Presidential Library, National Archives and Records Administration.)

ACKNOWLEDGMENTS

This book could not have been completed without the generous support of many individuals and institutions. In Peru, my *cuñados*, Ignacio Basombrio and Felipe Valcárcel, assisted me in my research and provided me with their special insights into Peruvian history and politics. Miriam Campodonico helped enormously in arranging the interviews I conducted in Lima in the summer of 2003. I owe a great debt to those interviewed—former foreign ministers General Edgardo Mercado Jarrín and José de la Puente Radbill, former Peruvian ambassador Celso Pastor de la Torre, and former government minister and close friend of President Fernando Belaúnde Terry, Octavio Mongrut—for taking the time to talk with me. Rosa Garibaldi, a pioneer Peruvian diplomat and accomplished historian, was especially helpful in aiding me in gaining access to the Foreign Ministry archives and to the correspondence of Peru's ambassadors to the United States. In the archive, its director, Iván Pinto Román and his staff, were welcoming and attentive and made my work there both pleasant and productive. The staff of the Biblioteca Nacional del Peru were also most helpful. Finally, my niece, María Pía Valcárcel helped me enormously in acquiring the photographs from the archives of *El Comercio*.

In the United States, my research was greatly aided by the efforts of the staff at the National Archives in College Park, Maryland; the Lyndon Baines Johnson Library and Museum in Austin, Texas; and the Olin Library at Washington University. The dean of the faculty at Washington University in St. Louis, Edward Macias, provided generous research support over the years this project proceeded. Washington University students Gilles Bissonnette and Tanya Roth aided me in my research and the preparation of the book manuscript. I also owe thanks to Dan Hellinger, Peter Klaren, Cynthia McClintock, and Daniel M. Masterson for their advice and assistance.

Finally, as always, this book could not have been completed without the constant support and assistance of my wife, Susana, always by my side.

INTRODUCTION

Historically, relations between Peru and the United States have been, as representatives from both sides have frequently stated, "warm and friendly." As a result, Peru has rarely been a top priority or concern for the United States in formulating and implementing its overall policies toward Latin America. Between 1960 and 1975, however, some notable exceptions occurred. In 1962, a military coup in Peru provided an important test case for the administration of John F. Kennedy in trying to promote civilian democracy in the region as it wrestled with whether to recognize the military government. The ultimate decision to extend recognition had significant repercussions not only for relations between the two nations but also for Latin America. Between 1963 and 1968, the administration of Lyndon B. Johnson tangled with Peru over issues involving the expropriation of a major U.S. investor in that country, the International Petroleum Company (IPC), and Peru's determination to establish a 200-mile limit for its territorial waters. These matters, as well as a counterguerrilla campaign in 1965 and 1966, attracted a fair amount of U.S. press coverage. Finally, between 1968 and 1975, the administrations of Richard M. Nixon and Gerald R. Ford had to grapple with the nationalist policies of a reformist military regime that took an even harder position on issues of expropriation and fishing rights than did its civilian predecessor and which also sought to chart a more independent foreign policy that included establishing relations, both diplomatic and commercial, with the Soviet Union, the People's Republic of China, and Cuba.

The general outlines of these developments are well known and have been covered extensively in a variety of essays, articles, and books. Drawing on a wide range of primary and secondary material, especially recently declassified U.S. State Department records, as well as from the Foreign Ministry archives of Peru, I intend in this study to provide a more detailed and nuanced examination of relations between the two nations in these years. Moreover, unlike other treatments of the diplomatic history of this period, I shall try to give equal weight to both sides of the story, the United States' and Peru's. Much attention will be paid to the views and roles of the respective ambassadors of the two nations. Their actions, in turn, will be placed within the context of larger political, economic, and diplomatic developments.

While many studies of U.S.–Latin American relations have emphasized the role of U.S. policy-makers and diplomats, the reverse has been less true. Prominent U.S. ambassadors to the region have written their own extensive memoirs, which usually justify or explain more fully their actions at their posts. Again, this has not typically been the case for Latin American diplomats. By highlighting the role of Peru's ambassadors to the United States, then, I am attempting again to redress the balance and to provide a fuller picture of the overall relationship. Much of my discussion of the Peruvian ambassadors' activities in Washington, D.C., comes from their correspondence to the Foreign Ministry in Lima, drawing on material that hitherto has not been used by historians of that nation's relationship with the United States.

With one notable exception, these Peruvian and North American ambassadors were either career diplomats or persons with considerable experience in living and studying abroad. They were also, mostly, keen observers of the domestic political scene in their respective posts and showed a serious commitment to their responsibilities of representing their nations' best interests. There was, of course, an asymmetry in their positions. The ambassador of the United States, representing the major power in the hemisphere, if not the world, oversaw an embassy of more than one hundred officials and staff and was clearly the most important foreign representative in the country. The Peruvian embassy, however, had officials and staff of between fifteen and twenty persons, representing a mid-level Latin American country, and was overshadowed in significance not only by the diplomatic missions of the major global powers but also by the larger and more influential Latin American nations. As a result, the Peruvian ambassador had only infrequent contact with and access to the president of the United States and met only a bit more frequently with the secretary of state. Most of his major connections and conversations were with the assistant secretary of state for Inter-American Affairs and State Department desk officers. The U.S. ambassador in Peru, however, had much greater access to the president of that country as well as his foreign minister and other important governmental figures. Indeed, on at least one occasion, during an attempt in 1968 to resolve the IPC controversy, the U.S. ambassador was a vital player in the Peruvian government's actions. Of perhaps greater value to the historian, however, this access allowed the U.S. ambassador to report, often in confidence, back to Washington certain insights into and details about the Peruvian presidents that allow for a much fuller picture of their personalities, their motivations, and their actions than has heretofore been available. Recently declassified material from the diplomatic records also sheds greater light on some of the behind-the-scenes maneuvering that took place as both sides addressed the challenges and crises that arose in the relationship.

The four main ambassadors of this period, two for the United States and two for Peru, had the advantage of serving for a significant time. For the United States, Ambassador John Wesley Jones was in Lima from 1963 to 1969 during most of the presidency of Fernando Belaúnde Terry (1963–1968) and the beginnings of the military government of General Juan Velasco Alvarado (1968–1975). His successor, Taylor Belcher, served from 1969 to 1974 and was followed by another career diplomat, Robert Dean. For Peru, Fernando Berckemeyer had already been in place as ambassador for some time when Kennedy was elected president in 1960, and he served until the election of Belaúnde in 1963. He returned to his post in 1968 and served until 1974, when he was replaced by Admiral José Arce Larco. Between 1963 and 1968, Belaúnde's brother-in-law, Celso Pastor de la Torre, was Peru's representative in Washington. Such extensive service aided their comprehension of the political dynamics in their respective posts (not to say that it was always precise or perfect) and in establishing the necessary personal and professional contacts to advance the policies and the interests of their respective nations.

Using the ambassadors and their actions as a basic framework, a number of questions will be addressed in this study. For example, to what extent did these representatives have an accurate understanding of the larger society in which they operated, and how perceptive were they with regard to political developments in their respective posts? It is often alleged that diplomatic difficulties and strains in relations develop because of a failure of one side to understand or appreciate the position of the other or, in the particular case of the United States, to show sensitivity to the culture in which its representatives operate. Popularly, they often have been derided as "striped-pants cookie pushers." Was that the case for the U.S. representatives in Peru?

Were failures to communicate common and important in the relationship? On the U.S. side, what was the role of the ambassador and the U.S. embassy in promoting and protecting the interests of the U.S. business community in Peru, especially with regard to the IPC? Was the embassy, as many charged at the time and afterward, simply acting as the company's advocate or were there also larger concerns at play? What role did personal factors play in this and other aspects of U.S.-Peruvian interaction in these years?

There are other questions to be addressed. What was the role of the U.S. Central Intelligence Agency (CIA) in Peru during this period? Some assert that the agency was active in both the counterinsurgency campaign of the mid-1960s and in efforts to weaken or to encourage the overthrow of the Velasco regime. What does the evidence suggest? Did the CIA intervene directly in the nation's internal affairs? Moreover, how accurate were the CIA's predictions about the course of events in Peru in these years?

The actions of the CIA in Peru were usually clandestine, and charges of interference usually lacked hard proof. However, another form of what Peruvians considered intervention and intimidation in their internal affairs involved various amendments to foreign aid bills passed by the U.S. Congress during the 1960s to punish any nation that expropriated U.S.-owned properties without compensation or captured U.S. fishing vessels in disputed waters. While Peru was only one of a large number of nations to which these amendments could be applied, it appeared to be a principal target of them. What role did these amendments play in the overall relationship between the two countries and how effective were they?

In seeking to answer these questions, I will follow a straightforward chronological and narrative trajectory. The chronological parameters have been determined to some extent by this gap in the literature as well as the availability of the documentary evidence. From the Peruvian side, the story begins essentially near the end of the administration of President Manuel Prado y Ugarteche (1956–1962) and ends with the resignation of General Velasco from the presidency in late 1975. From the U.S. side, I start basically from the presidency of John F. Kennedy (1961–1963) and conclude in the middle of the administration of Gerald R. Ford (1974–1977). The major presidential players, however, were Johnson and Belaúnde and Nixon and Velasco. I am also aware that there are many aspects of the relationship between Peru and the United States that had little to do with presidents, secretaries of state, foreign ministers, and ambassadors, and I mention some of these in the conclusion. These factors, including cultural exchanges, investment patterns, and the movement of Peruvians to live in the United

States, provide an important part of the larger context in which diplomats and statesmen operated.

This is an attempt to give equal time to the perspectives and actions of both nations during challenges and crises between the two. As such, it may aid policy-makers to avoid some of the misperceptions and mistakes of the past to ensure that U.S-Peruvian relations remain "warm and friendly" in the future.

1

PERU AND JFK

As was the case with most Latin Americans, Peruvians welcomed the election of John F. Kennedy as president of the United States in 1960, seeing it as the possibility of a fresh start in relations between the two nations. The announcement and implementation of an ambitious program of assistance, the much-ballyhooed Alliance for Progress, designed to encourage social and economic development to forestall violent revolution and to promote democracy in the region, bolstered these hopes. Peru was to be one of the main targets for Alliance for Progress funding and received considerable attention from Kennedy and his advisors. Alliance hopes for Peru, however, as in many instances in Latin America, encountered some rough sledding as idealistic visions ran into the harsh realities of domestic politics that forced the Kennedy administration to change the course of its relations with that nation on several occasions. A military coup in 1962, moreover, posed a serious dilemma for administration policy-makers, the consequences of which were substantial and long term. Throughout this period, Peru was at or near the top of the U.S. foreign policy agenda regarding Latin America.

Strains in the Relationship and the Role of Peru's Ambassador to the United States

In the years immediately before Kennedy's election, certain strains had developed in Peruvian-U.S. relations. The hostile reception accorded to Vice

President Richard M. Nixon in Lima during his ill-fated 1958 good will tour of South America, highlighted by a violent confrontation with students at the University of San Marcos, led many North Americans to believe that Peru was a hotbed of anti-American sentiment.[1] Complicating matters further was a perception that aid funds to Peru were not being used efficiently or specifically for the purposes they were intended, prompting the State Department to carry out a special audit and to assert publicly that such concerns were overstated.[2] Members of Congress, however, were not convinced. On August 9, 1961, after the Alliance for Progress had been announced, Republican Congressman George Meader of Michigan read into the *Congressional Record* a committee report that alleged the aid program to Peru was characterized by "maladministration, conflict of interest, diversion of funds contrary to regulations, and incompetence." These deficiencies, he observed, were long ago reported to the appropriate aid agencies and to the State Department, apparently to little effect.[3] Finally, while Conservative Peruvian President Manuel Prado (1956–1962) had been targeted by San Marcos students during the anti-Nixon riots as a tool of Peru's oligarchy and as subservient to the interests of U.S. capital, he was, in fact, trying to reorient Peru's policies away from dependence on the United States and to achieve a greater balance in the relationship by drawing closer to Europe.[4]

Peru's ambassador in Washington, D.C., during the Prado administration, who was responsible for dealing with these strains, was Fernando Berckemeyer. Married to a North American, fluent in English, and from one of Peru's elite families, Berckemeyer was known as a "representative of big business," particularly the coastal cotton and sugar plantation owners prominent in the Sociedad Nacional Agraria (SNA, or National Agrarian Society), and was particularly concerned with trying to convince the U.S. Congress to increase its quota for the import of those commodities.[5] A State Department biography at the time described Berckemeyer as "pro-American and anti-communist and while without any clear political affiliation, close to conservative family interests influential in the [Manuel] Odría regime

---

1. Carey, *Peru and the United States, 1900–1962*, 197–98. Nixon's own view of the encounter can be found in his *Six Crises*, 192–210. The view of the students who protested the visit can be found in Reyes Flores, "San Marcos y Richard Nixon 8 de mayo de 1958."
2. U.S. Department of State, *Department of State Bulletin* [hereafter as *DOSB*] (Washington, D.C.: Government Printing Office, June 12, 1961), 923.
3. U.S. Congress, *Congressional Record—House* (Washington, D.C.: Government Printing Office, August 9, 1961), 15280–81.
4. St. John, *The Foreign Policy of Peru*, 188–19.
5. Bourricaud, *Power and Society in Contemporary Peru*, 335–36.

[1950–1956]." He was also considered strongly supportive of the Spanish dictator Francisco Franco and had received a decoration from the Spanish government. The memo also described Berckemeyer as "not a man of great intellectual ability and professional acumen, but [he] possesses poise, dignity of bearing and considerable charm" albeit at times "somewhat flamboyant." Having served as Peru's ambassador to the United States for fifteen years, longer than any of his Latin American counterparts, he and his wife had a wide circle of friends and were "very active socially."[6]

Berckemeyer's communications to Lima in the early months of 1960 provide a flavor of his activities and duties. Several dealt with the ramifications of planned visits by U.S. statesmen and opinion makers to Peru. In January, he wrote of his disappointment that President Eisenhower would not be visiting Peru on his upcoming tour of Latin America, a tour intended to take some of the sting out of Nixon's ill-fated visit to the region. In his report to the foreign minister, he appended a letter from Peter Grace (whose family company had gotten its start in Peru and still had substantial investments there), who urged the president to include Lima on his itinerary since "a visit by you would provide Peru with an opportunity to make clear that the unfortunate incidents which occurred during the visit of the Vice President in no way represents the true feelings of the Peruvians."[7] In a later communication, Berckemeyer was optimistic about plans for several North American journalists to visit Peru, where they would have an opportunity to gauge the public opinion of the country and to gain "a fuller idea of the level of development reached by South American countries in general, and to better appreciate the severe problems that they face, as well as to assess the urgency of the economic and technical assistance required from the more developed countries, especially from the United States."[8]

While most of Berckemeyer's attention was focused on Peru's relationship with the United States, he also kept the Foreign Ministry informed of any developments that might affect its relations with other Latin American nations, most especially its immediate neighbors. In late 1960, for example, he wrote about historian A. Curtis Wilgus's book *Latin America in Maps*,

6. From a memorandum of December 9, 1963, from Benjamin A. Read, executive secretary of the U.S. Department of State, to National Security Advisor McGeorge Bundy based on a biography of September 1961. National Security File [hereafter NSF], Country File, Peru Cables, Volume I, Box 72, Folder Seven, Lyndon Baines Johnson Library [hereafter LBJ Library].

7. República del Perú, Ministerio de Relaciones Exteriores, Archivo Central Raúl Porras Barrenechea, *Correspondencia desde la embajada del Perú en Washington, D.C. al Ministro de Relaciones Exteriores* (Lima: 1960–1975) (5-3-A/1), January 13, 1960, 1. Hereafter as *Correspondencia* with file number and date. For more on the Grace Company, see Clayton, *W. R. Grace and Co.*

8. *Correspondencia* (5-3-A/5) (February 26, 1960), 1–2.

in which Wilgus allegedly had incorrectly delineated the frontier between Ecuador and Peru, a matter that had led to war between the two countries in the early 1940s and which still festered as a matter of concern.[9] In response, the foreign minister, Luis Alvarado Garrido, saw this as a serious matter that could lead to misconceptions by all who consulted the book and "serve as an instrument of Ecuadorean propaganda," and he urged the ambassador to contact Wilgus and the press to set the record straight. He added that if these "errors" were not corrected, the Peruvian government might consider placing an embargo on all books produced by the presses associated with the publication.[10] Two months later, Wilgus diplomatically responded that he appreciated the points that had been brought to his attention and when the revised edition of the work was prepared he would, without guaranteeing any changes, take these "interesting and valuable" observations into account.[11]

There is no follow-up in the correspondence about what finally transpired in this affair. While it might seem trivial on the surface, it underscored the seriousness with which Peru viewed the matter and the nation's sensitivity with regard to its boundaries, especially its boundaries with Ecuador.

With regard to larger hemispheric issues, Berckemeyer reflected the Prado government's strong anticommunist position, which was accentuated and reinforced after the Cuban Revolution. An apparently trumped-up raid on the Cuban embassy in Lima late in 1960 uncovered documents that "proved" some Peruvian officials were being paid by the Fidel Castro regime, leading to the arrest of certain opponents of the Prado administration and a break in relations with Cuba as part of an overall campaign to crack down on communism and communist activities in Peru.[12] In his own reports and activities, Berckemeyer consistently stressed what he saw as the impending threat of communism in the Americas. In February 1961, for example, he gave a strongly anticommunist speech, warning of the dangers of Castroism, at Tulane University in New Orleans.[13] Like many, he also saw this threat as an opportunity for Latin American nations to press the United States for economic assistance to address the root causes of poverty and underdevelopment on which communism fed. Writing to Lima in September 1960, he saw some promising signs from the Eisenhower administration: "The new plan of assistance for Latin America proposed by the United

---

9. *Correspondencia* (5–3-A/209) (October 14, 1960), 1–2.
10. *Correspondencia* (5–3-A/215) (November 29, 1960), 1.
11. *Correspondencia* (5–3-A/6) (January 5, 1961), 1.
12. For more, see Philip, *The Rise and Fall of the Peruvian Military Radicals, 1968–1976*, 64–65.
13. *Correspondencia* (5–3-A/51) (February 23, 1961), 1.

States and approved at [the inter-American economic conference in] Bogotá underscores the importance of aid dedicated to social works and has signaled a fundamental shift in the traditional and rigid *yanqui* [*sic*] economic policy with regard to Latin America."[14]

Not all of the ambassador's correspondence with Lima dealt with such weighty matters. Throughout his assignment, Berckemeyer rather consistently complained of the lack of funds to run the embassy in an efficient manner. In one communication, he quoted from a *Time* magazine article on the difficulties a New Jersey metalworker was having in trying to adopt a child because his monthly salary of $515.67 was considered inadequate, observing that this salary was substantially higher than that of several employees of the embassy.[15] He, or another official, constantly provided detailed accounts of embassy expenditures to show their budgetary constraints. These kinds of concerns rarely, if ever, appeared in the reports of the U.S. ambassador to Lima.

Whatever the fiscal constraints, they did not prevent the ambassador and his wife from hosting some of the most lavish diplomatic receptions in the capital. An article on such affairs in the *Saturday Evening Post* observed that "at the palatial Peruvian Embassy, set on thirty wooded acres in northwest Washington, Ambassador and Mrs. Fernando Berckemeyer give the most impressive dinners in the diplomatic corps. Only on rare occasions is a native Peruvian dish served. The ambassador and his American wife prefer to let their priceless Spanish and Peruvian antiques, paintings, and tapestries lend a Latin atmosphere, while their guests are served French cuisine [prepared by a chef brought by the ambassador from France] which the Berckemeyers feel is most appropriate for formal entertaining."[16] In this regard, the culinary tastes of the Berckemeyers seemed to coincide beautifully with those of the sophisticated new U.S. president and his even more sophisticated wife.

Peru and the Election of JFK

The Peruvian press covered the hard-fought presidential campaign of 1960 with considerable interest. Most commentary on John F. Kennedy's election was favorable. The lead editorial in *El Comercio*, the nation's oldest

---

14. *Correspondencia* (5–3-A/220) (September 19, 1960), 1–2. For more on the Bogotá conference and the shift in the Eisenhower administration's policies with regard to economic assistance for Latin America, see Rabe, *Eisenhower and Latin America*, 142–44.

15. *Correspondencia* (5–3-A/75) (March 22, 1960), 1.

16. Cahn, "Washington Hostesses Serve Their National Specialties as Diplomatic Delicacies," 61.

and most prominent newspaper, a few days after the election underscored both Kennedy's youth and his Catholicism and attributed his victory to "his good looks, his extraordinary dynamism and willingness to confront problems in a straightforward manner without sweeping them under the rug, his imaginative and creative impetus, [and] his ability to bring hope and promote beneficial changes in his own country and abroad."[17] *La Tribuna*, the organ of the Aprista Party (Alianza Popular Revolucionaria Americana, or APRA), echoed these sentiments, comparing Kennedy with Franklin Roosevelt and predicting that in this young and gifted politician the West had found a leader with "the intellectual brilliance and sufficient courage to face off against the spectacular figure of [Nikita] Khrushchev [the current Soviet leader]."[18] At the other end of the political spectrum, the conservative *La Prensa*, whose owner, Pedro Beltrán, was Prado's prime minister, saw Kennedy's election as opening the way for a more innovative and imaginative foreign policy than had previously been the case and as countering the advances made by communist nations in recent years.[19] Following Kennedy's inauguration, a spokesman for the center-left Acción Popular (Popular Action) Party hailed the new president's mention of the importance of Latin America in his address and concluded that the United States now had the opportunity to promote progressive change and social justice in the region.[20]

Writing from Washington, Ambassador Berckemeyer was more restrained in his reaction. One of his postelection communications reported that, because of a lack of coordination with the staff of the Democratic Party, many letters of congratulations to Kennedy on his victory from various heads of state, including Prado of Peru, had arrived two weeks late.[21] He did agree, however, that the new administration heralded the real possibility of significant change with regard to foreign policy. Commenting on the appointment of Dean Rusk as Kennedy's secretary of state, Berckemeyer noted that it was the plan of the new administration to implement a new policy "to reaffirm the prestige of the United States in the world." From his understanding of Rusk's publications, this new policy would include a better coordination of the international, economic, and cultural policies of the United States with other countries, "especially those in Latin America." He

---

17. *El Comercio*, November 10, 1960, 2.
18. *La Tribuna*, November 10, 1960, 4.
19. *La Prensa*, November 10, 1960, 2.
20. *Caretas*, 11, 213 (Lima: February 1–15, 1961), 7, 43, 46. The author of these remarks was the party's secretary-general, Fernando Schwalb, who would later serve as foreign minister under the administration of Fernando Belaúnde Terry (1963–1968).
21. *Correspondencia* (A-5-3/247) (November 28, 1960), 1.

also wrote that Rusk had shown interest in the culture of Peru, that he knew the secretary-designate reasonably well, and that his wife and Mrs. Rusk "shared a sincere and cordial friendship."[22] In a follow-up communication on the composition of Kennedy's entire cabinet, he remarked on its religious and party diversity and commented favorably on the confirmation of George Cabot Lodge as assistant secretary of labor as someone whom Peruvian diplomats had been able to work well with in the past.[23]

Peru and the Alliance for Progress

Determined to distinguish himself from his predecessor with regard to Latin America, Kennedy, at a meeting of the diplomatic corps of the Latin American republics on March 13, 1961, announced a bold, new initiative for the region, the Alliance for Progress.[24] The alliance called for a substantial commitment from the United States to provide Latin American nations with economic assistance, responding directly to long-standing complaints that the region's problems had for too long been ignored, and proposed an ambitious agenda for encouraging fundamental changes, including promoting agrarian reform, social justice, and political democracy. While Berckemeyer did not comment directly on this initiative, about which he may have had some reservations, he nonetheless immediately forwarded the full text of Kennedy's address in Spanish translation to Lima.[25]

As with Kennedy's election, the Peruvian press was generally positive in its response to this new initiative. An editorial in *La Tribuna* hailed Kennedy's speech on the alliance as "one of the most auspicious documents ever to have emerged from Washington."[26] The conservative *La Prensa* was equally enthusiastic, claiming that the promise of the alliance was an "extraordinary stimulus" to developments already under way in Peru to transform the nation.[27] Another publication, however, was more cautious in its optimism.

---

22. *Correspondencia* (5-3-A/262) (December 27, 1960), 2.
23. *Correspondencia* (5-3-A/52) (February 6, 1961), 1.
24. There is an abundant literature on the Alliance for Progress. For its origins, see Goodwin, *Remembering America*, 108–9, and Schlesinger, *A Thousand Days*, 186–205. A good overview and analysis is provided by Levinson and de Onís, *The Alliance That Lost Its Way*. Another, briefer summary, is Smith, "The Alliance for Progress," 71–89. For an excellent analysis of how the alliance fit into Kennedy's overall plan to contain the spread of communism in Latin America, see Rabe, *The Most Dangerous Area in the World*. See also Packenham, *Liberal America and the Third World*.
25. *Correspondencia* (5-3-A/108) (March 15, 1961).
26. *La Tribuna* (March 15, 1961), 4.
27. *La Prensa*, March 15, 1961, 2.

In an open letter to Kennedy published in the popular newsmagazine *Caretas* a month after the announcement of the program, the author pointed out the significant power held by a few in Peru, a "dominant class" that controlled the economy and the government and who labeled as "extremists" any who dared to oppose their power. Moreover, various foreign companies often engaged in practices that would be forbidden in the United States and worked at cross-purposes to the stated goals of that nation's policies, a not-too-disguised reference to the International Petroleum Company. Most Peruvians had lost faith in the many unfulfilled promises of would-be reformers. For the alliance to succeed, it had to be a cooperative effort with popular support and the United States had to abandon its habitual practice of unilateral interventionism in the internal affairs of Latin American countries.[28]

The man who would represent the United States in Peru and try to confront these challenges was well known in Washington. Soon after unveiling the alliance, Kennedy named Joseph Loeb as the new U.S. ambassador to Peru. Loeb had been a high school teacher, executive assistant to the director of the Mutual Security Agency, and co-owner of a newspaper but had most distinguished himself as founder and president of the anticommunist liberal advocacy group Americans for Democratic Action. While he had had no previous diplomatic experience in Latin America, the appointment of such a high-profile personality indicated a certain amount of administration concern with Peru.[29]

Prado's Visit to the United States

As a sign of the high priority the new administration had assigned to Peru, in September 1961, President Prado became the first Latin American head of state to visit Washington after Kennedy's inauguration. Prado addressed a joint session of the U.S. Congress. Much of his speech dealt with the threat of Cuba and communism, claiming that direct intervention to forestall that danger would be justified in light of the Castro regime's own interventionist policies. He also strongly supported the main thrust of the Alliance for Progress, arguing that meeting Latin America's pressing social and economic needs was essential to slowing potential communist advances. Any

28. *Caretas*, 11, 218 (April 14–28, 1961), 5.
29. Information on Loeb from, in part, U.S. Department of State, *The Biographic Register, 1963* (Washington, D.C.: Government Printing Office, 1963), 274.

delays in implementing or limitations on the program, he warned, "can be an open door for the enemy."[30]

In Prado's private meeting with Kennedy, he pressed the president to be more aggressive with constraining Castro and urged him to consider working more closely with sympathetic Latin American allies and the Organization of American States (OAS) in this endeavor. Given the disaster of the attempted intervention in Cuba in April at the Bay of Pigs and a generally jaundiced U.S. view of the effectiveness of the OAS, these suggestions were ignored. Other issues discussed included the ongoing boundary dispute between Peru and Ecuador and the possibility of additional loans to further development efforts, especially in the southern Andean region. In this regard, Kennedy suggested that Peru's minister of public works get in touch with the appropriate U.S. agencies to work on the details. After the meeting, a joint communiqué was issued, which one participant noted had "more words than substance." In his memo summarizing the meeting, then Assistant Secretary of State for Inter-American Affairs Robert Woodward concluded that "so far President Prado and his party seem happy with the visit."[31] The Peruvians were made even happier when, a few weeks later, the embassy in Washington reported that the Inter-American Development Bank had approved two loans for $22.8 million and $1 million each to fund public housing projects in Peru, apparently a result of the Kennedy-Prado discussions.[32]

In the six months following Prado's visit, U.S.-Peruvian relations entered into what newly appointed Assistant Secretary of State for Inter-American Affairs Edward Martin labeled a "tranquil" period.[33] The activities of the Peruvian embassy in Washington generally reflected this tranquillity, but there were growing concerns with just how new aid packages would be formulated and directed. In addition, Berckemeyer regularly informed Lima of some of the difficulties he was encountering in trying to get clear answers about the maintenance of import quota levels for Peruvian products,

---

30. As reprinted in *DOSB* (October 31, 1961), 674–78. In preparation for his speech to Congress, Berckemeyer forwarded to Prado, through the foreign ministry, copies of similar recent addresses by other Latin American presidents. *Correspondencia* (5–3-A/282) (September 5, 1961).

31. "Memorandum from the Assistant Secretary of State for Inter-American Affairs (Woodward) to Secretary of State Rusk," September 20, 1961, in Edward C. Keefer et al., *Foreign Relations of the United States, 1961–1963* [hereafter *FRUS*], vol. 12, *American Republics* (Washington, D.C.: Government Printing Office, 1996), 854–56. Comments and information on the Prado visit, including the remark about the joint communiqué's lack of substance, can be found in Martin, *Kennedy and Latin America*, 341, 380n.

32. *Correspondencia* (5–3-A/348) (no date).

33. Martin, *Kennedy and Latin America*, 34.

especially cotton and sugar. In January 1962, he met with Robert Woodward at the State Department to emphasize the importance to Peru of the U.S. market for these products and referred to a general discussion on quotas that had taken place earlier between Prado and Kennedy. During these discussions, the U.S. president had promised that his administration "would keep very much in mind the interests of Peru in this matter."[34] When the U.S. Congress, however, considered reducing the quota for Peruvian sugar, Berckemeyer forwarded testimony from John C. Duncan of W. R. Grace and Company, which had substantial investments in northern sugar plantations, to the Committee on Agriculture of the House of Representatives on May 22, 1962, in which Duncan strongly defended maintaining the existing quota. "It is inconceivable," he stated, "that this commodity agreement which has worked so well for 28 years and which, particularly in the last two years, contributed so much toward the economic development of Peru should be upset at the very time when the U.S., under the Alliance for Progress, is rendering urgent financial aid to Peru and other Latin American countries to achieve the same objective."[35]

With regard to cotton, the embassy's second-in-command, Arturo García, had met with Richard Poole, desk officer for Peru, and others in the State Department in early March to protest the reduction of the Peruvian quota. He was told that the decision was not so much that of the executive branch as from congressional pressure to protect domestic producers. Not satisfied with this response, García underscored the negative consequences of the decision for the Peruvian economy.[36] A few months later, Ambassador Berckemeyer forwarded a three-page aide-memoire to the State Department strongly objecting to a U.S. decision to sell cotton to Chile under the provisions of Public Law 480, arguing that such action "will certainly affect the international trade [its own sale of cotton to its southern neighbor] adversely."[37]

Although it was sometimes lost in the shuffle of more spectacular political developments, the U.S. quota for Peru's exports would remain a prominent concern for the embassy throughout this period. In the instances noted, the various embassy efforts appeared to have no effect in changing the minds of the administration or the Congress.

---

34. *Correspondencia* (5–3-A/14) (January 12, 1962), 1.
35. *Correspondencia* (5–3-A/159) (May 29, 1962), 1.
36. *Correspondencia* (5–3-Y/8) (March 8, 1962), 3–4. The "Y" designation indicates that this was a confidential communication.
37. *Correspondencia* (5–3-Y/19) (July 12, 1962), 3.

The Military Coup of 1962

Peru's presidential elections, scheduled for June 10, 1962, did much to disrupt the tranquillity. After some complicated maneuverings, three major candidates emerged. Returning from exile in late 1961, former president Manuel Odría entered the political arena as the candidate of the Unión Nacional Odriista (National Odrista Union, or UNO), a clearly personal vehicle. Labeling himself a "socialist of the right," Odría sought to appeal to an unusual coalition of the urban working classes and the business-industrial groups that had benefited from his previous regime, especially his extensive public works programs. While Edwin Martin described Odría in 1962 as a "well-respected figure, no longer tied to the military," his authoritarian past made him an unlikely choice to receive the backing of the United States at this time.[38]

The candidate who seemed to fit most of the prerequisites for U.S. support as an Alliance for Progress democrat was Fernando Belaúnde Terry. Young, intelligent, and articulate, Belaúnde and his Popular Action Party promised substantial reform by democratic means. However, the Kennedy administration was less than enthusiastic about him. As Martin described him, Belaúnde was a "somewhat charismatic speaker, probably left of center," who in 1956 had run as the candidate of a party "with some communist supporters in its lower ranks."[39] As far as the administration was concerned, doubt about the solidity of Belaúnde's anticommunist credentials was sufficient reason to withhold support.

Washington's preferred candidate was neither a new face nor, by 1962, much of a reformer. Once again, Víctor Raúl Haya de la Torre, founder and leader of the Aprista Party, entered a presidential campaign with hopes of election. While careful not to embrace Haya openly, it was no secret that the United States hoped he was the candidate who would emerge triumphant. The reasons seemed evident. As Martin reported, "In February, 1962, Assistant Secretary Woodward wrote that Haya was *our* [emphasis mine] candidate as APRA was the strongest anti-communist force in Peru."[40] Arthur Schlesinger cited Ambassador Loeb as saying virtually the same thing, adding that APRA was "the best means of keeping the working class from communism."[41] Leftist journalist Carleton Beals claimed that APRA had

---

38. Martin, *Kennedy and Latin America*, 345.
39. Ibid.
40. Ibid.
41. Schlesinger, *A Thousand Days*, 786.

close links with anti-Castro Cubans in Peru and that Haya was "the chosen C. I. A. candidate and was getting the support of U.S. money."[42]

Despite the United States' enthusiasm for Haya, major figures in the Peruvian military made it abundantly clear that they strongly opposed his candidacy and if he were to be elected the military would move to prevent his installation as president. Aware of this resistance, Ambassador Loeb and the administration worked feverishly to prevent military intervention, a course of action that would run counter to the democratic ideals of the Alliance for Progress. In the months preceding the election, Loeb and others met on numerous occasions with Peruvian political and military leaders, warning them that the consequences of a coup would lead to a break in diplomatic relations and a suspension of economic assistance. They also argued that military intervention would only serve to strengthen the pro-Castro left. To sway the Peruvian military, at Loeb's urging, a group of high-ranking U.S. army officers came to Lima to try to influence their Peruvian colleagues to desist from their intended course.[43]

As the date for the elections approached, it became increasingly clear that none of these efforts would work. A telegram from Secretary of State Rusk to the U.S. embassy in Lima on June 7 implied that military intervention was almost a foregone conclusion and laid out possible U.S. reactions if such action occurred. Among the five scenarios listed, the second proved the most prophetic. It foresaw an APRA victory followed soon by military intervention, which in turn would lead to suspending relations, recalling the ambassador, and withholding aid programs. This scenario did not envision much chance of getting the armed forces to step down immediately once in power and hoped at best for some sort of compromise that would lead to a return to civilian control.[44]

The expected occurred. The election was supervised by the armed forces, and there was general agreement that it had proceeded fairly and honestly. Despite the large number of candidates, most votes went to the three major contenders. None of the three, however, were able to achieve the constitutionally mandated one-third of the total, although Haya, with 32.95 percent, was within a hair's breadth of that figure, followed closely by Belaúnde with 32.13 percent and Odría with 28.88 percent.

As the slow vote count proceeded, the United States continued to try to

---

42. Beals, *Latin America*, 112.
43. Martin, *Kennedy and Latin America*, 348–50.
44. "Telegram from the Department of State to the Embassy in Peru, June 7, 1962," *FRUS (1961–1963)*, 861–62.

forestall military action. On June 12, Kennedy referred to the recent contest in Peru as an example of "what a vigorous democracy we have in the hemisphere."[45] That vigor, however, was being sorely tested. The military held firm in its opposition to Haya and the Apristas, claiming that fraud had been committed in certain districts that had supported the party and placing pressure on Prado to annul the entire process and call for new elections. This was something Prado refused to do even in the face of threats from the military that this was the only course that would allow him to finish his term.[46] A few days before the coup, Secretary Rusk sent a telegram to Loeb to encourage Prado in his position and to offer any assistance possible. Prado expressed his appreciation for the gesture but rather poignantly but accurately said that there was nothing the United States could do, "either privately or publicly, to assist."[47]

Prado's pessimism was understandable. On July 18, the Peruvian armed forces, defying all U.S. pressures, moved against his government. According to the military, the charges of electoral fraud were the prime motivations for their actions. According to Edwin Martin and others, it was the specter of a deal between the Apristas and Odría to support the former general as president that led to the armed forces' action.[48]

Kennedy's Dilemma

The Peruvian military's actions posed a serious dilemma for the Kennedy administration. Deposing elected governments, even conservative ones, ran counter to the democratic ideals of the Alliance for Progress. The administration already had acceded, with only minor objections, to the overthrow of the elected government of Arturo Frondizi in Argentina in March. To accept yet another Latin American military coup only a few months later would seriously undercut the alliance's message of democratic reform. But the practical realities of the situation meant that, unless Washington could rally considerable backing for a hard-line position in opposition to the new junta from other Latin American nations, it ultimately would have to

45. As quoted in Martin, *Kennedy and Latin America*, 350.
46. For more on the complex maneuvering surrounding the election, see Masterson, *Militarism and Politics in Latin America*, 165–77.
47. "Telegram from the Department of State to the Embassy in Peru, July 12, 1962," *FRUS (1961–1963)*, 863.
48. Martin, *Kennedy and Latin America*, 351. See also Masterson, *Militarism and Politics*, 175–77; Pike, *The United States and the Andean Republics*, 318–19; Rabe, *The Most Dangerous Area in the World*, 119–20; and Tamarzi Lúcar, *Historia del poder*, 327–34.

accept the new regime as the legitimate government of Peru and deal with it accordingly.

The initial U.S. reaction followed more or less the steps recommended in Rusk's June 7 telegram. Kennedy was informed of the coup at his July 18 staff meeting. That same day the State Department issued a statement deploring the coup and announcing the suspension of diplomatic relations.[49] The following day, Kennedy made his own statement in which he underscored his "great concern" over the coup, which, he said, represented "a serious setback" for hopes for hemispheric democracy. Simultaneously, the State Department announced that it was suspending all assistance programs to Peru except for those "where important humanitarian factors are involved."[50] Ambassador Loeb was then recalled for consultations in Washington.

Over the next few weeks, Kennedy was subjected to conflicting advice and pressures about how best to resolve the Peruvian situation. On July 27, the day following Loeb's recall, Under Secretary of State George Ball sent an extensive memorandum to Kennedy on the matter. He advised the president to adhere to his current policy of suspending recognition and aid, arguing that it would serve to forestall potential coups in other Latin American countries, most notably in Venezuela and the Dominican Republic, two intended showcases of the Alliance for Progress. He suggested, too, placing as much pressure as possible on the junta to schedule new elections and urged getting other Latin American nations to aid in the process, mentioning in particular the pro-U.S. government of Venezuela's President Rómulo Betancourt as a likely ally.[51] At the same time, using Loeb as an intermediary, Haya de la Torre, far from a disinterested party, assured Kennedy that his policy of withholding recognition had "produced [an] extraordinarily favorable reaction" among most Peruvians, an assurance that bore little relationship to the facts on the ground.[52] Stopping off in New York on his way to Parisian exile, now former president Prado met with Assistant Secretary Martin and took pains to praise the activities of Ambassador Loeb and to encourage the administration in its position.[53]

These words of encouragement, however welcome, did little to resolve Kennedy's dilemma. In Congress, some of the early support for the administration's position had begun to erode. Republican Congressman John P.

---

49. *DOSB*, xlvii, 1206 (August 6, 1962), 327–34.
50. Ibid.
51. "Memorandum from the Under Secretary of State (Ball) to President Kennedy, July 27, 1962," *FRUS (1961–1963)*, 864–67.
52. "Telegram from the Department of State to the Embassy in Peru, July 28, 1962," *FRUS (1961–1963)*, 868–69.
53. Martin, *Kennedy and Latin America*, 355.

Saylor of Pennsylvania on July 31 argued that the State Department had been "too hasty" in applying sanctions against Peru and concluded that "no nation should be deprived of diplomatic status with this country simply because we do not approve of the local government."[54] On the following day, Republican Senator Barry Goldwater of Arizona, beginning to emerge as a possible opponent of Kennedy's in the 1964 presidential election, alleged, without providing any detail, that the U.S. policy toward Peru was starting to have "adverse effects" on the rest of Latin America. The United States, he asserted, "cannot impose our system of government on others either by force or threat." He also argued that backing Haya de la Torre, who, he claimed, was "a proved Socialist, a fellow traveler of Communists, and an opportunist," had been a serious mistake.[55]

These pressures and the limited options available began to have their effect. In a meeting with Kennedy in early August, the Venezuelan foreign minister claimed that the United States was doing "a wonderful thing" in denying recognition to the Peruvian junta and recommended that a meeting of the foreign ministers of the OAS be called to encourage a blanket condemnation of all military coups. While Kennedy did not altogether discount this strategy, he underscored the tenuous position of the United States. There were, he said, legitimate doubts about the electoral process in June. More important, from all he could tell, there had been a general acquiescence to the coup and the junta in Peru, making it "difficult for the United States to adopt an attitude of outrage." He was also concerned about the growing perception that, by withholding recognition of the new government, the United States was in danger of being perceived as trying to unduly influence internal developments in Peru.[56]

Kennedy's concerns were justified. A few days later, the OAS determined not to consider a Venezuelan proposal for a statement on coups. As Kennedy had feared, most Latin American nations, especially Brazil, Mexico, and Argentina, saw the U.S. position as undue intervention in Peru's internal affairs. Bowing to reality, the administration determined to recognize the new government and to restore normal relations and economic assistance along with the Peace Corps program. In a statement issued on August 17, the State Department claimed that the junta was in "effective control" of the country and had pledged to honor its international obligations. It had set June 9, 1963, as the date for new elections, promised that

---

54. Saylor's remarks were read into the Senate record. *Congressional Record—Senate* (July 31, 1962), 15186.
55. *Congressional Record—Senate* (August 1, 1962), 15207.
56. "Memorandum of Conversation, August 2, 1962," *FRUS (1961–1963)*, 872–75.

these elections would be completely open to outside inspection, that in the meantime constitutional guarantees would be restored, that all political parties could operate freely, and that the electoral outcome would be respected whatever the result. Following these elections, power would be transferred back to civilian authority on July 28, Peru's Independence Day.[57]

The Peruvian Reaction

In his overview of Peru's foreign policy, Ronald Bruce St. John highlighted the reaction to Kennedy's position on recognition of the junta as one that had a significant long-term effect. "Virtually all Peruvians, especially those affiliated with the military, resented what they viewed as an unacceptable level of U.S. interference in Peruvian internal affairs."[58] An example of this resentment could be seen in an article in an August edition of *Caretas*, which argued that the United States and other Latin American nations had fallen victim to erroneous press reports about the situation in Peru and had failed to understand the true nature of events. The actions of the junta, it claimed, actually were legal within the spirit of the Alliance for Progress in terms of respecting democratic procedures by responding forcefully to a fraudulent election. The junta fulfilled all the conditions for recognition of a de facto government, and the U.S. efforts to reverse the coup, it alleged, were a "puerile attempt to restore Prado to the presidency." It took particular aim at the activities of Venezuela's Betancourt and José Figueres of Costa Rica, asserting that they were backing U.S. policy to advance the interests of the "APRA indoamericana." The driving force behind the U.S. position, it suggested, came from some hotheads (*termocéfalos*) in the administration, who were urging a stance that meant, as Kennedy rightly feared it would be perceived, direct intervention in Peru's internal affairs. The article urged the Peruvian government to resist such pressure and concluded that, if "North American aid, civilian or military, has to come at the price of sacrificing our dignity and our liberty of action within the international sphere, then it is preferable not to receive such aid."[59]

Articles and editorials in *El Comercio* echoed these sentiments, placing an even stronger emphasis on what it saw as Aprista maneuvering and influence behind U.S. policy. It also carried in full the July 26 press conference

57. *DOSB*, xivii, 1210 (September 3, 1962), 348–49.
58. St. John, *The Foreign Policy of Peru*, 195.
59. *Caretas*, xii, no. 249 (August 3–August 15, 1962), 10–11.

of the leader of the junta, General Ricardo Pérez Godoy, who accused Ambassador Loeb of showing undue favoritism for the candidacy of Haya de la Torre. He added that "we have no complaints against the U.S. government as a whole, but rather with the actions of Loeb" and promised that the harder the United States pushed to interfere in Peruvian affairs the harder the Peruvians would resist.[60]

Not all was negative. Not surprisingly, *La Tribuna* favored the U.S. policy. In one editorial, it claimed that intervention to promote democracy, as was the case in this instance, was not really "intervention."[61] *La Prensa* covered the whole recognition question in some detail but had little to say about the matter editorially. When recognition was granted, it welcomed the move as providing an opportunity for restoring democracy and for Peru to enjoy "the benefits of the Alliance for Progress."[62] Some weeks later, *Caretas* reported favorably on the arrival to Peru of 250 Peace Corps volunteers. It was almost inconceivable, the magazine observed, that a well-to-do Peruvian would abandon his or her career and comfortable surroundings to live and work in the urban slums and to aid the poor, as many of the U.S. volunteers were doing. Whether the volunteers could actually do much good remained to be seen, but the effort and example were clearly admirable.[63]

Kennedy's Second Thoughts

In retrospect, Kennedy expressed his regrets that he had spoken so publicly and so soon in condemning the coup in Peru. Carving out a clear position so early, he believed, had hindered him in developing a more flexible and effective policy. He also seemed to agree with his critics that the position had "a taste of past U.S. intervention" that his administration was trying "to persuade the Latin Americans to forget."[64] His advisors, however, sought to reassure him that the policy had produced positive results. The junta had been forced to soften its own position and schedule new elections. Moreover, as presidential advisor Arthur Schlesinger, Jr., recalled, the administration had showed its willingness not to bow to the wishes of the U.S. business community in Peru, which had urged immediate recognition. This resistance, he asserted, "further consolidated the confidence of

60. *El Comercio*, July 27, 1962, 4.
61. *La Tribuna*, August 5, 1962, 1.
62. *La Prensa*, August 19, 1962, 12.
63. *Caretas*, xii, no. 252 (September 25–October 10, 1962), 26–27.
64. Martin, *Kennedy and Latin America*, 356.

democratic Latin Americans in the progressive purposes of the American President."⁶⁵

Kennedy, however, was probably correct in his concerns. Changing course after having taken an initial strong stand was seen as a serious reversal and probably served to undermine the confidence of democratic forces in the region. The president also seemed to have learned from the Peruvian experience. When the State Department recommended that certain limitations be placed on U.S. military assistance to Peru as a sign of continuing displeasure with the junta, Kennedy rejected their advice and ordered that it be fully restored.⁶⁶ When subsequent coups occurred in Ecuador, Guatemala, the Dominican Republic, and Honduras, he took a more ambivalent stance than he had with Peru. Failing to advance the alliance's goals in any of these instances, the administration, in Robert Packenham's words, "had learned something of the limits of its capacity to promote democracy in Latin America."⁶⁷ Later, in October 1963, Assistant Secretary Martin sent a message to all U.S. diplomatic posts in Latin America, laying out what he considered a more realistic approach toward coups in the region, crafting a policy that would try to combine recognition of military governments with a continued push to achieve democratic development.⁶⁸ While this would be a difficult balance to achieve, it underscored the larger repercussions of the Peruvian experience.

Berckemeyer and the Junta

Despite his own reservations, Berckemeyer remained as Peru's ambassador to Washington after the July coup.⁶⁹ He did what he could to get the Kennedy administration to extend recognition and resume normal relations. On July 26, he forwarded an extensive confidential memorandum to Lima, explaining in some detail what he and the embassy saw as the main reasons for the initial adverse reaction to the coup by the United States and making his own policy recommendations to deal with the situation. In this analysis, much of the emphasis was placed on the sympathy for Haya de la

65. Schlesinger, *A Thousand Days*, 788.
66. Rabe, *The Most Dangerous Area in the World*, 120–21.
67. Packenham, *Liberal America and the Third World*, 73.
68. Ibid., 73–75.
69. In a conversation with a State Department official the following year, Berckemeyer communicated his own objections to the coup, noting that in that instance he "had swallowed a pill," something he would be loath to do in the future. "Memorandum of Conversation, May 10, 1963," *FRUS (1961–1963)*, 882–83.

Torre and the Apristas displayed by most of the New Frontiersmen associated with the administration, "in which," he alleged, "the leftist ideas of certain groups from Harvard University have a preponderant influence." This group, and their sympathizers, seemed to believe that only the so-called democratic left in Latin America—men such as Betancourt of Venezuela, Figures of Costa Rica, Luis Muñoz Marín of Puerto Rico, and Haya of Peru—could truly produce democratic change. They and their allies also feared that the military takeover in Peru could well touch off similar actions in other nations such as Brazil and Venezuela. He also credited the Apristas, largely because of their extensive exile experience, with considerable sophistication in establishing contacts with sympathizers in the United States and elsewhere and having their position and points of view predominate in friendly public forums. Berckemeyer wrote, "For many in this country, Haya and APRA are synonymous with democracy and anti-communism and are seen as the only solution for Peru."

While these factors prevailed for the moment, he continued, there were also signs of a growing counterreaction. Many of his Latin American counterparts had expressed to him their concerns that the U.S. policy represented undue interference in Peru's internal affairs. He also saw signs that Kennedy was beginning to back away from his hard line on Peru at his press conference. The ambassador complained that he was having trouble contacting congressmen directly to present the Peruvian position and only had telephone access to State Department officials. Nonetheless, he and the embassy staff were in constant touch with "colleagues, personal friends, journalists, and businessmen tied to Peru" and were doing all they could to counter the negative image of the junta and to force a change in U.S. policy. While much of this activity had been restricted to New York and Washington, Berckemeyer planned to visit other parts of the country to try to spread the word regarding the Peruvian position and "to avoid finding myself in Washington during the first days of the arrival of Ambassador Loeb," underscoring his own displeasure with and disapproval of his counterpart's actions.

Berckemeyer concluded that, while it was clear that certain official hostility to the junta prevailed, there were also some optimistic signs. The State Department had informed him that there would be no reduction in the sugar quota for Peru, that Public Law 480 food shipments would continue, that a decision to divert Peace Corps volunteers to other countries had been suspended, that there had been no fundamental change in military advising programs, that the U.S. Agency for International Development (AID) was studying the resumption of suspended public health programs, and that the Inter-American Bank was still considering loans to Peru under the Alliance for Progress. Although it might have been difficult for the Kennedy administration to reverse its position, given the firm stance it had taken originally, events seemed to be moving in that direction. The announcement by the junta that elections would be scheduled and the strong, almost unanimous, reaction by most important groups in Peru against what was seen as U.S. interference in the nation's internal affairs were helping gradually to shift the balance. Finally, he advised, "It only remains for us to wait, without becoming impatient, for the U.S. Government to see itself obligated, before the persistent pressure that is being applied from all directions, to rectify its position."[70] As events proved, this was sound advice based on a solid understanding of the political and policy dynamics operating in Washington.

In his memo, Berckemeyer promised to keep the Foreign Ministry closely advised of developments regarding the recognition struggle. He sent on a steady stream of newspaper clippings and copies of congressional speeches for and against U.S. action. Among these were several commentaries that criticized the actions of Ambassador Loeb in Peru and predicted that he would not return to that country but be reassigned elsewhere. Observing that Loeb had many "influential friends" in Washington, Berckemeyer believed that they would try to convince the administration that a reassignment would not represent a "punishment" but rather a reward. Otherwise, it would have to admit to the failure of its policy toward the junta.[71]

By late October, any lingering repercussions for the administration over events in Peru were overshadowed by the Cuban Missile Crisis. Early in November, Berckemeyer sent on a detailed eight-page, single-spaced analysis of the crisis along with numerous press clippings. The ambassador concluded that in the future the Kennedy administration should be much tougher on both Cuba and the Soviet Union. While he lauded the withdrawal of Soviet missiles from Cuba, he felt that there were many aspects of the superpower confrontation still to be resolved if the United States were to retain its prestige and continue to defend "Western Christian values and, in a certain sense, the measure of its influence in the social revolution of the twentieth century." If, as was widely reported, the removal of the missiles was done at the cost of promising not to try to overthrow Castro, the result, then, was that "the United States had won only a superficial

---

70. *Correspondencia* (5–3-Y/24) (July 26, 1962), 1–6.
71. *Correspondencia* (5–3-Y/37) (August 17, 1962), 1.

and ephemeral psychological victory, leaving the Soviet Union with a deeper and more lasting conquest."[72]

On the domestic front, Berckemeyer saw recent congressional elections as having produced little change. However, without specifying, he also noted that there were "moderate elements" in both parties who were resisting certain aspects of the New Frontier. He also saw the election of Republican governors in the key states of Michigan, New York, and Pennsylvania as potentially significant for the presidential contest in 1964. He particularly singled out New York's Nelson Rockefeller as a strong possibility to lead the GOP ticket and as one who would likely provide effective leadership in international affairs.[73]

Another domestic political issue, somewhat lost in the light of larger events and one on which Berckemeyer failed to comment (or at least there is nothing in his correspondence file), was the passage of the so-called Hickenlooper amendment to the Foreign Assistance Act of 1962. Introduced by Senator Bourke Hickenlooper, Republican of Iowa, the amendment stipulated that, in the event of expropriation or nationalization of U.S. capital enterprises by a foreign nation, if no agreement to a reasonable settlement with regard to compensation was arrived at within six months of the action, then the president was to suspend assistance to that government until a settlement was reached. Despite the objections of the State Department, which felt that the measure was too punitive and restrictive and would seriously hinder its ability to negotiate outstanding disputes, the measure was approved as a sign of a "popular feeling of frustration" among the North American public directed at governments in Latin America and elsewhere that took over U.S.-owned properties without compensation and then expected foreign aid to continue.[74] This amendment, as will be seen, would have very significant consequences for U.S.-Peruvian relations.

A New U.S. Ambassador to Peru

By the end of the year, it was clear that Loeb would not return to Peru as the U.S. representative. Whether fairly or not, he was seen as too closely associated with a policy that favored Haya de la Torre in the presidential election. Named to succeed him was John Wesley Jones, a career diplomat.

---

72. *Correspondencia* (5–3-A/379) (November 3, 1962), 7–8.
73. *Correspondencia* (5–3-A/383) (November 12, 1962), 1–2.
74. For more, see Bernstein, *Foreign Investment in Latin America*, 186–211.

After graduating from George Washington University in 1930 with a liberal arts degree, Jones had entered the foreign service the following year and had served extensively in Europe, mostly in Italy, but also for a while in Madrid, where he became fluent in Spanish. In Peru, he gave some of his speeches in Spanish and retained the particular Castilian accent, which, he later recalled, "was rather a plus for me because it sort of impressed people."

Other than his Spanish language skills, there was little in his résumé that indicated any experience in or knowledge of Latin America beyond a brief stint early in his career in the Saltillo, Mexico, consulate. He had, however, served five years as ambassador to Libya, where he had successfully handled negotiations over rights to an airbase there. In Libya, too, he had been present when major oil strikes had been made by Standard Oil, turning that nation into a major world petroleum producer. His contacts with Standard Oil would continue in Peru but with less favorable results. Returning to Washington in October 1962, he first met President Kennedy, whom he greatly admired, in the company of the Libyan crown prince. Briefing the president on the prince's visit at the height of the Cuban Missile Crisis, Jones appeared to have made a favorable impression, and that might have been the reason he was chosen to replace Loeb. As Jones later recalled it, the administration, having been burned by Loeb's association with the Apristas, was looking for "an Ambassador that didn't have any previous connections with Peru and couldn't possibly be accused of having any political preferences for one party or another . . . [and] so the story was that they appointed Johnny Jones Ambassador because he didn't 'know nothing' about Peru."[75]

Despite his lack of experience in Peru, Jones was a quick learner and would prove to be a conscientious and able ambassador with a challenging and complex assignment. Before his departure in January 1963, his Peruvian counterpart, Berckemeyer, hosted an embassy banquet for him, attended by Assistant Secretary Martin and other State Department officials, along with representatives of the Cerro de Pasco Mining Company, W. R. Grace, and other major U.S. investors. The businessmen, in particular, were critical of former ambassador Loeb and were pleased to see him replaced by a career diplomat. Berckemeyer, as he informed Lima, had met with Jones on several occasions before the banquet and had formed of him "the best

---

75. From an interview with Jones conducted by Horace G. Torbert on May 11, 1988, as part of *The Foreign Affairs Oral History Collection of the Association for Diplomatic Studies and Training*, available at http://memory.loc.gov/cgi-bin/query/D?mfdip:1:temp/-ammend_LOco, pp. 16–17. See also U.S. Department of State, *The Biographic Register* (July, 1970), 207.

impression, not only because of his background and capabilities but also because of his disposition [presumably, sympathetic and friendly] towards Peru."[76]

On his arrival in Lima, Jones presented his credentials to the leader of the junta, General Pérez Godoy. Later, he said that the general was "not one of my favorites, but there were some good military in that government from well-established Peruvian families who did want a return to constitutional government."[77] He also found an embassy with a staff of ninety-four; there were also five members in the recently opened consulate in the southern city of Arequipa.[78] In terms of total personnel, this was about eight times the size of the Peruvian embassy in Washington and reflected the predominance of U.S. missions and diplomats in Latin America in general.[79]

The 1963 Elections in Peru

Jones's arrival in Peru coincided with the run-up to the presidential elections scheduled for June. The three main candidates were Belaúnde, Haya, and Odría. This time, the United States and its ambassador were careful not to be seen as favoring any of the three. Behind the scenes, however, there were still some concerns at the State Department and elsewhere that Belaúnde was soft on communism, a concern that was alleviated somewhat when he allied his party with the moderate Christian Democrats, further solidifying his already strong position.[80]

In Washington, Jones's counterpart, Berckemeyer, met with Secretary of State Rusk in early May before a visit home and discussed with him the upcoming elections. He told the secretary that the junta was committed to carrying these out freely and would respect the results regardless of the outcome. When asked if there was any danger that extremist elements might prevail, he assured Rusk that the 1962 elections had shown that moderates were in the majority. Revealing what may have been his own distance from events, or more likely his own inclinations, he said that of the three candidates, Odría had gained the most ground and had done well in 1962 in the Lima-Callao area, "where the 'quality vote' is cast; i.e., the intellectuals,

---

76. *Correspondencia* (5-3-Y/5) (January 25, 1963), 2.
77. Jones interview, *Foreign Affairs Oral History Collection*, 17.
78. U.S. Department of State, *Foreign Service List* (Washington, D.C.: Government Printing Office, April 1963), 123.
79. For more on this point, see Goldhamer, *The Foreign Powers in Latin America*, 200–202.
80. Martin, *Kennedy and Latin America*, 357.

business, government servants, industrial labor, etc." His wife was also a major political asset. As far as Belaúnde was concerned, there were "too many unknowns" and the leaders of APRA, notably Haya de la Torre, were "too old" to triumph. Rusk replied that he hoped the ambassador was correct in his belief that the "quality vote" would prevail and asked him to report back to him on his return.[81]

Following his trip home, Berckemeyer met with Rusk on May 31 and provided an upbeat assessment of the situation in Peru. The economy, he asserted, was "very healthy," the election preparations were going forward in a climate of considerable freedom, and his contacts had assured him that the junta would respect the results even if Haya should win. He reiterated his belief that Odría was doing well and had to be considered the favorite at this point. Divisions within APRA, he reported, were weakening Haya's support and Belaúnde, he averred, was "falling behind," due in part to "communist support." While some still suspected the U.S. embassy of backing Haya, Ambassador Jones, he reported, had done a good deal to instill confidence "between the Embassy and the Peruvians" and to allay such suspicions.[82]

A week before this meeting, the Peruvian embassy's Arturo García had sent a confidential communication to the Foreign Ministry in Lima, laying out what he saw as the U.S. position on the upcoming elections. At this point, he believed that the United States had abandoned its previous inclination to favor APRA as well as its objections to both Belaúnde (too far to the left) and Odría (too far to the right) and had determined "to work closely" with whomever might emerge triumphant. He saw as a sign of this "new realism" the warm welcome afforded recent visitors representing the upper ranks of Acción Popular, including Belaúnde's brother-in-law, Celso Pastor de la Torre, who would soon be named Peruvian ambassador to the United States. These visitors met with the directors of the Alliance for Progress, prominent congressmen, and White House officials "in an atmosphere of great cordiality." García also reported that what seemed to concern U.S. officials the most was the possibility of another coup, either before or soon after the elections, and the serious implications that would have on other hemisphere nations, notably Argentina, Brazil, and Venezuela, and on the prospects for the Alliance for Progress.[83] In this case, the second-in-command at the Peruvian embassy, García, seemed to have a firmer grasp on the political

---

81. "Memorandum of Conversation, May 10, 1963," *FRUS (1961–1963)*, 882–83.
82. "Memorandum of Conversation, May 31, 1963," *FRUS (1961–1963)*, 883–86.
83. *Correspondencia* (5-3-Y/38) (May 24, 1963), 2.

situation in Washington than his superior, Berckemeyer, had of the situation in Peru.

Belaúnde and JFK

As almost everyone except Ambassador Berckemeyer seemed to expect, Fernando Belaúnde won the 1963 elections rather easily. Polling almost 40 percent of the vote, he comfortably outdistanced Haya, who received a little more than 34 percent, and Odría, with only a bit more than 25 percent. More ominous for Belaúnde was that his Acción Popular–Christian Democratic coalition won only 44.4 percent of the seats in the Senate and only 35.7 percent of those in the Chamber of Deputies. An alliance of convenience between APRA and UNO would frustrate many of the new president's legislative initiatives and would prove a major factor in the political difficulties he faced throughout his term in office.[84]

On the surface, from the U.S. point of view, Belaúnde appeared to be the ideal choice to fulfill the goals of the Alliance for Progress. Strongly committed to democracy, he came from a family of distinguished public figures and diplomats. A graduate of the School of Architecture at the University of Texas at Austin in 1935, he had resided in both the United States and Europe for many years. Initiating his political career in the 1950s, he had founded Acción Popular as the vehicle that would carry him to the presidency. He also had seen as much of Peru as possible; in the late 1950s, he traveled throughout the country by foot, by mule, by horseback, and by car to learn of the Peruvian reality first hand. One of the results was a book published in 1959 entitled *La conquista del Perú por los Peruanos* (*Peru's Own Conquest*), in which he drew on Peru's indigenous past and its immense resources to sketch an optimistic picture of the future. Among the most notable elements of this vision was an emphasis on what he called "agrarian justice" that aimed to increase the areas of land under cultivation and to undermine the latifundio system that had prevailed up to that point. He also called for the implementation of what he called *cooperación popular*, a kind of local communal effort to construct public works for the common good. Finally, his favorite proposal, reflecting his professional training as an architect, would be the *carretera marginal*, or "marginal jungle highway," that would link the eastern jungle area of Peru with the coast and open up

---

84. For more on the elections, see Astiz, *Pressure Groups and Power Elites in Peruvian Politics*, 102–5, and Masterson, *Militarism and Politics*, 197–98.

new areas of colonization as well as eventually tie the eastern interior regions of the Andean nations together by means of a modern road system.

The realization of these ambitious plans would be difficult under any circumstances. The dogged opposition of UNO and APRA made it doubly so. However, at least initially, Belaúnde enjoyed the support of the nation's most influential political constituency, namely, the armed forces. With his election, the military "gained their most important civilian presidential ally in the twentieth century," and many of the more progressive officers shared his "grand vision for Peru's future."[85] Over time, however, that alliance became badly frayed and ultimately ruptured.

Belaúnde laid out his program in his inaugural address on July 28. It contained three main points. First was a promise to overhaul the tax system, which was seen as controlled by the elite to their own benefit. Second was to resolve the long-standing dispute with the International Petroleum Company within three months, a promise that was wildly off the mark. Third was to introduce soon a land-reform proposal.

Among the first U.S. officials to meet with Belaúnde at the inauguration were Assistant Secretary of State Martin and Ralph Dungan, a special advisor to the president. Martin recalled that the principal items in two lengthy discussions with the new president involved requests for increased U.S. economic assistance for projects that were, to his mind, "more imaginative than practical." From the U.S. side, the envoys, seeking to further the alliance goal of strengthening civilian authority through the armed forces, tried to pressure Belaúnde to cut spending on the military, which in terms of gross national product was the largest in Latin America. The new president, however, was resistant, arguing that the military were "the best friends the United States had" in Peru. Finally, there was a brief discussion of the IPC issue, with Belaúnde emphasizing the Peruvian desire to own and control its subsoil resources. Martin concluded from these talks that the new president was "a fine architect but didn't know any contractors."[86] This impression of Belaúnde as too much the visionary and too little the pragmatist is one that would persist among U.S. policy-makers throughout his administration.

In the United States, the public reaction to Belaúnde assuming Peru's presidency was positive. Berckemeyer sent on various clippings from U.S. newspapers attesting to the "enormous interest" the elections had aroused and "the very favorable atmosphere that the new government's program has

---

85. Masterson, *Militarism and Politics*, 203.
86. Martin, *Kennedy and Latin America*, 357–58.

awakened in the press."⁸⁷ In the U.S. Senate, Democrat Hubert Humphrey of Minnesota hailed the election of Belaúnde as initiating a "new trend" of democratic governments in Latin America and predicted that Peru's new president would have "the strong support of the U.S. government and Congress in his efforts to implement the Alliance for Progress programs in his country."⁸⁸ In a meeting with the new Peruvian foreign minister, Fernando Schwalb, on September 23, Secretary of State Rusk promised that Peru could count on the United States for assistance and expressed his pleasure with the reform proposals made by the new administration. However, he also uttered some words of caution. While the United States and the alliance favored agrarian reform in Latin America, he warned that any such program should be carefully crafted to avoid what he considered some of the mistakes Mexico had made in this regard. He also said that it was equally important to develop a climate in which foreign and domestic capital felt confident and could flourish. In other words, reform was all well and good, but it should not proceed too far and too fast. He concluded by stating that the relationship between the two countries had weathered a difficult eighteen months and was now on a more stable footing, and he urged the new Peruvian government to "do everything possible to maintain this positive position."⁸⁹

Belaúnde, the IPC Issue, and the Kennedy Administration

Schwalb seemed to take Rusk's admonitions to heart. In a meeting a few days later with Teodoro Moscoso, director of the Alliance for Progress, and Assistant Secretary Martin, he and Berckemeyer, who accompanied him, thanked these officials for AID loan requests for Peru that had been recently approved. Schwalb assured them that agrarian reform in Peru would be carried out in a way that would not cause undue disruption or a decline in production. He also said the Belaúnde government shared U.S. concerns about communist influence in labor unions and among students and would do what it could to address this issue. Then, addressing what was often the "elephant in the room" in meetings between officials of the two governments at this time, the foreign minister declared, without going into detail that

---

87. *Correspondencia* (5–3-A/204) (June 14, 1963), 1, and (5–3-A/261) (August 29, 1963), 1.
88. *Congressional Record—Senate* (June 28, 1963), 12010.
89. "Memorandum of Conversation, September 23, 1963," *FRUS (1961–1963)*, 887–89.

he was "optimistic" that a solution to the IPC dispute could be found that would be satisfactory to all sides.[90]

Shwalb's optimism was premature. On the Peruvian side, pressure had been building for some time to nationalize the holdings of the U.S.-owned oil company, which had been operating in Peru since the 1920s and which, through its practices, had aroused considerable and widespread popular resentment. From the U.S. side, the State Department and the executive branch, under pressure from the Hickenlooper amendment and public perceptions that U.S. interests were being abused by nationalist regimes—perceptions intensified by Fidel Castro's confiscation of North American properties in Cuba—worked to ensure that, at the least, expropriated U.S. companies would receive adequate compensation for any takeovers that occurred. These conflicting pressures produced ongoing problems for both governments as each tried to protect their respective interests and respond to their respective constituencies. A stalemate over this issue was a major stumbling block in Peruvian-U.S. relations for more than a decade and proved to be particularly damaging to the Belaúnde administration.[91]

In his inaugural address, Belaúnde had promised to address the IPC issue immediately. Although not advocating outright nationalization, he proposed legislation to assert greater Peruvian control over the company's La Brea y Pariñas fields in the northern coastal area of Talara. As he proceeded, he met on several occasions with Ambassador Jones to try to work out, in private, some solution that would satisfy both the company and the Peruvians. These negotiations proved unsuccessful, and in late October, Belaúnde submitted to Congress a law that would restore to the Peruvian government the subsoil rights to the oil fields that had been surrendered in 1922. Congress substituted two laws of its own for this proposal, which in effect had the same result of revoking the rights of the original agreements and which were passed by large majorities.

In reaction to these actions, the United States set in motion a policy to apply pressure on the Peruvians to accommodate the company by withholding economic assistance until a satisfactory resolution on compensation and other matters had been reached. There is some debate and confusion about exactly when this policy was applied. According to Kennedy advisor Richard Goodwin, Alliance for Progress director Moscoso had assured

90. "Telegram from the Department of State to the Embassy in Peru, October 2, 1963," *FRUS (1961–1963)*, 890–92.
91. For more on this complicated issue, see Goodsell, *American Corporations and Peruvian Politics*; Ingram, *Expropriation of U.S. Property in South America*; and Pinelo, *The Multinational Corporation as a Force in Latin American Politics*.

Belaúnde soon after his inauguration that the United States would withhold a decision on assistance until the ninety days in which he had promised to resolve the IPC matter were up and that "the aid was to flow whatever the outcome might be." Goodwin argued that the real hard line with regard to holding up aid to Peru was not established until later, under the administration of Lyndon B. Johnson.[92] However, in an October 2 meeting with Ambassador Jones, Belaúnde was already complaining that U.S. assistance was slow to arrive, that his political enemies, including some in the press, were hoping for him to fail, and that he "needed desperately some tangible evidence of progress." He appealed through Jones to Washington for some sort of "emergency measure of temporary authorization to move ahead at least on the projects already approved," an appeal that went unanswered.[93] On November 8, Jones met again with Belaúnde to discuss the IPC case, but the president refused to engage him on it. Jones then "made it clear that the continued provision of U.S. economic assistance to Peru was contingent on the satisfactory resolution of the issue."[94] This punitive policy aimed to support the IPC, then, seemed to be already well in place by the time Lyndon B. Johnson assumed the presidency later in the month.

Transition and the Kennedy Legacy

With the election of Belaúnde, Fernando Berckemeyer's days as Peru's ambassador to the United States were numbered, and in October, he announced his resignation. In the interim, until his replacement arrived, he and Arturo García kept Lima informed of developments regarding the U.S. reaction to the IPC matter, which seemed to dominate most conversations with State Department officials. García, for example, reported on a luncheon in late October attended by the visiting minister of education of Peru and the director of the national library, with, among others, Taylor Belcher, the State Department's director of Pacific Coast Affairs at the time (and later U.S. ambassador to Peru), in which there was an extensive discussion, as García put it, of "the law by which our government seeks full control and total possession of the oil fields of La Brea and Pariñas."[95] Then, in a confidential communication a few days later, García reported on the general disappointment

92. Richard Goodwin, "Letter from Peru," 58–60.
93. "Telegram 234 from Jones to Department of State, October 4, 1963," Personal Papers of John Wesley Jones, Box 21, Folder 9, LBJ Library.
94. "Editorial Note," *FRUS (1961–1963)*, 887.
95. *Correspondencia* (5-3-A/362) (November 1, 1963), 1–2.

expressed by Assistant Secretary Martin and others that no agreement had been reached on the IPC matter. García took advantage of a meeting with Martin to present forcefully the Peruvian position and argued that the company could continue to operate profitably in Peru if it would show some signs of accommodation. He also added that while Peru appreciated and needed the economic assistance provided by the United States and the Alliance for Progress, it would not allow those needs to overcome what it considered "our principles and our dignity." The entire issue, he concluded, had to be resolved "within the context of the Peruvian constitution and legal system."[96] There could not have been a clearer exposition of the nationalism that drove the Peruvian position, but its effect on U.S. policy-makers was minimal as they continued to pursue a policy that privileged the company's interests over those of providing badly needed economic assistance to a recently elected democratic regime.

Berckemeyer was still acting ambassador when President Kennedy was struck down by an assassin's bullets on November 22, 1963. Víctor Andrés Belaúnde, the president's uncle, his country's representative at the United Nations, and one of the country's most distinguished diplomats, represented Peru at the funeral. In Peru, as elsewhere, there was shock, dismay, and sadness at this tragic turn of events, which was felt perhaps most keenly in Latin America where the general response to the young and dynamic Kennedy, so closely associated with initiatives such as the Alliance for Progress and the Peace Corps, as well as being the United States' first Catholic president, had been favorable and enthusiastic.

As the 1960s progressed, the United States seemed to abandon the Alliance for Progress and became less interested in Latin America under Kennedy's successor, Lyndon Johnson. As U.S. relations with Peru became more strained, there were those in that country, especially those associated with the Belaúnde administration, who argued that such strains might not have developed if Kennedy had not been assassinated. They believed Kennedy would have been more sympathetic with and supportive of Belaúnde's reform aspirations than was Johnson and would not have been as susceptible to the pressures applied by the IPC.

Whether this would have been the case, of course, cannot be determined. However, Kennedy's support for reform through the alliance was only one part of his strategy for Latin America. Equally, if not more, important was the development of counterinsurgency programs that would allow the United States not only to contain and isolate Cuba but also, by reorienting Latin

---

96. *Correspondencia* (5–3-Y/63) (November 9, 1963), 4.

American militaries away from preparing to fight their neighbors and toward confronting internal threats, to deter Cuban attempts to interfere directly in other hemisphere nations. The administration significantly stepped up its military assistance programs to the region, including to Peru, and recruited more Latin American officers to study at the School of the Americas in the Panama Canal Zone, where training was refashioned to emphasize the new counterguerrilla tactics. In addition, in August 1962, Kennedy issued a directive to establish a program to help assist and train police forces in the third world to deal with insurgent threats in urban areas: the Office of Public Safety, which would operate under the Agency for International Development.[97] By the end of 1963, moreover, Kennedy and his advisors were disappointed with the results of the Alliance for Progress and were more inclined to support a greater role for the Latin American armed forces and the counterinsurgency doctrine than had been the case two years earlier.[98]

Kennedy's concern with containing communism was a constant throughout his administration. As Steven Rabe has argued, he saw Latin America as "the most dangerous area in the world," an area ripe for the repetition of the Cuban Revolution unless thwarted. Peru was perhaps not as susceptible to radical change as some other Latin American nations, but it was clearly part of the larger picture. In May 1963, a U.S. intelligence report suggested the possibility of radical forces gaining strength in that nation. According to Rabe, Kennedy was concerned that Peru might come under the influence of "international communism" and communicated to Ambassador Jones before his departure these concerns and the "primary place" of Latin America in the larger strategy of combating such threats.[99]

As the 1960s progressed, the "hard line" associated with counterinsurgency would come to predominate over the "soft line" associated with the Alliance for Progress. The pattern of military coups and governing juntas that characterized the early years of the decade would persist and become more common and institutionalized. While there were differences between Kennedy and Johnson policies toward Latin America, they were often more differences of style and emphasis than of content and ultimate purpose. Cold War considerations remained paramount throughout, and there was a great deal more continuity between the two Democratic administrations than admirers of the New Frontier, both at home and abroad, might be willing to admit. In sum, while it is conceivable that Kennedy, if he had

---

97. Rabe, *The Most Dangerous Area in the World*, 131.
98. Walker, "Mixing the Sweet with the Sour," 55.
99. Rabe, *The Most Dangerous Area in the World*, 121.

lived, would have been more supportive of Belaúnde and more accommodating on the IPC issue than was Johnson, it is equally plausible that, if he had perceived the Peruvian president's course as running contrary to his own anticommunist vision, he would not have behaved much differently from his successor.[100] Contrary to Goodwin's assertions, it appears that the punitive policy of withholding assistance to Peru, which favored the IPC, was initiated during the Kennedy years, a policy that under Johnson would be elaborated on and applied with even more rigor.

100. For more on this matter, see Packenham, *Liberal America and the Third World*, 75–98; Rabe, *The Most Dangerous Area in the World*, 125–47; and Walker, "Mixing the Sweet with the Sour," 42–69. For more on counterinsurgency, see Barber and Ronning, *Internal Security and Military Power*, and Shafer, *Deadly Paradigms*.

2

BELAÚNDE, LBJ, AND THE "MANN DOCTRINE"

The administration of Fernando Belaúnde, inaugurated on July 28, 1963, overlapped for only a few months with the last stages of John F. Kennedy's administration. For the rest of his time in office, Belaúnde would deal with the administration of Kennedy's successor, Lyndon Baines Johnson. On the surface, relations between the two administrations should have been smooth and cooperative given Belaúnde's democratic-reformist nature, and in some ways they were. There were, however, a number of disagreements that made the relationship sometimes rocky. The major area of discord was over the International Petroleum Company (IPC) matter. Differences on this issue had emerged during the first months of the Belaúnde administration, when Kennedy was still alive, and they only deepened in the first years of the Johnson administration. The issue would burden Belaúnde throughout his term, finally contributing significantly to break the back of his presidency. In addition, there were other areas of contention over such matters as the U.S. contribution to an antiguerrilla campaign in 1965, the Peruvian claim to a 200-mile limit off its shores for fishing rights, and the purchase of supersonic aircraft from France. Also playing a role, it would appear, was the persistent U.S. impression of Belaúnde as a visionary as opposed to a hardheaded realist, an impression that seemed to be shared by many in the Johnson administration, including the president.

Johnson and Mann

Johnson assumed the presidency with limited experience in or appreciation of foreign affairs and foreign policy. A masterful domestic politician, he knew relatively little of the world and lacked both the cosmopolitanism and interest in foreign policy of his charismatic predecessor. One area of the world he claimed to know well, however, was Latin America. Born and raised in Texas, he had taught Mexican American children as a young schoolteacher and was something of a hero on both sides of the border for his actions as a U.S. senator regarding the burial of a Mexican American casualty of the Korean War. As Senate majority leader, he had visited Mexico and established good relations with its president, Adolfo López Mateos. He apparently assumed that the rest of Latin America was or should be like Mexico, with its orderly one-party state. There were some, too, who believed that he shared with many North Americans, and perhaps especially Texans, a paternalistic and patronizing attitude toward Latin America and Latin Americans.[1]

Johnson shared Kennedy's anticommunism and commitment to contain Cuba and to prevent the replication of the Cuban Revolution anywhere else in the hemisphere. At least initially, he also seemed to back the goals of the Alliance for Progress. On November 27, 1963, at a meeting of ambassadors from Latin America, his first official gathering after assuming the presidency, he assured the assembly "that he would do everything in his power to expand the Alliance and make it work."[2]

While Johnson shared many of Kennedy's goals and tried to emphasize continuity, there were also some significant differences. One of these differences might have played a significant role in his attitude toward Belaúnde and Peru. Unlike Kennedy, he did not seem as enamored with leaders of the "non-Communist left" as had been his predecessor, nor did he believe that military governments necessarily led to an increase in "hard swings to the left."[3] The implication of this stance was that Johnson would agonize less than Kennedy over whether to recognize military governments that appeared during his term. Indeed, in at least one notable incident, that of the military coup in Brazil in April 1964, the administration actively encouraged such a development.[4]

---

1. For more, see Geyelin, *Lyndon B. Johnson and the World*, 24–27, and LaFeber, "Latin American Policy," 63–64.
2. Tulchin, "The Promise of Progress," 218.
3. Geyelin, *Lyndon B. Johnson and the World*, 26–27.
4. See, for example, Parker, *Brazil and the Quiet Intervention, 1964*, and Weis, *Cold Warriors and Coups d'État*, 141–69.

Johnson's greatest differences from Kennedy, however, were probably in personality and in methods of operation than in substance. Johnson was one of the most skilled domestic politicians of his era, coming to dominate the U.S. Senate to a greater extent than anyone before him. The keys to his success were in making backroom deals, exerting behind-the-scenes pressure, and manipulating others. He did not have the public skills and presence of his predecessor, and this proved to be a serious liability for him when dealing with Latin America. In Latin America, in particular, Kennedy was a tough act to follow.[5]

This negative image can be seen relatively early on in Peru. The leftist magazine *Oiga*, for example, provided extensive coverage of the Kennedy assassination during and after the event, including detailed articles speculating on a conspiracy behind the assault. But there is scarcely any mention of Johnson in these accounts.[6] In its edition before the November 1964 elections in the United States, *Caretas* described the contest between Johnson and Barry Goldwater as basically a race between two different kinds of conservatives and observed that Johnson was the first Democratic candidate in some time to have strong backing from the business community.[7] Nothing was said about Johnson's progressive domestic policies or the general appreciation for his ability to rally the nation after one of the greatest tragedies in its history.

Although Johnson appeared committed to the Alliance for Progress, he, like Kennedy in the latter stages of his administration, was concerned about its management and the sparse results to date. U.S. policy toward Latin America, he reasoned, had been too much in the hands of "idealists" little versed in the region, who operated in an uncoordinated and often amateurish manner that greatly reduced the effectiveness of policy directives. To correct this problem and to give the policy new and, as he perceived it, firmer direction, in the first major appointment of his new administration, on December 14, he recalled Thomas Mann as ambassador to Mexico and named him assistant secretary for Inter-American Affairs in the State Department as well as special assistant to the president. A few days later, he also appointed him as coordinator of the Alliance for Progress. This unprecedented concentration of power in one man was clearly intended to give Latin American policy more coherence and more direction.

The appointment was controversial. Mann, a career diplomat, was considered by many as a conservative who would be much less committed to

---

5. Geyelin, *Lyndon B. Johnson and the World*, 66.
6. Various editions of *Oiga* (published in Lima) in late 1963 and early 1964.
7. *Caretas*, 14, 300 (November 3–17, 1964), 28.

the democratic goals of the alliance than the Kennedy team. Many on that team resented the shift his appointment represented and the changes in policy the appointment portended. The changes, however, were perhaps less significant than partisans suggested. Again, there was considerable continuity. Kennedy had been contemplating placing the direction of the alliance in the hands of one man, his brother-in-law Sargent Shriver.[8]

Because both Johnson and Mann were from Texas, it was sometimes assumed that they had a close personal relationship, which explained the appointment. However, this was not the case. Undoubtedly, the connection helped, and apparently the recommendation of some Texas businessmen had some role in the choice, but, as Walter LaFeber noted, "Mann was apparently not so much a presidential intimate as a proponent of the President's view of Latin American strategy."[9] And that view was to be one characterized by hardheaded pragmatism as opposed to the "ideological" bent of the Kennedy team. Moreover, Mann would represent for Johnson a clear change in style As one author put it, he was a man of few words who "not only didn't have charisma, he didn't believe in it."[10]

Whatever Mann's deficiencies with regard to his public personality, he did have long and deep experience in Latin America. Born in Laredo along the Texas-Mexican border, he was fluent in Spanish and had served in several important diplomatic posts in the region.[11] During his career, he had developed a strong antipathy to what he considered "ultra-nationalism" of the kind, for example, associated with Argentina's Juan Perón. He was also an advocate of free markets and free trade as the best way for Latin America to develop and, while a strong anticommunist, was dubious about the value of direct intervention in Latin American affairs as the best way to promote U.S. interests.[12] These ideas helped inform an important speech Mann gave on March 18, 1964, to U.S. officials serving in Latin America. When the supposedly off-the-record remarks were reported by Tad Szulc in the *New York Times* the following day, they eventually came to be known as composing the Mann Doctrine for Latin America. In essence, the argument was for U.S. policy in the region to be less ideologically driven and more pragmatic and to have four main objectives: "economic growth . . . the protection of $9 billion in United States investments there, non-intervention

---

8. Geyelin, *Lyndon B. Johnson and the World*, 95.
9. LaFeber, "Latin American Policy," 64.
10. Geyelin, *Lyndon B. Johnson and the World*, 97.
11. For more on Mann's diplomatic career before 1963, see LaFeber, "Thomas C. Mann and the Devolution of Latin American Policy," 166–86.
12. Ibid., 170–71.

in the internal affairs of the hemisphere's republics, and opposition to Communism."[13]

The application of the doctrine and other policies pursued by Johnson and Mann could be seen in some ways as a change in emphasis rather than a radical break with the past. Private sector investment had always been encouraged under the alliance; now it would receive more attention and prominence. Military assistance would be increased, building on policies already in place. Some might argue that major changes could be seen in downplaying social reform as a goal and, in the political realm, less of a commitment to democracy and a greater willingness to condone military coups and regimes. Here, too, however, there was continuity. Although Kennedy had originally strongly supported liberal democracy in Latin America at the beginning of his administration, he had moved to a more pragmatic "moderate" position near the end. Johnson and Mann simply accelerated this pragmatic trend.[14]

Perhaps the most controversial and complicated aspect of the Mann Doctrine concerned intervention. As it happened, and as could have been foreseen, a commitment to nonintervention and a commitment to halt the spread of communism (real or perceived) in the region would often prove incompatible. During Mann's time in office, there were three major U.S. interventions in Latin America, two more or less covert (in the Brazilian coup of April 1964 and in support of Eduardo Frei in the Chilean elections of September of that same year) and one directly in the Dominican Republic in 1965. These interventions produced varying reactions throughout the region, with the most adverse stemming from the Dominican case. In the case of the Brazilian coup, an article in *Caretas* was scathingly critical of the role of the United States in this action, driven by a "simplistic anti-leftist position" and one that revealed Mann as "a mistaken pragmatist without constraint," concluding that "this is all very lamentable and censurable."[15]

While there was no U.S. intervention on this scale in Peru during the Johnson-Mann years, decisions were made early on that would have long-range implications for the Belaúnde administration. The Peruvian government's position with regard to IPC put the Johnson administration in a bind. On the one hand, there was a desire to see Belaúnde succeed, if only to forestall less attractive alternatives. On the other hand, if the Peruvian hard line against IPC prevailed, the administration might be forced to apply the Hickenlooper amendment, the application of which could well stir

13. Ibid., 187.
14. Packenham, *Liberal America and the Third World*, 95.
15. *Caretas*, 14, 287 (April 14–24, 1964), 14–15, 50.

violent nationalist sentiments and turn moderate regimes into radical ones. In addition, from the beginning, there was apparent concern that, if Peru was able to nationalize the IPC holdings, it would help start a chain of such actions against U.S.-owned properties in other parts of Latin America. Therefore, in early February 1964, Mann and other top advisors determined to withhold any program loans to Peru until Belaúnde assured the United States that no "confiscatory action" would be taken against the IPC. According to George Ingram, Mann was the principal architect of this policy and carried it out without informing Lima, disguising it as a matter of "bureaucratic inefficiency."[16] Again, while this was a significant ratcheting up of the pressure on Belaúnde, even if he was not to be directly aware of it, the threat of a cutoff of economic assistance over the IPC issue was already a matter of record before Johnson assumed the presidency and Mann took over Latin American affairs.

Almost from the beginning, Mann became something of a bête noire, not only for Kennedy partisans but also for many Latin Americans. He seemed to personify what many perceived to be a radical shift in policy away from the idealism of the popular Alliance for Progress and to a more no-nonsense approach that seemed unduly to favor U.S. business interests in the region and accepted military regimes as viable solutions to Latin America's many social and economic problems. Later, when he resigned his post in May 1966 at age fifty-three, the *New York Times* described him as "a complicated man of private charm and public abrasiveness."[17] Despite the image, the demeanor, and occasional unfortunate and patronizing remarks, Mann seemed to relate well to Latin Americans on a personal basis. As Walter LaFeber put it, "Deeply experienced in, and respectful of, Latin cultures, Mann, at least until the Dominican intervention, was probably more highly respected by Latin Americans than any other U.S. official who specialized in the region."[18] That certainly seemed to be the case with regard to Peru's new ambassador to Washington.

A New Man in Washington

Even before Belaúnde's new emissary presented his credentials in Washington, the embassy was reporting favorably on the appointment of Mann to

---

16. Ingram, *Expropriation of U.S. Property in South America*, 51. Another source, citing a personal interview with a U.S. government official, reaffirmed that Mann was the principal decision maker in this regard, a decision that was made in secret without Peruvian authorities being fully informed of it. Peeler, "The Politics of the Alliance for Progress in Peru," 63.

17. As quoted in LaFeber, "Thomas C. Mann and the Devolution of Latin American Policy," 197.

18. Ibid., 198.

direct Latin American affairs. Chargé Arturo García saw the step as heralding new and positive changes in the State Department with regard to the region and destined "to set in motion a more dynamic United States policy with regard to the Alliance for Progress." García endorsed granting additional power to Mann and saw his nomination as having "special significance." He also saw the Texas link as important and mistakenly believed, as did many, that the president and the new assistant secretary had enjoyed a close friendship of many years.[19]

On January 30, 1964, the new Peruvian ambassador, Celso Pastor de la Torre, met with Mann for the first time. He brought with him some impressive credentials. Born in Lima in 1914, the son of a diplomat, he had studied in Colombia and in Berlin, where he received his bachelor's degree while his father was Peru's ambassador to Germany. Back home, he earned his law degree from the Catholic University and was admitted to the bar in 1959. Active in business and law, he was a prominent member of Acción Popular (AP) and one of Belaúnde's closest advisors. He married the president's sister, Mercedes, and had three children. As a State Department memorandum described it, he was fluent in German and French and a "somewhat labored English."[20] He also had a superb collection of Peruvian colonial art, which he soon arranged to have exhibited in the United States.

Pastor initiated his meeting with Mann by reminding the new assistant secretary that the United States had promised to aid Peru after the successful completion of the elections and that the nation would be an excellent showcase for the Alliance for Progress. Mann, he reported, showed particular interest in the new government's plans for tax and agrarian reform. He then asked how things were going on the IPC issue, to which Pastor responded that it had aroused considerable nationalist sentiments but that the government was committed to finding a fair solution to the dispute. Pastor then raised the matter of aid loans to Peru, which, he reported, seemed to produce "some confusion" among the State Department officials, including Taylor Belcher, in charge of Pacific Coast Affairs, and Richard Poole, in charge of the Peruvian desk, who were present, and an attempt, he noticed, "to avoid a firm reply." Mann stepped in to say that he had been absorbed by the current crisis in Panama and had not had time to address

---

19. *Correspondencia* (5-3-A/405) (December 17, 1963), 1–2. In an earlier communication, García had sent on without comment a clipping from the *Washington Post* that described the close ties between Johnson and Texas oil interests. Given the ongoing dispute with IPC, this was probably not just of passing interest. *Correspondencia* (5-3-A/401) (December 10, 1963).

20. "Confidential Memo for McGeorge Bundy from Benjamin Read, executive secretary, Department of State, February 7, 1964," CO 206, Box 11, LBJ Library.

fully Peruvian issues but promised to do so in the near future. In a clear reference to the IPC matter, he reminded Pastor of the complications of the Hickenlooper amendment and said, according to the ambassador, in that regard, "Let me see what I can do." Calling the meeting "frank and very cordial," Pastor informed the Foreign Ministry, in his confidential communication, that he had a "very good impression of Mann and I trust that he can find a way to avoid the Hickenlooper amendment."[21]

Pastor's description of this meeting suggested that Mann already had determined to implement the hard line on withholding loans to Peru to force a favorable settlement on the IPC issue, hence the "confusion" of the accompanying officials when Pastor raised the point. Mann also tried to convince Pastor that he would do what he could to avoid the Hickenlooper sanctions while at the same time hiding his true intentions and underlying policy, seeking to maintain a good personal relationship with the ambassador throughout, something that Pastor seemed to appreciate. The mutual courtship continued a few days later when Pastor hosted a banquet for Mann at the embassy residence, also attended, ironically, given what was supposed to be tension between the New Frontiersmen and the new assistant secretary, by Democratic Senator Edward Kennedy of Massachusetts. At the banquet, Mann praised Peruvian democracy and expressed his conviction that the historically good relations between the two countries would be strengthened in the future. Both Kennedy and Mann stayed until 2 A.M., something that Pastor said was unusual in the Washington diplomatic circuit, and after the banquet he hoped that "the cordial relationship established with Mann will be advantageous for our country."[22]

A few days later, on February 11, Pastor presented his credentials to President Johnson. In preparing Johnson for this meeting, national security advisor McGeorge Bundy informed the president of the danger of the administration being forced to apply the Hickenlooper amendment due to the IPC issue and a policy adopted by that time to grant Peru small loans but to defer approval of major loans. However, he added, "*We do not want to admit any such connection to the Peruvians*" (emphasis mine). Pastor, he observed, would be directly involved and play a major role in the negotiations over this matter. Therefore, Bundy suggested to Johnson that he clarify the U.S. concerns over the IPC issues and his hopes that it would be resolved equitably, but if Pastor made any connection "between the IPC problem and the delays in U.S. Agency for International Development

---

21. *Correspondencia* (5-3-Y/4) (February 1, 1964), 3.
22. *Correspondencia* (5-3-Y/6) (February 7, 1964), 3.

(AID) programs . . . that you side-step the question by making the general comment that, if the Peruvians would make a sincere effort to find a solution to the problem we have raised and if we do likewise with the problems the Peruvians have raised, the outlook will be optimistic for fruitful cooperation in achieving our mutual objectives."[23]

The only account of this meeting comes from Pastor, who does not mention the IPC matter being raised. Reporting to Lima on his conversation with Johnson and Mann, who also attended, Pastor presented a positive impression of this encounter. Johnson, he observed, made a special point of referring most matters to Mann, who, he emphasized, would be responsible for directing the Alliance for Progress, a program to which all parties present pledged their continuing commitment. The major initiative that Pastor presented was to try to reinforce the Texas connection, noting that Belaúnde had received his architecture degree from the state university and suggesting that some sort of cooperative relationship could be established between that state and Peru, an idea that appeared to produce a favorable reaction. The main point of his communication, however, was to underscore the close relationship he saw between Mann and Johnson and his impression that the appointment of Mann was a very positive development for Latin America and for Peru. As he stated, "I praised Mr. Mann's fine qualities and the good impression he made on us because of the knowledge he has of our problems and his willingness to contribute to their solution with a strong spirit of understanding. I ended by saying that we considered the appointment of Mr. Mann as a very good decision by the President of the United States." In response, Johnson reasserted his own confidence in Mann and asked Pastor to send his warmest regards to Belaúnde "with the hopes that Peru will continue on the road to progress"[24]

Pastor's effusive tribute to Mann certainly ran counter to popular impressions at the time. It seemed to reflect the assistant secretary's skillful cultivation of the Peruvian representative in their first meetings. Throughout Mann's time in office, Pastor would continue to have a good personal relationship with and a favorable impression of Johnson's man in charge of Latin American affairs. Indeed, forty years later, in an interview with me, Pastor repeated his high opinion of Mann, who throughout the IPC dispute claimed that his own hands were tied by the provisions of the Hickenlooper amendment in trying to work out a negotiated settlement. At one point, Pastor

23. "Conference Memorandum from McGeorge Bundy, February 7, 1964," CO 234, LBJ Library.
24. *Correspondencia* (5–3-A/56) (February 12, 1964), 1–2.

related, Mann suggested to the ambassador that Belaúnde could expropriate the IPC holdings and then compensate the company with money borrowed from the United States. Pastor relayed this offer to the Peruvian president, who rejected it.[25]

In his interview with me, Pastor also recalled that his post in Washington had been demanding and difficult. Pastor began to hint at some of these difficulties in his next communication to Lima. Meeting in the State Department with Belcher and Poole, he began with a proposal, following up on his conversations with Johnson and Mann, to establish contacts between Peru and Texas, something that these U.S. officials urged him to pursue. The main items on the agenda, however, were requests for economic assistance. In this regard, they were joined by AID official Robert Busemberg, in charge of Peruvian affairs, "who," in Pastor's words, "affirmed that intense collaboration with our country had already begun with a recently-signed agreement to provide financing for food purchases." Pastor then turned to loan funds for road-building projects, especially one to connect Pomacocha to Tarapoto and, at this point, was informed that "the process of granting these funds had been delayed within the Federal Reserve and the Treasury Department, who were raising certain questions with regard to the Hickenlooper amendment and a satisfactory resolution of the IPC matter." Pastor persisted with requests for information on promised assistance in airport construction, which he insisted were of the highest priority. He also raised questions about loans to support Belaúnde's agrarian reform proposals, with which the U.S. officials expressed considerable sympathy, but nothing concrete. In the end, he reported, "From this conversation I have received the impression that the directives of Mr. Thomas Mann in the sense of providing loans to Peru are going forward, but that their final resolution is being slowed for procedural reasons."[26]

Pastor's report on this meeting indicates pretty clearly that by this time the decision had been made to suspend assistance to Peru as a means to pressure the government on the IPC matter. However, as this kabuki-like policy unfolded, at least as far as Pastor was concerned, the real "message" had not yet been clearly received, or at least it was one he was reluctant to acknowledge. The slowdown, he concluded, was due more to "bureaucratic inefficiency" than to any punitive policy, and his admiration and friendly feelings toward Mann continued unabated.

---

25. Personal interview with Celso Pastor de la Torre, Lima, Peru, June 23, 2004.
26. *Correspondencia* (5–3-A/70) (February 18, 1964), 1–2.

Getting the Message

Pastor returned to Peru for a brief visit at the end of March. *Caretas* offered a flattering portrait, describing him as a particularly effective and hardworking diplomat who had succeeded in getting commitments for 1,200,000 soles in loans. (The sol, the Peruvian currency, at the time was trading at 3.75 to the dollar.) His diplomatic style, the magazine averred, was "of the most modern" and was characterized by a U.S. journalist as infused by "a contagious enthusiasm" and had "awakened in the important newspapers of the United States a new appreciation of Peru thanks to the ambassador's actions." Formerly, it concluded, only the Chileans had been so successful in gaining access to the North American press to the benefit of their country. Now, because of Pastor, Peru could compete on equal terms with its major South American rival.[27] In an interview with *La Prensa*, Pastor expressed his own satisfaction with "the interest that Peru has provoked in the United States" and asserted that the actions of the Belaúnde government had "created a favorable and welcoming environment for Peru." He also listed a number of U.S.-backed loans granted to Peru with more in the pipeline.[28]

Belaúnde was less upbeat, and there were increasing signs that he, at least, was beginning to get some of the message that Mann intended. On February 28, 1964, speaking extemporaneously at graduation ceremonies at the National Agrarian University (La Molina), with the U.S. ambassador and AID representative present, Belaúnde "sharply criticized the slowness of aid through the Alliance for Progress," and, in apparent reference to the IPC, "claimed that the noble purposes of the Alliance were being obstructed by private interests." Whether Belaúnde saw this lack of action as directly linked to the new policies proposed by Mann is not clear. He did, however, suggest that his administration might begin to look elsewhere for assistance, with some in the press taking this to mean opening up commercial relations with communist countries. Foreign Minister Fernando Schwalb soon clarified this to mean seeking such relations with Western as opposed to Eastern European states.[29]

An article on Peru published in the June 1964 *Commentary* by Norman Gall reiterated Belaúnde's complaints. Citing a recent interview with the

---

27. *Caretas*, 14, 286 (March 24–April 8, 1964), 10.
28. *La Prensa*, March 19, 1964, 2.
29. "Limited Official Use Airgram from Haahr, March 4, 1964," U.S. Department of State, *Records of the Department of State Relating to Internal Affairs of Peru (1964–1966)*, Record Group 59, United States National Archives [hereafter USNA], Box 2574, 1–2.

president, Gall repeated his complaints that so far there had been little real U.S. assistance provided to support his ambitious reform plans. Gall sympathized with Belaúnde and agreed that the United States had failed to give him the necessary support to take on the Peruvian oligarchy and to implement the kind of social and economic reforms that would underpin a real "democratic revolution." Part of the problem, Gall argued, was due to what he described as a serious asymmetry in the U.S. aid mission, "bizarrely overstaffed in its comfortable Lima office and understaffed in the field." If it were not for the 450 Peace Corps volunteers in the country, the impact of the U.S. aid effort in Peru would be barely negligible.[30] Some of these problems were of long standing and had little to do with Mann's decision to withhold assistance.[31] That decision, however, would do little to alleviate the problems to which both Belaúnde and Gall alluded.

Back in Washington, Pastor reported on a Johnson press conference following the coup in Brazil in which the U.S. president responded to critics who claimed that he was paying less attention to Latin America than had his predecessor. In that conference, Johnson reiterated his confidence in Mann, announced the naming of White House advisor Walt Rostow—another pragmatist—to replace Moscoso as the U.S. representative on the directive board of the Alliance for Progress and reemphasized his commitment to providing assistance to the southern hemisphere. In this connection, he also announced his intention to extend his recently proclaimed War on Poverty to Latin America.[32]

Pastor did what he could to direct Alliance funding toward Peru. In early May, he reported on a speech he had given to the U.S. Foreign Service Institute, wherein he made the argument that his country could serve as a model for the alliance, "achieving within a brief time the kind of social and economic progress" that the program envisioned. Therefore, he encouraged his listeners to supply "*immediately* [emphasis mine] all the financial and technical resources necessary" to realize this vision.[33] In mid-June, he visited San Antonio, Texas, where he was the principal speaker at a banquet to inaugurate a committee of the so-called Partners of the Alliance that would establish a cooperative program of state-to-nation assistance. During his visit, he called for extending the War on Poverty to Latin America; underscored the Texas links among Johnson, Mann, and Belaúnde; and

---

30. Gall, "Letter from Peru," 68.
31. For a fuller account of U.S. assistance operations in Peru in the 1960s, see Peeler, "The Politics of the Alliance for Progress in Peru."
32. *Correspondencia* (5-3-A/160) (April 8, 1964), 1.
33. *Correspondencia* (5-3-A/215) (May 4, 1964), 1-2.

repeated the argument that Peru could be a showcase for the alliance.³⁴ In Congress, Democratic Representative Henry B. Gonzalez of San Antonio trumpeted the agreement as establishing a unique kind of partnership that "will help assure the people of Latin America of our concern for their struggle to rise above poverty and despair."³⁵ Whether any concrete actions would flow from these promising words remained to be seen.

Behind the scenes, Pastor finally seemed to be getting the message on the connection between assistance and the IPC. On May 14, he met with Mann to express frustration with the delays in providing assistance to Peru. He also pointed out that currently more U.S. assistance was going to dictatorships in Latin America like Brazil than to democracies like Peru. He also complained that both Chile and Colombia seemed to be receiving much more aid than his country. Mann reassured him that Peru would receive as much aid as Colombia in 1965 and that about one-fifth of a $40 million loan to Peru already had been disbursed. Once again, Mann's magic seemed to work with Pastor. Reporting back on his "long, frank, and cordial conversation," the ambassador observed that "I received with great joy these most emphatic, most enthusiastic, and most cordial manifestations of Mr. Mann."³⁶

In early July, Pastor tried to defend Peru's interests on another front. On July 10, President Johnson, along with assistant secretaries of state George Ball and Thomas Mann, spoke to an assembly of all the Latin American ambassadors to the United States called to the White House for a frank exchange of ideas. The president repeated his commitment to the region and to the Alliance for Progress. According to Pastor, most of the diplomats reported rather optimistically of progress in their respective countries, but when the Peruvian ambassador's turn came, he decided to honor the stated purpose of the gathering and to speak his mind. While Peru was, Pastor reminded the assembly, "an authentic democracy, with economic liberty and a solid currency," it, like all Latin American nations, was suffering from unfavorable terms of trade with the United States. In essence, it was receiving less for the goods, mostly raw materials, it was selling to the United States and paying more for the imports it bought from that country. In particular, he raised concerns about quotas imposed on exports, especially on Peruvian sugar. This, he realized, was a complicated problem, but it was one, he believed, that had to be addressed. Pastor noted that other regions had

---

34. *Correspondencia* (5–3-A/283) (July 7, 1964), 1.
35. *Congressional Record—House* (June 25, 1964), 15007–8.
36. *Correspondencia* (5–3-Y/22) (May 18, 1964), 1–4.

created trade blocs to resolve some of these issues, but this was not the case between the United States and Latin America. Despite Ball's attempts to have Johnson evade this issue (according to Pastor), the president seemed to respond favorably. As usual, he asked Mann to look into the matter. Mann, in turn, said that not only would the present quota for Peruvian sugar be maintained but also increased. In his report to Lima, Pastor concluded that his action at that meeting promised positive results and that he had been congratulated by other diplomats for presenting Peru's position so forcefully.[37]

Pastor was also encouraged by a letter he received from Mann a few days later. Before the meeting on the tenth, Pastor had communicated to the assistant secretary his concerns that, as had been reported in the press, the administration was planning to recommend to Congress that the quota for imported sugar in general be revised and reduced. In reply, Mann assured Pastor that he knew of no plans to revise the Sugar Act to the detriment of Peru or of any other country.[38] Despite these reassurances, Tad Szulc reported in the September 24 *New York Times* that Latin American nations remained worried that the U.S. Congress would act to limit imports of coffee, meat, and sugar, an article that Pastor forwarded to Lima.[39] Reports of such possible action led *Caretas* to comment that cutting Peru's sugar quota would have serious economic consequences and ran contrary to "the spirit that inspired the policy of President Kennedy in his relations with Latin America."[40] In light of this threat, Pastor continued to press various officials in the State Department and the Department of Agriculture to look out for his nation's interests on this issue, arguing as he had throughout that cutting the sugar quota would undermine the "ideals that sustained the Alliance for Progress."[41]

While Pastor appeared to continue to have a good impression and a good personal relationship with Mann, little was being accomplished to loosen the U.S. aid purse strings. In late August, Pastor had yet another three-hour "cordial" conversation with Mann to discuss various issues, with the assistant secretary underscoring the importance of resolving the IPC issue

---

37. *Correspondencia* (5-3-A/296) (July 13, 1964), 5. In his interview with me in 2004, Pastor recalled that he had a good impression of Johnson and believed that he had a good relationship with him. What appeared to be the positive results of the July 1964 encounter might be evidence of this.
38. *Correspondencia* (5-3-A/304) (July 16, 1964), 2.
39. *Correspondencia* (5-3-A/392) (September 24, 1964), 1–3.
40. *Caretas*, 14, 297 (September 18–25, 1964), 10.
41. Near the end of the year, Pastor provided the foreign ministry with a detailed accounting of his meeting with various U.S. officials on the sugar quota question and made several specific recommendations for points that the government should make in promoting the nation's position on this matter. *Correspondencia* (5-3-A/405) (October 6, 1964), 1.

and expressing his confidence that such a resolution could be found.[42] The words of confidence, however, had no immediate result. In October, the president of Peru's Chamber of Deputies asked for the ambassador's help in getting the United States to approve an $18 million AID loan to finish airport construction in the country's major cities, including Lima. As the congressional leader noted, there had been a delay of more than a year in delivering the promised funds. Pastor forwarded the request to the appropriate officials in the State Department and spoke personally with Mann about the matter, but with no satisfactory response.[43] Clearly, the unspoken hard-line policy was still in effect.

The Belaúnde Administration Through the Eyes of the U.S. Embassy

Enjoying something of a honeymoon, Belaúnde was able to notch some early accomplishments despite the unfavorable congressional lineup. He managed, for example, to initiate his Cooperación Popular program with some success and to achieve something of a start on public works development, especially road building. In May 1964, Congress approved his agrarian reform proposal, which, while watered down, was still a beginning in trying to address the problems associated with *latifundio*, especially in the Peruvian sierra. Earlier, he carried through on his promise to hold municipal elections. These had been provided for in the Constitution of 1933 but had never been held nationwide. When they were, in December 1963, the Acción Popular–Christian Democratic slate won almost 48 percent of the vote to the Aprista Party–Unión Nacional Odriista coalition's 44 percent. In Lima, it was thought that Odría's wife, María Delgado, who enjoyed considerable popularity because of her charitable works (sometimes likened to Eva Perón in this regard), would carry the day. Instead, Luis Bedoya Reyes, a close friend of the president and an important figure in the Christian Democratic Party, won an overwhelming victory.[44]

These victories aside, that the opposition controlled Congress and was determined to stymie any major initiatives from Belaúnde severely constrained his field of action. They constantly blocked his more innovative initiatives and often called his ministers to account, using a power of interpellation that led to frequent changes in the cabinet. He was also hemmed

---

42. *Correspondencia* (5-3-Y/45) (September 1, 1964), 1–5.
43. *Correspondencia* (5-3-A/405) (October 6, 1964), 1.
44. Astiz, *Pressure Groups and Power Elites in Peruvian Politics*, 110.

in by constitutional provisions that gave Congress great power in budget making, especially in approving new taxes and, unlike most presidents elsewhere in the Americas, he had no veto power. There were some who urged him to bypass Congress through referenda or by appointing an all-military cabinet. Belaúnde, however, remained steadfastly committed to democracy and tried mightily to convince the opposition to see things his way. Despite good personal relations with many of the opposition leaders, including Haya de la Torre, this was something he was unable to do. However admirable Belaúnde's vision of trying to be a different kind of democratic leader for Peru, critics chastised him for being weak (*sin pantalones*) in the face of determined opposition, a view that might well have been shared by some in the U.S. embassy and State Department.[45]

Reports from Ambassador John Wesley Jones and others reflected what the U.S. embassy in Lima saw as the strengths and weaknesses of Belaúnde's first months in office. The municipal elections were described as a significant victory for the government, the principal results of which, one commentator suggested, would be to force the Apristas to change their leadership and their "style in the face of the challenge from the new progressivism represented by Belaúnde's AP-DC Alliance."[46] However, various reports underscored a continuing concern with what appeared to be increasing activity and support for the extreme left in Peru, especially among young people. In early February, Ernest V. Siracusa, deputy chief of mission of the embassy, met with up-and-coming Peruvian diplomat Javier Pérez de Cuellar (later secretary-general of the United Nations), serving then as acting secretary-general of the Foreign Ministry, to discuss evidence of Castro-inspired subversive activity in Peru and to explore the possibility of bringing such activity to the attention of the Organization of American States.[47]

A few days later, James Haahr of the embassy staff forwarded a report on a public meeting held in Lima's Plaza San Martín on February 7, 1964, to unite all the major leftist groups in the country. In attendance were the Frente de Liberación Nacional (National Liberation Front, or FLN), the Frente de Izquierda Revolucionaria (Leftist Revolutionary Front, or FIR), the pro-Peking branch of the Communist Party, and the Movimiento de Izquierda Revolucionaria (Leftist Revolutionary Movement, or MIR). The most dynamic and effective speech of the night was delivered by the head

---

45. For more on this aspect of Belaúnde's personality, see Jaquette, *The Politics of Development in Peru*, 140–41.
46. "Limited Official Use Airgram from Haahr, January 12, 1964," USNA (1964–1966) (Box 2575), 5.
47. "Confidential Airgram A/602, February 9, 1964," USNA (1964–1966) (Box 2576), 1.

of the MIR, Luis de la Puente Uceda, whose call for violent revolution was received "enthusiastically" by those in attendance.[48]

Soon after this public meeting, another source, probably a Central Intelligence Agency "mole," reported back to Washington on de la Puente's revolutionary agenda. According to this source, at a secret meeting in Lima, de la Puente claimed that the MIR had arms assembled in various neighboring countries ready for import into Peru as well as about $3 million contributed by the Chinese government to finance the revolutionary effort located in Swiss banks as well as other funds available in various Chinese embassies in Europe.[49] At another secret meeting two days later, de la Puente informed his colleagues that the MIR would begin operations in two or three months. He also claimed to have received a letter from Mao Tse-Tung encouraging him in his efforts and recommending that all parties of the left unite.[50]

In addition to following the activities of de la Puente and others, U.S. diplomats throughout these years carefully monitored what they saw as growing leftist influence within Peru's universities. The U.S. consul in Arequipa, George C. Mitchell, for example, reported on a meeting held in that city on January 24, 1964, wherein student and labor leaders lambasted the Johnson administration for its recent "aggression" and "imperialism" in putting down student-led riots in Panama. One of the speakers criticized the Peace Corps for the work it was doing in Arequipa's slums (*barriadas*), arguing that by emphasizing general improvement of their properties rather than by teaching slum dwellers industrial skills, the volunteers were contributing to the "colonial" mentality that the United States allegedly wanted to maintain in Peru. He also urged the local University of San Agustín to expel the five volunteers who were teaching there on the grounds that they were "imperialist" agents. According to Mitchell, this was part of a larger communist-inspired campaign to remove all volunteers from Peru's universities, something that they had been able to accomplish the previous year at the National University of Huamanga in Ayacucho (later to be the birthplace of Sendero Luminoso, or Shining Path).[51]

---

48. "Airgram from Haahr, February 13, 1964," USNA (1964–1966) (Box 2574), 1. In his speech, de la Puente declared Belaúnde's government already a "bankrupt failure" and claimed that "the strongest economic sectors are represented in the present Parliament [and are] . . . unconditional lackeys of the North American monopolies. . . ." As quoted in Jaquette, *The Politics of Development in Peru*, 143.

49. U.S. Central Intelligence Agency, Intelligence Information Cable, "Decision by the Movimiento de Izquierda Revolucionaria to begin Preparations for Revolution, February 11, 1964," NSF, LBJ Library.

50. United States Central Intelligence Agency, Intelligence Information Cable, "Plans of the MIR for Revolutionary Action, February 12, 1964," 3, NSF, LBJ Library.

51. "Airgram from George C. Mitchell, Arequipa, January 26, 1964," USNA (1964–1966) (Box 2574), 1.

The main preoccupation of the embassy in these months, however, remained primarily focused on how the Belaúnde administration was responding to U.S. attempts to pressure it on the IPC issue. In a January 15, 1964, confidential telegram to Mann, Ambassador Jones reported on the current state of affairs on this issue, with the United States "dragging its feet" on supplying $64 million in AID funding for Peru in an attempt to get the Belaúnde administration to restart negotiations with IPC. Following this course, which in effect was applying the Hickenlooper sanctions without actually doing so, Jones saw as treading "on dangerous ground," and he expressed his own hope "that we can resume a normal pace of operations at [the] earliest possible moment." Jones also added his rather favorable impression of the Belaúnde government, describing it as "respectable, democratic and progressive [with] every evidence of a desire for close collaboration and warm friendship with [the] US." Peru, he believed, was a country that could "achieve real progress" under the alliance, and he encouraged Mann to meet as soon as possible with Ambassador Pastor (which he did on January 30) and to impress on him the importance of "renewing actual negotiations (on the IPC matter) and, eventually, of achieving [a] bilateral solution of this problem."[52]

One month later, reporting on Foreign Minister Schwalb's maiden speech to Congress in February, the embassy noted the minister's heavy emphasis on the oil issue and his implication that receiving economic assistance from the United States was "excessively conditioned" on a resolution favorable to IPC. The dispatch also noted that "his criticism of the Alliance for Progress and foreign aid was especially strong. In talking with Ambassador Jones before his presentation, however, he said that his remarks on the Alliance should not be interpreted as an unfriendly reference to the United States. He said that his Government was very grateful for whatever help it received from the Alliance and depended on it very much. His remarks were to be understood as an expression of urgent need for more help."[53] They could also be understood as an expression of the frustration the new Peruvian

---

52. "Confidential Telegram 822 from Jones to Mann, January 15, 1964," in *FRUS, 1964–1968*, vol. 31, *South and Central America; Mexico* (Washington, D.C.: Government Printing Office, 2004), 988–89. On February 12, Mann discussed the IPC situation with President Johnson by telephone and advised him that he did not see it as a major problem at the moment, with Belaúnde reported to have plans for a takeover of the company some thirty years down the road. However, Mann said, "I'm going to have to warn about expropriation and the Hickenlooper Amendment applies to this," but there is no indication of just how and when this would be done or to whom the warning would be directed. Ibid., 988–89n7.

53. "Limited Official Use Airgram from Haahr, February 15, 1964," USNA (1964–1966) (Box 2575), 1.

administration felt at being caught between the nationalist demands of its political supporters (and opponents) and the need to maintain good relations with the United States.

Belaúnde's own frustrations, as revealed in his February 28 remarks at La Molina, have already been referred to. By late March, the embassy was beginning to report that the honeymoon was already over for the new president, with the IPC issue as only one of several mounting problems. Tensions were emerging within the governing coalition. The Christian Democrats apparently were willing to allow Belaúnde considerable latitude in resolving the confrontation with Standard Oil, while members of his own party were expressing concerns that the president would make unnecessary concessions to resolve the dispute. His supporters were also growing impatient with what they perceived to be Belaúnde's unwillingness to confront the opposition Apristas and Odriistas, who were continuing to block the administration's initiatives in Congress. Increasingly, too, the opposition accused Belaúnde of being "soft on communism," responsible, they charged, for a number of labor disturbances over the past few months (while progovernment spokesmen blamed the Apristas for stirring up their own unions as behind these protests) and leveling accusations against Minister of Education Francisco Miro Quesada for allegedly turning his ministry into a "nest of communism."

The embassy's explanation for the administration's difficulties emphasized Belaúnde's lack of experience and pragmatism. According to one analysis, Belaúnde and his team were new to the job, and it was taking some time for them to learn the political ropes. They were also finding how difficult it was to turn visionary promises into concrete reality. There were some signs, however, that the president was beginning to develop a surer political footing and was working to effect some changes in the way he dealt with Congress. Moreover, while some saw the president as becoming too closed off from the public and too dependent on a small group of advisors, the analysis concluded that for all his growing difficulties "Belaunde still appears to be in control and it should be recalled that his political career generally has been characterized by ups and downs in popularity and prestige. However, he is now in the driver's seat which is a much more difficult and demanding position than he ever has had in the past."[54]

The difficulties for Belaúnde were more than evident when the leaders

---

54. "Confidential Airgram from Haahr on 'Current Problems Faced by President Belaunde,' March 18, 1964," USNA (1964–1966) (Box 2575), 1–6.

of Acción Popular met in Ayacucho at the end of May. At that meeting, they took their most radical position yet on the IPC issue, calling for the complete nationalization of the company's oil fields and refinery. This position went further than the positions of both Belaúnde and his coalition partner, the Christian Democrats.[55] In response, Belaúnde tried to distance himself from the party's left wing, making clear in another meeting a few days later that he "wanted nothing to do with any talk about Moscow, Peking or any other similar place," and, in the words of the reporting officer, with regard to the leftist faction, "might not be unhappy if this group decided to leave AP at some future date." Then, a few days after the meeting, the AP Directive Committee announced that Mario Villaran Rivera had been separated from the party. Villaran, a deputy from Lima, had been with Belaúnde since 1956 and was considered the number two official within Acción Popular. According to the embassy dispatch, "Villaran was, and probably remains, the leader of the left wing of the party and some consider him to be a communist."[56]

How much these actions against the left wing of the governing party were related to the IPC issue cannot be determined, but there seems little doubt it played a role. In midyear, too, Belaúnde made some cabinet changes, appointing as his minister of government a former naval officer, Miguel Rotalde Romana. An apolitical native of Belaúnde's home city of Arequipa, he was described by a former U.S. naval attaché as "strongly and seriously anti-communist" and "extremely pro-US."[57]

Not all members of the Peruvian armed forces in government positions were as sympathetic to U.S. interests. In a confidential communication dated April 15, 1964, Ambassador Jones reported on a lengthy luncheon discussion he had with General Pedro Puente, director of the National Telecommunications Board, regarding a rate hike requested by the Peruvian Telephone Company (PERUTELCO), a subsidiary of International Telephone and Telegraph (IT&T). Despite Jones's arguments on behalf of the company's position, the general stated that he and the board would reject any increase in rates and made clear his and the board's "antagonistic attitude" toward the company. Any rate increases at this point, he argued, "are out of the

55. "Confidential Airgram from Haahr, June 21, 1964," USNA (1964–1966) (Box 2574), 1. In a meeting with Ambassador Jones on May 6, Belaúnde had assured him that contrary to certain rumors there would be no expropriation of the IPC holdings. Jones, in turn, asserted that "we are not using our AID programs to protect U.S. private interests" and that the embassy stood ready to provide its good offices for a negotiation of the dispute. "Confidential Telegram 1287 from Jones to DOS, May 6, 1964," NSF, Box 72, Folder 7, LBJ Library.
56. "Airgram from Haahr, June 18, 1964," USNA (1964–1966) (Box 2574), 1.
57. "Limited Official Use Airgram from Haahr, August 10, 1964," USNA (1964–1966) (Box 2575), 2.

question because of local political factors," and "if the Executive authorized such increases the Congress would only annul them."[58]

This case, while enjoying a much lower profile than that of IPC, seemed to fit a common pattern. In 1930, IT&T had come to control much of the nation's phone service, especially in Lima. For the next thirty years, and particularly under the Odría administration, it had been able to expand and improve its service at an acceptable pace. After Odría, however, it faced a growing Peruvian nationalism directed toward foreign enterprises, especially foreign monopolies, which made getting rate increases politically difficult, if not impossible. Without rate hikes, the company argued, it could not maintain the level of service required. The quality of service deteriorated rapidly, making the argument for rate increases even weaker and leading for calls from many for a government takeover of this foreign-owned enterprise.[59]

While there were concerns over these and other matters, embassy reports on the Peruvian reaction to the election of Christian Democrat Eduardo Frei as president of Chile in September were clearly upbeat. The Johnson administration, primarily through the CIA, had worked hard to assure Frei's victory. As the embassy reported back to Washington, the reaction to the Chilean result "was unanimously favorable among all sectors of democratic opinion in Peru." It saw the Frei triumph as significantly strengthening the hand of the Christian Democrats in Peru: "Although overconfidence and excessive demands for power within present or future coalitions may be a danger in the short run, the future of the PDC in Peru seems considerably brighter after the events in Chile."[60] By implication, a stronger Christian Democratic partner might also help Belaúnde maintain a more moderate course within his own governing coalition.

Belaúnde and Mann

The two main protagonists in the IPC matter finally met face to face at the end of 1964. Arriving in Lima on December 4 for a meeting of the Inter-American Social and Economic Council, Mann publicly praised the economic situation in Peru, claiming that it was producing a "very good impression" in the United States.[61] On the next day, in the company of

---

58. "Confidential Airgram from Jones, April 15, 1964," USNA (1964–1966) (Box 2575), 1.
59. Goodsell, *American Corporations and Peruvian Politics*, 54–55.
60. "Limited Official Use Airgram, October 4, 1964," USNA (1964–1966) (Box 2575), 1.
61. *El Comercio*, December 5, 1964, 1.

Jones and Siracusa, he held a two-and-half-hour discussion with Belaúnde in the presidential palace. After the usual exchange of niceties, during which Mann complimented Belaúnde "as heading the kind of progressive, democratic and socially conscious government which the United States likes to see and cooperate with in Latin America," the Peruvian president began an extensive presentation of what he believed were some of the major accomplishments of his administration, as well as his vision for the future. These included efforts at agrarian reform and, of course, his ambitious road-building plans, both of which required considerable financial investment. While he admitted that congressional opposition was a continuing problem, he believed that he had good personal relationships with the leaders of UNO and APRA, with whom he often lunched or dined "in an harmonious and friendly atmosphere." He also claimed to have significantly reduced the attraction that many young Peruvians felt for Castroism "to the point where it is no longer a threat." Progress had also been achieved on the international front, with improved relations with Peru's immediate neighbors.

Throughout his early remarks, Belaúnde underscored what he considered was an "excellent relationship" between his government and that of the United States. He especially praised the warm ties established with Ambassador Jones, the work of Peace Corps volunteers, the close cooperation on military affairs, and the general coincidence between the two nations on foreign policy issues. As he often did, Belaúnde then turned to a rather detailed description of his vision for the *carretera marginal*. This discussion, however, simply provided an interlude for what all knew was the main purpose of the meeting—how, if possible, to resolve the IPC dispute. For his part, Belaúnde defended his administration's treatment of foreign investment in general, its desire to continue to attract such investment, and what he considered his "sound and sober" economic and fiscal policies. But, he added, support from the Alliance for Progress had been slow and uncertain and program grants "are for some reason (apart from their merit) being held up." He mentioned in particular the slowdown in getting funds to complete airport construction.

Mann's response was twofold. First, he argued that U.S. assistance funds were scarce and difficult to get approved in a Congress that was growing increasingly skeptical about foreign aid in general. Second, this matter was clearly related to the IPC case and for Mann it was a matter of principle— "the principle being the deeply ingrained respect in the American society for the rights of private property and its protection under the law." However, Mann did not explicitly say that it was his decision to condition funds to Peru on a satisfactory resolution of the IPC matter but rather the difficulties he faced in getting congressional approval for assistance in light of larger political concerns over the possible expropriation of U.S.-owned properties. Mann then made a serious tactical mistake by mentioning the forthcoming announcement of some $600 million in aid to Brazil and Chile "to ward off economic disaster," implying that this commitment would constrain efforts to aid other Latin American nations.

With this, Mann touched a sensitive nerve. Belaúnde responded rather heatedly that it would be a disaster if it were to be known publicly that the United States considered the governments of those two nations more worthy of support than his own. "It would be a blow to Peru, to his government and to him personally." After implying that the lesson of favoritism toward neighboring republics would be to pursue irresponsible fiscal policies and to play on Cold War fears as a way to curry favor and support from the United States, he concluded that "he was disheartened and disillusioned by what Mr. Mann had told him." Belaúnde's frustrations could not have been clearer.

Mann did what he could to mollify the president by trying to explain the reasons for the support to Brazil and Chile at this particular time. If either country "had gone left," as had seemed likely, it would have produced "a true disaster of continental proportions." He then went on to try to emphasize the importance of property rights within the North American legal system, placing the IPC case within that context. Belaúnde responded forcefully that IPC had undertaken "a campaign of propaganda and lies which had created a totally false image" with regard to the truth. Despite what he considered the company's unethical behavior, he was nonetheless in favor of allowing the company to continue to operate in Peru under the terms of a new contract more in line with the nation's constitutional norms than the present one. He also emphasized that there was no question of expropriation or confiscation.

Mann replied by agreeing to consider the president's position but again reiterated the importance of the principle of protecting the sanctity of private property. He asked for a timetable for a new contract, but Belaúnde emphasized the difficulty of negotiating this matter on the home front and the delicate problem of dealing with the Christian Democrats, who were moving from a more moderate to a more extreme position on this issue. Nonetheless, he hoped some new proposal could be put together in the next few weeks. Mann was encouraged by this prospect and Belaúnde's assurances but also warned the president about "the danger in an ill-defined situation without adequate guarantees, of confiscation by taxation, or other means of attrition and harassment." He then suggested that the dispute could be taken to an international tribunal for resolution. Belaúnde, however, rejected this possibility, reflecting a general Peruvian distrust that their position would be treated favorably in such a setting. "The only problem," he concluded, was "to achieve agreement with the IPC Company, and he emphasized again his desire to do so."[62]

Mann and Belaúnde were slated to continue their discussions at a later date, but no record in the files exists of what transpired. However, neither side emerged very satisfied with the exchange, and even though this appeared to be a frank and open conversation, both sides were hiding things from the other. Mann was still trying to convey his hard-line message that aid was being used as a lever to get a favorable resolution on the IPC dispute without coming right out and saying so.[63] Belaúnde must have recognized by this time that this was the strategy being employed but also appeared reluctant to bring it out on the table in a forthright manner. The meeting, in the end, while giving the Peruvian president an opportunity to vent his frustrations, did little to change Mann's and the United States' position; economic assistance was still withheld, and no progress was made on the Peruvian side in resolving the IPC dilemma, which would continue to fester for several more years.

62. "Secret Memorandum of Conversation, December 5, 1964," USNA (1964–1966) (Box 2575), 1–8.
63. In an oral interview several years later, Mann recalled that he had impressed on Belaúnde the need to compensate the IPC if its holdings were expropriated but made no mention of withholding aid to Peru until this principle was adhered to. Transcript, Thomas C. Mann Oral History Interview I, November 4, 1968, by Joe B. Frantz, Internet Copy, LBJ Library, 23–24.

3

BELAÚNDE, THE COUNTERGUERRILLA CAMPAIGN, AND THE ROLE OF THE UNITED STATES

For Fernando Belaúnde Terry and Peru in 1965 and into 1966, there were some encouraging developments on the economic front. Significant progress was made in public works. In addition to construction proceeding on the *carretera marginal*, there were major advances in port expansion, housing, health care, water and sewerage, and irrigation. The economy continued to grow at a healthy rate, especially in the fishing, fish meal, and manufacturing sectors. Wages for white-collar and blue-collar workers rose, employment opportunities expanded, and the regime faced few major strikes in this period. Despite the ongoing difficulties with the IPC issue and the slowness in U.S. public assistance, private investment in Peru, particularly from the United States, continued to increase. Overall, the book value of U.S. direct investment grew from 436 million in 1961 to 605 million in 1967, with mining and manufacturing leading the way.[1]

Economic progress aside, Belaúnde faced some daunting challenges in 1965. The most significant was a guerrilla uprising that, for a time, posed a serious threat. While the threat was ultimately thwarted, the campaign had significant long-term consequences. On the diplomatic front, Peruvian-U.S. relations experienced some tensions. Peru strongly disapproved of the

---

1. Kuczynski, *Peruvian Democracy Under Economic Stress*, 10. For more on the economic growth of these years, see Parodi Trece, *Perú 1960–2000*, 81–85.

U.S. intervention in the Dominican Republic, and a serious dispute arose over fishing rights off the Peruvian coast. The IPC issue continued to fester, and a visit by Robert F. Kennedy to Peru in late 1965 served to roil rather than to calm the diplomatic waters.

A "Model" Alliance President

Despite certain disagreements and disputes, the public impression of Belaúnde in the United States was enhanced by some favorable press coverage. His picture graced the cover of the March 12, 1965, edition of *Time* magazine, one of the few Latin American leaders, especially democratic leaders, to receive such attention in the 1960s. The article, detailing the challenges that Belaúnde and other democratic reformers faced, was laudatory, claiming that the Peruvian leader "has captured the imagination of his people as no one before" and that "as far as the U.S. is concerned, he is the very model of an *Alianza* President." The article praised the economic growth that had been achieved: "Nurtured along by Belaúnde's firm hand and the president's vision for the future." It also observed that the former fiery orator was now "calmer, [and] more tolerant" and described his agrarian reform bill as "one of the most sensible in Latin America." Belaúnde not only had been able to attract substantial U.S. investment, but also his reformist regime had stymied any significant communist advance in the country. According to *Time*, "the Communists are few and out of date in Peru. The country is too busy working on Fernando Belaúnde's Peruvian architecture to pay much attention to foreign voices."[2]

A somewhat more sober although essentially upbeat assessment was provided by historian James C. Carey, in the December 1965 issue of *Current History*. Despite what he called the "razzle-dazzle" of the government's political efforts, there had been little real amelioration of Peru's fundamental social and economic problems. While some small gains had been made in road building and public housing, most of this had been achieved through U.S. loans and barely scratched the surface of the nation's essential needs to reduce the glaring gap between the few rich and many poor. However, Belaúnde had managed to get many of the nation's competing constituencies to cooperate on certain essential matters, and despite the challenges and difficulties, the chances for future success, he asserted, "are better than they have been in 20 years." And, if Belaúnde were to succeed, it would also

2. "Peru: The New Conquest," *Time*, March 12, 1965, 32–42.

prove a significant success for the ideals behind the Alliance for Progress. Trying to achieve a balance between Peruvian nationalist sentiments and pressures from Washington, Belaúnde's somewhat independent foreign policy, Carey concluded, "seems to be a more accurate reflection of the feeling of many Peruvians" than had been the case in the past.[3]

Pastor's View from Washington

As Belaúnde sought to chart a more independent course regarding the United States, Ambassador Celso Pastor de la Torre continued to press his government's interests in Washington and to report back to Lima on what he considered the most important developments that might affect Peru. In a communication at the beginning of the year, he reiterated his continued favorable impression of Mann, praising him for resolving several ongoing problems between the United States and various Latin American nations and relayed reports that the assistant secretary was being mentioned as a possible successor to Secretary of State Dean Rusk, an eventuality that Pastor seemed to favor.[4] At about the same time, in a secret communication, the ambassador reported on a three-hour conversation he had had with Vice President Hubert Humphrey when both had been in Puerto Rico for the installation of a new governor. The main item discussed was the IPC issue, with Pastor complaining of the slowness of Alliance aid to Peru that, it was becoming increasingly clear, was being used as a lever for his nation to accommodate the company's interests. He called this policy "myopic" and counterproductive and blamed it on "the unwise eagerness of some functionaries to lend their ample support to petroleum interests, without taking into account the larger picture and without taking into account, equally, that that policy could have a grave impact on the old and cordial relations that unite our two peoples." Humphrey promised to look into the matter upon his return to Washington and warmly praised Belaúnde's democratic orientation and reform efforts.[5] Nothing concrete, however, resulted.

In subsequent reports, Pastor emphasized his repeated efforts to speed up U.S. assistance to Peru and the continued frustrations he encountered in this regard. Nonetheless, he still maintained both good relations with and

---

3. Carey, "Peru," 323–27.
4. *Correspondencia* (5–3-A/21) (January 14, 1965), 1.
5. *Correspondencia* (5–3-Y/1) (January 6, 1965), 1.

a good impression of Mann, who he still saw as a "friend of Peru" and who, apparently, he did not see as among those "functionaries" who were acting on behalf of "petroleum interests" in blocking aid to his nation. When he met in February with Jack Hood Vaughn, who replaced Mann as assistant secretary of state for Inter-American Affairs, he reported that Vaughn had assured him of continuity in policy. "I am Mann's man," Vaughn claimed. This Pastor saw as a positive statement in that "Mr. Mann at all times has revealed a great sympathy towards our nation and favors the idea of providing Peru with the greatest economic and technical assistance possible."[6]

While it is impossible to know exactly why Pastor continued to adhere to such a favorable view of Mann, it certainly seemed to run counter to that of many others. Pastor sent a report to Lima in late March that included protestations from the Argentine and Chilean governments about Mann's alleged "geo-strategic plan" to have the United States dominate Latin America.[7] Whatever the truth of those allegations, it is hard to explain why Pastor would look favorably on the individual who was the main architect of the policy to withhold aid to Peru over the IPC issue unless the ambassador truly believed that policy was being carried out by "underlings" in the State Department on their own, an unlikely occurrence given the unusual authority over Latin American policy that Mann possessed. Perhaps, too, Pastor was reluctant to admit that Mann might be the main figure in the policy, given what appeared to be a good personal chemistry between the two men, which Pastor might have hoped could overcome any policy differences and work to his and Peru's advantage. Whatever the reasons, there is no indication in either Pastor's nonconfidential or confidential communications to Lima that Mann was responsible for the "go-slow" policy with regard to alliance aid and was anything other than friendly toward Peru's interests.

Pastor also had a favorable impression, at least initially, of Vaughn. He described him to Lima as intelligent, fluent in Spanish, and knowledgeable of the region and the "idiosyncrasies of its population."[8] Although subsequent communications showed that Pastor had a good working relationship with Vaughn, he did not seem to hold him in as high a regard as Mann, and there is no mention of the possible benefits for Peru if he might become secretary of state.

6. *Correspondencia* (5–3-Y/4) (February 15, 1965), 1.
7. *Correspondencia* (5–3-A/107) (March 29, 1965), 1–2.
8. *Correspondencia* (5–3-Y/8) (March 23, 1965), 2.

Peru and the U.S. Intervention in the Dominican Republic

When the Johnson administration dispatched Marines to occupy a portion of the Dominican Republic in April 1965, the reaction in Peru was largely unfavorable. The Peruvian Congress passed a resolution condemning the action and calling for a prompt end to the intervention. The Christian Democrats were outspoken in their criticism as were the Apristas, supposedly U.S. favorites. A May 7 statement from that party's national executive committee described the intervention as a return to the Big Stick diplomacy of the past that would only serve to stir Latin American resentment and would only strengthen sympathy for communism in the hemisphere. Citing its long-standing opposition to both communism and imperialism, the committee called for an immediate withdrawal of U.S. forces from the island.[9] Articles and editorials in *La Tribuna* reflected these sentiments.[10]

The editor of the leftist *Oiga* described the intervention as "barbarous, brutal, and stupid," contravening well-established principles of nonintervention. A detailed article on the affair highlighted in approving tones the Peruvian government's criticism of and opposition to the intervention, asserting that "it has received the unanimous and impressive support of the public opinion of the nation."[11] At the other end of the spectrum, *La Prensa* also condemned the intervention and rejected the reasons the United States had given for it.[12]

Also commenting critically on the intervention, *Caretas* saw the action as an "alarming" sign of a return to unilateralism by the United States, deciding on its own when there was a "threat to democracy" in the region. It traced this turn to the ascendancy of "hard-liners" in the Johnson administration, who had decided to ignore "the diplomatic and political changes introduced by Franklin Delano Roosevelt and consolidated by John F. Kennedy."[13] In a confidential message to Lima about a month later, Ambassador Pastor reaffirmed this analysis. According to his sources, the growing interventionism of the Johnson administration, as evidenced in the Dominican situation (on which he had reported extensively) and which could be seen

---

9. "Embassy Dispatch, May 13, 1965," USNA (1964–1966) (Box 2574), 1.

10. For example, *La Tribuna* (May 8, 1965), 4.

11. In a poll of 499 persons, the magazine found that 327 interviewed saw the intervention as either "hasty" (*apresurado*) or "incorrect" (*incorrecto*). Nonetheless, 131, or about a third, judged it as "correct." One columnist, however, described the excuses given by the Johnson administration for the intervention flimsier than those put forth by Adolf Hitler for the invasion of Czechoslovakia. *Oiga*, 123, 2 (May 7, 1965), 3–9.

12. *La Prensa*, May 2, 1965, 16.

13. *Caretas*, 15, 311 (May 7–20, 1965), 7–9.

most clearly in the growing U.S. involvement in Vietnam, represented a policy that many considered "inefficient and negative," and a "radical change" away from it was required. He also reported on the growing domestic opposition to this policy, especially with regard to the Vietnam War.[14]

The 200-Mile Limit

In June, a more serious irritant was added to Peru-U.S. relations. As in the IPC case, it involved the accentuation of a long-standing issue. For some years, Peru had claimed that its territorial waters extended 200 miles from its coastline and that it had jurisdiction over all fishing that took place within those parameters, a claim also asserted by Ecuador. For its part, the United States recognized only a three-mile limit. Over the years, there had been various incidents involving U.S.-based vessels that refused to recognize the 200-mile boundary. In June, the Peruvian Navy had seized two U.S. tuna clippers, the *Hornet* and the *San Juan*, some ninety miles offshore and had taken them into port under arrest for not having the required licenses. These actions received considerable attention in the U.S. press and led to an amendment introduced by Republican Senator Thomas Kuchel of California, where most of the U.S. tuna fleet was located, to the Foreign Assistance Act of 1961. Labeled the "Freedom of the Seas Amendment," it stated that any sanctions or fines levied against U.S. vessels fishing in what the United States considered international waters would be a factor to be considered in determining whether the country that imposed these penalties should receive foreign aid.[15] During debate on the amendment, Senator Edward Kennedy, along with Democratic Senator William Fulbright of Arkansas, opposed the proposal, arguing that it constrained diplomatic maneuvering. Moreover, in Kennedy's words, "The adoption of this amendment in effect tells the people of Peru that they must alter their position on fishing limitations or we will not assist their growth into a strong and democratic nation."[16] Despite these objections, the amendment was approved by the Senate on June 14 by an overwhelming vote of 59 to 24.[17]

The introduction of the Kuchel amendment produced a predictably strong reaction from Ambassador Pastor. Perhaps in anticipation, Secretary

---

14. *Correspondencia* (5-3-Y/18) (June 17, 1965).
15. For more on this matter and the overall background of the issue, see Loring, "The Fisheries Dispute," in Sharp, *U.S. Foreign Policy and Peru*, 57–124.
16. *Congressional Record—Senate* (June 14, 1965), 13, 502.
17. Ibid., 13, 501.

of State Dean Rusk sent a letter to Peru's ambassador on June 15, notifying him that the introduction of the amendment came as a "great surprise" to him and went out of his way to indicate that some of the harsher criticisms of Peru uttered on the Senate floor during discussion of the amendment in no way represented his or the State Department's opinions.[18] These reassurances did little to mollify the Peruvian representative. Soon thereafter, he met with Robert Sayre, special advisor to the president, filling in for Jack Hood Vaughn, who was in the Dominican Republic. He began by communicating his government's "most energetic" protests against the amendment and the potential harm that it could do to future relations. If U.S. vessels were to have unrestricted access to fish in Peruvian waters, it would threaten directly one of the nation's most vital natural resources. This threat, on top of the difficulties revolving around the IT&T and IPC issues, was inclining the Peruvian government, he warned, to withdraw from the Alliance for Progress altogether. In response, Sayre sought to reassure Pastor that the U.S. government was committed to finding an "amicable" solution to the disputes between the two nations and that the State Department would do what it could to see that the Kuchel amendment not be included in the final text of the foreign aid bill.[19] Whatever the efforts of the department in this regard, the amendment was finally approved by Congress on September 7.[20]

Belaúnde and the Guerrillas

Belaúnde faced one of the most serious challenges to his administration during the second half of 1965 when he was forced to confront a small but determined guerrilla threat in the Andes. Although he was initially slow to respond, he ultimately gave the army free rein to deal with the revolutionary forces, and after several months of counterinsurgency combat, the major insurgent leaders were either killed or captured and their forces neutralized or eliminated.

The story of the guerrilla movement against Belaúnde is well known and will only be summarized here.[21] The two main groups involved were

---

18. "Rusk to Pastor, June 15, 1965," USNA (1964–1966) (Box 2576), 1.
19. *Correspondencia* (5–3–Y/20) (June 17, 1965), 1–3.
20. The provisions of the amendment, which gave the president considerable discretion in applying sanctions, however, were not applied to Peru during these years. As will be seen, however, they were applied in 1969. Loring, "The Fisheries Dispute," 83–84.
21. For more, see Béjar, *Peru 1965*; Campbell, "The Historiography of the Peruvian Guerrilla Movement, 1960–1965," 45–70; Gott, *Guerrilla Movements in Latin America*, 305–94; Mercado, *Las guerrillas en el Perú*; and Petras, "Revolution and Guerrilla Movements in Latin America," 329–69.

the Movement of the Revolutionary Left (MIR), led by Luis de la Puente Uceda, and the National Liberation Army (Ejerctio de Liberación Nacional, or ELN), led by Héctor Béjar. The MIR was the larger of the two groups and was composed mostly of younger, dissident Apristas who believed the party had become too conservative and out of touch. According to the U.S. embassy, by mid-1965 the MIR had twelve hundred members and perhaps three thousand sympathizers.[22] The ELN was a much smaller force, beginning, again according to the embassy, with "about 50 Peruvians trained in Cuba in 1962 at the same time as many members of the MIR."[23]

Both groups had clearly been inspired by the Cuban Revolution and like many similar organizations throughout the region sought to emulate that example in their own country. They put forth a radical agenda for change with sweeping agrarian reform and nationalization of foreign-owned companies as principal goals. They also saw a strong link between the oligarchy that allegedly directed the nation and foreign imperialism, mostly emanating from the United States. Both, too, argued that Belaúnde had failed to address adequately Peru's pressing social, economic, and political problems.

Despite the general programmatic agreements, the two organizations had evolved separately. This was due to the general fragmentation of the Peruvian left as a result of the growing Sino-Soviet split, with the more radical elements adhering to the Peking line and the more moderate to Moscow.[24] Ultimately, both would join in a joint guerrilla struggle. However, according to Héctor Béjar, they never could overcome certain basic differences. These differences were based on their origins and their respective strategies. The MIR had emerged from the Apristas and already had something of an established organization and leadership, while most of the ELN leadership came from the communists and believed "that both party and leadership ought to arise from the struggle itself."[25] In the end, these differences, along with a variety of other factors, would doom the revolutionary effort.

The first major guerrilla operation occurred on June 9, 1965, with an

22. "Confidential Airgram A-751, June 26, 1966," USNA (1964–1966) (Box 2575), 2.
23. Ibid., 3.
24. The mainline Peruvian Communist Party (Partido Comunista del Perú) had split into pro-Chinese and pro-Soviet factions in January 1964. In addition to the MIR and the ELN, the embassy reported that by mid-1965 there were several other, smaller revolutionary groups in Peru, including the Revolutionary Party of Workers and Campesinos (PROC), "a miniscule splinter group of the Workers Revolutionary Party (POR/T), the official Trotskyist party in Peru," the National Liberation Front (FLN), and the Armed Forces of National Liberation (FALN). All, to one degree or another, pledged support to the MIR's revolutionary efforts. "Confidential Airgram A-751."
25. Béjar, *Peru 1965*, 68.

MIR attack and raid on a mining center near the town of Satipo in the Department of Junín in the center of the Andean region. This attack had been preceded by about two years of activity in setting up guerrilla camps in the south in La Convención Province in the Department of Cuzco, not far from the popular tourist destination of Machu Pichu and site of Trotskyite Hugo Blanco's early efforts to organize the peasantry and carry out land reform, the Satipo area, and in the north in Ayabac Province in the Department of Piura. By mid-1965, according to the U.S. embassy, a significant percentage of those who manned these camps had received guerrilla training abroad in socialist countries.[26]

At first, Belaúnde downplayed the guerrillas' presence, initially dismissing them as "cattle rustlers" and "rural bandits." On June 7, however, a guerrilla group ambushed a contingent of Civil Guards near the town of Yaharina in the Department of Huancavelica, killing nine and wounding nine more. A few weeks later it was revealed that the guards had been tortured before being killed.[27] On July 4, the struggle was brought to the heart of Lima when bombs exploded at the exclusive Hotel Crillón and the even more exclusive Club Nacional, the principal social institution of the nation's elite. Although there were no serious injuries and no group claimed responsibility, the message that revolutionaries were prepared to strike at will anywhere in the country was unmistakable.

Responding to these attacks and pressure from his political opposition, Belaúnde began to take action. On July 7, he suspended certain constitutional guarantees throughout Peru for thirty days to give the armed forces and the police greater latitude in the counterguerrilla struggle. In mid-July, facing a threat of an "institutional coup" by the armed forces, he gave the military direct control over all counterinsurgency operations. Given this authority, they acted with dispatch and ruthlessness, which included the use of napalm against suspected guerrilla hideouts and sympathizers and other "American counter-insurgency techniques."[28]

Despite the aggressiveness of the campaign, the guerrillas continued to hold out and to operate with some success for several months. Again, Belaúnde found himself caught in the middle of competing forces. The opposition continued to hammer him for what they saw as his failure to act more decisively and, despite his increasingly strong statements about the "red peril" and the "foreign support" for the Peruvian insurgency, still accused

26. "Confidential Airgram A-751," 4.
27. A page 1 article in *El Comercio* of August 3 reported in some detail on the torture.
28. Jaquette, *The Politics of Development in Peru*, 146.

him of being "soft on communism." In mid-September, he was forced to shuffle his cabinet, replacing some of the younger, reform-minded members with moderates more acceptable to the UNO-APRA coalition.[29] At about the same time, he sought to downplay reported U.S. concerns that, next to the Dominican Republic, Peru represented the second likeliest target in Latin America for communist penetration. He responded to this concern with a sharp note to Ambassador Jones, expressing his government's "surprise and displeasure" over this assessment and expressing confidence that the armed forces would eliminate the revolutionary bands in two or three months.[30]

This confidence proved well placed. On October 23, the armed forces tracked down and killed the MIR's leader, Luis de la Puente Uceda, and seven of his followers, virtually eliminating the guerrilla threat in the southern zone and dealing a deadly blow to the insurgency overall. Attention then shifted to the area around Ayacucho, where the ELN had been active. There, after engagements in November and December, the armed forces again prevailed. Although Héctor Béjar initially avoided capture, he was ultimately tracked down and imprisoned. Finally, on January 5, 1966, Guillermo Lobatón, the MIR's most effective military leader, met the same fate as that of de la Puente Uceda, ending the struggle in the central zone.[31]

Although the campaign was ultimately successful, it was not without costs. Since few prisoners were taken and the guerrillas often disposed of their own dead and wounded, the number of revolutionaries killed cannot be precisely determined. The U.S. embassy estimated between fifty and seventy-five.[32] The peasant population absorbed the greatest casualties because they were often caught in the crossfire or subjected to indiscriminate fire and bombing. Several estimates put the numbers of *campesinos* killed at eight thousand, with nineteen thousand forced to relocate and with fourteen thousand hectares of their land destroyed. Officially, the armed forces

---

29. *New York Times*, September 16, 1965, 17. The U.S. embassy later reported that the cabinet changes were due primarily to ongoing attempts by the opposition to exert greater control over the executive branch, taking advantage of a low point for the government in its counterguerrilla campaign. *Confidential Airgram* A-751, 8–9.

30. *New York Times*, September 10, 1965, 7. *El Comercio* reported that the assertion of the communist danger in Peru had been made by an unnamed State Department official at the annual meeting of the American Political Science Association; *El Comercio*, September 10, 1965, 4. It also reported the next day on efforts by State Department spokesman Robert McCloskey to downplay the significance of the assessment. *El Comercio*, September 11, 1965, 4.

31. For more on the details of the campaign, see Gott, *Guerrilla Movements in Latin America*, 336–94.

32. "Confidential Airgram A-751," 11.

put their own losses at thirty-two although another estimate suggested fifty-six killed.[33]

The United States and the Counterinsurgency Campaign

The United States' role in the counterguerrilla struggle is a matter of debate. Former CIA official Victor Marchetti and former State Department intelligence analyst John D. Marks contend that the United States was deeply involved through the actions of Special Forces, or Green Beret, advisors. Their actions in Peru, they allege, were part of a larger policy of dispatching such elements from Fort Gulick in the Panama Canal Zone to various Latin American hot spots either under CIA or Pentagon direction. According to their account, when the guerrilla insurgency emerged, the Belaúnde government urgently requested U.S. assistance, "which was immediately and covertly forthcoming." Such assistance included the establishment of a base camp in the Peruvian jungle, "a miniature Fort Bragg." In addition, the United States provided helicopters and other equipment as well as on-site training and advice. Because of these efforts, they conclude, "the local guerrillas were largely wiped out."[34]

Drawing from Marchetti and Marks, William Blum describes the CIA's role in similar terms. He also acknowledges that "the extent to which American military personnel engaged directly in combat is not known."[35] In his account, former CIA agent Philip Agee argues that he had enjoyed considerable success in penetrating the MIR and locating their base camps and their urban infrastructure.[36] In his history of the struggle, Rogger Mercado claims that "North American advisers participated directly in the conduct of the 'anti-subversive' actions" of the Peruvian military.[37] In 1985, Daniel Masterson interviewed a former U.S. army officer who claimed the CIA had an advisor assigned to the Guardia Civil forces who fought the guerrillas.[38]

Other sources also allude, if not as directly, to the presence of U.S. advisors. Héctor Béjar suggests that the Peruvian military benefited greatly from the experiences provided by their U.S. military advisors, although he does

---

33. Jaquette, *The Politics of Development in Peru*, 147; and Masterson, *Militarism and Politics in Latin America*, 216.
34. Marchetti and Marks, *The CIA and the Cult of Intelligence*, 137–38.
35. William Blum, *The CIA: A Forgotten History*, 194.
36. Agee, *Inside the Company*, 313.
37. Mercado, *Las guerrillas del Perú y la Revolución de Trujillo*, 163.
38. Masterson, *Militarism and Politics in Latin America*, 238–39n64.

not claim these advisors were actually present at the time of the struggle.[39] Pedro-Paul Kuczynski, who was a government official at the time, wrote that once Belaúnde had ordered military action against the would-be revolutionaries, "the army sent its crack 'Ranger' troops—*which appear to have received some covert U.S. government training and support* [emphasis mine]—and in a few months the guerrilla-like tactics of the Rangers had wiped out the rebels."[40] Richard Gott claimed that in the Mesa Pelada combat zone "at least one United States army counter-insurgency expert was said to have helped plan and direct the attack."[41]

Although parts or all of these assertions may be correct, information from U.S. State Department records and other sources present a different account. In a secret outgoing telegram dated July 17, 1965, among the first documents to deal with the question of Peruvian requests for U.S. assistance in the struggle, Robert M. Sayre in the State Department recommended a positive response to requests for communication equipment and helicopters to aid in the effort. However, also included was a request for napalm. Sayre suggested that the embassy respond with a "low key turn down" while pointing out to the local armed forces the danger its use would pose to their larger public image and questioning its "usefulness" in the counterinsurgency effort.[42]

On July 17, in a secret telegram, Jones reported back to Washington on a meeting with Belaúnde about the guerrillas. In this discussion, the Peruvian president said that he was planning "to eliminate what he called 'Cuba-trained malcontents' as soon as possible." He also requested a speed-up in the delivery of helicopters. With regard to the request for napalm, both men sought to avoid a direct confrontation on this issue. When Jones suggested that the use of napalm might prove counterproductive, Belaúnde replied that he left such matters up to the military and hoped that the use of such a weapon would not be necessary. In Jones's mind, Belaúnde did not seem aware of the request for napalm, and therefore it was not necessary at that point to provide the "low-key" rejection.[43]

A few days later, however, Jones reported that the commander of the U.S. Military Assistance Group in Peru on July 27 had informed the Peruvian air minister that the United States would not provide the requested

---

39. Béjar, *Peru 1965*, 115.
40. Kuczynski, *Peruvian Democracy Under Economic Stress*, 66.
41. Ibid., 370.
42. "Outgoing Secret Telegram from State to U.S. Embassy, Lima, on 'Anti-Guerrilla Activities,' July 17, 1965," USNA (1964–1966) (Box 2576), 1.
43. "Secret Telegram from Jones, July 20, 1965," USNA (1964–1966) (Box 2576), 1.

napalm. According to the report, the minister saw the napalm as essential to the counterinsurgency effort and asserted that if the United States would not supply it, the Peruvians would look elsewhere and added that he found U.S. policy in this instance "difficult to understand."[44] With regard to supplying napalm, then, it seems clear that the United States was drawing a firm line on how far it would go to assist the Peruvian antiguerrilla campaign, adopting a policy that seemed sensible at the time but that led to some resentment from the Peruvian armed forces.

As the counterinsurgency effort intensified in the Mesa Pelada area in early September, the embassy was forced to confront another aspect of possible U.S. involvement. In describing the details of this campaign, *New York Times* reporter Henry Raymont wrote, "At least one United States Army counter-insurgency expert was said to have helped plan and direct the attack."[45] The appearance of this report prompted the State Department, apparently with Secretary of State Rusk involved, to ask the Lima embassy whether there was any substance to it.[46] In a confidential telegram on September 15, Jones reported back that Raymont had received his information in a rumor from an Aprista source and that the U.S. military attaché had "denied categorically that [the] U.S. military [was] giving field advice to [the] Peruvian army in this effort."[47] This denial was consistent with other embassy assertions throughout these months that the United States was not providing direct military advice and assistance to the Peruvian military in the counterinsurgency campaign. It seems unlikely that the embassy would try to hide such assistance from the State Department, and it seems to reflect a belief on the embassy's part that what it was reporting was the truth.

During the counterinsurgency campaign, Belaúnde downplayed any U.S. involvement. In a special report to the *New York Times*, Henry Raymont wrote that the Peruvian president was confident that the nation's armed forces could handle the guerrilla threat on their own and what was needed from the United States were helicopters and planes that could aid in the operation. According to Raymont, who a month earlier had reported that a U.S. counterinsurgency expert had been involved in the Mesa Pelada operation, Belaúnde "denied that United States officers had been invited to act as advisers in the field."[48] The statement, of course, did not assert that U.S.

44. "Secret Telegram from Jones, July 30, 1965," USNA (1964–1966) (Box 2576), 1–2.
45. *New York Times*, September 12, 1965, 32:4. This was the report on which Gott based his assertion. See page 370.
46. "Outgoing Telegram from State to Embassy, September 14, 1965," USNA (1964–1966) (Box 2576), 1.
47. "Confidential Telegram from Jones, September 15, 1965," USNA (1964–1966) (Box 2576), 1.
48. *New York Times*, October 11, 1965, 1.

advisors had not helped out in other areas removed from actual combat. It is also possible that Belaúnde was dissembling or even did not know of the full scope of U.S. activities in the campaign.

More conclusive is the confidential report prepared by Ambassador Jones on the role of the United States in the campaign:

> The operations against the MIR guerrillas by the Peruvian Armed Forces *were almost entirely an all-Peruvian effort* [emphasis mine]. Although the U.S. Air Attaché accompanied Peruvian Air Force staff personnel on an aerial reconnaissance of the Pucutá-Satipo area on August 12, 1965, otherwise no foreign visitors were permitted to approach the areas of military operations, including the foreign military attachés. While U.S. Military Group personnel continued to perform their normal duties with MAP-supported units, the Peruvian military did not at any time ask the Military Group for advisory involvement in the counter-insurgency effort.

The United States had rejected the Peruvian request for napalm and limited provisions to field rations and radio equipment. The delivery of helicopters already purchased and in the pipeline was accelerated, and some medical equipment and assistance was also supplied. The AID Public Safety program "during the period of guerrilla insurgency also assisted the Civil Guard in establishing a Special Police Emergency Unit for use in insurgency situations and for civic action missions. This latter assistance, however, was an ongoing project antedating the outbreak of MIR guerrilla activity." In conclusion, Jones asserted, "Peru is the only country in the world, so far as the Embassy is aware, which by its own efforts and resources had overcome an outbreak of armed communist insurgency."[49]

Negotiations to establish the Special Police Emergency Unit (SPEU) with U.S. training and assistance began at the behest of the Peruvian government in mid-1964. After about a year of discussions, an agreement to establish the unit was signed by representatives of the two governments on June 26, 1965. According to a secret memo included in a confidential airgram from the embassy on September 16, 1965, "The SPEU is designed to carry out pre-military tasks of a limited nature, where a small number of men can quell a disturbance, prevent subversive activities, or reinforce regular police units in a given operation. When the operation exceeds the capabilities of the police, or when it becomes a military mission, it is assumed that the

---

49. "Confidential Air-gram A-751," 13–14.

Peruvian Army will take control over the operation and of the auxiliaries involved."[50] The unit was to number 150 men, to be mobile, and to operate easily and quickly in the more remote areas of the nation. A base camp was established in the Mazamari-Satipo area, and by August 1965 a twelve-hundred-meter airstrip had been cleared, six tents had been set up, and fifty recruits had been accepted into the program. Funds and equipment were provided by both governments.[51]

This camp may well have been the "Fort Bragg" in the jungle referred to by Marchetti and Marks. However, there is little evidence that the SPEU was in a position at the time to participate in the larger antiguerrilla campaign of the end of the year. A confidential airgram from the embassy on September 26, 1965, indicated that while the unit had completed its training and was ready to move into the field, it had not yet done so, awaiting approval for coordination with the armed forces.[52] Given these circumstances, it appears that this unit played little if any role in the counterinsurgency campaign.[53]

While SPEU might not have been ready to act against the guerrillas, the Peruvian army, as we have seen, certainly was. And while no U.S. personnel appeared to have been directly involved in their efforts, many had received advanced training in counterinsurgency tactics and had received military hardware for this effort from the United States. By 1964, 805 Peruvian officers had graduated from the United States Army School of the Americas in the Panama Canal Zone, where they, along with many others from Latin America, took courses "designed to strengthen the internal security of their republics in peace and war."[54] Moreover, the Peruvian military, with assistance from the Agency for International Development, had been among the leaders in Latin America in carrying out programs of "civic action," particularly in road building and other infrastructure projects, intended to promote economic development and to undercut the appeal of radical elements in the country.[55] The U.S. embassy saw this program as proceeding

---

50. "Secret Memorandum to Doctor Octavio Mongrut Muñoz, Minister of Government and Police, August 23, 1965, in Airgram from Lima, A-132," USNA (1964–1966) (Box 2575), 5.

51. Ibid., 1–5.

52. "Confidential Airgram A-202, from James Haahr, September 26, 1965," USNA (1964–1966) (Box 2575), 1. In a secret communication to Jones in October, Assistant Secretary Vaughn reported that the Peruvian military was "dragging its feet in helping to coordinate with [the] new unit," apparently confident it could deal with the guerrilla threat on its own. "Secret from Vaughn to Jones, October 19, 1965," Personal Papers of John Wesley Jones, Box 23, Folder 11, LBJ Library.

53. For more on the Special Police Unit and the possible involvement of North Americans in the counterinsurgency operation, see Brown and Fernández, *War of Shadows*, 107–9, 141–63.

54. Barber and Ronning, *Internal Security and Military Power*, 145.

55. Ibid., 190–91.

smoothly and achieving real results.[56] Finally, from 1950 to 1965, the United States had provided Peru with about $124 million in military assistance, the third largest amount for Latin America after Brazil and Chile. In 1965, it supplied almost $3 million for assistance in the counterinsurgency campaign.[57]

The Peruvian military's counterguerrilla operation should be seen in the context of overall U.S. policy toward the region in these years, which emphasized training Latin American armed forces to deal specifically with the kind of threat that appeared in Peru in 1965. However, again, there is little to indicate the kind of involvement and direction that Marchetti and Marks assert. First, the United States was reluctant to supply all that the armed forces requested, particularly napalm. Second, once the campaign was concluded, the Peruvian military took great pride in what it had accomplished on its own. Belaúnde denied the presence of U.S. advisors in the effort. Moreover, in an interview with me in 2003, Dr. Octavio Mongrut, who had been minister of Government and Police in 1965, admitted the development of SPEU, with which he had been closely involved, but he asserted that the counterguerrilla campaign was strictly a Peruvian operation.[58] Further points to be considered are the refutation of the Raymont report of a U.S. advisor in the Mesa Pelada area, that no Peruvian publication reported on any role for the United States (although press access to the combat zone was admittedly limited), and no indication from the dispatches of Celso Pastor, the Peruvian ambassador in Washington, that the CIA or any other agency of the U.S. government, was playing a role in the struggle. Perhaps most convincing were the assertions and conclusions of Ambassador Jones, who, in his confidential and detailed report summarizing the campaign, emphasized the largely Peruvian nature of the effort. Moreover, while it is conceivable that the CIA had participated in the counterinsurgency effort without the ambassador's knowledge, Jones, in a later interview, recalled that he had "a very good relationship with my CIA chief" and was "kept informed of all principal plans and actions and projects that were going to be developed and carried out in a covert manner."[59] Finally, a secret CIA report on the insurgency claimed that there was "no indication of agency action or intervention" in dealing with the guerrilla threat.[60]

56. "Confidential Airgram No. A-204, September 26, 1965," USNA (1964–1966) (Box 2575), 4.
57. Villanueva, *Ejército peruano: Del caudillaje anárquico al militarismo reformista* (Lima: Libreria-Editorial Juan Mejía Baca, 1973), 317. For more, see Luigi Einaudi, "U.S. Relations with the Peruvian Military," in Sharp, ed., *U.S. Foreign Policy and Peru*, 15–48.
58. Interview with Dr. Octavio Mongrut, July 25, 2003, Lima, Peru.
59. Oral Interview with John Wesley Jones, 24.
60. "Special Memorandum No. 19-65, Secret CIA Office of National Estimates, July 29, 1965," NSF, Country File, Box 72, LBJ Library.

Long-Term Consequences

The legacy of the counterguerrilla campaign was substantial. While the revolutionary effort was probably doomed from the start because of various internal weaknesses, the military still took great pride in having successfully put it down in a few months. As Jones observed, Peru was the first nation in the world to have defeated an armed communist insurgency. Some Peruvian military leaders would later contrast their successes with the failures of the United States in Vietnam. At the same time, certain aspects of the campaign increased tensions between the Peruvian armed forces and the United States, especially the rejection of the request for napalm, which, according to one Peruvian, "could be considered as one of the most important factors in the cooling of relations between the Peruvian military and the North Americans."[61] Equally important was the effect of the experience on the military. Many of those involved in the campaign were from coastal Peru and were shocked by the social and economic conditions they encountered in the highlands and in the jungle. This awakened in some a social consciousness and determination to do something about these circumstances. They also became even more acutely aware of the need to address the root causes of backwardness and underdevelopment that provided the seedbed for the kinds of radical movements they had just defeated. If not, their victory would only be temporary.[62] As an unnamed high military official had put it at the end of the campaign, "with a little more peasant support, nobody would have been able to stop the guerrillas."[63]

In his analysis of the results of the victory over the guerrillas, Ambassador Jones was upbeat and optimistic. He saw the successful action as suggesting "that Peru's democratic institutions have emerged from the test of communist guerrilla violence stronger and more vigorous than before."[64] Although this analysis may been correct, it failed to recognize some of the longer-term consequences. On the surface, it would appear that Belaúnde could only be strengthened by this success. However, his initial slowness to react to the threat concerned both his civilian and, most significantly, military critics, who questioned his decisiveness in a crisis.[65] This lack of

---

61. Villanueva, *Ejército peruano*, 304.

62. For more on this point, see Einaudi, "U.S. Relations with the Peruvian Military," 23; Masterson, *Militarism and Politics in Latin America*, 219; and Villanueva *Ejército peruano*, 302–3.

63. *Caretas*, 15, 324 (December 20, 1965–January 13, 1966), 9.

64. "Confidential Airgram A-751," 14–15.

65. Masterson, *Militarism and Politics in Latin America*, 219–20. For more on Belaúnde's relationship with the military, see Villanueva, *Ejército peruano*, 312–16.

confidence would increase as time passed and Belaúnde proved incapable of carrying out the reforms he had promised in 1963, leaving basically untouched the kind of social and economic problems that so preoccupied the military. Ultimately, these failures would contribute significantly to the military's decision to remove Belaúnde from office in October 1968 and to embark on an ambitious reform program of its own.

Belaúnde's Continuing Problems with the IPC

The antiguerrilla campaign did little to help Belaúnde with his government's ongoing problems with the IPC issue. In May, the administration's coalition partner, the Christian Democratic Party, had announced that it favored nationalization of the oil company through expropriation with compensation. In explaining his party's position on this matter, Senator Héctor Cornejo Chávez claimed that it was a matter of "national dignity" to take control of this resource no matter what the reaction from the IPC or the U.S. government. He also suggested that the compensation could be provided by canceling the taxes he claimed the company owed the government but had not paid. He also said that the IPC, because of its history of unfair dealings with Peru, was a special case, and the party's stance did not imply a "chauvinistic or rabidly anti-foreign position."[66]

The Partido Demócrata Cristiana's declaration was clearly in line with public opinion. Taking a poll soon afterward, *Caretas* found 76 percent of the respondents in favor of nationalization as a measure that would benefit the nation (only 16 percent believed it would not and 8 percent thought it would benefit Peru only to a certain extent).[67] These growing pressures led the president's party, at its annual convention in Ayacucho at the end of May and the beginning of June, to go on record as also favoring complete nationalization of the oil fields and the IPC refinery. Compensation might be provided, but that issue, the party determined, should not hold up government action. As the U.S. embassy reported, this resolution went further than Belaúnde had recommended and placed the AP in a position, "once again, more radical than its partner the PDC."[68]

The issue continued to exacerbate tensions between Peru and the United States, even as the counterinsurgency campaign unfolded. Over the next

66. *El Comercio*, May 20, 1965, 4.
67. *Caretas*, 15, 311 (May 28–June 7, 1965), 7.
68. "Confidential Airgram from Haahr, June 21, 1965," USNA (1964–1966) (Box 2574), 1–2.

several months, various Peruvian constituencies and the press pushed for assertive action to nationalize the company's holdings while the United States held firm to its policy of withholding assistance to force an accommodation. Belaúnde did his best to pressure the United States to accept his administration's position on the IPC matter and to resume the stalled flow of economic assistance. In an interview with the *New York Times* in late September, he expressed his confidence "that under present circumstances the United States will give urgent attention to Peru's economic needs and to that common interest that our redevelopment efforts move ahead in peace and security." He also proclaimed Peru as a "key partner" in the Alliance for Progress and urged the United States to put aside the IPC issue "at least until we have overcome the present difficulties [of the counterguerrilla campaign]."[69]

Belaúnde met with Jones and the IPC representative, Fernando J. Espinosa, several times over the next few months to try to get the United States to be more flexible in its policy. There were few positive results. In one such meeting with Espinosa, on November 20, as Jones reported it, while the Peruvian president remained "friendly and cordial," his frustrations were clear. He complained of the lack of U.S. aid for Peru, observing that more was being given to Chile, Colombia, Bolivia, and "even" Ecuador, which was under a military government. He saw a direct correlation between the lack of aid from the United States and the intransigence of the IPC, and he suggested to Espinosa that to resolve the dilemma "his company advise the State Department to change its policy. This, he said, would provide an atmosphere in which it would be easier to solve the IPC problem."[70]

In late December, members of the Peruvian Senate joined Belaúnde in complaining about the pressures applied on behalf of the IPC. They argued that Peru should not submit to this kind of blackmail, expressed their support for Belaúnde's refusal to give in to State Department demands, and asked the minister of finance to look into this matter and report back to them.[71] All of these positions and actions notwithstanding, by the end of

---

69. *New York Times*, September 28, 1965, supplement.

70. The source of this information is not entirely clear. It was found in a "Limited Official Use Telegram," apparently from the U.S. embassy in Rio de Janeiro, dated November 20, 1965. USNA (1964–1966) (Box 2574), 1–2. In early December, Jones communicated to Vaughn his concerns that a continued hard line on loans to Peru over the IPC matter would not only hurt Belaúnde but also his new minister of development, [Sixto] Gutiérrez, "a staunch friend of the U.S." He urged flexibility on a particular loan project for an electrification project in the Andes, but there is no response to the suggestion in the records. "Limited Official Use Telegram from Jones to Vaughn, December 6, 1965," Personal Papers of John Wesley Jones, Box 23, Folder 11, LBJ Library.

71. *El Comercio*, December 22, 1965, 1.

1965, the impasse between the Peruvian government and the IPC was no closer to resolution than it had been at the beginning of the year.

Pastor's Efforts in Washington

In Washington, Ambassador Pastor continued to do what he could to advance Peru's interests with regard to the IPC matter. On June 30, he had a lengthy discussion with Assistant Secretary Vaughn before the latter's visit to Lima for the U.S. chiefs of mission conference. In that discussion, he focused on the IPC case and the problems the U.S. position were causing for the Belaúnde government. Showing his own frustration, he suggested that, at the moment, the Alliance for Progress was doing Peru more harm than good and that the nation might be better off withdrawing from the program rather than remaining within it and having so many difficulties in getting the kind of assistance for development that it promised. This was probably an empty threat, but it did apply some pressure on the United States, which was still committed to making the alliance work and which considered Peru one of the program's showcase countries. In addition, Pastor claimed that the U.S. government's position on the dispute was damaging the nation's image in Peru, especially in the Congress, and that U.S. pressure on the company's behalf was delaying a satisfactory resolution and severely weakening Belaúnde overall.

Vaughn responded that he considered the situation described by Pastor as "extremely serious" and that the United States still had confidence that Peru could make some substantial social and economic progress through the alliance. He also claimed that regarding the IPC there were a variety of possible solutions, and the U.S. government was not committed to any single one although the implications of the Hickenlooper amendment were clear and the "strong political repercussions here in the U.S. to any unilateral Government of Peru (GOP) action should be obvious." The United States, he explained, preferred some mutually agreed on resolution between the Peruvian government and the company as opposed to any unilateral action and believed that President Belaúnde had sufficient influence and prestige to "secure Congressional approval and public acceptance of such a settlement." Pastor took some exception to this assertion, stating that Belaúnde could have ignored the matter from the beginning but had taken the politically courageous step of addressing it from the onset of his administration, but for a number of reasons was increasingly constrained in his ability to find a satisfactory resolution that would gain both congressional and public acceptance. Vaughn promised to discuss the issue when he met with Belaúnde in early July, but these discussions led nowhere.[72]

Vaughn met with Pastor again on September 22 to discuss further the stalled negotiations over the IPC matter. The Peruvian ambassador suggested that he might request from Belaúnde "plenipotentiary powers" to serve as a mediator of the dispute, adding that he might request the assistance of several Peruvian experts in serving in this role. Vaughn apparently was noncommittal, but at his subsequent meeting with State Department officials on September 30, he, along with Mann and others, expressed their disenchantment in general with "Ambassador Pastor's contribution toward improving U.S.-Peruvian relations. The consensus seemed to be that Pastor has not been able to look beyond Peru's boundaries during his service as Ambassador here, and apparently cannot see, let alone convey to his Government, a larger view of U.S. or free world interest in many of the issues confronting his and our Government."[73] While Pastor undoubtedly would have been chagrined if he had known of these negative opinions, the reasons on which they were based did not seem particularly solid. His responsibility, after all, was to represent the interests of his own nation to the best of his ability and not necessarily to concern himself with the larger view Mann, Vaughn, and others were pursuing, whatever that might be. Reading between the lines, it would seem that the negative view U.S. officials had of both Belaúnde and Pastor had more to do with their own frustrations over a failure to pressure the Peruvians to resolve the IPC dispute to the company's liking than with any particular personal failings of the president and the ambassador.

In early October, Pastor met directly with President Johnson to discuss U.S. policy with regard to import quotas on products such as sugar and cotton, a constant concern of the Peruvian government. Pastor took the opportunity to present his own "larger view of U.S. [and] free world interests" by underscoring the growing threat of communism in the region, inspired, as he saw it, by Cuba and the Soviet Union. The communists, he claimed, were spending large sums in Latin America to stir up trouble and to advance their cause, and the United States, particularly its intelligence agencies, was, in his eyes, failing to recognize the full extent of these efforts and the danger they posed. In response to a question from Johnson on the role of agrarian reform, Pastor asserted that such programs as carried out in places

---

72. "Department of State, Memorandum of Conversation, June 30, 1965," USNA (1964–1966) (Box 2576), 1–3.
73. "Barnebey to Jones, September 30, 1965," *FRUS (1964–1968)*, 992.

like Peru were important ingredients in measures to forestall the communist advance and were fully deserving of more assistance from the Agency for International Development. While there was nothing in Pastor's report to indicate that this assertion was in any way directly related to the difficulty Peru was having in getting assistance from the United States because of the IPC matter, it could certainly have been read that way. There was no recorded response from Johnson on this matter, but Vaughn, who was also in attendance, agreed that agrarian reform was "making progress" in Peru but that in other Latin American countries the process was "more complicated."[74]

Pastor was acutely aware of the sensitivities in Washington of agrarian reform efforts that appeared "too radical." In November, he advised the Foreign Ministry that a proposal in the Peruvian Congress to include three hundred thousand hectares of land owned by the U.S.-based Cerro de Pasco Corporation could have serious negative repercussions for overall U.S.-Peruvian relations. Such a move could be seen as the kind of nationalization of foreign-owned private property that many North Americans associated with socialism and which could prove a profound disincentive for foreign investors. The Peruvian government, he noted, had made a "supreme effort" to instill confidence in such investors, and such confidence should not be undermined by the proposed actions against Cerro de Pasco. Moreover, he observed, Peru was becoming even more dependent on its economic ties with the United States as a trading partner and as a source of credits than it had been in the past. Peru, too, was asking the United States for special consideration for the sale of products like sugar and cotton, and now was not the time to throw up obstacles to those negotiations. North Americans, Pastor claimed, were particularly sensitive to the nationalization of U.S. properties abroad, especially if no or inadequate compensation were provided and believed that such actions were particularly egregious if they occurred in countries like Peru that had been or were receiving U.S. assistance. In conclusion, he argued that action against Cerro de Pasco, which had promised to aid in certain development efforts, would produce "the certain hostility of North American capital toward Peru." He believed that this situation was serious enough to be brought to the attention of President Belaúnde and he requested that the foreign minister do so.[75] Although it is not known whether this request was honored, Belaúnde proceeded with plans to expropriate a two-hundred-thousand-hectare sheep farm owned

---

74. *Correspondencia* (5-3-Y/44) (October 7, 1965), 1–3.
75. *Correspondencia* (5-3-Y/47) (November 1, 1965), 1–5.

by Cerro de Pasco in the Central Sierra, although the final decree implementing the measure was not signed before Belaúnde was forced from office.[76]

The Visit of Robert F. Kennedy to Peru

In November, Pastor reported on the upcoming tour of South America, which would include a stop in Peru, by New York's new Democratic senator, Robert F. Kennedy, the slain president's younger brother. In two dispatches, each containing articles from U.S. newspapers, Pastor communicated that Kennedy had strong disagreements with both President Johnson and Assistant Secretary Jack Hood Vaughn over U.S. policy toward Latin America. This was a continuation and an exacerbation of the differences that originated between the New Frontiersmen who had crafted the Alliance for Progress under President Kennedy and the change of direction under Johnson signaled by the appointment of Thomas Mann as assistant secretary for Latin American affairs. According to one of Pastor's reports, Senator Kennedy disagreed in particular with the policy toward Peru over the IPC issue wherein Vaughn was seen as following Mann's lead in denying that country assistance until the issue was resolved to the company's and the U.S. government's satisfaction.[77] In a private conversation with the senator before his trip, Pastor urged him not to bring up the IPC issue during his visit to Peru because it was, in his words, "too complicated."[78]

Kennedy's arrival in Peru stimulated considerable excitement and interest. He was seen as the heir apparent to his fallen brother's legacy. Many Peruvians were disenchanted with Johnson and his policy toward the region in general and their country in particular. This disenchantment was reinforced by the United States' intervention in the Dominican Republic; they saw the newly elected senator as representing the potential for the restoration of the bright promise of the New Frontier and the Alliance for Progress. Friendly and enthusiastic crowds greeted each of the senator's public

---

76. Kuczynski, *Peruvian Democracy Under Economic Stress*, 69. White House Official William Bowdler notified National Security Advisor Bundy about the proposed Cerro de Pasco expropriation in mid-October and found it "disturbing" that such action would be taken "against an efficient and responsible foreign operation." He was unsure as to what it implied for the IPC negotiations but suggested that the State Department investigate the matter. "Limited Official Use Memo for Bundy from William Bowdler, October 15, 1965," NSF, Country File, Box 72, LBJ Library.

77. *Correspondencia* (5–3-Y/53, November 18, 1965), 1–3, and (5–3-Y/55, November 19, 1965), 1–2.

78. Interview with Celso Pastor de la Torre, June 23, 2004.

appearances and there was considerable and mostly favorable press coverage of his visit.[79]

According to Richard Goodwin, who accompanied Kennedy, the senator took advantage of his visit to confront Ambassador Jones and his staff on the withholding of assistance to Peru over the IPC matter. In his account, the senator expressed his "outrage" over the policy and stated that "'Peru has a democratic government' [and] 'We ought to be helping them succeed, not tearing them down just because some oil company doesn't like their policies.'"[80] He also promised to address this issue personally when he returned to Washington.

Later, at a private meeting with Peruvian artists, writers, and journalists arranged by Goodwin, in response to steady criticism of U.S. "imperialist" policies, particularly over the IPC issue, he took an even stronger stand. Again, according to Goodwin, he responded to their complaints in the following manner: "Well, if it's so important to you, why don't you just go ahead and nationalize the damn oil company? It's your country. . . . The U.S. government isn't going to send destroyers or anything like that. So if you want to assert your nationhood, why don't you just do it?" Taken aback, some of those in attendance pointed out that in a recent visit of his own, Chase Manhattan's David Rockefeller had warned that action against IPC would mean an end to all assistance. Kennedy's rather intemperate response was not to worry about Rockefeller, "We Kennedys," he said, "eat Rockefellers for breakfast," a statement that, unfortunately for him, appeared in the press and was widely circulated.[81]

Kennedy was more circumspect in public. In an interview with *Caretas*, for example, he asserted that Peru as a sovereign nation had a perfect right to take over holdings such as those of the IPC. But he also emphasized that "the law and justice require there be adequate compensation for expropriated property."[82] *El Comercio*, however, strongly in favor of nationalizing the IPC holdings, chose to highlight the senator's private musings, running a cartoon that reinforced the senator's claim that expropriation would not unduly affect U.S.-Peruvian relations and in an editorial highlighting his

---

79. *La Prensa*, for example, followed Kennedy's visit every step of the way and gave it several pages of coverage each day. In a Sunday supplement article, the author praised the senator for the "firmness of his ideas and the courage of his opinions." *La Prensa*, November 14, 1965, 8.
80. Goodwin, *Remembering America*, 438.
81. Ibid., 438–39. The gist of his remarks were reported in a supplement of *El Comercio*, November 14, 1965.
82. *Caretas*, 15, 321 (November 10–22, 1965), 18.

belief that the dispute should not have led to a slowdown in U.S. assistance to Peru.[83]

While Kennedy's visit might have warmed the heart of Peruvian nationalists, as Pastor reported later in November, it had the opposite effect in Washington. Many in the North American press, he wrote to Lima, saw the South American trip as laying the groundwork for a possible challenge to President Johnson for the Democratic nomination in 1968. Many believed that on his tour Kennedy had "operated with too much audacity and irresponsibility, without stopping to think that his words were often inflammatory and could be perceived by the lower classes as an incitement to rebellion." On Peru in particular, the senator's "declarations . . . with regard to such delicate problems as those dealing with la Brea and Pariñas, have produced disquiet, and such a frank invitation [on his part] for a policy of expropriation has concerned many possible investors due to the repercussions such advice might have on the political circles of Peru."[84] In the final analysis, then, Kennedy had done little to further the cause of some sort of resolution of the long-standing IPC dispute, which was continuing to frustrate the Belaúnde administration in its efforts to fulfill the lofty aspirations of the programs of social and economic change so eloquently articulated by President Kennedy. The following year, however, would witness some improvement in Peruvian-U.S. relations overall and a resumption of some of the assistance that had previously been withheld, even though no final resolution of the standoff over the IPC would be achieved.

83. *El Comercio*, November 15, 1965, 2.
84. *Correspondencia* (5–3-Y/58) (November 29, 1965), 1–2.

4

BELAÚNDE'S POSITION BEGINS TO CRUMBLE

The successful conclusion of the counterguerrilla campaign represented a high-water mark for the Belaúnde administration. Over the next two and half years, the president's political position underwent a steady deterioration, fueled to some extent by economic difficulties and the continued intransigence of his domestic opposition. Increasingly, Peru's armed forces saw Fernando Belaúnde Terry as so weakened that some sort of leftist takeover might be possible, inclining them to intercede to prevent such a possibility. The Johnson administration, and particularly Ambassador John Wesley Jones, were aware of Belaúnde's difficulties, especially the threat of a military coup, and undertook steps to try to salvage his administration. While some progress was made in working toward a resolution of the International Petroleum Company (IPC) controversy, it still remained as a major stumbling block in bilateral relations, and failure to come to a satisfactory agreement helped accelerate the overall slide of Peru's democratically elected government.

An Apparent Breakthrough

There were some important measures taken by both sides to ease U.S.-Peruvian tensions at the beginning of 1966. In February, special presidential advisor Walt Rostow arrived in Lima to discuss some resolution to the

IPC controversy with Belaúnde. By establishing a good personal relationship with the Peruvian leader, Rostow was able to get Belaúnde to promise that under "no circumstances" did he intend to confiscate the company's holdings, a promise that was communicated directly to President Johnson along with a recommendation that assistance to Peru be resumed.[1]

After countering an assertion in the *New York Times* that the Rostow-Belaúnde negotiations represented a sharp reversal of the Mann Doctrine, the administration began to loosen the purse strings.[2] In early March, the Inter-American Development Bank issued a $20 million loan to Peru aimed at raising living standards in seven largely indigenous areas of that nation, containing over a million persons, who were mostly dependent on subsistence farming.[3] The assistance was to be coordinated with matching funds from the Peruvian government with ongoing agrarian reform programs previously initiated in 1964. One goal of the program was to halt the continuing exodus from the highlands to the coast and the accompanying growing income gap between the two regions.[4]

Whether the program would do much good for either the intended beneficiaries or the Belaúnde administration remained unclear. Although the renewed flow of U.S. assistance was welcomed, difficulties in getting the opposition in Congress to allow for the matching funds from the Peruvian side continued.[5] Moreover, by this time, loosening U.S. purse strings may have been too late to accomplish much in terms of Belaúnde achieving any substantial success in his reform efforts given growing economic difficulties and the continued strength of the recalcitrant opposition in Congress. Moreover, as an editorial in *El Comercio* pointed out later in the year, the U.S. Senate had voted to approve only $543 million for Alliance for Progress funds overall for the following year, tracing this relatively small amount to the increasing demands of the Vietnam War, where the United States was spending in one year the amount earmarked for ten years of the alliance.[6] These limitations, of course, meant less assistance available for Peru at a time when such assistance was badly needed.[7] Finally, whatever Belaúnde's

---

1. "Secret Telegram from Rostow, forwarded by Jones, February 5, 1966," USNA (1964–1966) (Box 2576), 1–2.
2. *New York Times*, February 10, 1966, 5.
3. *New York Times*, March 5, 1966, 39.
4. *New York Times*, March 27, 1966, 5.
5. Ibid.
6. *El Comercio*, August 1, 1966, 2.
7. An article in a midyear edition of the *Reporter* provided a rather downbeat assessment of Belaúnde's chances of accomplishing much in the final years of his term given the problems in receiving U.S. support for his reform efforts and the obstacles thrown up by his domestic opposition. This was

promises to Rostow and Johnson, domestic forces were pushing him even harder to take aggressive action against the IPC. For its part, the company continued to resist any measure that did not include compensation.

Jones and Belaúnde

In an 1988 interview, then former ambassador Jones recalled that he "had very cordial relations" with Belaúnde and "came to be very fond of him and got to know him very well."[8] Nonetheless, the meetings between the two men frequently had their moments of strain and tension. While the difficulties over the IPC issue abated somewhat after the February agreement with Rostow, Peru's persistent defense of its 200-mile fishing limit led to some uneasy confrontations during the year. The capture and fining of the *Mayflower*, a U.S. fishing vessel, in February led to a series of protests from the State Department with Secretary of State Dean Rusk actively involved. Jones met on several occasions with the Peruvian president to warn him of the possible adverse consequences of adhering to what the United States perceived as an instransigent position, potentially provoking retaliatory action by the U.S. Congress. At one such meeting, Belaúnde proposed that the dispute could be resolved if U.S. vessels applied for licenses to fish in Peruvian waters, but he maintained his stance on the 200-mile limit as a defense of one of the nation's most important natural resources.[9] In further discussions during 1966, no significant progress was made to breach the differences over this matter.

Belaúnde's own domestic position had been strengthened somewhat with a second round of municipal elections in November 1966. The results were more or less a draw between the candidates of the governmental alliance and the opposition coalition, with both declining somewhat in strength in previous strongholds and gaining strength at the expense of their rivals in other areas. Foreign policy issues played little role. Jones saw the results "as a ratification of the status quo of present policies and of the division of power between the two blocs."[10]

In a meeting with Jones and Jack Hood Vaughn, now director of the

---

a notable change from the more optimistic reporting in various U.S. magazines and newspapers a year earlier. See Rodman, "Peruvian Politics Stalls Belaúnde's Reforms," 37–40.

8. "Interview with John Wesley Jones, 1988," 16.
9. "Limited Official Use Telegram from Jones, April 3, 1966," USNA (1964–1966) (Box 2578), 1–2.
10. "Confidential Airgram from Jones, December 21, 1966," USNA (1963–66) (Box 2575), 1–3.

Peace Corps, soon after the election, Belaúnde tried to turn his interpretation of the results to his advantage. The success of the Unión Nacional Odriista (UNO) coalition in former alliance strongholds of Arequipa and Cuzco, he argued, were more apparent than real. He claimed it was communist gains in those areas that had undermined the alliance's position. He called this increase "alarming" and said that it was accompanied by "considerable anti-American sentiment." He traced this growing communist strength to a lack of important public works and development projects in the south and used this argument to press both men for increased U.S. assistance to counter this danger.[11]

While Jones might not have agreed with the specifics of Belaúnde's argument, he did show sympathy with the basic message that the president sought to convey on the need for further economic assistance to counter any possible communist threat. In his communications to the State Department at the end of the year, Jones admitted some of the weaknesses of Belaúnde and his administration but argued that it remained the best alternative and deserved whatever support could be provided. "The present government," he emphasized, "is democratic, constitutionally elected and has the support of a broad base of the population." Therefore, policies that strengthened the social and economic reform agenda of the administration should be maintained and even expanded. "While our assistance *per se* will not mean the difference between Belaúnde's 'success' or 'failure,' our aid should enable us to exert meaningful influence on the GOP [Government of Peru] in three key areas: government policies as related to the private sector; government development and investment policy; and, government policies in fields linked with social and economic reform, particularly agriculture and education." In conclusion, he encouraged maintaining planned levels of economic and military assistance and keeping the number of Peace Corps volunteers at about four hundred while restoring assistance to cultural and exchange programs that had recently been cut to previous levels.[12]

As a follow-up to these recommendations, Jones urged the State Department to suggest to the White House that President Johnson invite Belaúnde on a special visit to the United States. Such an invitation already had been extended to Chile's President Eduardo Frei, who, Jones observed, had

---

11. "Limited Official Use Telegram from Jones, November 23, 1966," USNA (1964–1966) (Box 2575), 1–4. Reports from the U.S. consul in Arequipa, George Mitchell, referred to various anti-U.S. demonstrations carried out by leftist students but said nothing about growing communist influence in the municipal elections. "Airgram from Mitchell, October 19, 1966" and "Limited Official Use Airgram from Mitchell, November 30, 1966," USNA (1964–1966) (Box 2576), 1–2.

12. "Secret Airgram from Jones, A-288, November 30, 1966," USNA (1964–1966) (Box 2576), 1–6.

been in office for a shorter time than had Belaúnde. Moreover, the Peruvian leader, he asserted, "is one of the most outstanding democratic leaders in the hemisphere and a highly personable individual representative of the kind of new image in Latin American leadership which we are trying to cultivate under the Alliance for Progress."[13] Despite Jones's recommendation, however, for whatever reason, there was no invitation forthcoming from the U.S. president to Belaúnde for an official visit and there would be none throughout the remainder of his term, a glaring omission considering the number of other Latin American leaders, both democratic and authoritarian, who visited Washington in these years. According to one close confidant of Belaúnde, the president, who had spent much of his adult life abroad, was reluctant to leave Peru during his term in office.[14]

The View from Washington

Peru's Ambassador Pastor, of course, had less access to and much less influence on President Johnson than was the case with Jones and Belaúnde. Nonetheless, he had enough exposure to the president and other high officials to keep Lima informed of major developments. Throughout the year, he reported back that the administration overall was increasingly consumed with the Vietnam War and was beginning to place much less emphasis on the importance of the Alliance for Progress than it had previously, a development that was obvious to all. A sign of the lower priority the administration was affording Latin America, according to Pastor, was a decision by Johnson at the end of 1966 to postpone a scheduled summit meeting of the heads of state of the Americas until the following year.[15]

There were some positive developments to report. State Department officials had seemed to respond favorably to Pastor's concerns about continued Soviet and Cuban attempts to subvert the Peruvian government, a concern that might translate into increased assistance.[16] Later in the year, the embassy notified Lima that it seemed unlikely that the punitive provisions of the Kuchel amendment to cut off assistance to countries that captured U.S. fishing vessels in disputed waters would be applied by President Johnson.[17]

In September, however, Pastor reported on a possible point of additional

13. "Confidential Telegram from Jones, December 28, 1966," USNA (1964–1966) (Box 2575), 1.
14. Interview with Osvaldo Mongrut, Lima, July 25, 2003.
15. *Correspondencia* (5-3-Y/34) (October 10, 1966), 1–2.
16. *Correspondencia* (5-3-Y/7) (January 24, 1966), 1–3.
17. *Correspondencia* (5-3-Y/24) (July 25, 1966), 3.

strain in Peruvian-U.S. relations. At a lunch with special advisor Rostow, the two men discussed a recent decision by the Peruvian Senate to earmark 900 million soles for the purchase of advanced fighter aircraft for the Peruvian Air Force. Rostow, who emphasized how pleased he was with the course of Peru's social and economic development under Belaúnde, believed that such a purchase would create a "deplorable impression" in the United States and would hinder future Peruvian attempts to receive assistance for social and economic projects. He asked Pastor to communicate these concerns to Belaúnde and assured the ambassador that he remained an admirer of the kinds of changes the Peruvian president was carrying out and hoped to see these continue.[18] It is not clear whether Belaúnde received these words of warning from Rostow, but matters of arms purchases from the United States, including ongoing efforts to obtain two destroyers from the U.S. Navy, would continue to complicate U.S.-Peruvian relations for some time.

In midyear, Pastor commented on the shuffling of positions among Johnson's Latin American policy-makers. These changes included Mann's resignation from the State Department for health reasons, the shifting of Jack Hood Vaughn from assistant secretary to head of the Peace Corps, and the naming of the former ambassador to Brazil, Lincoln Gordon, as the new assistant secretary for Latin American Affairs. According to Pastor's second-in-command, Carlos Gerberding, Gordon was seen as a more independent figure than Mann, who was, as he saw it, quite close to Johnson. In his words, "Mr. Gordon has clearly shown, from the beginning, a will to act with complete independence and following his own criterion in relations with our countries."[19]

Pastor took the occasion to reiterate his favorable impression of Mann, who, according to him, consistently had shown "a cordial friendship with and a full understanding of and sympathy toward Peru."[20] At no point in this extensive communication or, indeed, in any of his dispatches did Pastor blame Mann for the policy of withholding assistance to Peru over the IPC issue. Indeed, in his year-end summary for Lima, Pastor referred specifically to the many reports that the Department of State had followed such a policy, mentioning also that Senator Robert Kennedy had cited the delay in granting a loan to support the Cooperación Popular program as part of this overall strategy. Pastor, however, asserted forcefully that "never has a functionary of the Government of the United States accepted this

---

18. *Correspondencia* (5-3-Y/30) (September 29, 1966), 1-2.
19. *Correspondencia* (5-3-Y/15) (May 2, 1966), 3.
20. *Correspondencia* (5-3-Y/18) (May 24, 1966), 1-4.

interpretation and, if such a policy had existed, it would have been rejected with all vigor by this embassy, especially if it concerned the petroleum problem."[21] He then went on to list specific grants over the past years from various U.S. and international aid and loan agencies.

Just why Pastor, in confidential dispatches to Lima, would deny the existence of a policy that just about everyone recognized as having been in effect until early 1966 is still a mystery. Perhaps, given his admiration of Mann and his apparently good personal relationship with him, he was reluctant to admit that the Texan had been behind the policy decision and took him at his word that it was the threat of the Hickenlooper amendment that constrained him in encouraging more assistance to Peru. Indeed, there might have been more than a grain of truth in this assessment. Another explanation might be that Pastor was covering himself from potential criticism for not doing more to get the restoration of U.S. economic assistance to Peru with the argument that the policy of deliberately withholding assistance did not exist or at least he could not find anyone to admit that it did. Certainly, as earlier dispatches indicated, Pastor was aware of the damage the IPC issue was doing to Peruvian-U.S. relations. It could be that his own equivocation about who was responsible for the hard-line policy reflected his own confusions and frustrations in dealing with the matter.

Brighter Prospects

At the beginning of 1967, the Peruvian economy appeared to be in reasonably good shape. As the *New York Times* reported in January, over the past year, "impressive gains" had been made in industry and in commerce and an almost "insatiable demand for all consumer goods" had been spurred by increased employment and purchasing power, especially among the middle classes. Inflation, which had been 16 percent in 1965, was reduced to 10 percent in 1966. High world prices for metals, especially copper, as well as a rebound for fish meal, helped drive economic growth.[22] In February, the government placed a seven-page advertisement in the *New York Times* extolling Peru's economic potential and political stability as a way to encourage further foreign investment. One article in the supplement underscored the assertion that Peru and the United States were "old friends."[23]

21. *Correspondencia* (5–3-Y/41) (December 19, 1966), 53.
22. *New York Times,* January 23, 1967, 56.
23. *New York Times,* February 9, 1967, 57.

President Johnson referred to developments in Peru in his annual message to Congress on foreign aid. Per capita income, he noted, had grown from $325 in 1961 to $378 in 1966. "The critical job now," he stated, "is to bring more people into the economic mainstream, while further stimulating the developed coastal area. U.S. contributions," he promised, "will be heavy in the areas of agriculture and education."[24] Two months later, in his message to Congress on foreign assistance, Secretary of State Rusk pointed to the municipal elections in Peru in late 1966 as a sign of the kind of democratic progress that the U.S. policies in the region were trying to cultivate and encourage.[25]

However, the same article in the *New York Times* that reported on Peru's "excellent economic year" also underscored some danger signs for the nation's future. These included growing trade and fiscal deficits, with the government borrowing heavily to cover the gap, leading to an expanding foreign debt, a decline in foreign exchange reserves, and pressure on the sol. A devaluation of the currency seemed likely as did a consistent struggle to keep up with population growth and continuing movement from the countryside to the cities, especially to Lima. As a result, the demand for food had grown, leading to increasing imports of meat and wheat. Belaúnde's plans to aid the poor were viewed as necessary and well intentioned but also costly, hampered by the nation's dependence on mineral exports and fish meal, which were subject to fluctuating supply and demand. Whatever the dangers of these conditions, the article concluded, "President Belaúnde and his Administration appear more concerned with the four-fifths of the population that still exist on the fringes of the economy and the greater danger posed by their growing awareness of how the other fifth live."[26]

Renewed Fishing Disputes and the Pelly Amendment

While Belaúnde wrestled with these problems, the fishing dispute again heated up. In February, Ambassador Pastor reported to Lima that in conversations with unnamed U.S. government officials, he had received their confidential expressions of concern over the repeated incidents involving the Peruvian navy and U.S. fishing boats. These officials said they were under considerable pressure from Congress and from large fishing companies

24. *DOSB*, 56, 1445 (March 6, 1967), 382.
25. *DOSB*, 56, 1457 (May 29, 1967), 829.
26. *New York Times*, January 23, 1967, 56. For more on the economic policies, and difficulties, of the Belaúnde administration, see Wise, *Reinventing the State*, 55–81.

to take a hard line on this matter. The U.S. Agency for International Development (AID), he wrote, was particularly alarmed that this dispute could hinder further assistance to Peru. This issue was receiving the highest priority, and the position of the United States increasingly did not allow the repetition of actions against its vessels that fished in what they considered international waters. However, Pastor also observed that some U.S. fishing interests wanted to extend the nation's own territorial waters to a 200-mile limit to deal with the increasing competition from Japanese and Russian fishing vessels.[27]

A few weeks after these messages, Pastor met with the Peruvian-Ecuadorian desk officer in the State Department, Malcolm R. Barnebey, to discuss the matter. Barnebey reported that the United States was considering holding a conference to work out a negotiated compromise. The desk officer, who was "very cordial" throughout the meeting, said he "lamented" the current situation and implied, without saying so directly, that the State Department was not in agreement with the Kuchel amendment, which, he asserted, was driven by "the enormous political force of the fishing interests of California, which the senator, being from that state, felt himself obligated to defend." The occasion of this meeting, Pastor noted, was a memo to the ministry of foreign relations by Ambassador Jones asserting that the United States would not recognize Peruvian sovereignty over waters it considered international.[28]

The congressional pressure to which Pastor alluded in this instance came from the House of Representatives as well as the Senate. In January, Democratic Congressman Lionel Van Deerlin of California had urged a strengthening of the Fishermen's Protective Act to compensate those who had been fined or otherwise penalized for fishing in international waters and who, "in effect, have become pawns in the internal political power struggles of our neighbors to the south." He did not at the moment favor penalizing these countries by reducing foreign aid since it "would limit the State Department's flexibility to use foreign aid as a viable instrument of our foreign policy" and because he had been assured by Under Secretary of State Eugene V. Rostow that a new policy was being formulated to deal with the problem.[29]

These assurances, however, were not enough for Republican Congressman Thomas Pelly of Washington state. In February, he called the continued seizure of U.S. fishing vessels in international waters action akin to that of the Barbary pirates of the early nineteenth century. Over the past fifteen years, he claimed, Latin American nations had seized, held, and fined eighty

27. *Correspondencia* (5–3-Y/13) (February 18, 1967), 1–2.
28. *Correspondencia* (5–3-Y/22) (March 9, 1967), 1.
29. *Congressional Record—House* (January 30, 1967), 1861.

tuna vessels, and in the first month of 1967, Ecuador and Peru had seized six more. In each case, the State Department had protested but to no avail. Ironically, he noted, some of these seizures were carried out by naval warships provided to the offending country by the U.S. government. Accordingly, he called for the government to provide rapid and full reimbursement to the owners of the ships seized, to make it mandatory that the secretary of state "take all 'necessary' action to collect on claims for such reimbursement paid," and, "if not paid within 120 days, then to advise the President when such claims are not paid and thereupon the President must suspend all assistance to such offending country under the Foreign Assistance Act of 1961 until the claims are paid."[30]

A few months later, Congressman Van Deerlin again entered the debate discussing a bill authorizing the loan of U.S. warships to foreign nations. Amplifying the point made previously by Pelly, he particularly singled out Peru for its use of U.S.-provided ships to seize U.S. fishing boats, actions "that have shocked public opinion with their outrageous, high seas forays against American fishermen." Under these circumstances, he urged that in the future the government deny the loan of any U.S. vessel "to nations that would turn our own warships against us."[31]

Ultimately, both these proposals, somewhat modified, became law. Section 5 of the Fishermen's Protective Act of 1967 established that, if a government that had seized a U.S. fishing vessel had failed to provide full compensation payment within 120 days, the secretary of state (not the president) "shall withhold, pending such payment, an amount equal to such unpaid claim from any funds programmed for the current fiscal year for assistance." In addition, Pelly had the Foreign Military Sales Act of 1968 amended to prohibit the U.S. government from selling a "defense article or service . . . to any country that seizes or takes into custody or fines an American fishing vessel engaged in fishing more than 12 miles from the coast of that country."[32] In other words, presuming this provision were to be enforced, no longer would Congressman Van Deerlin have to confront future photographs of "a gun-slinging Peruvian officer pausing between shots at the crew of a San Diego tunaboat, the *Mayflower* [a name dripping with patriotic symbolism]" from the deck of a "a large, seagoing, American-built tug—a dubious gift from the U.S. Government," such as the one he currently had in his office.[33]

30. *Congressional Record—House* (February 1, 1967), 2143–44.
31. *Congressional Record—House* (April 19, 1967), 10045.
32. Loring, "The Fisheries Dispute," 84.
33. *Congressional Record—House* (April 19, 1967), 10045.

Passions were aroused in Lima as well. On February 23, State Department spokesman Robert McClosky had announced that the United States would consider suspending assistance to any nation that seized U.S. fishing boats within the 200-mile limit that Peru and other nations claimed. On the following day, Belaúnde called Ambassador Jones to his office for an urgent meeting, expressing his concerns that some sort of sanctions would be applied and calling the threat "Anti-Alliance for Progress." The president also took the occasion to complain of the "slow pace" of AID programs and his concern that if such punitive measures were applied, the Peruvian public, given Belaúnde's own "well-known pro-American sentiments," would see his policy of trying to placate U.S. interests, particularly private interests, as a failure. He concluded, in Jones's words, "by saying that he did not become president of Peru to strip (*despojar*) [the] country of its territorial rights. [He] assured me he would not leave Peru with less than when he took office: that he had no territorial ambitions to add one square meter to Peruvian frontiers but by [the] same token would not permit any diminution," implying that, as he saw it, the 200-mile ocean limit was actual Peruvian territory.[34]

Belaúnde's strong reaction to McClosky's announcement reflected public opinion. In Lima, students from the Aprista Party–dominated Federico Villareal University marched on the U.S. embassy to register their protest. The police broke up the demonstration before it could reach its destination. All political parties condemned the action. *La Prensa*, generally sympathetic to the United States, asserted that while Peru needed assistance, it should not come at the price of national independence.[35]

Jones met with Belaúnde on March 15 to discuss the matter further. He began by noting how important it was for the Peruvian president to avoid any unnecessary confrontations with the United States before a planned summit meeting of the American heads of state slated for next month. Belaúnde said the matter could be easily settled if the U.S. fishing vessels simply bought licenses for fishing within the 200-mile limit, which, given the profits earned from tuna fishing, they could comfortably afford. He also reiterated his firm position in favor of the 200-mile claim, a position that was "expected by all Peruvians." Jones, in response, called for restraint, something that the U.S. government had urged on the tuna industry in California, but something that was much easier for a sovereign head of state like

---

34. "Confidential Telegram from Jones, February 24, 1967," USNA (1967–1969) (Box 2425, Folder 4), 1–2.
35. *La Prensa*, February 25, 1967, 10.

Belaúnde to enforce when it involved forces under his direct command. He concluded by recognizing that both sides held firm to strongly contrasting positions on the issue but expressed his own optimism that some sort of compromise could be reached.[36] Whether because of Jones's advice, or for other reasons, there were no further seizures of U.S. fishing vessels by Peruvian forces over the next months. There were, however, other points of conflict.

Belaúnde at the Summit

In early April, President Belaúnde made his first trip outside of Peru since his inauguration to attend the summit meeting of American heads of state at Punta del Este.[37] The meeting had been called at the behest of the Johnson administration to discuss ways Latin America and the United States could cooperate in efforts toward economic integration. The agenda reflected the changes that had occurred in the alliance, which was optimistically launched at the same venue some six years earlier. As Levinson and de Onis observed, "The first meeting at Punta del Este had produced a call for political and social reform; the second dealt with essentially technical concerns."[38]

In Peru, disillusionment with the alliance and U.S. policy in general was palpable. Articles in *Caretas* before the summit questioned the overall utility of what relatively little assistance the United States provided Latin America in general and Peru in particular, especially when it was used as a weapon to try to force the nation to yield on nationalist issues such as the expropriation of foreign-owned properties and enforcement of the 200-mile limit. In the face of the dubious benefits and unreliability of U.S. assistance, *Caretas* argued that "nobody ought to doubt that it is indispensable to explore immediately the possibility of aid from the Soviet bloc. It will have

---

36. "Limited Official Use Airgram A-548 from Jones, March 2, 1967," USNA (1967–1969) (Box 2422), 1–2.

37. According to Johnson's ambassador to the OAS at the time, Sol Linowitz, Belaúnde had threatened not to attend the summit if it included proposals on weapons restraints, seeing this as running counter to his own attempts to modernize the Peruvian military (and keep the armed forces happy). Linowitz was able to overcome Belaúnde's reluctance by having President Johnson agree to the unprecedented use of Air Force One to transfer the remains of the Peruvian leader's recently deceased uncle, Víctor Andrés Belaúnde, from New York to Lima. "When I met with Belaunde . . . and told him what the President was doing," Linowitz recalled, "he burst into tears. Before our interview ended, he agreed to come to Punta del Este, even though the agenda retained the item on military expenditures." Linowitz, *The Making of a Public Man*, 16. The fishing dispute and the threat to cut aid had also been factors in Belaúnde's initial resistance to attending the summit.

38. Levinson and de Onis, *The Alliance That Lost Its Way*, 98.

its limitations, but this is of little importance for a country such as Peru."[39] With regard to the summit, *Caretas* suggested that Peru would oppose the establishment of any multinational military force to be used for interventionist purposes, would object to quotas placed on its principal exports, and take a "go-slow" position regarding regional economic integration.[40]

Although Belaúnde might not have made all these points as forcefully as *Caretas* might have liked, his performance at the summit was regarded by the magazine and the Lima press as a smashing success. According to their accounts, his speech at the meeting was the highlight of the event, delivered eloquently and interrupted more frequently than any others by applause. Returning from the summit, Belaúnde received a hero's welcome at the new Jorge Chávez airport in Lima, which he had helped oversee to final construction.[41]

To the U.S. embassy, Belaúnde's triumph at Punta del Este provided a badly needed boost to his popularity and overall standing.[42] The summit also provided Belaúnde with his first opportunity to meet privately (or publicly) with President Johnson. At his postreturn press conference, he said that the meeting had been "frank and cordial" but "without concessions." He also reported, "I told him that it was necessary to renovate the philosophy of President Roosevelt [apparently referring to the Good Neighbor Policy of nonintervention] and I pointed out that action and action now is needed." Johnson, he claimed, was surprised at the urgency of these remarks given the amounts of U.S. assistance that already had been provided to Latin America, and "I told him that figures did not interest us but rather our objectives. I said we had not come to claim or ask for something but rather to work on a level of equality without offending or flattering anybody."[43]

Several days after Belaúnde's return, Foreign Minister Jorge Vázquez Salas reported to the Peruvian Senate on the results of the hemisphere conference.

39. *Caretas*, 17, 348 (March 9–23, 1967), 20. This suggestion was a harbinger of a policy to pursue aid from the Soviet bloc that would be followed by the military regime that overthrew Belaúnde.
40. *Caretas*, 17, 350 (April 10–24, 1967), 9–12.
41. *Caretas*, 17, 351 (April 27—May 11, 1967), 14–17. According to accounts of the summit in the *New York Times*, Chile's Eduardo Frei, who had given the meeting's "most acclaimed address," was the main Latin American star of the get-together, although Belaúnde was mentioned along with Frei as one of the "few leaders of continental scale," aside from Johnson, of course, at the summit. *New York Times*, April 13, 1967, 14, and April 14, 1967, 18.
42. "Airgram A-614 from Jones, April 16, 1967," USNA (1967–1969) (Box 2419, Folder 1), 2–3.
43. "Telegram No. 4915 from Jones, April 17, 1967," USNA (1967–1969) (Box 2422, Folder 1), 2. In a later meeting with Jones, Belaúnde told the ambassador that his meeting with LBJ "had been very agreeable." "Report of Meeting with President Belaúnde, May 10, 1967," Personal Papers of John Wesley Jones, LBJ Library.

He presented a rather downbeat assessment, labeling it a meeting that had produced little consensus and only vague promises of U.S. assistance for education, agricultural development, and continued work on the Pan-American highways system.[44] Ambassador Jones met with the minister to express his disappointment with the tone of his remarks. He also pressed him to throw his support behind U.S. plans for economic integration. While this might have been a priority for the Johnson administration, it was clear that for Belaúnde a commitment from the United States to support his various plans for social and economic development was paramount on his own agenda.[45]

The Mirage Issue

Despite lingering tensions in the U.S.-Peruvian relationship following the summit, in late April and early May, some old wounds were healed. On April 27, the AID mission in Peru signed a $1.1 million project agreement with the Ministry of Agriculture, the Peruvian Research and Extension Service, and the National Agrarian University designed to increase the production of potatoes, livestock, beans, fruit, and rice and to encourage a better coordination of agricultural research. In early May, former vice president Richard Nixon returned to Peru for the first time since his ill-fated visit of 1958 as part of a fact-finding tour to prepare for his return to the political arena in the United States. This time, after meeting with Belaúnde and other major Peruvian leaders, he received a warm welcome in three Lima *barriadas*, where in one, residents hoisted him on to their shoulders with cries of "Viva Nixon!" Whether memories were short or these appearances were staged cannot be determined. It seems unlikely that the reception reflected any larger favorable Peruvian sentiment with regard to U.S. policy overall but was rather, perhaps, an attempt by Peruvians to put the incident that had embarrassed both sides in the past. Whatever the interpretation, Ambassador Jones considered the Nixon visit "to have been completely successful."[46]

Near the end of May, there seemed to be additional positive developments for the Peruvians, although they might not have been fully aware of them. On May 19, Special Assistant Walt Rostow sent a confidential memorandum to President Johnson encouraging approval for a $40 million aid request jointly from the Inter-American Development Bank and the International

44. Levinson and de Onis, *The Alliance That Lost Its Way*, 98.
45. "Telegram No. 5089 from Jones, April 27, 1967," USNA (1967–1969) (Box 2422, Folder 1), 1.
46. "Confidential Airgram A-699 from Jones, May 16, 1967," USNA (1967–1969) (Box 2419, Folder 1), 1.

Monetary Fund to enable Belaúnde to deal with his ever-growing budget deficit. The conditions of the loan included a commitment by the Peruvian Congress to authorize measures to raise $116 million in new revenues, to cut expenditures by $15 million (the budget deficit for the coming fiscal year was estimated at $186 million), and, as would prove most significant, to reject the military's $30 million request to purchase supersonic jets. In recommending approval, Rostow emphasized that Belaúnde was among "a new generation of political leaders of democratic bent" who were "deeply interested in modernizing their countries." Claiming that Belaúnde had so far fulfilled his promise "not to impair the position of the International Petroleum Company," Rostow argued that in the end, despite lingering problems on this and the fishing issue, "We have a stake in seeing Belaunde and his program succeed" and that the loan agreement would be an important step in that direction.[47]

Johnson asked Rostow whether others in the foreign policy bureaucracy, including Secretary of State Rusk, were in agreement. Rostow assured him that they were, and after some further deliberations and consultations, Johnson determined to approve Rostow's recommendation and to make clear that any agreements reached with Peru would be submitted to him for his "review prior to signature."[48] That Johnson was determined to be so deeply involved in the Peruvian negotiations not only may have reflected his own personal interest in and concern with the matter but also may have been part of a larger pattern of behavior that extended famously to choosing specific bombing targets during the Vietnam War.

If the AID grant, the Nixon visit, and the prospects of the $40 million loan had contributed to any improvements in U.S.-Peruvian relations, the effects did not last long. On June 19, the *Washington Post* published a story revealing that Peru was about to purchase supersonic *Mirage* fighter jets from France. The following day the *Post* published an editorial severely criticizing that decision. The editorial was then translated and published in Lima's *La Prensa*, provoking, in the U.S. embassy's words, "a swift and unanimously angry reaction in Peru." The choice of words in the editorial, it continued, had "emotionally united all Peru's political factions and the military, which have interpreted them as an offense to Peru's national dignity."[49]

47. "Memorandum from the President's Special Assistant (Rostow) to President Johnson, May 19, 1967," *FRUS (1964–1968)*, 1009–10.
48. "Telegram from the President's Special Assistant (Rostow) to President Johnson in Texas, May 29, 1967," *FRUS (1964–1968)*, 1011–12.
49. "Limited Official Use Airgram A-802, June 25, 1967," USNA (1967–1969) (Box 2419, Folder 1), 2–3. Not all of the press was so critical. An article in *Caretas* attacked the expenditure for the sophisticated jets as unnecessary and said it was promoted by the "personal interests" of certain Air Force

This latest nationalist brouhaha could not have happened at a worse time for Belaúnde. Already enmeshed in a lengthy battle with Congress over tax and tariff policy, he was trying to resist pressures to devalue the sol. Two days before the story on the intended *Mirage* purchase, Secretary of State Rusk had instructed Ambassador Jones to meet with Belaúnde and to inform him that such a purchase would preclude any possibility of the $40 million program loan as it would directly violate one of the explicit conditions for such an arrangement.[50]

Belaúnde once again found himself squeezed between two opposing forces. On the one hand was the pressure from the State Department and on the other hand the desires of his most important constituency, the Peruvian armed forces. The decision to purchase the French fighter jets had come only after the U.S. State and Defense departments had delayed action on an earlier Peruvian request to purchase less sophisticated F-5 jets from the United States. The delay added to the nationalist resentments of the Peruvian military, especially the air force, which chafed at their dependence on what they saw as basically outmoded U.S. equipment.[51]

Writing from Washington, Ambassador Pastor promised that the Peruvian embassy was doing and would continue to do all that it could to lessen the tensions produced because of "the publications of the *Washington Post*."[52] Other developments, however, would make that a difficult task. In early July, there was a widespread outcry from spokesmen of Peru's major parties, echoed in the press, of the possibility that the U.S. Congress would approve reduced quotas on the imports of Peruvian lead, zinc, and cotton, calling this proposal a "grave threat" to the nation's economy. The Apristas described the measure as a "new economic aggression" on the part of the United States.[53]

IPC Once Again

An additional example of "economic aggression" reemerged. In June and July, Christian Democrats, Apristas, and Odriistas in the Peruvian Congress

---

officers rather than with the broader needs of the nation and the military in mind. It opposed the purchase, which it called an "irrational assault on the economy of the country." *Caretas*, 17, 355 (July 3–12, 1967), 24–26.

50. "Telegram from the Department of State to the Embassy in Peru, June 17, 1967," *FRUS (1964–1968)*, 1012–13.

51. See Kuczynski, *Peruvian Democracy Under Economic Stress*, 152–59, and Masterson, *Militarism and Politics in Latin America*, 221–22.

52. *Correspondencia* (5-3-Y/36) (June 29, 1967), 3.

53. "Unclassified Airgram A-005 from Jones, July 9, 1967," USNA (1967–1969) (Box 2419, Folder 1), 3.

pushed again for nationalization of the IPC. Concerned with its own deteriorating popularity and position, Acción Popular also joined the chorus, albeit with a somewhat more moderate proposal. The more radical position prevailed, however, and on July 8, in one of the few measures on which most of Congress could agree, they sent to Belaúnde a bill that called for the transfer of the La Brea y Pariñas fields to state control. The bill also empowered the president "to establish an exploitation plan 'most consistent with the national interest'" and also authorized him to take over any company assets required to operate the fields. Finally, he was given a thirty-day limit for carrying out the provisions of the law once enacted.[54]

Belaúnde signed the law on July 26. Just before this decision, U.S. Ambassador Jones communicated to him the proposal for the aforementioned program loan to help with the current fiscal crisis, repeating the requirements, which included "non-impairment of the position of the International Petroleum Company." "The President," Jones wrote, "reacted quite strongly to the conditions and is now consulting with his advisors."[55]

Just how strongly the president reacted was detailed in a follow-up memorandum from Jones on his conversation with Belaúnde on July 25, the day before he signed the IPC bill. The ambassador pressed the president to negotiate a contract with the company in the thirty-day period allowed him by the proposed legislation, thereby avoiding outright expropriation and finally setting the matter to rest. Belaúnde responded that this period was too short to carry out such complicated negotiations and that the opposition—as well as members of his own party and coalition partner Christian Democrats—was opposed to such a step. He was, he claimed, "all alone in trying to reach an agreement with IPC." Nor, he asserted, was the company being helpful and argued that its own legal position was weak. Moreover, while the company seemed to be operating efficiently and fairly, previously it had earned "enormous profits" in league with dictatorial and corrupt Peruvian governments. As Jones reported, in discussing the company, Belaúnde "worked himself up to a relatively high degree of emotion (for him) on this subject, saying that when he considered what IPC had done to obstruct his plans for the development of Peru these past four years, the best thing for Peru would be that the Company and its holdings up north all go up in a big explosion." As the ambassador observed, "when Belaunde

---

54. Pinelo, *The Multinational Corporation as a Force in Latin American Politics*, 134. See also Ingram, *Expropriation of U.S. Property in South America*, 54–55, and Kuczynski, *Peruvian Democracy Under Economic Stress*, 159–60.

55. "Confidential Airgram A-43 from Jones, July 30, 1967," USNA (1967–1969) (Box 2419, Folder 1), 2.

is scratched on this subject, he is basically as anti-IPC as any other member of his party."

The conversation then turned to other matters. On the proposed *Mirage* purchases, Belaúnde expressed bewilderment about a policy decision that seemed to be designed purposely to alienate the armed forces, "who were our best friends in Peru." He then went on to declare that he would not accept any conditions for the proposed program loan that would limit Peruvian sovereignty or seem to interfere in the nation's internal affairs, leading Jones to respond that "political realities" in the United States demanded the conditions that had been imposed. In addition, the president complained that the original offer of assistance was only in the amount of $15 million, with the ambassador responding that an additional $25 million could be forthcoming if all proceeded according to plan.

Belaúnde took the occasion to unburden himself of some long-standing complaints. Betraying perhaps a bit of paranoia, he expressed his belief that "there was a kind of conspiracy against Peru," aided by its hemisphere neighbors, designed to keep the country from developing. The Alliance for Progress, he asserted, had neglected Peru in favor of Chile and Colombia. What made these slights especially hurtful, he argued, was that "there had never been a President of Peru who was a greater friend of the United States than he who had been educated in the U.S.; that he felt sure we would never have a president in the *Palacio de Gobierno* as partisan to the United States." Then, in a statement that proved prophetic, he predicted "that the next president of Peru we would find more difficult to deal with than he."

Belaúnde's frustration with U.S.-Peruvian relations was not new. However, it seemed to have deepened over the years and, combined with the current domestic political crisis, had produced both a clear bitterness and sense of resignation in a man many considered still the archetype of the Alliance for Progress reforming democrat. At the end of the discussion, Jones observed, "Belaúnde lapsed into silence, apparently dejected by the [relatively small] size of the Program Loan offer and the political difficulties posed by the conditions surrounding it." Jones urged the president to consider ways to meet the conditions for the loan. "The President sighed," Jones wrote, "and indicated his agreement. On leaving we felt he had come to the conclusion, without much enthusiasm, that he would have to make a try for the $15 million."[56]

While controversy continued to swirl over the issues Jones and Belaúnde

---

56. "Confidential Airgram A-44 from Jones, July 27, 1967," USNA (1967–1969) (Box 2419, Folder 1). Also in *FRUS (1964–1968)*, 1021–23.

had discussed, another nationalist sore spot was removed through successful arbitration between the government and the IT&T-owned Peruvian Telephone Company (PERUTELCO). On July 18, the company agreed to supply equipment for sixty-seven thousand new lines and then sell all its shares to the government in 1971. Ambassador Jones saw this agreement as successfully resolving "one of the long-standing problems between the United States and Peru" and significantly improving the overall investment climate. Both sides, too, believed there would be little congressional opposition to the accord, suggesting, perhaps, that a similar agreement might be reached with the IPC.[57]

Continued Difficulties for Belaúnde

The IT&T (International Telephone and Telegraph) agreement offered Belaúnde little respite. His relations with Congress had deteriorated to the point that he was unable to deliver his annual July 28 State of the Nation speech. The stalemate persisted into early August, when the government announced that it would reject the U.S. program loan offer as too restrictive for the amounts involved. Given the current circumstances, it was almost impossible for Belaúnde to accept the U.S. offer. On the one hand, Congress was adamantly opposing any attempt to raise taxes that would hurt the lower classes to close the current budget deficit, while the United States was demanding deflationary measures and new revenues before funds could be disbursed.[58] The result, the U.S. embassy reported, was that the inability to provide economic assistance to the beleaguered Belaúnde would contribute to a "further cooling of U.S.-Peru relations," which "have not been at such a low ebb for several years."[59]

Trying to bolster his sagging position, Belaúnde reshuffled his cabinet in September. Working behind the scenes, Ambassador Jones did what he could to bolster Belaúnde's increasingly precarious position and improve the overall relationship between the two countries. He encouraged the State Department to make a counteroffer of F-5 fighter jets to the *Mirage* purchases, although he admitted that such an offer might already be too late, and pushed for a renewed effort on the program loan to shore up the lagging public and private confidence in the democratically elected government. If

---

57. "Unclassified Airgram A-57 from Jones, August 7, 1967," USNA (1967–1969) (Box 2419, Folder 1), 3.
58. *New York Times*, August 13, 1967, 29.
59. *FRUS (1964–1968)*, 1023n4.

such confidence were not restored over the next few months, he warned, "it is our judgment that authoritarian intervention in one form or another is highly likely."[60]

The momentary resolution of the internal political crisis and Jones's efforts on his behalf (which were perhaps unknown to him, at least regarding specifics) did little to improve Belaúnde's relationship with the United States. In a private conversation with Fernando Espinoza, the general manager of the IPC in Peru, Belaúnde expressed his disappointment that delays and constraints in providing a program loan had led him to devalue the sol, for which he was paying a heavy political price. He also criticized the actions of certain unnamed U.S. companies that bought up large amounts of dollars before the devaluation as contributing to the economic crisis he was facing.[61] Several weeks later, Belaúnde went public with the same complaints. In a radio address on October 23, he claimed that the Alliance for Progress had failed to fulfill its commitments to Peru, while Peru had more than met its obligations, pointing in particular to the successful conclusion of the antiguerrilla campaign. As Jones reported, these were Belaúnde's "first public criticisms of [the] U.S. in relation to Peru's current financial problems."[62]

Meanwhile, the IPC and *Mirage* jets issues continued to fester. With regard to the former, a definitive resolution was still being negotiated. In the meantime, the company was allowed to operate its La Brea y Pariñas fields under a temporary accord. Complicating ongoing negotiations was the introduction, as a result of the July 26 decree, of the question of debts owed by the company to the government. In a September 7 meeting with Belaúnde, company manager Espinosa had promised to supply the Peruvian government with information on the value of the company's assets, and in return, the company wanted the president "to take a single positive, concrete step which could convince IPC management that [the] GOP [was] moving along [a] clear course to settle with [the] company."[63] Given the pressures under which he was laboring, that would be a step Belaúnde would be slow to take.

---

60. "Telegram from the Embassy in Peru to the Department of State, September 27, 1967," *FRUS (1964–1968)*, 1025–26.
61. "Confidential Telegram 1138 from Jones, September 8, 1967," USNA (1967–1969) (Box 1371, Folder 4), 1.
62. "Confidential Telegram 1948 from Jones, October 23, 1967," USNA (1967–1969) (Box 2422, Folder 1), 1–2.
63. "Confidential Telegram 1138 from Jones, September 8, 1967," USNA (1967–1969) (Box 2422, Folder 1), 1.

In early October, the *Mirage* purchase decision became front-page news in the United States. Various articles in the *New York Times*, for example, related the decision to an accelerating arms race in Latin America.[64] The Johnson administration was also concerned. When news of the purchase decision surfaced, Special Assistant Rostow contacted the president and warned him that Peru's action "threatens a supersonic aircraft race among the larger South American countries." Detailing Belaúnde's precarious position, he recommended that, after consultation with congressional leaders, the president renew the offer of the $40 million program loan and offer as well the sale of F-5 aircraft in place of the *Mirage*s, with the understanding that the loan would not be forthcoming if the *Mirage* sale held. "I am convinced," Rostow added, "that unless we help Belaunde reverse the action taken by his military, we will be in deep trouble in Peru, and our ability to support . . . [the] Alliance for Progress seriously weakened."[65]

With Johnson's approval, the State Department reversed its previous position and announced that it would allow Peru to purchase the F-5 jets. However, the new policy came too late to dissuade the Peruvians from pursuing the purchase of the *Mirage*s, which they saw as a clearly superior aircraft to the F-5.[66] Writing from Lima, John Goshko of the *Washington Post*, who had first broken the story about the purchase, commented that the change of policy "has touched off a wave of undisguised chortling in Peruvian political and press circles about what is regarded here as the hypocrisy and inconsistency of the U.S. position. It also is known to have caused great gloom among U.S. embassy and AID officials who feel the action has seriously undermined their ability to influence the Peruvian government on matters related to the jet deal."[67]

U.S. congressional action did not make the embassy's task any easier. Throughout October, various representatives and senators, mostly liberal Democrats, assailed both the Peruvian decision to purchase the jets and the inconsistent policies of the United States in this regard. These critics urged efforts to dampen the arms race, which ran contrary to the principles of the Alliance for Progress, by reducing economic assistance in equal amounts to arms purchases.[68] As Congress considered the issue, State Department

64. *New York Times*, October 4, 1967, 1, 5, and October 8, 1967, 19, section 4, 4.
65. "Secret Memorandum from the President's Special Assistant (Rostow) to President Johnson, October 5, 1967," *FRUS (1964–1968)*, 1027–29.
66. Kuczynski, *Peruvian Democracy Under Economic Stress*, 159.
67. As reprinted in the *Congressional Record—Senate* (October 26, 1967), 30131–32.
68. Among those prominent in speaking out on the issue were Democratic Congressmen Clarence D. Long of Maryland, Henry S. Reuss of Wisconsin, William F. Ryan of New York, and Democratic

officials Richard J. Bloomfield and Robert Sayre met with Peruvian Ambassador Pastor to inform him of the difficulties the *Mirage* purchase had engendered in terms of possible cutbacks in economic assistance, including Alliance for Progress funds slated for Peru. They urged Pastor to communicate these complications to Lima and to recommend postponing a final decision to buy the jets. "Instead of indicating his understanding of or sensitivity to our Congressional problems," Bloomfield wrote, "Pastor's reaction to these points was to fulminate against Peru's Congressional critics. The conversation left me with an unhappy impression of Pastor as a conveyor and interpreter of events here."[69]

Whatever Pastor might have done, it seems unlikely that it would have had any effect on the congressional debate. The result of this debate was the Conte-Long (Democratic congressmen Silvio Conte of Massachusetts and Clarence D. Long of Maryland) amendment to the Foreign Assistance Act, which withheld aid to Latin American nations that purchased sophisticated weapons. As U.S. officials interpreted the Peruvian situation, the F-5s were not considered sophisticated, but the *Mirage*s were—a bit of sophistry that did little to strengthen the U.S. position in Lima.[70]

The weakness of that position was suggested in a confidential communication from Ambassador Jones at the end of October. The economic situation in Peru, he reported, was gloomy, the devaluation of the sol having slowed growth, and the prospect for the next few months suggested the possibility of inflation combined with a recession. There was little the United States could do at this juncture, he wrote, to change this prospect in any significant manner.[71] This assessment followed on a personal meeting Jones had with Belaúnde the previous day. Hoping to break the stalemate that had developed over the *Mirage* purchase and the program loan refusal, the ambassador reported that he had approached Belaúnde as an "old friend and personal admirer" but had found the president adamant in his position

---

Senator Frank Church of Idaho. *Congressional Record—House* (October 18, 1967), 29348–49; (October 20, 1967), 29581–82; and *Congressional Record—*Senate (October 26, 1967), 30131–32.

69. "Letter from Bloomfield to Jones, October 16, 1967," Personal Papers of John Wesley Jones, Box 23, Folder 1, LBJ Library.

70. Kuczynski, *Peruvian Democracy Under Economic Stress*, 159. On October 17, Secretary of State Rusk had sent a secret telegram to Ambassador Jones laying out the conditions he should relay to Belaúnde for renewing the program loan offer and the sale of F-5s, conditions that were quite restrictive and, had they become known or adhered to, would undoubtedly have produced additional political headaches for the Peruvian leader and done little to strengthen his already weak political position. "Telegram from the Department of State to the Embassy in Lima, October 17, 1967," *FRUS (1964–1968)*, 1029–31.

71. "Confidential Airgram A-233 from Jones, October 25, 1967," USNA (1967–1969) (Box 2422, Folder 1), 6.

that at this point it was impossible to cancel the contract for the French fighters and that such an action would be seen as a "national scandal." Moreover, he complained of the great difficulties he faced in dealing with nettlesome domestic issues and claimed that "Communist agitators" were taking advantage of his current dilemma. Given these circumstances and sentiments, Jones concluded, there seemed little sense in pursuing these matters further, although he believed that having Northrop (the manufacturer of the F-5s) representatives come to Lima to make a direct sales pitch might be worth trying.[72]

Belaúnde and Johnson

Jones's pessimism was shared in the State Department. A secret intelligence note of October 27 to the secretary of state reported that the deteriorating situation for Belaúnde might well lead to a military takeover. The armed forces at the moment, the report stated, were probably reluctant to take action and to assume responsibility in the present circumstances, but events might force them to move regardless. Such a takeover "would lead to a deterioration of our relations with Peru." Military leaders there still resented U.S. policy in delaying the recognition of the junta that assumed power in 1962 and were particularly disturbed by the resistance to the purchase of the *Mirage* jets. A "reliable clandestine source" had reported that a military government would likely order the U.S. military mission to leave the country and might well look elsewhere, perhaps to Europe, for financial assistance.[73]

On October 31, Rostow informed President Johnson directly of the precarious situation in Peru. Drawing on the intelligence note as well as CIA reports, he warned the president of the possibility of a military coup in that country, one "which would seriously undermine your Alliance for Progress effort." He saw the *Mirage* issue as the major sticking point and added, "What I find disturbing is that neither our Embassy nor State are applying imagination and energy to finding a formula for heading off the catastrophe." He suggested that they get in touch with key political and military

---

72. "Secret Telegram from the Embassy in Peru to the Department of State, October 24, 1967," *FRUS (1964–1968)*, 1032–33.
73. "Secret Intelligence Note of October 27, 1967 from Thomas L. Hughes to the Secretary of State on Peru," USNA (1967–1969) (Box 2418, Folder 1), 1–6. A report from the CIA the next day began, "We see some danger that Belaunde might be overthrown within the next few weeks." "Secret Special Memorandum from the CIA Board of National Estimates, October 28, 1967," NSF, Country File, Box 72, Folder 7, LBJ Library.

officials in Peru and find ways to get around the current impasse, including a cancellation of the *Mirage* decision.[74] Over the next several days, Johnson spent some time on the matter, discussing the situation with, among others, former president Dwight Eisenhower, claiming that Belaúnde's decision to buy the *Mirages* had put the United States "in a hell of a mess" and suggesting that Eisenhower's brother, Milton, who had considerable experience in Latin America, might be sent as a special envoy to Belaúnde to try to resolve the situation. The former president indicated that his brother "might be receptive" to such a mission, but there is no indication that sending Milton Eisenhower or any other high-ranking emissaries was ever seriously considered.[75]

While Rostow and Johnson pondered the Peruvian situation, matters there seemed to worsen. Another secret intelligence note in early November reiterated the growing possibility of a military coup and noted Belaúnde's increasingly dispirited "state of mind," which appeared to make him "psychologically incapable of taking any action" to deal with the current crisis.[76]

In the late afternoon of November 8, Belaúnde's predicament became the main topic of a White House meeting that included Johnson, Ambassador Jones, who had come to Washington to discuss the current crisis, Covey T. Oliver (another Texan), now assistant secretary of state for Inter-American Affairs, and Special Assistant William Bowdler. Jones's report was discouraging. The economic situation there was bad and had the prospects of worsening. Belaúnde had not prepared the population for the consequences of the devaluation of the sol and indeed had consistently promised that it would not happen, which seriously undermined his credibility. While a military coup might not be immediately imminent, a further worsening of the overall situation made one increasingly likely.

During this discussion, Johnson made it clear that he did not have a very high opinion of Belaúnde. After having met with him at the Latin American summit, he rated him at the bottom of current hemisphere leaders, barely above President Otto Arosemena of Ecuador, who had been the United States's bitterest critic at that meeting. At his personal meeting with the Peruvian leader, a sleep-deprived Johnson had concluded, after Belaúnde

---

74. "Secret Memorandum from the President's Special Assistant (Rostow) to President Johnson, October 31, 1967," *FRUS (1964–1968)*, 1034–36.

75. "Memorandum from the President's Special Assistant (Rostow) to President Johnson, November 6, 1967," *FRUS (1964–1968)*, 1036–37.

76. "Secret Intelligence Note 895 from Thomas L. Hughes to the Secretary of State, November 7, 1967," USNA (1967–1969) (Box 2418, Folder 1), 1–2.

had rattled on about his grandiose plans for the "marginal highway" and South American physical integration, that Belaúnde "not only has his head in the clouds, he's got his feet in the clouds, too."[77] Johnson recognized, however, that Jones had a good opinion of the Peruvian leader. The ambassador pointed out that in terms of promoting Alliance for Progress goals of democracy and adhering to constitutional principles, there really was "no alternative to the Belaunde Administration." While he admitted that Belaúnde was something of a visionary, he was also interested in the overall development of Peru. Moreover, if he completed his term in office, he would be only the fifth Peruvian president to do so, which made him worth supporting. Therefore, Jones requested flexibility in dealing with such matters as the *Mirage* purchase and the program loan. Johnson expressed skepticism that any of Jones's efforts would bear fruit but gave him the go-ahead to try to do what he could to salvage what seemed to be a nearly hopeless situation. At the end of the meeting, Johnson "again expressed his doubts about President Belaunde and his ability and political convictions."[78]

It seems unlikely that Belaúnde knew of Johnson's rather low regard for him. It certainly seemed to run counter to the Peruvian leader's public statements on his private meeting with Johnson following his return from the summit. It also is not clear whether this is an opinion Johnson had held for some time or was more recently formed or whether it really made any significant difference in the long run. Whatever his personal doubts about Belaúnde, Johnson seemed willing to allow Jones and others a certain degree of latitude in trying to assist Peru in its hour of need and to prevent a military takeover. At this point, and unlike in some other cases, most notably in Brazil in 1964, there was little if any real communist threat in Peru to justify—or at least to provide a rationale for—U.S. support for a move by the armed forces. Moreover, a military coup and government in Peru might be even more hostile to U.S. interests than any conceivable civilian alternative. Therefore, if only on purely pragmatic grounds, a continued attempt to bolster Belaúnde seemed the most logical policy to pursue at the time.

77. Johnson's comments were recalled by Lincoln Gordon, who was present at the meeting and who himself thought that Johnson's observations concerning Belaúnde were on target. "Oral Interview with Lincoln Gordon," LBJ Library, 50.

78. "Secret Memorandum of Conversation 19701, November 8, 1967," *FRUS (1964–1968)*, 1038–39. According to Sol Linowitz, the Latin American leader who had most impressed Johnson at the summit was the head of the military regime in Brazil, Artur de Costa e Silva. "That fella from Brazil," Linowitz recalled LBJ commenting, "When he looks you in the eye and he tells you he's with you, you know he means it," a quality lacking, apparently, as Johnson saw it, among democratic leaders like Belaúnde. Linowitz, *The Making of a Public Man*, 27n.

Belaúnde's Downward Spiral Continues

In the final months of 1967, things went from bad to worse for Belaúnde. In November, alliance candidates suffered stinging losses in special elections, and the Christian Democrats formally abandoned the coalition. Before the election, a Peruvian court had found that the government had the authority to collect back taxes on "illegal enrichment" by the IPC since 1959.[79] While the decision pleased nationalists, it only complicated Belaúnde's negotiations with the company.

Responding to these developments, in late November, Belaúnde once again shuffled his cabinet. Reporting on these changes, Ambassador Jones was cautiously optimistic that the appointment of Raúl Ferrero as the new prime minister would help strengthen Belaúnde's overall position.[80]

Once in office, Ferrero did his best to tackle the difficult budgetary problems that influenced much of the economic turmoil and uncertainty of these months. At the same time, Ferrero and the government pushed the IPC to pay what it claimed were the back taxes owed to the state. While the company appealed the claim, its assets were frozen in late November, and in response, it was forced to pay the tax bill despite its appeals. In the face of this action, the company continued to argue its case, to the Peruvian government, the State Department, and the U.S. embassy, that it should not have to pay these taxes. Among its complaints was the charge that it was getting "conflicting statements" from various cabinet ministers in response to its claims, "indicating the 'chaotic' situation vis-à-vis the IPC case prevailing within the GOP."[81]

Ambassador Jones sought to bring some order to this chaos. Operating as an "honest broker," he met frequently with company representatives and high Peruvian officials, including Belaúnde and his foreign minister, to try to reach an agreement on the continuing imbroglio. While urging flexibility on both sides, throughout his many meetings, he continued to emphasize the State Department position that if the IPC properties were expropriated, some compensation should be provided. By this time, however, both sides seemed to have become more intransigent. Reports from both Jones

79. "Confidential Airgram A-275 from Jones, November 19, 1967," USNA (1967–1969) (Box 2419, Folder 1), 5–6.
80. "Confidential Airgram A-275 from Jones, November 19, 1967," USNA (1967–1969) (Box 2419, Folder 1), 2. For more on these developments, see Kuczynski, *Peruvian Democracy Under Economic Stress*, 196–97, and *New York Times*, November 14, 1967, 33.
81. "Limited Official Use Airgram A-309, December 3, 1967," USNA (1967–1969) (Box 2419, Folder 1), 2–3.

and the company's main negotiator indicated that Belaúnde, under increasing domestic pressure, was disinclined to provide the company with any leeway and might well leave the matter up to his successor.[82] The company refused to give up its demands for compensation and found the new demand for payment of alleged debts through back taxes as totally unacceptable.

A successful negotiation of the IPC matter would have clearly strengthened Belaúnde's ever-weakening political position. However, any sign that he was giving in to company demands would prove fatal. While both sides wanted a breakthrough, none seemed possible under current conditions. And the longer the stalemate continued and the president's difficulties mounted, the greater the chances that, as Jones reported, a coup became a matter of when, not if.[83]

---

82. "Limited Official Use Telegram 2590 from Jones, December 6, 1967," USNA (1967–1969) (Box 1371, Folder 3), 2–3.

83. "Secret Telegram 2319 from Jones to the Secretary of State, November 17, 1967," USNA (1967–1969) (Box 2423, Folder 5), 1–5.

5

THE END OF THE BELAÚNDE ADMINISTRATION

President Fernando Belaúnde Terry's political position, already battered by the stunning losses of his party's candidates in the November 1967 by-elections, continued to deteriorate over the course of the following year. Deepening divisions within Acción Popular combined with a persistent and tenacious opposition left him with little room to maneuver and few legislative successes. While the economy showed some signs of recovery from the shock of the devaluation, there was insufficient relief to allow him to continue with his ambitious reform plans, which remained stalled and largely ineffective. Relations with the United States, particularly over the International Petroleum Company (IPC) issue but also involving other matters, remained rocky, highlighted by another withholding of assistance in midyear. In August, it appeared that he had managed finally to resolve the dispute with IPC, but the victory proved ephemeral, and on October 3, a military coup led by the army forced him from office and into exile. The role of U.S. policy in these events was often ambiguous and contradictory, with Ambassador John Wesley Jones and the State Department caught in the dilemma of trying to support the democratically elected regime in Lima while protecting the interests of the IPC. The result was a failure to do either.

The IPC Dispute Enters a New Stage

A State Department Intelligence note of January 10, 1968, painted a rather dismal picture of the state of U.S.-Peruvian relations. In addition to the still festering IPC imbroglio, continuing disputes over fishing rights, the *Mirage* purchases, and a threat that the U.S. Congress might cut back on the Peruvian cotton quota further complicated matters. The Peruvians, the note observed, believed that they were being unfairly targeted for punitive measures and that "the US is taking a harder line towards their country than toward any other Latin country," citing the holdup in U.S. assistance between 1963 and 1966 as an example.[1] A CIA report at the end of the month speculated that, if Belaúnde had buckled on the *Mirage* purchases, the military probably would have taken over. In the future, any restrictions on U.S. assistance to Peru mandated by congressional amendments "would jeopardize the survival of the civilian reformist government."[2]

In Lima, Ambassador Jones seemed to share these rather gloomy assessments. Nonetheless, he continued to do what he could to try to resolve the IPC dispute, meeting on several occasions with the finance minister and with Belaúnde and suggesting to the State Department that a special envoy, perhaps even Walt Rostow, who seemed to have a good relationship with the Peruvian leader, be sent to break the logjam. These efforts, however, proved to no avail, and on January 26, he informed Washington that in his opinion the IPC issue was at "a virtual impasse."[3]

There was something of a breakthrough the next day. On January 27, Belaúnde issued a decree by which henceforth negotiations on the La Brea y Pariñas matter would take place between the state oil company, Empresa Petrolera Fiscal (EPF), and the IPC. As a later State Department review put it, this was a clever move by Belaúnde: "EPF is legally autonomous and separate from the central government, and Peruvian nationalists have viewed the entity as the appropriate vehicle to operate the LBP [La Brea y Pariñas] properties. Should EPF—on its own volition so to speak—arrive at a settlement with IPC, nationalists would find it more difficult to criticize Belaúnde personally for the solution." This decision, the report speculated, was the result of Belaúnde having resumed a "moderate" position on the issue after a temporary hard line, seen as an "aberration," as a result of domestic political pressures.[4] What the report did not mention, however, was that

---

1. "Confidential Intelligence Note 30 from Thomas L. Hughes, January 10, 1968," USNA (1967–1969) (Box 2425, Folder 1), 1–3.
2. "Secret Special National Intelligence Estimate Submitted by the Director of the CIA, January 29, 1968," National Intelligence Estimates, Box 8, LBJ Library.
3. "Confidential Telegram 3159 from Jones, January 19, 1968," USNA (1967–1969) (Box 1372, Folder 3), 1–3.
4. "Confidential/No Foreign Dissemination Research Memorandum from Thomas L. Hughes, Department of State, March 14, 1968," USNA (1967–1969) (Box 1372, Folder 1), 5–8.

the EPF had desired full control of La Brea y Pariñas for some time, and this decree was a major step in that direction. Belaúnde, however, had serious doubts that EPF could operate the fields efficiently and had long been opposed to their assumption of this responsibility. As George M. Ingram observes, "His granting EPF the authority to negotiate with the company demonstrates how strong the pressures for outright nationalization had become."[5]

While the path now seemed cleared for a final resolution, Ambassador Jones remained cautious and skeptical. On January 29, he met with Prime Minister Raúl Ferrero to reiterate his concern over the matter of compensation, which still remained pending, and the continued obstacle of the "unjust enrichment" problem. He reminded Ferrero of the implications of both the Sugar Act and the Hickenlooper amendment. Ferrero, for his part, assured the ambassador that the Peruvian government "would take no action which would prejudice its credit standing abroad."[6]

The State Department was closely monitoring these developments. Officials there were eager to see the two parties reach an agreement "without our intervention." One unnamed official, however, expressed worries about how the IPC was dealing with current developments.[7] These worries, in turn, may have reflected divisions among the company's directors. In 1968, the Standard Oil management was divided between "doves" and "hawks" with regard to the Peruvian situation. The former wanted some sort of resolution that would avoid confiscation and favored a flexible response and some concessions. The latter, however, were concerned about the implications of giving in too readily to Peruvian demands on their operations around the globe. Therefore, "'backing down' in Peru would be construed as a sign of weakness." In this struggle, the hawks prevailed.[8]

Against this background, on February 7, Assistant Secretary Covey T. Oliver, along with four other State Department officials, met with IPC president Howard Kauffmann. From the memorandum reporting on the meeting it is difficult to tell whether Kauffmann, who dominated the proceedings, was a hawk or a dove as his conversation seemed to indicate elements of both, although perhaps more of the former than the latter. He began by observing that he believed the decision to have IPC negotiate directly with the EPF was "on balance . . . favorable." He did not, however, have a very

---

5. Ingram, *Expropriation of U.S. Property in South America*, 56.
6. Ibid.
7. "Confidential Telegram 107707 to Lima, from Department of State, January 31, 1968," USNA (1967–1969) (Box 1372, Folder 3), 1–2.
8. Goodsell, *American Corporations and Peruvian Politics*, 129.

favorable view of the state oil company's director, Carlos Loret de Mola, who, he said, was "not a heavyweight" and who was appointed because of "the Peruvians having run out of other people." However, as head of the state enterprise, Loret de Mola also seemed immune to the kind of nationalist attacks that newspapers like *El Comercio*, the press leader of the campaign against the company, might employ, and he saw this as a plus in the current climate. That climate, overall, was not necessarily "ripe for agreement," nonetheless "has never been better" from the company's point of view.

With regard to the negotiations themselves, Kauffmann indicated that the IPC had little more to give on substance but was willing to show flexibility on certain issues that might be politically important. These included giving EPF assurances that it would receive control of productive parts of La Brea y Pariñas and taking over subsurface and surface property with an operator's contract to Esso Peruana. He also expressed some optimism that the question of "unjust enrichment" could be resolved through an exchange of assets in compensation for state operation of the fields. In return for surrendering control of La Brea y Pariñas, the company would continue to operate production units at Lobitos and other areas, continue its marketing activity, and continue operating the refinery at Talara. This flexibility aside, an indication that Kauffmann sided with (or perhaps led) the hawks was his observation that the "IPC will sign off on anything re La Brea y Pariñas property which *will not give Jersey problems in Venezuela* [emphasis mine], but wishes to hold back a bit of negotiating flexibility for the current EPF discussions with particular reference to the terms of a service contract." He also argued that such a contract must have Peruvian congressional approval, not just the agreement of EPF.

While Kauffmann indicated his willingness to negotiate and compromise, he also pushed the State Department to take "bold action" at this juncture. He stated that the possibility of U.S. action on the sugar quota had helped create the atmosphere that had led Belaúnde to issue the January 27 decree. Sugar interests, he noted, were "powerful" in Peru and had considerable influence over the president. The "guildmiesters [*sic*—referring to one of the best-known family owned enterprises in Peru, Gildemesiter, with extensive haciendas on the north coast of the country]," he claimed, "treat the President like a little boy."[9] To ratchet up the pressure on the president, Kauffmann urged that the State Department, through Ambassador Jones and perhaps including Ambassador Celso Pastor de la Torre, set a deadline by which Belaúnde would have to come to a definitive

---

9. For more on these interests, see Klaren, *Modernization, Dislocation, and Aprismo*.

decision, perhaps six months from the time the La Brea y Pariñas fields were registered with the state.

State Department officials seemed cool to this request. Richard Bloomfield responded "that it is one thing for the company to push—another thing for the USG [United States government] to push. The latter would have very serious implications." Ambassador Jones, he observed, had communicated official concerns to Belaúnde and there was already a kind of implicit deadline agreed on. Kauffmann was not assured and continued to argue for a definitive date by which Belaúnde had to act, claiming that "he won't respond otherwise." Oliver, however, after observing that he saw "hopeful" signs in what had transpired so far and that the climate for negotiation was about as propitious as the IPC could expect, also expressed his reluctance to have the U.S. government overly involved or pushing too hard to advance the company's interests. While some discussions between Jones and Belaúnde might be "useful," there should be no "blandishment" of the kind that Kauffmann was urging.[10]

As this exchange reveals, the State Department seemed caught in the same bind as its ambassador, trying to represent and protect the interests of the IPC while minimizing the damage being done by the dispute to the overall relationship between the United States and Peru. Following the meeting, the department sent a confidential telegram to Jones summarizing the conversation with Kauffmann. The communication reiterated Oliver's resistance to the IPC president's demand that Belaúnde be given a deadline that could in any way be seen as an ultimatum delivered by the U.S. government.[11] Much the same point was made in another communication to Jones a week later. In it, the ambassador was told that Kauffmann had been informed that on an upcoming visit to Lima, Oliver would press upon Belaúnde the urgency of finding a resolution to the IPC case but that this would only be one of a number of issues discussed. And if Kauffmann again raised the question of setting a deadline, "we will point out to him that setting such a deadline would constitute [an] ultimatum to [the] GOP and we do not believe [the] present situation warrants consideration of that course of action."[12]

Oliver arrived in Lima later that month. His conversations with Belaúnde

---

10. "Confidential Memorandum of Conversation, Department of State, February 7, 1968," USNA (1967–1969) (Box 1372, Folder 3), 1–3.

11. "Confidential Telegram 112933 from Department of State, February 9, 1968," USNA (1967–1969) (Box 1372, Folder 3), 1–3.

12. "Confidential Telegram 116638 from Department of State, February 16, 1968," Stamped by Rusk, USNA (1967–1969) (Box 1372, Folder 3), 1.

apparently provided little opportunity to discuss the IPC case. However, in a separate conversation with Prime Minister Ferrero, he was able to press on him his belief that "all the elements for a good settlement were at hand." He expressed his hope that Ferrero could prevail on Belaúnde to work toward a resolution on the matter and "eliminate this international legal hangnail." Writing to Jones on his return to Washington, Oliver also made the point that "we must both make it clear to IPC representatives that I have not in any sense intruded upon their negotiations. While in Peru what I did was to urge [the] GOP representatives to work for [a] solution now. I did not add to or detract from the elements of [a] solution that are in play. IPC representatives may be assured that in my opinion [the] GOP representatives [were] fully aware [of the] Hickenlooper and Sugar Act incentives to [a] settlement."[13]

Over the next few months after Oliver's visit, negotiations between the IPC and the EPF proceeded in a fitful and sporadic manner. Company official Fernando J. Espinosa, the principal in the discussions with Loret de Mola, continued to report regularly to Jones. These reports reflected the various ups and downs of the negotiations, with moments of discouragement followed by hopeful signs that something could be resolved. In most of these exchanges, Espinosa repeated the oft-heard refrain that the U.S. government was not sufficiently defending the company's interests. For his part, Jones continued to act as an intermediary between the two parties without becoming directly involved, seeking as best he could to maintain a balancing act that was becoming progressively more difficult and, in terms of the basic U.S. interest of maintaining Belaúnde in power, more dangerous.

Pastor Battles on Many Fronts

In Washington, Ambassador Pastor had been called to the State Department in early April to discuss the IPC negotiations. At that meeting, U.S. officials communicated their fears that the Belaúnde administration might take a rash action and seize the company's holdings without compensation. Pastor, in turn, agreed to communicate these concerns directly to the Peruvian president.[14] Pastor, however, apparently had other issues beyond the

---

13. "Secret Department of State Telegram 123578 from Oliver to Jones, March 1, 1968," USNA (1967–1969) (Box 1372, Folder 1), 1.

14. "Confidential Telegram 141486 from Department of State to Lima, April 4, 1968," USNA (1967–1969) (Box 1372, Folder 1), 1–2.

IPC dispute on his mind. Indeed, in his confidential correspondence back to Lima, there is scant mention of the IPC case, although, as in this instance, he did engage in several discussions with State Department personnel over the issue. What his correspondence does show are frequent meetings over the withholding of economic assistance due to disagreements over the *Mirage* purchase and the continuing problem of the 200-mile limit and the ongoing fishing dispute.

On February 13, 1968, for example, Pastor reported to Lima on the United States' decision to veto a Peruvian bid for a $10 million loan from the Inter-American Development Bank for industrial development. The decision had been based on an amendment to the Foreign Assistance Act introduced by Democratic Senator Stuart Symington of Missouri intended to discourage arms sales to third world countries receiving U.S. aid. Once the decision had been announced, Pastor met with Under-Secretary of State Nicholas Katzenbach to protest the action. He said that denying aid under these circumstances threatened to strain further U.S.-Peruvian relations. Katzenbach responded bluntly that the Peruvian government had been warned on many occasions of congressional opposition to the *Mirage* purchases and the implications this would have for future assistance. The Belaúnde administration, he stated, had to confront the reality of the Symington amendment. He recognized that Peru was a sovereign nation, free to make its own choices, but it also needed to accept the consequences of these choices. With regard to the amendment, he asserted, there was little the State Department could do legally but enforce it when the occasion arose.

Pastor responded, apparently rather heatedly, that it was "lamentable" that the administration was giving in to the expositions of some congressmen and journalists, who apparently wanted to convert the armed forces of Latin America into "simple police organizations." It was this attitude, he averred, that had allowed communism to establish bases in the hemisphere, and he tied U.S. opponents to aiding Latin America to those who also favored a withdrawal from Vietnam. In reply, Katzenbach assured Pastor that the administration continued to appreciate the "democratic advances" that had been made in Peru under Belaúnde and said that he would urge a reconsideration of the veto decision. Pastor argued that such reconsideration should not be unduly delayed, as doing so would threaten to strain even further U.S.-Peruvian relations. He reported separately to the Foreign Ministry that Peru should expect further "difficulties" with the Symington amendment and that it, and all other matters involving relations with the United States within the context of the "complex and uncertain electoral situation of this country," presumably referring to the upcoming Democratic primaries wherein President Johnson was being seriously challenged by Democratic senator Eugene McCarthy over the Vietnam War.[15]

On April 5, 1968, Katzenbach sent a telegram to Lima informing the embassy that another Kuchel amendment to the Foreign Assistance Act had been passed by a large margin in the Senate. That amendment was designed to put more teeth into the earlier one and stated that, in the case of any nation imposing fines or sanctions on U.S. vessels fishing in "international waters," such action should be taken into consideration "in determining whether or not [to] furnish assistance.'"[16] Katzenbach said that the department would try to prevent the approval of something similar by the House but given the current political climate was doubtful that it would succeed. In these circumstances, Jones should relay to the Peruvian government again the importance of trying to avoid future incidents on the high seas.[17]

Once the Kuchel amendment had been passed, Pastor sought to communicate to Lima its implications and what he was trying to do in Washington to counter its effects. He noted that the State Department was trying to change or at least alleviate the consequences of the amendment but like Katzenbach was dubious that in the current political climate much could be done in this regard. Nonetheless, he promised to continue to press Peru's position on this matter. He had sent a note on April 8 to the State Department reiterating his nation's 200-mile claim and arguing that it ran contrary to the "noble goals" of the Alliance for Progress to withhold assistance to a Latin American country that was seeking to carry out ambitious reforms simply to protect certain "particular interests."[18] He also sought to form alliances with other Latin American nations to protest the amendment but with mixed results. While El Salvador, Costa Rica, and Colombia offered "full support," he was disappointed that Ecuador and Chile, at least for the moment, "not only have shown no enthusiasm but have given the impression that they do not desire to participate in such an effort."[19]

---

15. *Correspondencia* (5-3-Y/6 [D] [H]), February 13, 1968, 4–5. For more on the withholding of economic assistance to Peru at this time, see Hayter, *Aid as Imperialism*, 146–49.

16. Loring, "The Fisheries Dispute," 83–84. Kuchel cosponsored this amendment along with Democratic Senators Warren Magnuson of Washington State and E. L. Bartlett of Alaska, two other states with powerful fishing interests. Kuchel and Magnuson explicitly mentioned Peru's actions in capturing and fining U.S. fishing vessels as prompting their new amendment. Their previous efforts, they claimed, had been largely vitiated by executive branch failure to enforce the needed penalties. Their current proposal sought to make aid cuts to offending nations mandatory. *Congressional Record—Senate* (April 3, 1968), 8854–65.

17. "Outgoing Department of State Telegram from Katzenbach to Lima, April 5, 1968," USNA (1967–1969) (Box 2425, Folder 4), 2.

18. *Correspondencia* (5-3-Y/11) (April 9, 1968), 2–3.

19. *Correspondencia* (5-3-Y/13) (May 3, 1968), 1.

On May 14, Pastor met with Richard Bloomfield and John Shumate at the State Department to discuss the response to his April 8 note. They reiterated the U.S. government's position of nonrecognition of the 200-mile limit but also said the department was doing all it could to prevent a companion measure to the Kuchel amendment from being passed in the House of Representatives. They repeated, too, the observation that their chances for success were not very good. They did express some optimism, however, that a potential meeting involving Chile, Ecuador, and Peru might lead to some flexibility and help to avoid further problems.[20] As a follow-up, Pastor, along with the ambassadors of Chile and Ecuador, met with Donald McKernan, the State Department's expert on the fishing problem, who repeated the department's opposition to the Kuchel amendment and stated his belief that a compromise solution could be achieved. He tried to reassure the assembled diplomats that he would spare no effort in fighting the amendment, and while "he could not guarantee anything, he hoped that he could at least help produce a new measure with a less inconvenient text."[21]

More Trouble for Belaúnde

While Pastor pressed the United States on the fishing dispute, Belaúnde continued to face mounting difficulties and pressures at home. The first months of the year found him confronting a smuggling scandal that appeared to involve members of the police, the armed forces, and figures in his own administration. Stories and allegations related to the charges dominated much of the Lima press from March to May. Although there was nothing particularly new about the details of what had been a common practice under many governments, critics took the Belaúnde administration to task for a lackadaisical and cavalier attitude toward the affair. Content to leave the matter to the courts, Belaúnde's management of the matter seemed maladroit and yet another example of his administration appearing weak and feckless.[22]

In late April, a State Department officer reported renewed rumors of an impending military coup. This news came from C. W. Robinson, president of the powerful Marcona Mining Corporation, who had just arrived from Lima and who met with John P. Shumate at the State Department

---

20. *Correspondencia* (5–3-Y/14) (May 14, 1968), 1–2.
21. *Correspondencia* (5–3-Y/15) (May 18, 1968), 1–2.
22. Kuczynski, *Peruvian Democracy Under Economic Stress*, 215–16.

on April 25. According to Robinson, information had reached him that a group of military officers were planning to remove Belaúnde from office without the participation of the war minister, General Julio Doig Sánchez. Indeed, they already had approached the president and had asked him to resign, a request Belaúnde had rejected. Although this effort may have failed, it was Robinson's opinion that "Peru cannot survive fourteen more months of drift under Belaúnde." He also hoped "that if a coup . . . to arrest the drift in Peru were to take place, the United States Government would not react in a punitive fashion," to which Shumate replied that the United States "was opposed to a coup of any description against the constitutional government."[23] Whether Robinson's view of Belaúnde's weaknesses and his own apparent willingness to accept a military takeover were typical of the broader community of U.S. investors in Peru at the time cannot be exactly determined. However, it seems safe to speculate that his was not an isolated voice.[24]

At about the same time Robinson was meeting with Shumate, the position of the military became even more complicated. At a joint press conference by the three leaders of the armed forces designed to address the investigation into the possible involvement of certain uniformed officers in the smuggling scandal, with Doig as the principal spokesman, the military seemed to imply that it was abandoning its long-standing opposition toward the possibility of an Aprista president if one should be elected. While this was not an explicitly stated position, Doig did say that "the word 'veto' has been erased for some time from the dictionary of the armed forces." One interpretation of the possible turnaround was that the armed forces saw Belaúnde and his party as severely weakened and unlikely to prevail in the upcoming elections and therefore were displaying their willingness to support the likely winner. Whatever the reason, the implications of this turnaround, which was openly celebrated by the Apristas, suggested strongly that the military would not move against Belaúnde at this time and instead would allow him to finish his term and for the upcoming elections to be

23. "Confidential Memorandum of Conversation, Department of State, April 26, 1968," USNA (1967–1969) (Box 2418, Folder 1), 1–2.
24. In a survey conducted of top personnel in U.S. companies operating in Peru in mid-1968, which asked them to compare the past three civilian administrations as to "Best for Peru" and "Best for U.S. Business in Peru," the respondents rated Belaúnde at the top of the first category and at the bottom of the second. During the Belaúnde administration, despite some of the uncertainties associated with it, there had been a "moderate expansion" of direct private U.S. investment in the country. Goodsell, *American Corporations and Peruvian Politics*, 78–82. For Belaúnde's relationship with the predominantly U.S.-owned mining sector, of which Robinson was a leading figure, as well as information on U.S. direct investment in Peru in the 1960s, see Kuczynski, *Peruvian Democracy Under Economic Stress*, 7–10.

held as scheduled in 1969 as a likely Aprista victory no longer appeared to be a concern.

Not all top officers supported this shift. General José Rodríguez Razzeto, head of the powerful Lima garrison and a strong anti-Aprista, at a subsequent meeting of the army high command "demanded a full discussion of Doig's remarks." In response, Doig tried to get Rodríguez to resign his post. When he refused, he and Army Chief of Staff Juan Velasco Alvarado pressured Belaúnde to enforce their demand. In a compromise, the president sent the dissident general to Washington to fill a vacancy on the Inter-American Defense Board.[25]

In mid-May, the already beleaguered Belaúnde received another blow. On May 16, the State Department announced that pursuant to the Long-Conte amendment and as a result of the Peruvian decision to go ahead with the *Mirage* jet purchase for more than $20 million, all U.S. development assistance to that country was suspended for the rest of the fiscal year. Interviewed on the decision, which Peruvian diplomats claimed caught them by surprise, Congressman Clarence D. Long suggested that the renewal of assistance would depend on the size of the portion of the Peruvian budget for the following year devoted to defense. He also argued that "a country is perfectly free to divert its own resources from economic development to defense but not United States funds." He was also critical of the lack of progress in Peru, with the current government "unable to collect taxes from Peruvians who can afford to help finance their own country's growth" and with half of the nation's population, mostly the Andean Indians, "living at standards 'lower than when Columbus discovered America.'"[26]

While he might have been caught unawares, Ambassador Pastor was not slow to respond to this new development. Calling the comments of Long and others "mistaken" and "distorted," he requested and received an urgent meeting with Assistant Secretary Oliver to protest this recent action. Unburdening himself of long-standing complaints, he argued that even before this recent decision Peru had scarcely received any aid from the United States for at least the past two years, most of which, he said, with perhaps some

---

25. Kuczynski, *Peruvian Democracy Under Economic Stress*, 178n, and *Washington Post*, May 3, 1968, 22. Kuczynski claimed that Rodríguez was a "strong supporter of Belaúnde" and that his removal to Washington weakened the president's position overall with the military. At this time, too, "It was said in Lima . . . that Doig had started plotting a coup." Marcona's Robinson, however, asserted that it was Rodríguez who, for reasons of "personal ambition," was behind the plan he reported to remove Belaúnde from office and that it was Doig who defended the administration by forcing him out. "Confidential Memorandum of Conversation, April 26, 1968," 1–2.

26. *New York Times*, May 17, 1968, 1.

exaggeration, was only barely enough to cover the administrative costs of the Peace Corps and the U.S. Agency for International Development (AID) mission in Lima. He suggested that various congressmen and senators lacked accurate information or were misinformed about conditions in Peru and the actual amounts of aid provided to the country in the recent past.

In the face of this barrage, Oliver replied that the State Department had no control over what individual congressmen might say or do and that his own role in trying to balance U.S. and Peruvian interests in matters such as this was "complex." He hoped that the recent controversy would not lead to further "misunderstandings" and suggested that perhaps the Peruvians were "overreacting" to this decision. These words did little to mollify Pastor, who continued to object strongly to the cutoff of assistance, which he labeled as "coercive" and reflective of attitudes and policies that his nation "could not tolerate." Peruvians, he asserted, were working hard to achieve their "own progress with our own resources and our own efforts," and U.S. aid should be used to further and enhance those efforts, not place obstacles in their way. He concluded by observing, as he and others had in the past, that this action by the U.S. government seemed to run counter to the spirit of the Alliance for Progress, and if policies like these continued to be pursued then perhaps the charter of Punta del Este should be abandoned so that it "could not be utilized as a means of political pressure."[27]

Pastor's barely concealed anger over the aid suspension decision echoed an even more strident response in Lima. There, political factions from right to left strongly condemned the U.S. action, producing a rare unanimity in an increasingly divided and contentious political climate. Editorials in APRA's *La Tribuna* attacked the decision as blackmail and stated that the party strongly objected to such imperialist actions.[28] *La Prensa* chimed in with an editorial blasting the decision and arguing that Peru should not be subjected to the economic "tutelage" of the United States.[29] Christian Democratic senator Héctor Cornejo Chávez introduced a measure to expropriate all U.S. private investment in Peru in light of the aid suspension, a proposal that was ultimately rejected as too extreme but which showed the depth of feeling on the matter. Prime Minister Ferrero stated "that the United States would never be able to dictate policy to Peru." Defenders of the *Mirage* jet purchase, which had triggered the decision, claimed that the money to pay for the planes had been accumulated over the past five years,

---

27. *Correspondencia* (5-3-Y/17) (May 22, 1968), 3–4.
28. *La Tribuna* (May 17, 1968), 4, and (May 23, 1968), 4.
29. *La Prensa*, May 18, 1968, 12.

countering the argument that this was an "excessive" expenditure, part of the rationale for the application of the Long-Conte provisions, and that the modernization of equipment was badly needed, especially to keep pace with the Chileans.[30]

The U.S. embassy tried to calm the storm by announcing that certain aid and loan requests for Peru had been approved at the end of April. These included a $7.5 million AID loan for the Peruvian packaging and processing industry and a general loan of $15.1 million from the Inter-American Development Bank.[31] In a subsequent communication to Washington, Ambassador Jones reported that while the initial "flurry of passion, grievance and misunderstanding" occasioned by the aid cutoff had diminished, the overall climate created by the episode made the likelihood of major breakthroughs on outstanding issues less likely for the moment.[32]

The aid suspension decision was only one of several crises Belaúnde had to deal with at the end of May. On May 23, his finance minister of only two months, General Francisco Morales Bermúdez (later president of Peru from 1975 to 1980), submitted his resignation in frustration over his inability to institute changes in tax policy. Six days later, the entire Ferrero cabinet also resigned. Belaúnde immediately named his sixth cabinet, one that included five members of the previous cabinet, including Pablo Carriquiry as minister of development, headed by Osvaldo Hercelles, a physician who also served as foreign minister. This cabinet was seen as less dominated by Acción Popular and more acceptable to the Apristas than its predecessor. In retrospect, one of the most fateful choices Belaúnde made was to pass over Army Commander Juan Velasco Alvarado as his war minister, instead naming his second-in-command, General Roberto Dianderas, to the post. Belaúnde, it was asserted, did not trust Velasco. According to one account, Velasco was already planning the coup he would lead in October and maneuvered to have Dianderas accept the war ministry appointment in his stead.[33]

Further Developments on the IPC Front

The new cabinet, undoubtedly aware that only bold action could forestall a military coup, moved quickly to address some of the nation's most

---

30. *New York Times*, May 24, 1968, 7.
31. Ibid.
32. "Confidential Telegram 5139 from Jones, May 20, 1968," USNA (1967–1969) (Box 1372, Folder 1), 1.
33. For a more detailed account of these developments, see Kuczynski, *Peruvian Democracy Under Economic Stress*, 205–30. The point about Velasco is drawn from Zimmerman, *El Plan Inca. Objetivo*, and cited by Kuczynski, 219n.

important economic problems. Playing a leading role was the new finance minister, Manuel Ulloa, who, along with Prime Minister Hercelles, immediately began negotiating with APRA leaders to get their approval for emergency measures to confront the current crisis. As a result, on July 19 the Congress passed Public Law 17044, which gave the executive a sixty-day period to try to narrow both the budget and balance-of-payments deficits and stimulate economic growth. Using this authority to great effect, the government initiated a successful series of tax reforms that enhanced public revenues, negotiated with foreign-owned mining companies to encourage renewed investment in that vital sector of the economy, and refinanced the external public debt through negotiations with U.S. and Canadian banks and the International Monetary Fund. These measures produced hopes for an improving fiscal situation and, in the words of one observer, also held the promise that the nation was poised "to enter a period of rapid economic growth."[34]

Also on the new cabinet's agenda was a renewed commitment to resolve the IPC dispute. Beginning in June and extending into July, the U.S. embassy provided Washington with increasingly optimistic reports that a breakthrough might be in the works. Indeed, even before the new cabinet was installed, there were a few hopeful signs on the horizon. Communications from both Ambassador Jones and Ernest V. Siracusa, reporting on their meetings with various high government officials and political leaders, indicated a growing number of favorable developments that seemed to promise a final solution to this nettlesome problem. At a July 4 embassy reception, Siracusa reported on a private conversation with Hercelles, who told him that while the two sides in public still seemed far apart, a *criollo* (Peruvian-style) solution was in the works. He added that while Belaúnde was "keenly interested" in the matter, the "cabinet [was] even more interested and their interest was for a solution."[35]

By mid-July, the pace of negotiations had indeed quickened. On July 13, Ambassador Jones, who continued to try to play the role of "honest broker," reported that he had met with the new IPC president, James Dean, and company manager Espinosa to discuss strategy for impending talks with Belaúnde. After considering various alternatives, Jones urged the company officials to be "as flexible and forthcoming as possible."[36] In a subsequent communication, Jones saw the replacement of Kauffmann as company

---

34. Ibid., 261. Again, the details of these developments can be found in ibid., 219–58.
35. "Confidential Telegram 6074 from Siracusa, July 5, 1968," USNA (1967–1969) (Box 1372, Folder 1), 1.
36. "Confidential Telegram 6193 from Jones, July 13, 1968," USNA (1967–1969) (Box 1372, Folder 1), 2.

president with Dean as a hopeful sign (although not mentioning or identifying him as either a hawk or a dove) that a settlement could be reached. He also added that "we think the time has come, therefore, for the U.S. government to assert some new positive pressures for a solution now" to prevent the situation from becoming "an even worse albatross weighing against good relations . . . with the Belaunde administration." Jones then mentioned several specific ways in which an arrangement might be made to satisfy both sides, including the company's surrender of its claims to La Brea y Pariñas in exchange for rights to explore for oil in the jungle.[37]

The apparent willingness of the company to compromise at this point coincided with Belaúnde's increasingly precarious political position, adding to the complexity of the negotiations. Any resolution that seemed to favor the company unduly would not only arouse nationalist ire but also might serve as the excuse for a military takeover. There was some speculation that a proposal from Loret de Mola and EPF in March that would continue to allow for an IPC presence in La Brea y Pariñas, a proposal that Belaúnde rejected, would have produced just such a result.[38] Adding to the pressures on him was the decision of Acción Popular on June 1 to name left-winger Edgardo Seoane as the presidential candidate to succeed him in office and to call for outright expropriation of IPC. On July 7, the Apristas, as expected, nominated Haya de la Torre as their candidate for the presidency.[39]

At the end of July, the IPC acted to break the logjam. On July 25, company officials met with the minister of development and told him they were now ready to transfer the La Brea y Pariñas fields to the state. They also agreed to renounce all subsoil claims and to give up demands for an operating contract. The company asked the government to abandon its insistence on payment of back debts and to allow it to continue its other operations in the country. "The government," in the words of one source, "reacted 'first with incredulity, and subsequently with unsurpassed delight.'"[40]

What led the company to "drop this bombshell" is not clear. Perhaps it was concern that failing an agreement with Belaúnde another regime, either military or civilian, would take a more radical course. Perhaps it was the

---

37. "Confidential Telegram 6245 from Jones, July 17, 1968," USNA (1967–1969) (Box 1372, Folder 1), 2–3.

38. For more on this, see Pinelo, *The Multinational Corporation as a Force in Latin American Politics*, 137–38.

39. Ingram, *Expropriation of U.S. Properties in South America*, 57.

40. Pinelo, *The Multinational Corporation as a Force in Latin American Politics*, 139. See also, Goodsell, *American Corporations and Peruvian Politics*, 129, and Ingram, *Expropriation of U.S. Properties in South America*, 57.

"flexibility" that Jones, Oliver, and others saw with Dean at the helm of the company as opposed to Kauffmann that led to this sudden reversal. Perhaps, too, the urgings of the State Department and the embassy played some role in convincing the company to approach the government with this offer, which President Belaúnde later speculated, if presented five years earlier, would have allowed the company to operate in Peru indefinitely.[41]

On July 26, the day following the "bombshell" announcement, Espinosa met with Jones and Siracusa to brief them on his meeting with Belaúnde. The major difference in the new agreement from past proposals, he reported, was that the IPC would completely disassociate from the La Brea y Pariñas operations, except as a purchaser of crude oil produced there by EPF in return for concessions elsewhere in the country. Jones wrote to Washington that this was a most promising development. "We believe," he stated, "such a proposal should have broad appeal and that it provides a viable and generous basis for settlement of this long-standing controversy which ought to soothe Peruvian psychological sensitivities which have been aroused over the years." But he also issued a word of warning: "It must be pointed out, however, that even though the president announces a solution, a great deal of negotiation lies ahead and Belaúnde has consistently shown himself to be always unpredictable and often erratic insofar as this problem is concerned. Please keep details above," Jones concluded, "in strict confidence."[42]

Belaúnde took advantage of the annual July 28 address to the nation to announce the results of the most recent negotiations. While emphasizing the point that the EPF would take over the La Brea y Pariñas fields, he also made clear that further details remained to be worked out. He was hopeful that this could be accomplished quickly and that he could personally travel north to the Talara refinery to sign the final agreement.[43] In Washington, Oliver sent Secretary of State Dean Rusk a memorandum informing him of what appeared to be the "satisfactory solution" of the long-standing dispute, removing "one of the most vexing obstacles to greater U.S.-Peruvian cooperation."[44] On the following day, Jones communicated to the department the general reaction to Belaúnde's announcement and emphasized that in his statement the president had referred to the "compensatory attitude" on the part of the IPC in coming to this agreement. The use of the

---

41. Goodsell, *American Corporations and Peruvian Politics*, 129.
42. "Confidential Telegram 6443 from Jones, July 26, 1968," USNA (1967–1969) (Box 1372, Folder 1), 1–3.
43. Pinelo, *The Multinational Corporation as a Force in Latin American Politics*, 139.
44. "Confidential Memorandum from Oliver to Rusk, July 29, 1968," USNA (1967–1969) (Box 1372, Folder 1), 1–2.

word "compensatory" had already begun to cause problems and indicated that much still needed to be done to hammer out the final details of the accord. Jones wrote, "We urge . . . that the Department avoid statements on the subject, and particularly that it avoid going into details other than to express pleasure that agreement in principle has been reached. We also believe it important that the department coordinate closely in possible future comments with IPC, Coral Gables and/or the Jersey board."[45]

Reaching a Final Agreement

Jones's warning that "the devil would be in the details" in reaching a satisfactory resolution proved prescient. Meeting with Espinosa and his assistant manager on the night of August 2, Belaúnde pushed hard for an agreement that could be concluded by August 10, the date he had set for the handover ceremony at Talara. The IPC officials, however, insisted that before they could agree to this they had to be assured that the act of transfer included a clause that guaranteed the company would not be assessed for past debts and that this guarantee had to be provided not only by Belaúnde but also by Congress. Belaúnde argued vehemently that congressional approval was not needed with the company representatives arguing just as vehemently that it was. At times, they reported to Jones, "the meeting . . . grew exceedingly tense . . . with neither side yielding. Eventually . . . the president threatened Espinosa with an embargo of the company's assets and with 'exposure' before Congress and the people if he did not have his way." Leaving for Coral Gables to report to headquarters that night, Espinosa expressed to Jones his concerns that the company's rights would not be protected under the pressure of rushed negotiations driven by an artificial deadline.[46] From Belaúnde's perspective, of course, the deadline was far from artificial. Under increasing political pressure from all sides, he badly needed this problem resolved to keep alive whatever hopes he had for finishing his elected term. Moreover, the special sixty-day authority given to the executive, which was nonrenewable, was due to expire on August 19.

Belaúnde discussed the negotiations further with Jones and OAS Ambassador Sol Linowitz during a luncheon meeting on August 6. He reiterated

---

45. "Limited Official Use Telegram 6459 from Jones, July 30, 1968," USNA (1967–1969) (Box 1372, Folder 1), 1–2.

46. "Confidential Telegram 6544 from Jones, August 3, 1968," USNA (1967–1969) (Box 1372, Folder 3), 1–2.

his objection to the company's insistence on congressional approval. Jones, continuing his role as mediator between the company and the government, reported that he had met with Dean and Espinosa the previous day, and they had made clear to him their reluctance to sign a new agreement without congressional approval, having already been stung by that body's demand they pay back taxes. In response, Belaúnde gave in somewhat, arguing that it would not be "inconvenient" to present the new contract to Congress but that he did not want such a commitment as a written provision in the agreement. What he suggested instead was that he and the company come to an oral agreement on the contract, which would then be submitted to Congress as a fait accompli. Otherwise, he feared that it would become bogged down in congressional debate and never ratified. Jones continued to press the company's position, arguing that Dean "had brought a great deal of imagination and courage to the solution of this old problem and that his quid pro quo was to assure that all past obligations of the company alleged or otherwise were considered discharged not only by the government but by congressional action. I urged the president to see Mr. Dean while he was here and to meet him half way in his requirements." When Jones reported his conversation to Dean and Espinosa, they repeated their insistence that congressional approval was essential to protect their interests. Once the company's assets were transferred officially to the state, they argued, they had no lever to assure that Congress might not push again for collection of alleged past debts. They were encouraged, however, that Belaúnde seemed now to be willing to postpone his planned transfer of the assets at Talara for at least a few days.[47]

In addition to the question of congressional ratification of any ensuing contract, there were other issues at play in the negotiations. Among the company's demands were an agreement by EPF to provide it with at least 80 percent of the crude oil produced at La Brea y Pariñas at the price of $1.80 per barrel, to retain more than one hundred of the company's workers at the fields, and to give IPC concessions to explore in the jungle regions of the country. Belaúnde and his negotiating team refused to give on these and other issues, and there was little movement on either side. These discussions occurred on Saturday and Sunday. On Monday, El Comercio published a report on the "impasse," listing the company's demands in detail. Since these details had become public, the government said that the company had to drop them for the negotiations to succeed. The IPC representatives agreed

---

47. "Confidential Telegram 6619 from Jones, August 7, 1968," USNA (1967–1969) (Box 1372, Folder 3), 1–3.

to give up the request for future concessions in the jungle but held firm to its demand for a fixed share of the crude oil purchased from the EPF at a fixed price. On the same day that the story on the impasse appeared in *El Comercio*, August 12, Ambassador Jones reported to Washington that "the situation remains fluid and tense and the outcome is not assured."[48]

Further negotiations that day between the company and Belaúnde and his team produced no breakthroughs. Therefore, early in the morning of August 12, the president proposed and the cabinet agreed to a measure that would simply expropriate the IPC holdings. In one last attempt to reach an agreement, Hercelles telephoned Jones to inform him of the government's plans. Jones then requested a delay of several hours so that he could convince Espinosa to return to the presidential palace and agree to the government's position. The ambassador was apparently successful in those efforts, and Espinosa finally accepted the government's terms. These included an agreement that the EPF would take on 167 IPC workers and the rest would remain with the company. Regarding oil purchases, the price per barrel was set at $1.97, and the amount of crude to be provided to IPC would be determined by EPF. This agreement was signed by both parties at 5:30 A.M. on August 13. Later in the day, Belaúnde and other high-government officials and party representatives flew to Talara and signed the official document, the Acta de Talara, that transferred the IPC holdings to the Peruvian government. Also on that day, special advisor Rostow informed President Johnson that the IPC problem had finally been resolved, "thereby removing this dangerous matter from U.S.-Peruvian relations once and for all."[49] As events would soon show, this judgment was premature.

In his report to the State Department on the negotiations and their results, Jones said nothing about his own role in these developments. Drawing on his conversations with Espinosa and his assistant general manager, Jones wrote that the major sticking point had been the price to be paid for crude oil, and the major obstacle to the agreement had been the recalcitrance of the EPF's Loret de Mola, who seemed determined "to torpedo the entire agreement if he possibly could." The IPC representatives claimed that Hercelles and other cabinet members had worn down the reluctant Loret de Mola and "almost literally held his hand while he signed" the contractual agreement. With regard to Belaúnde, Espinosa believed that he had "conducted himself very well throughout this trying night and was especially

---

48. "Confidential Telegram 6718 from Jones, August 12, 1968," USNA, 1.

49. "Information Memorandum from William G. Bowdler of the National Security Staff to President Johnson, July 30, 1968," *FRUS (1964–1968)*, 1050–51n2.

appreciative of the courteous and sensitive tone of the president's remarks at Talara next day." He also had high praise for Finance Minister Ulloa, "who interceded forcefully and intelligently at several key points throughout the night" and without whom "there would not have been an agreement." While Espinosa felt the company had emerged as best it could have under the circumstances, the result was certainly "no victory" for its position. "His main concern," Jones wrote, "is that much of the implementation will depend upon Loret de Mola and EPF and he is afraid that many problems will be deliberately generated from this quarter."[50] While things did not play out exactly as Espinosa had feared, these concerns, on the whole, proved well justified.

Belaúnde Tries to Hang On

While the Act of Talara seemed to resolve the long-running IPC dispute, other issues remained to complicate U.S.-Peruvian relations. In early August, the U.S. Congress passed the Pelly amendment to the Foreign Assistance Act that, as mentioned, cut off U.S. assistance to any country that seized U.S. fishing vessels outside of the recognized twelve-mile limit. On August 16, Ambassador Pastor communicated to Lima the latest developments on this front and promised to send a formal letter of protest to the State Department, arguing that the amendment "contradicts the spirit and the substance of the Alliance for Progress" and favors important U.S. economic interests without taking into consideration "the vital significance to Perú of its ichthyological richness within its jurisdictional waters."[51] True to his word, on August 19 Pastor sent a strong letter to Secretary of State Rusk protesting the Pelly amendment as "an inadmissible act of pressure that undermines the principles of the Alliance for Progress," the implications of which his country could not accept. He also declared that the United States' attempts to call a meeting of the South Pacific Coast nations to discuss these issues would be inopportune and "imprudent" in light of the current controversy generated by this amendment, "whose text contains pressure that a free and sovereign nation cannot accept."[52]

In Lima, Ambassador Jones encountered a similar response. Reporting on a mid-August meeting with a former foreign minister, Admiral Luis

---

50. "Confidential Telegram 6791 from Jones, August 15, 1968," USNA (1967–1969) (Box 1372, Folder 3), 2.
51. *Correspondencia* (5-3-Y/24) (August 16, 1968), 3.
52. "Letter from Pastor to Rusk, August 19, 1968," USNA (1967–1969) (Box 2425, Folder 4), 1–2.

Edgardo Llosa, with whom he claimed to have had "a long and friendly relationship," he found similar doubts about the utility of a proposed conference in Santiago for a multination discussion of the 200-mile-limit dispute. Furthermore, "When we clarified that the new act would only reduce aid by the amount of licenses and fines and would not cut off aid entirely he recognized the effect would be less onerous but still objected to the principle."[53] He received much the same message from Prime Minister Hercelles a week later, who told him that it would be better "not [to] press [the] matter now but 'let it cool' since [the] furor caused by [the] Pelley amendment both here and in Ecuador was such that no government could agree now to go to [a] conference with [the] USG on this subject."[54]

President Belaúnde addressed the issue in an interview with the *New York Times* that appeared on August 21. Claiming that current strains in U.S.-Peruvian relations were based primarily on "dangerous misunderstandings," he first defended the purchase of the *Mirage* fighters as a legitimate right of a sovereign nation to make such a choice. He added that "we also are peaceful and believe that Latin America will remain peaceful. But our armed forces must be prepared for emergencies. Our armed forces are never aggressive and the training their members receive is useful to the whole society." On the 200-mile-limit controversy, the president was circumspect, not wanting to provide detailed commentary "at this sensitive stage." However, he repeated the argument that the fish off Peru's coast were one of the nation's most vital natural resources and that "they can be gravely endangered by indiscriminate fishing." It was a national duty, he concluded, "to protect this important resource."[55]

The Final Act

Any comfort Belaúnde might have received from the apparent resolution of the IPC issue proved short-lived. At the end of August, Jones informed Washington that while the president and Development Minister Carriquiry were "fulfilling in every way their commitments to IPC. . . , the same is not true of [EPF director] Loreta de Mola." IPC manager Espinosa, he reported, was "considerably worried about the attitude of Loret de Mola

---

53. "Confidential Telegram from Jones, August 14, 1968," USNA (1967–1969) (Box 2425, Folder 4), 2.
54. "Limited Official Use Telegram from Jones, August 21, 1968," USNA (1967–1969) (Box 2425, Folder 4), 2.
55. *New York Times*, August 21, 1968, 9.

and the kinds of problems he is creating and can create" but not worried enough to postpone a three-month holiday.[56]

Espinosa's departure was poorly timed. There were still important details of the Talara agreement to be discussed and resolved. As negotiations proceeded, Loret de Mola and his team became frustrated by what they considered lack of support from Carriquiry and continued inflexibility from the company. On September 6, Loret de Mola, along with three members of the EPF board of directors, resigned, claiming that when they tried to assume control of the La Brea y Pariñas fields, the IPC had responded that its interpretation of the Act of Talara was that they could continue to operate there until the end of the year. More significant for the now former EPF director, however, was what he considered a failure to reach a definitive agreement on the minimum price of the crude oil that IPC would purchase from the state company. On September 10, Loret de Mola went on television to charge that page 11 of the contract on which this agreement appeared was missing. He suggested collusion between the Belaúnde administration and the company and that page 11 had been purposely mislaid to ensure the final agreement without publicly acknowledging that the company had received special treatment.[57]

The Lima press, especially *El Comercio* and *La Prensa*, leapt on these accusations to severely criticize both the Belaúnde administration and the IPC. Reporting on these reactions, Jones told Washington, in what was a considerable understatement, that "it appears that debate on [the] IPC case is far from over."[58] In a subsequent communication, based on a report from a "high palace source," he saw the controversy as weakening the president's position within his own party but believed that Aprista backing on this issue would be sufficient for him to survive, even though the revelation of the missing page 11 had severely eroded the original popular backing he had gained with the Act of Talara.[59]

Jones's cautious optimism notwithstanding, by this time, Belaúnde's position was becoming increasingly tenuous. Loret de Mola's accusations had served to accentuate political tensions and divisions and to encourage

---

56. "Confidential Telegram 7011 from Jones, August 28, 1968," USNA (1967–1969) (Box 1372, Folder 3), 1–2.

57. For more on this complicated matter, see Goodwin, "Letter from Perú," 88–89; Ingram, *Expropriation of U.S. Property in South America*, 58–59; Kuczynski, *Peruvian Democracy Under Economic Stress*, 266–72; and Pinelo, *The Multinational Corporation as a Force in Latin American Politics*, 141–42.

58. "Limited Official Use Telegram 7285 from Jones, September 12, 1968," USNA (1967–1969) (Box 1372, Folder 3), 2.

59. "Limited Official Use Telegram 7308 from Jones, September 13, 1968," USNA (1967–1969) (Box 1372, Folder 3), 3.

military elements plotting a coup to proceed with their efforts. While the question of whether the missing page 11 had ever existed remained a matter of controversy, most of the public seemed to agree that it had and to accept Loret de Mola's description and interpretation of events. Representatives of the IPC argued that there never had been a page 11 and so informed the U.S. embassy, providing it with a photostatic copy of the crude oil sales contract signed on August 13, a copy that contained only ten pages and which Jones forwarded to Washington.[60] As far as the political dynamics in Peru were concerned, however, the company's claim had no real effect, a not unsurprising result given the overwhelming nationalist sentiment against the IPC.

On the same day that he forwarded the contract copy to Washington, Jones met with Belaúnde to discuss the resumption of certain AID projects. The president spent much of the meeting reviewing the long and complicated efforts to resolve the IPC controversy, claiming it was a problem that stretched back 142 years, from "Bolívar to Belaúnde." As president, he claimed, he always had wanted to settle the matter, but it was only with the present cabinet that he had the kind of ministers who had the "determination" and the "will" to reach a solution. He was aware, he said, of the attacks he was getting from the opposition and the "incredible actions" of Loret de Mola but believed that the "matter was now terminated" and that his administration would stand by the agreement that had been reached. "However," Jones reported, "his government needed help for both political as well as financial reasons and he hoped that with this long-standing issue behind us [the] U.S. government would come forward with some material evidence of its support." In this regard, he made some specific requests for economic assistance.[61]

The tone of Jones's dispatch seemed to indicate a certain confidence on the part of Belaúnde that the IPC matter was indeed resolved and that he, his administration, and the U.S. government could now move on to other matters. This may have been an accurate reflection of the president's mood, a maneuver by him to speed up needed economic assistance to bolster his deteriorating position, or both. Nonetheless, it was clear to all that his position was becoming increasingly desperate. Writing to Secretary Rusk on September 20, Assistant Secretary Oliver provided a grim assessment of Belaúnde's prospects. The overall economic climate and the failure to resolve

60. "Confidential Airgram A-838 from Jones, September 18, 1968," USNA (1967–1969) (Box 1372, Folder 3), 1.
61. "Confidential Telegram 7382 from Jones, September 18, 1968," USNA (1967–1969) (Box 1372, Folder 3), 1–2.

the IPC matter appeared to mean that even a skilled politician like Belaúnde faced limited options. Under these circumstances, he concluded, there was little the United States could do, especially given the limits imposed by the various congressional amendments pertaining to expropriation of U.S. private interests, fishing rights, and arms sales.[62]

On September 21, trying to shore up his position with dramatic action, Belaúnde expelled Edgardo Seoane, who had called for an annulment of the Act of Talara and a dismissal of the current cabinet, from Acción Popular. This was followed by a direct attack by Seoane's supporters on party headquarters. On that same day, *El Comercio* reported that Air Force Minister José Gagliardi had denied the armed forces would act in an "unconstitutional" manner during the current crisis.[63] The next day, however, Army General Juan Velasco Alvarado claimed that Gagliardi's disavowal had "no validity." On the same day *El Comercio* reported Gagliardi's remarks, it also quoted Finance Minister Manuel Ulloa, who was on his way to London to arrange refinancing of the nation's external debt, as "very discouraged" by a recent announcement that Alliance for Progress funds would be cut for the coming year. "When it is convenient for its own political interests," he claimed, "the United States promises aid for Latin America, but in practice does not provide what it promises."[64]

In Washington, as these developments unfolded, State Department analyst Thomas Hughes discounted the possibility of a military coup "at the moment." He did acknowledge that the military had been following the current controversy over the IPC closely through its representative on the board of the EPF, and while the air minister and war minister seemed opposed to removing Belaúnde by force, the "bright and vigorous" commander and president of the joint chiefs, General Juan Velasco, had openly asserted that "the armed forces have a role to play in the IPC affair." Velasco, he said, had clearly come out on top in the exchange with Gagliardi and was "the principal figure of practically every coup rumor." While Belaúnde's immediate tenure might not be threatened, it seemed likely that he would change his cabinet, probably dismissing Prime Minister Hercelles and Finance Minister Ulloa and perhaps replacing them with military men. He also concluded that the sales contract between EPF and IPC would have to be rewritten, but that company representatives appeared ready "to live with the changes

---

62. "Information Memorandum from the Assistant Secretary of State for Inter-American Affairs (Oliver) to Secretary of State Rusk, September 20, 1968," *FRUS (1964–1968)*, 1052–54.

63. *El Comercio*, September 21, 1968, 4.

64. Ibid.

they envision, and . . . so far do not appear overly concerned."⁶⁵ A CIA Intelligence Information Cable of September 27 also asserted that the Belaúnde government "is not expected to be overthrown by the Peruvian armed forces *in the near future* [emphasis mine]."⁶⁶

A few days later, however, on September 28, Jones reported that a coup seemed likely. While divisions within the military continued, he wrote, the current political crisis "together with widespread mistrust of the government's handling of the IPC settlement has clearly reduced confidence in the democratic machinery and has doubtless encouraged many Peruvians to think along traditional lines of an authoritarian solution."⁶⁷ On October 1, in a last-ditch attempt to stave off the inevitable, Belaúnde named a new cabinet. Jones, recognizing the seriousness of the president's predicament, continued to lobby Washington on his behalf. In a confidential telegram on the day the new cabinet was named, he bemoaned the delays in granting the administration economic assistance following the Act of Talara and stressed the urgency of the current situation. "Belaúnde needs help," he pleaded, "and needs it now."⁶⁸

It is doubtful that any kind of U.S. action to support Belaúnde at this point would have done any good. The die was cast. Early in the morning of October 3, barely twelve hours after Belaúnde had sworn in his new cabinet, elements of the Peruvian army advanced on and surrounded the presidential palace in downtown Lima. A sleepy Belaúnde, still in his pajamas, was bundled into a waiting jeep and despite his protests and cries of "traitors" was taken to Jorge Chávez airport, which he had inaugurated with pride only a few years earlier, and put on a plane that took him into temporary exile in Buenos Aires. The experiment in reformist democracy that he had begun five years earlier was over.

The coup was carefully and effectively executed. The main instigators were the army's General Velasco and General Edgardo Mercado Jarrín, director of the Centro de Instrucción Militar del Perú and head of the army's

---

65. "Secret Intelligence Note (no foreign dissemination) 750 from Hughes, September 24, 1968," USNA (1967–1969) (Box 2422, Folder 6), 2–3.

66. "CIA Intelligence Information Cable, September 27, 1968," NSF, Country Files, Box 73, Folder 4, LBJ Library. The CIA report listed three conditions under which Belaúnde might be removed: (1) popular demonstrations against him; (2) a move on his part to remove Velasco from command; and (3) a likely victory by Haya de la Torre in the upcoming elections. None of these, with the possible exception of the third possibility, were factors in the coup.

67. "Confidential Telegram 7578 from Jones, September 28, 1968," USNA (1967–1969) (Box 2422, Folder 6), 1.

68. "Confidential Telegram 7619 from Jones, October 1, 1968," USNA (1967–1969) (Box 2421, Folder 5), 1.

Intelligence Service. Although there was some resistance within the armed forces initially, once the blow was struck, most in uniform fell into line. Air Force General Gagliardi, who had disavowed "unconstitutional" action by the military two weeks earlier, along with General Alejandro Sánchez Salazar, chief of the army's general staff, were placed under temporary house arrest. Aside from some brief disturbances by protesting students in the central streets of the capital, there was little public protest of the coup or defense of the fallen administration. The *New York Times* reported that on October 3 "a cardboard, hand-lettered sign was placed at the front gate of the United States Embassy saying 'Closed.' However, Ambassador J. Wesley Jones went ahead with a regularly scheduled weekly meeting in the embassy for American business in Lima."[69]

Belaúnde: An Opportunity Lost

The history of U.S. relations with the Belaúnde administration was replete with paradox and contradiction. On the one hand, the Peruvian president, by almost all accounts, was the ideal Alliance for Progress democratic reformer. Intelligent, charismatic, and committed to progressive change in Peru, he sought to address the fundamental problems of poverty and underdevelopment through a variety of innovative and generally well-conceived programs. He seemed, as many called his Chilean contemporary Eduardo Frei, "the last, best hope for democracy" in Peru.

On the other hand, almost from the beginning of his administration, Washington seemed more concerned with defending the interests of the International Petroleum Company than in supporting Belaúnde's reform agenda. The lack of aid clearly hurt and contributed significantly to Belaúnde's failures to achieve his reformist goals. Added to the IPC issue were the further complications of the fishing dispute and the *Mirage* jet purchase.

These specific issues aside, the State Department's and the executive branch's general view of Belaúnde rarely seemed particularly favorable. During the Kennedy administration and the 1962 presidential campaign in Peru, doubts had been raised about the strength of his anticommunist credentials at a time when the U.S. government clearly preferred the candidacy

---

69. *New York Times*, October 4, 1968, 1. For a more detailed account of these events and the background leading up to the coup, see Masterson, *Militarism and Politics in Latin America*, 226–34. See also Hoyos Osores, "Crisis de la democracia en el Perú," 7–31; Kuczynski, *Peruvian Democracy Under Economic Stress*, 270–76; and Tamarz Lúcar, *Historia del poder*, 337–42.

of Haya de la Torre. During the Johnson years, State Department documents often referred to Belaúnde as a "dreamer" and a "visionary" rather than as a practical, pragmatic, and hard-nosed leader capable of getting things done. President Johnson's own dim view of the Peruvian leader has already been mentioned and that view may have permeated through the executive branch to others. Belaúnde seems to have been one of the few Latin American leaders, especially its democratic leaders, who did not make an official (or even unofficial) visit to the United States during his presidency. Whether this was because of his own reluctance to leave Peru as claimed or because of lack of interest on Washington's part cannot be determined.

Ambassador Jones admired and had a good relationship with Belaúnde. He did his best to get Washington to support the increasingly beleaguered Peruvian president and to serve as a good-faith mediator in the seemingly never-ending wrangling over the IPC issue. In many ways, he was the classic "man in the middle," trying to get both sides to understand and to compromise with one another. In the end, he may have felt as frustrated as Belaúnde did with the failure of Washington to be more forthcoming with economic assistance.

Whatever Jones's good intentions, the U.S. policy toward Belaúnde must be judged a colossal failure. U.S. policy contributed not only to the weakening and ultimate downfall of the man *Time* magazine had labeled three years earlier as the "model" Alliance for Progress democrat, but it also led to a military government that would nationalize outright the IPC holdings as well as those of several other major U.S. investors and take a diplomatic posture that at least initially seemed to threaten a serious break in what traditionally had been a rather close relationship between the two nations.

Although the role of the U.S. in Belaúnde's downfall was clearly significant, it also should not be exaggerated. The Peruvian president faced many internal obstacles to his plans for reform that would have been difficult to achieve no matter what U.S. policy had been. Like many of his fellow Latin American reformers in the 1960s he had to deal with an obdurate and opportunistic opposition that controlled Congress throughout his term and consistently frustrated his bolder initiatives and hamstrung his administration as much as it could. Moreover, in addition to the opposition of the Apristas and Unión Nacional Odriista, he lost the support of his coalition partner Christian Democrats and saw his own party split, largely over the IPC issue. He also faced pressures from the extreme left, although he had enjoyed some success in crushing the guerrilla threat in 1965. Nonetheless, that experience had an important effect on the army, and the president's failures to address to their satisfaction the underlying conditions that produced the threat was an important factor in its decision to remove him from office. In addition, like any political leader, he made policy decisions that often did not produce the desired result. Critics, for example, often expressed skepticism about his determination to pursue his "marginal highway" scheme regardless of costs or other priorities.

Finally, it might be argued that the United States' withholding of economic assistance was not as detrimental as it might have seemed. While the public faucet was tightened, private investment from the United States flowed into Peru in considerable quantities in the 1960s. Moreover, despite some ups and downs, the economic performance of the administration was reasonably good throughout these years, and as late as September 1968, Peru was enjoying an export boom that was expected to produce a record $850 million in earnings by the end of the year.[70] One could argue that the withholding of U.S. assistance was of little overall consequence in the larger scheme. However, while the amounts withheld might have been relatively small, they could have gone to development projects with significant impact. Moreover, the perception was also important. The United States seemed to be singling out Peru for special punitive treatment over the IPC issue, a policy that not only exacerbated Peruvian resentment and a nationalistic reaction but also made Belaúnde's position ever more precarious. As he so often lamented to Ambassador Jones and others, the IPC matter had been a consistent thorn in his side throughout his administration and one that he struggled mightily to remove. Just when it seemed the issue had been settled, new complications emerged that accelerated the end of his administration. While it must remain in the realm of speculation, in retrospect a U.S. policy that placed less emphasis on defending the interests of a private company and more emphasis on supporting a democratic regime committed to reform might well have produced better results for both sides.

---

70. *New York Times*, September 5, 1968, 19.

6

THE COUP AND ITS AFTERMATH

The military action that ousted President Fernando Belaúnde Terry from office was certainly not unprecedented. A similar action had occurred in Peru six years earlier, and a longer tradition of armed forces intervention in the nation's political affairs stretched back to the early nineteenth century. Nor were such actions uncommon in Latin America generally. Despite the democratic aspirations of the Alliance for Progress, military coups and regimes had become commonplace throughout the region in the 1960s. It would soon become apparent, however, that the 1968 coup in Peru and the subsequent military regime were of a significantly different order from the commonplace. Faced with a new and complex challenge from the military reformers who came to power in Peru, it would take the U.S. government some time to react and to adapt to the unexpected challenge that this new reality posed to relations between the two nations.

Initial Reactions

The October 3 coup apparently caught both President Belaúnde and the U.S. embassy by surprise. Although rumors had been circulating for weeks that something was afoot, especially after the controversy over the missing page 11 erupted, Belaúnde continued to believe that the military would never move against him. He appeared to rely on what he considered good relations between himself and the armed forces, whose wishes he had sought to satisfy throughout his administration, and, when he was rousted in the middle of the night and unceremoniously removed from the presidential palace, Belaúnde reacted with shock and anger.[1]

While not as angry as the ousted president, the United States also seemed somewhat shocked by the turn of events.[2] As late as the last week of September both the State Department Intelligence Office and the CIA were discounting that a coup might be imminent. While Ambassador Jones was clearly aware that Belaúnde's situation was becoming increasingly desperate, he believed that disunity among the armed forces would forestall any immediate action. One explanation for these misperceptions might well have been that the coup plotters were a relatively small group of twelve army officers who took extreme measures to hide their intentions and their preparations for the takeover, even keeping their actions secret from their wives and choosing not to include the air force and the navy in their efforts.[3] Nonetheless, it does seem rather peculiar that the U.S. government apparently had no reliable sources within the military to keep both the embassy and Washington better informed about what would be a serious turn of events in Peru at a time of continuing tensions over various issues. A CIA cable on the day of the coup described it as "the product of many political factors" and mentioned in particular the cabinet changes that preceded it. On the whole, however, the report seemed basically clueless about what really had transpired and the forces that impelled the military to action.[4]

On the day of the coup, Ambassador Jones sought to provide Washington with what information he had available about its causes. In his interpretation, a desire to prevent an Aprista victory in the 1969 elections was paramount along with the general deterioration of the Belaúnde regime's position, exacerbated by the IPC imbroglio. He also speculated that many conservative Peruvians were pleased with the coup "and may have been

---

1. For a detailed account of Belaúnde's "arrest" and reaction, see Zimmermann Zavala, *El Plan Inca*, 174–80.
2. President Johnson was informed of the coup at 6:30 A.M. by a briefing officer at the White House. A few hours later, Rostow sent him a memo with more details, beginning by noting that the coup had occurred "contrary to our latest intelligence estimates" and that the question of recognition would soon have to be faced. He also said that for the moment AID would suspend any assistance plans for Peru. "Information Memorandum from the President's Special Assistant (Rostow) to President Johnson, October 3, 1968," *FRUS (1964–1968)*, 1057–58.
3. For more on the coup plotting, see Masterson, *Militarism and Politics in Latin America*, 230, and Zimmermann, *El Plan Inca*, 110–37.
4. "CIA Intelligence Information Cable of October 3, 1968," NSF, Country File 1–80, Box 73, Folder 4, LBJ Library. This cable, as with many, was heavily redacted, perhaps to protect the identity of CIA sources in Peru.

involved in it," largely in reaction to recent measures by the Belaúnde government and the Hercelles cabinet, particularly with regard to tax policies.[5] If that were the case, it would not take too long for them to regret such participation.

In another telegram on the same day, Jones provided what information he could about the leaders of the junta. Commenting on General Juan Velasco Alvarado, who had masterminded the coup and would lead the new military regime, he described him as "well known to the embassy as highly nationalistic and suspicious of U.S. policies." A report from the embassy's military attaché described Velasco as "ambitious, self-confident, not easily influenced, highly respected, extremely competent, and intelligent. He is strongly anti-communist and is also firmly anti-Apra."[6] The next day, Jones added an assessment of the new government as one made up of "technocrat" military officers who sought to "efficiently resolve Peru's problems."[7]

The State Department's first response to the coup was to inform Jones that it had the effect, although not yet officially announced, of suspending diplomatic relations between the two countries. It advised the ambassador to move cautiously in establishing contacts with the new regime. In the meantime, U.S. government officials were to work only in U.S. government offices or at home, and not be present in Peruvian government offices. Moreover, the department discouraged any official contacts but did recommend the continuation of any "unofficial contacts" that might provide useful information.[8] On the same day, the department also informed Jones that an unnamed source in the Peruvian embassy in Washington, who claimed to be the new regime's representative, had told a department officer that he had been authorized to inform him that "whatever happens to IPC, the Company will not be nationalized."[9] Whatever the source, this information

---

5. "Confidential Telegram 7661 from Jones, October 3, 1968," *FRUS (1964–1968)*, 1058–59.

6. "Confidential Telegram 7651 from Jones, October 3, 1968," USNA (1967–1969) (Box 2423, Folder 6), 1.

7. "Confidential Telegram 7705 from Jones, October 4, 1968," USNA (1967–1969) (Box 2423, Folder 1), 3. Apparently drawing on the information provided by Jones, Rostow reported to Johnson that the junta was "firmly in control in Peru," listed the main reasons for the coup, which reflected those underscored by Jones, and suggested that the recognition should await reactions from other American states. "Unlike the case of the Argentine coup in 1966," he added, "we have made no official statement condemning the action of the military leaders, although State officials have made our unhappiness clear on a background basis." "Information Memorandum From the President's Special Assistant (Rostow) to President Johnson," *FRUS (1964–1968)*, 1060–61.

8. "Confidential Telegram 249329 from Department of State (approved by Oliver and stamped by legal advisor Nicholas Katzenbach), October 2, 1968," USNA (1967–1969) (Box 2423, Folder 6), 1.

9. "Confidential Telegram 252362 from Department of State (stamped by Rusk), October 3, 1968," USNA (1967–1969) (Box 2422, Folder 4), 1.

could not have been more mistaken or more misleading. On October 4, in one of its first official acts, the new regime declared the Act of Talara of August 13 null and void, a harbinger of more radical action to come.

On that same day, the State Department announced that relations between the United States and the new government of Peru had been suspended but not formally broken. The U.S. embassy in Lima would continue to operate as normal while the administration consulted with other hemisphere nations on a future course of action. In the meantime, aid programs to Peru would be placed "under review." Privately, the *New York Times* reported, "United States officials . . . deplored the military take-over in Peru."[10]

In a more public forum, liberal Democratic Senator Ernest Greuning of Alaska made clear his own strong disapproval of the military action. In a speech to the Senate on October 3, he called the overthrow of Belaúnde "disgraceful" and "another example of the failure of US policies in Latin America." The main flaw of these policies, he argued, was an overreliance on military assistance to the region. He urged the State Department to suspend all aid to Peru until civilian democracy had been restored.[11] A fellow liberal Democrat, Senator Ralph Yarborough of Texas, made a similar argument in a speech to the Senate on the following day. He detailed his own sympathies for President Belaúnde and his attempts to bring about social and economic change within a democratic framework and bemoaned yet another Latin American military coup during a decade when such actions had become increasingly common. "The coup in Peru," he argued, "marked another victory in Latin America for the oligarchs." Moreover, "it is a tragedy when a constitutionally elected President is removed from his presidential palace in a predawn hour through the use of tanks and troops, but it is, I think, an added element of tragedy when the tanks bear the brand 'Made in U.S.A.' and the military leadership bears the stamp 'Trained in the U.S.A.'" In response, he urged the State Department to move with caution in recognizing the new regime and until it did to suspend military and economic assistance "except where it is clearly demonstrable that the aid will bring about social improvement."[12]

In the context of the time, Yarborough's reflections and reactions were understandable and probably rather widely shared. However, he, like many others, misread what had happened in Peru. The coup was hardly "another victory" for the oligarchs; indeed, in the Peruvian case, it turned out to be quite the opposite. Moreover, while the equipment and the training might

10. *New York Times*, October 5, 1968, 19.
11. *Congressional Record—Senate*, October 3, 1968, 29310.
12. *Congressional Record—Senate*, October 4, 1968, 29637–38.

have been "made in the U.S.A.," the coup was most certainly not, at least not directly, and relations between the United States and the military government would remain mostly difficult and strained for a substantial period.

Against the backdrop of this congressional condemnation of the coup, the State Department wrestled with the always knotty problem of recognition of the new government. In a series of secret communications with Jones, Assistant Secretary Covey T. Oliver not only expressed his own personal revulsion with the course of events in Peru but also sounded the envoy out about using the Peruvian example as a test case for a new policy that would express displeasure with the ousting of an elected government but would not lead to an outright break in diplomatic relations. Jones diplomatically replied that the current circumstances in Peru were perhaps not the best for such an experiment. Recognition, he reasoned, was eventually inevitable in that it was the only way the United States could expect to continue to protect and promote its interests in Peru. These included, in his view, not only the interests of private investors but also movement toward achieving the goals of the Alliance for Progress. Recognition should come, he concluded, once certain assurances had been made of a return to constitutional government.[13]

As these communications were exchanged in secret, the public response of the State Department to the coup and the recognition question remained critical but moderate in tone. In commenting on the new regime, the department stated that "it goes without saying that the United States believes in the principles of constitutional and elected governments. Obviously the disruption of constitutional government in Peru is of concern to us. It also is of concern to other countries in the hemisphere." Following this mild "rebuke," the *New York Times* reported on October 8, it seemed likely that following consultation with other hemisphere nations the United States would recognize the new Peruvian regime in the not too distant future.[14]

The Argentine Connection and the Chilean Reaction

Initial press reports on the military takeover in Peru compared it to a similar action in Argentina in 1966 when a junta there removed from office the democratically elected administration of Arturo Illia. The *New York Times*, quoting "qualified Peruvian sources," asserted that the Peruvian coup had

---

13. "Secret Telegram 7730 from Jones, October 6, 1968," USNA (1967–1969) (Box 2420, Folder 4), 1–2.

14. *New York Times*, October 8, 1968, 16.

been patterned after the Argentine example, with the most salient similarity being the plan for the military in Peru, as in Argentina, to remain in power "indefinitely, not merely on an interim basis."[15] Another *Times* article saw both military governments as nationalistic and prepared to turn to Europe to counterbalance the influence of the United States. This would be particularly pertinent in Peru, given the ongoing disputes over the 200-mile limit and the International Petroleum Company (IPC) case, among others. The military takeover in Peru was yet another in a series of reverses to "Washington's diplomatic efforts to encourage democracy."[16]

Initially, the possibility of Argentine involvement in the overthrow of Belaúnde was of considerable concern to Peru's southern neighbor, Chile. On October 9, U.S. officials met in Santiago with President Eduardo Frei's foreign minister, Gabriel Valdés, who expressed "great concern" over the coup and the possibility of his democratic country being squeezed between two authoritarian regimes. He claimed that his government had evidence of Argentine involvement both in the planning of the takeover and the events of October 2 and 3 and saw the new regime as a dangerous combination of the extreme right and left-wing nationalists. Valdés also manifested his concern that these events would force Chile to purchase more military equipment, which, at the moment, it could ill afford. Whatever the reservations, however, he also added that Chile would likely recognize the new regime within a couple of weeks, taking time to consult on the matter with Colombia, Ecuador, and Uruguay.[17]

Chilean suspicions of Argentine involvement in Peru were probably based on intuition rather than hard evidence. There were long-standing tensions between Chile and Peru dating from the War of the Pacific in the late nineteenth century, and relations between Peru and Argentina, which had both Chile and Brazil as common strategic concerns, had historically been close. But if the Argentine government had been directly involved in the Peruvian coup, it apparently was done without the knowledge of the Argentine ambassador to the United Nations, Nicanor Costa Mendez, who, in a conversation with Secretary of State Dean Rusk, claimed that the "coup had come as a surprise" to him as he had been somewhat optimistic that Belaúnde would be able to serve out his term.[18] A few weeks later, Ambassador

15. *New York Times*, October 5, 1968, 19.
16. *New York Times*, October 6, 1968, 29.
17. "Confidential Telegram 7002 from Santiago, October 10, 1968," USNA (1967–1969) (Box 2423, Folder 1), 1–2.
18. "Confidential Telegram 6953 from U.S. Mission at the U. N., October 8, 1968," USNA (1967–1969) (Box 2423, Folder 6), 1–2.

John Wesley Jones discounted the Chilean theory of Argentine involvement, noting that while there may have been some inspiration and some similarities, "we do not believe in the collaboration theory and in any case believe it was unnecessary" in that the Peruvian military junta was perfectly capable of acting on its own.[19] The Chilean reaction, too, underscored that it was not just the government of the United States that was somewhat befuddled by what had happened in Peru.

The Military Takes Over the Holdings of the IPC

While Chile was occupied with possible Argentine involvement in the coup and the United States wrestled with recognition, the new government took a bold but, by this time, not totally unexpected step. On the morning of October 9, in a speech to several hundred military officers assembled in the presidential palace and broadcast throughout the nation on radio and television, General Velasco announced that the new junta, by decree, was taking possession of the La Brea y Pariñas fields and that army troops were moving into Talara for that purpose as he spoke. This action, he proclaimed, was evidence of a "new emancipation" for the nation, intended to show that "the sovereignty of the Peruvian State from this moment on is not a mere phrase but rather an authentic reality." While most of the speech was suffused with similar nationalistic rhetoric, Velasco was careful to underscore that this action was a special case and that the "Revolution" would continue to welcome foreign investment so long as it operated "in accord with the legislation and the interests of Peru."[20]

This pledge was repeated less publicly by Development Minister General Alberto Maldonado Yanez, who had contacted three main U.S. mining companies operating in Peru (Southern Peru Copper, Cerro de Pasco, and Marcona) as well as oil companies Belco, Mobil, and Standard of California to assure them again that the IPC case was singular and "that their installations, their operations and their contracts with the government would be scrupulously respected." "Most local managers," Ambassador Jones reported, "have taken these assurances at face value." The exceptions were Mobil and Southern Peru Copper, whose president had been invited to Lima by the new prime minister, General Ernesto Montagne Sánchez, to assure him that his company, which was planning to develop a potentially massive

---

19. "Telegram 8282 from Jones to Oliver, November 5, 1968," USNA (1967–1969) (Box 2424, Folder 2), 1.

20. Zimmerman, *El Plan Inca*, 198.

copper deposit near its ongoing operations at Toquepala (the Cuajone project), would not be touched.²¹

These reassurances, of course, were not for public consumption. For the public, the decision to take over the IPC produced an outpouring of popular support for the new government. *El Comercio*, which had long been a leading opponent of the IPC and proponent of nationalization, titled its lead editorial "An Historic Day" and lauded the military government for its quick and decisive action. After only six days in power, the editorial observed, "The Revolutionary Government" had restored "the dignity of Peru and the rights usurped by a powerful foreign company. The ceremony realized yesterday in the Governmental Palace symbolizes one of the most beautiful episodes of our national life." This decision, it claimed, had given pride to all the nation's citizens, rich and poor, and had made clear that "the future of Peru is firmly in the hands of the Peruvians."²²

The reaction of the IPC and the U.S. government, of course, was much less laudatory. On the day of the announcement, a spokesman for the parent company, Standard Oil of New Jersey, called the Peruvian action "a clear violation of international law and the laws of Peru." Not yet taking a hard line, the spokesman also expressed his and the company's hope that the regime would soon recognize the illegality of its action and take the proper steps to align its measures within the proper legal framework.²³

Two days after the decree, IPC president James Dean and Acting General Manager Eduardo Elijaldo met with Minister of Development Maldonado to discuss the action. The minister stated that the takeover was an accomplished fact that had resolved a long-standing problem and in the end would benefit the IPC and lead to a better investment climate in the future. He emphasized that he hoped the company would continue to invest and operate in Peru and assured Dean and Elijaldo that the company's 50 percent interest in the Lobitos fields would remain untouched, as would its control over its distribution network, which left it still the largest supplier of petroleum products and largest producer of petroleum in the country.²⁴ Despite these reassurances, the company officials pressed Maldonado

---

21. "Limited Official Use Telegram 7865 from Jones, October 10, 1968," 1. For more on Southern Peru's operations and its difficulties with the Belaúnde government, see Goodsell, *American Corporations and Peruvian Politics*, 155–57. Prime Minister Montagne was described as, aside from Velasco, "the most important single figure in the coup." Philip, *The Rise and Fall of the Peruvian Military Radicals, 1968–1976*, 79–80.
22. *El Comercio*, October 10, 1968, 2.
23. *New York Times*, October 10, 1968, 1.
24. Ingram, *Expropriation of U.S. Property in South America*, 62.

on the legality of the expropriation and the question of compensation. The minister insisted that the expropriation was legal and dodged the question of compensation, which he said was not his department, and he repeated his claim that IPC was still welcome to invest in the country, perhaps working out some relationship with Empresa Petrolera Fiscal (EPF). Dean, however, countered that the company could not recommend to his shareholders continued operations in Peru until the legality of the expropriation and compensation had been resolved. At that point, the compensation matter seemed to involve consideration of the alleged debts owed by the IPC to Peru that would be used to cancel any Peruvian obligations for the properties taken, a position the company rejected.[25]

Little reassured by these discussions, company representatives, as they had so many times in the past, approached the State Department for assistance. In lengthy discussions on October 16 and 17 in Washington, IPC and Standard Oil representatives pressed the department to invoke the Hickenlooper amendment as well as the Sugar Act to suspend immediately all foreign assistance to Peru and to cut off U.S. imports of Peruvian sugar. The company representatives made it clear that they did not believe they would get fair treatment in Peruvian courts and that the new government was disinclined to negotiate further and that if the nationalization were to proceed unchallenged "the company's position in other countries would be gravely jeopardized." They also argued that the junta's nullification of the Act of Talara on October 4 voided the legal agreement between the government and the company, which meant that the effective date of expropriation was July 1967. Because more than six months had passed since that date, the provisions of the Hickenlooper amendment and the Sugar Act should be applied immediately.

The department's legal advisor did not agree, concluding that the real expropriation occurred on October 9 and that any punitive action should be taken six months from that date. Moreover, two weeks after the coup the armed forces had shown themselves in full control and had gained "popular support" through the expropriation. The junta had also promised "to respect international obligations," repeating that the IPC matter was a "special case" and that the IPC was free to pursue its claims regarding compensation in the courts. With regard to policy, the advisor recommended "a cool and correct stance with the military government" and that the U.S. take advantage of "appropriate opportunities to influence it to obtain a solution

---

25. "Confidential Telegram 7925 from Jones, October 14, 1968," USNA (1967–1969) (Box 2422, Folder 4), 1–2.

to the IPC problem satisfactory to us." He also advised that in the process of granting recognition the United States should emphasize the need for the new regime to agree to "the minimum accepted conduct of nations in the treatment of foreign citizens and properties in their countries." They should also be informed that the six-month clock on the Hickenlooper amendment had begun to run and that this would have significant implications for future economic assistance as well as the sugar quota.[26] As it turned out, these were the general guidelines followed by the department and the embassy.

The Problem of Recognition

The expropriation of October 9 occurred before the United States had officially recognized the new government, adding a further layer of complication to an already vexing issue. Publicly, the State Department announced that the junta's action against IPC would have no effect on its consultation with other nations of the hemisphere on the recognition issue.[27] Behind the scenes, the issue seemed a bit more complicated. Over the next two weeks, both the State Department and the White House struggled with the timing of what seemed an inevitable decision to accept the reality of the new regime and to avoid the Kennedy administration's apparent confusion and ultimate embarrassment in its delay in recognizing the military junta in 1962.

On October 11, Secretary of State Rusk informed President Johnson that while most Latin American governments would resume normal relations with Peru "relatively soon," it was "too early to judge" whether the United States should follow.[28] While the chronology and documents are somewhat confusing, Johnson apparently acted on his own without waiting for Rusk's recommendation. On October 14, Assistant Secretary Oliver sent a memo to Rusk informing him that the president had authorized resumption of relations with the government of Peru, leaving it up to the State Department to determine the exact date. Given what would transpire over the next several days, it is not entirely clear whether Johnson had provided Oliver with formal authority to take this course. In his memo, Oliver stated that "a prompt resumption is in our best interest" but that it "should not

---

26. "Confidential Memorandum 14061 from Oliver to Rostow, October 21, 1968," USNA (1967–1969) (Box 2422, Folder 4), 1–4.
27. *New York Times*, October 12, 1968, 13.
28. "Memorandum from Secretary of State Rusk to President Johnson, October 11, 1968," *FRUS (1964–1968)*, 1068–69.

be directly related to the IPC issue" and that a certain breathing space be created to discuss other issues before taking on the most nettlesome issue—how to confront the new government on the takeover of the oil company.[29]

Whatever the advice about "prompt resumption," Oliver, who earlier had expressed his "revulsion" with the turn of events in Peru, still seemed personally reluctant to move too quickly on the recognition issue. In a conversation with the Uruguayan foreign minister on the same day he sent his memo to Rusk, he made clear that he continued to view the military coup in Peru with some distaste, and although he was aware that recognition would have to come eventually, he wanted to wait at least as long as the Kennedy administration had in 1962.[30]

Pressure was building, however, for earlier action. Not surprisingly, Argentina had already been the first to recognize the new government, and other Latin American states were expected to follow. On October 16, U.S. Ambassador Edward Korry had reported from Santiago that Foreign Minister Valdés had informed him that after stopping off in Lima and having been informed by his own embassy officials that the IPC nationalization had received widespread backing throughout the nation and had thoroughly solidified popular support for the regime, Chile would soon recognize the new government.[31] The following day Ambassador Jones sent a confidential telegram to Oliver urging that the United States recognize the new regime as soon as possible. While there were continuing concerns about when new elections would be held and civilian government restored, overall "the situation in Peru is calm . . . and it appears that for the time being at least Peruvians generally either favor the revolutionary government or are willing to go along with it." Jones added that Foreign Minister General Edgardo Mercado Jarrín had assured him "that Peru's international obligations would be respected and that this included the property rights of foreigners." He also said that the courts would resolve the IPC compensation issue. Jones concluded "that further delay in resuming relations could only damage our own interests, and would deny us the opportunity to have contacts which might have a beneficial influence on the future action of the revolutionary government."[32]

---

29. "Confidential State Department Action Memorandum from Oliver to Secretary, October 14, 1968," USNA (1967–1969) (Box 2423, Folder 1), 1.

30. "Confidential State Department Memorandum of Conversation, October 14, 1968," USNA (1967–1969) (Box 2423, Folder 1), 1–2.

31. "Confidential Telegram 5706 from Korry, October 16, 1968," USNA (1967–1969) (Box 2423, Folder 1), 1–2.

32. "Confidential Telegram 7994 from Jones to Oliver, October 17, 1968," USNA (1967–1969)

Oliver responded to Jones that same day, urging patience. While he appreciated the ambassador's "local problems," he added that "our problem here involves a careful and exacting coordination of U.S. interests and timing, including some related but non-Peruvian factors."[33] Just what these "non-Peruvian factors" were was not spelled out. On the same day, Jones sent his own telegram to the State Department reiterating that the regime was firmly in control and suggesting that its revolutionary rhetoric often contradicted its more pragmatic and even conservative actions, such as its aim to balance the budget without raising taxes and other plans to strengthen the nation's fiscal position. It was also clear to the ambassador that the regime was fully aware of the importance of foreign investment and still sought to attract foreign capital. Moreover, it had no immediate plans to drastically rearrange the existing civilian bureaucracy. Overall, he found the junta, "although highly nationalistic and often suspicious of U.S. actions and motives," nonetheless "generally friendly to [the] U.S." However, Jones warned, "In any confrontation between Peruvian and American interests we believe they will react forcefully." While divisions might produce some internal infighting, he concluded, "Nonetheless, it is our judgment that for the present the revolutionary government is firmly in the saddle, will not be easily pulled off and is all set for a long ride."[34]

As recognition remained pending, the position of IPC continued to complicate matters. A new wrinkle appeared when a deadline neared for the company to purchase petroleum from the seized properties in Talara to provide for its distribution system. This would imply company recognition of the takeover and, in meetings with Oliver and Rostow, company president Dean and John White, the executive vice president for Latin America of the Standard Oil Company of New Jersey, expressed their extreme reluctance to submit to what they saw as undue pressure and asked for the

---

(Box 2422, Folder 5), 1–3. This telegram followed another sent the previous day reviewing a one-hour-and-ten-minute conversation Jones had had with Foreign Minister Edgardo Mercado Jarrín and the secretary-general of the Foreign Ministry, Javier Pérez de Cuellar, in the minister's home in which Mercado provided in some detail the rationale behind the military's actions and the general guidelines for the future governing of the country. Jones was little comforted, it appeared, by Mercado's rather vague references to a return to constitutional normality through a proposed referendum. "The atmosphere of the meeting was businesslike and cool," he wrote, "although not unfriendly as we have been closely associated for many years with Perez de Cuellar, a professional diplomat, and have also had some previous association with General Mercado on a friendly social basis." "Telegram from the Embassy in Peru to the Department of State, October 16, 1968," *FRUS (1964–1968)*, 1069–73.

33. "Secret Telegram 258165 from Oliver to Jones, October 18, 1968," USNA (1967–1969) (Box 2422, Folder 5), 1–2.

34. "Confidential Telegram 8021 from Jones to State, October 18, 1968," USNA (1967–1969) (Box 2423, Folder 1), 1–3.

department's help in this matter. In their conversations, they also clearly reflected their anger at what had happened to the IPC in Peru and their unwillingness to show any flexibility. Ultimately, Oliver and Rostow were able to convince Dean and White to resume negotiations with the new regime and informed them that recognition of the new government would soon be realized. Once that happened, they were assured, they could continue to press their position through the Peruvian judicial system, and the U.S. embassy in Lima would continue to offer its good offices in whatever negotiations they undertook.[35]

Against this backdrop, the U.S. government gradually decided on the recognition question. On October 19, Rostow sent Johnson a memorandum in which he informed the president that Secretary Rusk was requesting authorization to resume diplomatic relations with Peru. He observed that the junta was "in full control," that other key Latin American nations had been consulted and agreed with this course of action, "that the new government has assured it will honor its international obligations," and that it would hold a referendum for a new constitution. Recognition would not necessarily mean resumption of all economic assistance. "The IPC expropriation," he noted, "will gravely complicate our future relations, but should be kept separate from the diplomatic recognition question. Prompt recognition may help us protect IPC's interest in obtaining a reasonable settlement."[36]

At a luncheon meeting on October 22, Secretary Rusk finally made his recommendation that the United States recognize the new Peruvian regime. Johnson, apparently having not paid too much attention to the memos on the matter forwarded by Rostow, asked some rather fundamental questions about what would happen as a result of the recognition or withholding recognition. Rusk responded, "We don't get anywhere by not recognizing them." He added, "This is the 62nd coup I've lived through since I've been Secretary of State and Dick Helms [Richard Helms, head of the CIA and present at the lunch] did not cause a one of them—contrary to popular belief." Given the nature of the Peruvian case, at least in that instance Rusk's assertion appeared correct. At the end of the meeting, Johnson agreed to go ahead with recognition but apparently without much enthusiasm.[37]

---

35. The details of these discussions can be found in a series of communications between Washington and Lima between October 19 and 25 in USNA (1967–1969) (Box 2422, Folder 5).

36. "Action Memorandum From the President's Special Assistant (Rostow) to President Johnson, October 19, 1968," *FRUS (1964–1968)*, 1075–76.

37. According to Rostow, "the President had given Rusk a 'reluctant go-ahead to recognize, if that's what he [Rusk] wants to do.'" "Notes of Meeting, October 22, 1968," *FRUS (1964–1968)*, 1077.

The United States formally recognized the Peruvian regime on October 25. State Department spokesman Robert J. McCloskey made the public announcement, saying that it came after assurances from the regime that it would "return to constitutional government and would recognize its international obligations." It was also made, he added, after consultation with other American republics, thirteen of which already had extended recognition, and without consideration of the IPC takeover. When asked whether the Hickenlooper amendment would be applied in the Peruvian case, McCloskey refused comment, claiming that "this is a complicated issue involving legal points."[38]

In Lima, the press greeted the recognition decision with satisfaction. A cartoon in the October 27 issue of *El Comercio* depicted Uncle Sam tipping his hat and shaking hands with General Velasco, representing the "Nuevo Gobierno Peruano" (New Peruvian Government), while the IPC, drawn as a bewildered black sheep, hovered in the background; the implication was that the larger interest of good relations had overshadowed the interests of a particular company.[39]

But there were also indications that recognition did not necessarily mean a smooth road ahead. In Washington, there was a behind-the-scenes struggle between the Treasury Department's Under-Secretary Henry Fowler and the State Department over providing loans to Peru in light of the IPC takeover. Fowler's point of view was that the timetable for the Hickenlooper amendment to go into effect had already expired and "that if he were in charge of all U.S. financial transactions with Peru he would cut off all assistance."[40] On November 4, Rusk sent Fowler a memo in which he argued that, according to the State Department's view, the deadline for the Hickenlooper sanctions still had six months to run and, in the meantime, encouraged the Treasury Department not to impose any obstacles on loans to Peru, particularly as "we have just started a major diplomatic effort, with IPC, to reach a reasonable solution to the controversy."[41]

---

38. *New York Times*, October 26, 1968, 15. On that same day, Rostow had informed Johnson that the "low-key announcement" would be made and that the appropriate congressional leaders, including Senator Hickenlooper, had been notified and had offered no objections. "Information Memorandum from the President's Special Assistant (Rostow) to President Johnson, October 15, 1968," *FRUS (1964–1968)*, 1078.

39. *El Comercio*, October 27, 1968, 2.

40. "Official-Informal Telegram from William Stedman [Director of the Office of Ecuadorean/Peruvian Affairs at the Department of State] to Jones, October 29, 1968," Personal Papers of John Wesley Jones, Box 23, Folder 5, LBJ Library.

41. "Memorandum from Rusk to Fowler, November 4, 1968," Personal Papers of John Wesley Jones, Box 23, Folder 5, LBJ Library.

While this tug of war was going on, an article by Malcolm W. Browne in the *New York Times* in late October predicted a rocky road in the future for U.S.-Peruvian relations despite the recent recognition decision. There were, he reported, three main areas of disagreement: (1) the IPC matter, (2) no signs of any early return to constitutional government, and (3) Peru's plans to establish diplomatic and trade relations with communist nations. The article included comments from the junta's new foreign minister, Mercado Jarrín, who granted Browne his first interview with a foreign reporter. Mercado referred to the long-standing, good relationship between the United States and Peru, promised to remain a "staunch partner" in the Alliance for Progress, and "depicted himself as a close friend of private enterprise generally, provided its interests coincided with those of the nation." But the new government, he emphasized, was also fully committed to defending what it saw as the nation's sovereign rights and to follow a course best suited to the nation's interests. He also said the regime's takeover of the Talara field was now "a problem already solved." Peru's political freedom, he claimed, could only be achieved through economic freedom, "and this requires expanded markets and better prices. We need favorable credit arrangements to keep our payments in balance. This is why we are interested in the socialist countries." He saw no quick return to democracy and concluded that "the North American people should understand that social and economic changes required by the process of development are carried out in each country conforming to the imperatives in its own historic reality and within a process that has to be adapted to the roots of its individuality, without making facile generalizations."[42] Whether the North American people, not to mention the North American government, would come to this understanding, remained to be seen.

Peruvian Foreign Policy Immediately After the Coup

General Mercado Jarrín, the new foreign minister interviewed by Browne was well suited for the post. Born in Barranco, a suburb of Lima, in 1919, he had graduated from the Escuela Militar in nearby Chorrillos in 1940. He then had attended the Escuela Superior de Guerra in the early 1950s and studied at the U.S. Command and General Staff School at Fort Leavenworth, Kansas, in 1956–1957; he graduated first in his class of twelve hundred. He also studied at the Inter-American Defense College in Washington,

---

42. *New York Times*, October 27, 1968, 26.

D.C., in 1964. Through these experiences, he made many close friends with fellow North American officers.

By the time of the coup on October 3, in which he was a main ally of Velasco, he had established a considerable reputation as a military intellectual. Deeply concerned with strategic issues and a prolific writer, he had authored in the mid-1960s an essay entitled "El ejército de hoy y su proyección en nuestra sociedad en período de transición (1940–1965)" ("Today's Army and Its Projection in Our Society in a Period of Transition"), which laid out a new national role and responsibility for the armed forces in which he argued "that only the armed forces could save Peru from chaos," an article that became "one of the region's most widely read essays."[43] From January 1966 to January 1968, he served as director of Army Intelligence, from which post he moved to head of the Centro de Instrucción Militar del Perú (Center of Military Instruction of Peru), a position he held until the coup.

Given his background, Mercado was a natural choice for the all-important Foreign Ministry post, which, under the circumstances, could be considered the second-most important within the new regime and one replete with complicated and challenging issues.[44] According to Mercado, Velasco gave him free rein to run foreign affairs as he saw fit. His first and paramount concern was how to deal with the United States, which he saw as the main threat to Peruvian sovereignty and the kind of revolutionary and nationalistic policies the regime planned to implement. Recognizing the power of the United States and the relative weakness of Peru, he devised a strategy to try to counterbalance U.S. influence through various manipulations and maneuvers. These included establishing links with the Soviet Union, China, Cuba, and other communist nations, which he claimed was his idea. He also sought alliances with other Latin American nations to present a united front on certain issues such as the fishing rights controversy.

Not at all surprising for a military man, Mercado Jarrín reorganized the Foreign Ministry to make it more efficient and responsive. He emphasized the importance of planning to deal with current and future issues and brought in teams of competent professionals to work with existing personnel on particular problems. He also established the practice of having all ambassadors meet in Lima once a year for a debriefing to take advantage

---

43. Nunn, *The Time of the Generals*, 208–9.

44. According to Mercado, additional factors in Velasco's decision to appoint him as foreign minister were that he had "an elegant and attractive wife," Gladis Neumann Terán, with whom he had five children, and that they had a lovely home in which to entertain foreign guests. Personal interview with General Edgardo Mercado Jarrín, Lima, July 18, 2003. Biographical information from Frost, ed., *Latin American Government Leaders*, 109–10.

of their collective experiences. While consistently adhering to his nationalist beliefs, Mercado Jarrín also showed a pragmatic approach that emphasized competence and experience over ideology. When he told Velasco that he planned to name Fernando Berckemeyer to the all-important post of Peruvian ambassador to Washington, the president questioned the choice of a man so closely tied to the oligarchy at a time when the military was beginning to confront Peru's upper class on a variety of fronts. Mercado Jarrín responded that Berckemeyer had the intellectual and professional qualifications for the job, had many good contacts in the United States, both through his past posting and his North American wife, and he, Mercado, was convinced that he would serve well if, as indeed he was, named again as ambassador.[45]

Berckemeyer did not assume his post until later in the year. Meanwhile, in Washington, Carlos Alzamora, second-in-command at the embassy and a career diplomat, took over from Celso Pastor de la Torre, who resigned as soon as he received news of the coup.[46] Alzamora's first communication on October 4 included the usual press clippings dealing with the U.S. reaction to the coup, which, he observed, "given previous such cases, appears to be for the moment moderate in tone."[47] Later in the month, Alzamora sent a confidential cable on October 24, informing Lima that the United States would recognize the new regime on the following day. That recognition, which came in a third of the time taken by the United States in 1962, he credited in large measure to the "tireless efforts" of the embassy staff. He also underscored the importance of early recognition by Argentina in moving the process forward. He observed that the action against IPC and the coincidence of a coup in Panama at about the same time had mobilized "important conservative sectors tied to economic and financial interests" to demand a hard-line response from the U.S. government. The upcoming presidential elections, he observed, complicated matters as well, adding some fuel to the conservative fire in favor of a harder line. Nonetheless, in the end, recognition had been resolved, thanks in large measure to the efforts of "the team of young diplomats of the embassy, who used all their contacts inside and outside of the State Department to de-link the IPC matter from the larger question of recognition, and who did so in a manner that preserved the dignity of a country that retains its absolute freedom of action in the exercise of its legitimate and sovereign rights."[48]

45. Oral Interview with Mercado Jarrín, July 18, 2003.
46. *El Comercio*, October 10, 1968, 15.
47. *Correspondencia* (5–3-Y/32) (October 4, 1968), 1.
48. *Correspondencia* (5–3-Y/35) (October 25, 1968), 1–5.

In the United States, the recent events in Peru had produced a fair amount of press coverage. However, the news from South America was overshadowed in significant measure by the ongoing Vietnam War and the domestic controversy it had sparked, the decision by Lyndon Johnson not to seek reelection, making him a lame duck for most of the year, and the hotly contested election between Democrat Hubert Humphrey and Republican Richard Nixon. Reporting on the campaign and the implications of Nixon's ultimate victory over Humphrey, Alzamora observed that the Democratic candidate had, in his campaign, referred specifically to the military coups in Panama and Peru and had promised to cut military assistance to Latin America in the future while Nixon had made no such references. Indeed, Nixon had had relatively little to say about Latin America in general except to proclaim that the Alliance for Progress had been a failure and that the gap between the rich and the poor in the region was growing. While he judged Nixon's approach to Latin America as basically conservative, he also believed that the liberal wing of his party, led by former New York governor Nelson Rockefeller, would have quite a bit of influence on future policy toward the region.[49] Reporting on the congressional election results, Alzamora expressed his pleasure at the "departure from the Congress of the bitter critics of Perú, senators [Ernest] Gruening [D-Alaska], [Wayne] Morse [D-Oregon], and [Thomas] Kuchel [R-California]" and the replacement of Republican Senator Bourke Hickenlooper of Iowa, he of the infamous amendment, by a liberal Democrat, Harold E. Hughes.[50]

In his final confidential report to Lima, Alzamora presented a notably upbeat and positive assessment of relations between Peru and the United States at this point. The normalization of these relations, he asserted, had produced such beneficial effects as the decision by the International Monetary Fund to grant a $75 million loan to Peru and for the U.S. government to maintain in 1969 the sugar quota granted in 1968 (indicating that Rusk's position had prevailed over that of Fowler). The embassy's hard work to minimize the reaction to the IPC takeover, he claimed, had produced some success in keeping both the press and the Congress from adopting a harsher line toward Peru's actions than might have been expected. Most important, he saw the U.S. government, particularly the State Department, as committed to maintaining "cordial relations with Perú so as to create a climate that will favor the satisfactory resolution of all pending questions between the two nations." The department, in particular, he

---

49. *Correspondencia* (5–3-Y/37) (November 7, 1968), 1–5.
50. *Correspondencia* (5–3-Y/38) (November 14, 1968), 1–4.

concluded, had been working effectively to prevent any radical response to the IPC takeover.[51]

Taking over for Alzamora, Ambassador Berckemeyer's first confidential assessment of the reaction to the IPC takeover was less positive. Forwarding critical articles on the government's action from the *New York Times* and the *Washington Post*, he suggested that the writings of certain "anti-Peruvian" journalists would serve to discourage further U.S. investment in Peru and that efforts should be taken to counteract their influence.[52] On a somewhat more optimistic note, in early December, he made a courtesy call on Secretary of State Rusk, who informed him, in what must have been by now a numbingly familiar refrain, that the IPC issue was "one of the most serious that has faced U.S.-Peruvian relations" but that if both sides worked together, they could resolve this issue without employing "punitive measures." Berckemeyer agreed and said that "it would be his intention to promote such a solution."[53]

At about the same time as his meeting with Rusk, Berckemeyer reported on Nixon's choice of his close friend William P. Rogers as secretary of state. He observed that Rogers had little international experience and no significant knowledge of or contact with Latin America. Nonetheless, he was viewed as a pragmatist rather than an ideologue and was also known personally to the ambassador, who trusted that, over time, "he will develop a positive labor in the task of drawing near to our nations." Moreover, as far as Latin American affairs were concerned, the important choice was the appointment of the assistant secretary of state for Inter-American Affairs, which had yet to be made. In the meantime, the current incumbent, Covey T. Oliver, was slated to move on to the World Bank.[54]

Early Impressions of the Peruvian Junta

While Peruvian diplomats tried to gauge the character and orientation of the incoming Nixon administration, their U.S. counterparts in the State Department and in the embassy in Lima were still trying to get a handle on the nature of the new regime. The first State Department intelligence note on the junta stated that "no definitive picture of Peru's new government

51. *Correspondencia* (5–3-Y/41) (November 20, 1968), 1–3.
52. *Correspondencia* (5–3-Y/43) (December 2, 1968), 2.
53. "DOS Telegram 282180 to Lima, December 5, 1968," NSF, Country File 1–80, Box 73, Folder 6, LBJ Library.
54. *Correspondencia* (5–3-Y/45) (December 14, 1968), 5.

has emerged so far," although its quick expropriation of the IPC holdings clearly indicated its "nationalist" proclivities. That action notwithstanding, the note indicated that the junta would be pragmatic and receptive to continued foreign investment. On the domestic front, it also seemed committed to significant changes, and "they almost certainly will go well beyond the limited initiatives of the 1962–63 caretaker military regime." While divisions might emerge between conservatives and radicals within the junta, the military seemed determined to remain in power for some time.[55]

In retrospect, this analysis was not far from the mark. The prediction that the military would retain control for a lengthy period—for twelve years as it turned out—was accurate. Divisions within the military regime were evident from the beginning and persisted throughout its rule. Daniel Masterson divides the regime among "conservatives," primarily from the navy; "modernizers or moderates," including, among others, Mercado Jarrín; and "progressives," the group most responsible for the radical changes that took place over the next year or so. As Masterson describes it, "Most progressives were colonels at the time of the 3 October *coup*, with backgrounds in the Intelligence Service. They formed a firm cadre around Velasco in defense of an increasingly radical program of change. The military president appointed a number of these officers to key command positions in the armed forces, but their consistent power base was the *Comité de Asesoramiento de la Presidencia* (COAP) or Advisory Committee to the Presidency."[56]

George Philip, in his study of the regime, uses a somewhat different method of classification. He divides the initial Council of Ministers among "Velasco's Allies," "Conservatives" (including Vice Admiral Alfonso Navarro), and "Others" (including Mercado and Prime Minister Montagne). According to Philip, to consolidate his position, Velasco moved from a conservative to a more radical position by determining to take a hard line on the IPC takeover, a maneuver that proved successful. Therefore, by early 1969, a new alignment had evolved, which Philip listed as "Radicals and other Allies of Velasco," "Developmentalists" (Montagne and Mercado), and "Conservatives" (Navarro).[57]

Some indication of the divisions within the regime came with the resignation of Air Force General and Aviation Minister Alberto López Casilla in late October. López had not been a supporter of the coup nor was he happy with the new regime. He resigned because he objected to proposed

55. "U.S. Department of State Secret Intelligence Note 800, October 11, 1968," USNA (1967–1969) (Box 2422, Folder 5), 1–3.
56. Masterson, *Militarism and Politics*, 248.
57. Philip, *The Rise and Fall of the Peruvian Military Radicals, 1968–1976*, 82–92.

promotions that would place air force officers loyal to Velasco over more senior officers, which is what happened once he resigned.[58] The resignation gave rise to speculation of a countercoup by elements disaffected with the new regime, especially among the navy and the air force. Others, however, discounted such rumors, and the evidence suggested that Velasco was firmly in control and "confident of his base of power."[59]

For U.S. government officials, divisions within the regime and the IPC matter were not their only concerns. On November 1, another secret intelligence note in the State Department focused on the possibility of closer diplomatic and commercial ties between Peru and the Soviet Union. The note saw these as fundamentally only a continuation of overtures begun during the Belaúnde administration and in line with what other Latin American countries, most notably Argentina, were doing. There was also the possibility, however, that "the Junta's tendency toward radical nationalism might lead to adventurous commitments with the Soviets, in particular, which more experienced Latin American leaders in other countries have avoided." While it seemed clear that the contacts would be established, the note concluded that "it is unlikely that the Velasco regime will take any dramatic step (a la Aswan dam) which could entangle Peru with the Soviet Union in a troublesome fashion." The note also observed that the Soviets had at first condemned the coup of October 3 as "U.S.-inspired" but now referred to the junta as made up of "Creole Nasserists" and "honest officers with patriotic leanings."[60] It seemed that the Soviets, like many others, were having difficulties in determining the exact nature of this new kind of military regime. A CIA intelligence memo the following day speculated that the Soviets would be quick to take advantage of any serious "deterioration in Peruvian-U.S. relations" but that "its trade and aid will not compensate for a significant loss of US economic assistance and private investment, especially over the next year."[61] While some of the CIA's predictions with regard to Peru were less than accurate, this one proved to be generally on target.

More personal impressions of the new government were provided by Ambassador Jones, who, in early November, had his first official visit with Velasco since diplomatic relations had been resumed. Expressing his pleasure at the opportunity of meeting with the new Peruvian leader, Jones added

58. Ibid., 84.
59. *New York Times*, October 29, 1968, 26.
60. "U.S. Department of State Secret Intelligence Note 849, November 1, 1968," USNA (1967–1969) (Box 2419, Folder 1), 1–4.
61. "CIA Intelligence Memo of November 2, 1968," NSF, Country File, Box 73, Folder 4, LBJ Library.

that he hoped to continue to work with the new government as he had with the previous one "in the best interests of Peruvian-American relations." He then provided information on his previous talks with the prime minister and minister of foreign affairs, in which urgent bilateral issues such as the IPC matter and the fisheries dispute had been discussed; he hoped to be able to discuss these issues in the future with the president. Velasco assured him that "this was the case and that his 'door was always open to me.'"

Velasco informed Jones why the Revolution of October 3 had been so necessary. The country, he claimed, by that time was in a "mess," and the overall situation bordered on disaster. The military was particularly concerned about conditions in the sierra where many were close to starvation and where, not coincidentally, the mainly coastal armed forces had come into contact with the deprivation in that area during the counterguerrilla campaign of 1965. He admitted that the regime needed "help and understanding" from the United States, and he hoped that some assistance would be forthcoming in the future. "He said," Jones reported, "if they failed they would not only be hanged but the country would fall into either chaos or a Castro-type of government." The military regime had an overall plan for development, but it would only be revealed in stages. He was also particularly concerned about the situation in Peru's universities, "which he said were centers of subversion and political agitation rather than of higher education [a view shared by the military regimes—and others—in Argentina and Brazil of their own institutions of higher learning]." He promised to respect freedom of the press but had been forced to close temporarily *Caretas* and *Expreso* due to their personal attacks on members of the junta. Once the reforms the new regime envisioned were in place, the armed forces would "very happily go back to their homes," but not even an approximate date for that eventuality could be given. Finally, he informed Jones of how closely guarded the decision to remove Belaúnde had been, involving, so he claimed, "only six officers." Jones informed Velasco that Washington had formally accepted the naming of Berckemeyer as Peru's new ambassador. "Velasco," Jones reported, "expressed his pleasure at this news and his confidence that Berckemeyer would serve Peru well in this important post."[62]

In another communication several days later, Jones clearly indicated that he was not much convinced by Velasco's rationale for the military's action. The country by late 1968 was, he asserted, "again moving forward economically," and the coup, "on the basis of rational analysis, [was] unwarranted."

---

62. "Confidential Telegram 8336 from Jones, November 6, 1968," USNA (1967–1969) (Box 2421, Folder 5), 1–3. Also in *FRUS (1964–1968)*, 1079–80.

The military's action was attributable to a variety of complex causes. "In the final analysis," he concluded, "it was a growing concern for the future combined with personal ambition on the part of certain elements within the military, General Velasco in particular, and various officers in lower ranks in general, which, when supported by powerful civilian elements who were assuring the advancement of their own interests, which brought the experiment in popular democracy in Peru, over which Fernando Belaúnde Terry presided, to an abrupt end."[63] In his conclusion, Jones did not specifically mention the IPC controversy or the failure of the United States to provide adequate assistance to Belaúnde when it might have helped him when he needed it the most.

Two days before this communication, Jones had sent a confidential letter to a colleague in the U.S. embassy in Montevideo, Uruguay, lamenting the turn of events in Peru. As he put it, "The *golpe* was almost as hard on Ernie [Deputy Ernest Siracusa] and me as it was on Fernando Belaunde. We had hoped that he would make it until the end of his term and, as you know, had formulated our policy to support that end. Now I am back where I started and, in fact, find many old faces of my early days in 1963 under the then Military Junta reemerging in positions of importance. While this is helpful in many ways, it is also rather sad to have been here so long to see the cycle completed."[64] Two decades later, Jones would recall Velasco as "not a friend of the United States and curiously enough, was rather a Socialist in his outlook when he became President."[65]

Velasco's Move to Consolidate His Power and the U.S. Reaction

At the end of 1968 and the beginning of 1969, Velasco took several measures to strengthen his leadership position. He adopted an increasingly inflexible stance on the IPC issue, which would ensure continued popular support. With regard to his reform agenda, the government expropriated a property at Tahuanga for distribution and announced on November 4 that it would expropriate the land and livestock of the Cerro de Pasco Corporation. On the foreign policy front, diplomatic relations were established

---

63. "Confidential Airgram A-907 from Jones, November 10, 1968," USNA (1967–1969) (Box 2424, Folder 2), 1–9.
64. "Official—Informal—Confidential letter of November 8, 1968 from Jones to Nicholas V. McCausland, U.S. Embassy, Montevideo," Personal Papers of John Wesley Jones, Box 3, Folder 1, LBJ Library.
65. "Oral Interview with John Wesley Jones," 20.

with Yugoslavia and Czechoslovakia, and by early 1969, Foreign Minister Mercado was indicating clearly the government's intention to establish relations with the Soviet Union, although he discounted, for the moment, reports that relations with Cuba might be reestablished in the near future. Internally, the regime cracked down on student and labor protests, although not with the same ferocity as their Argentine and Brazilian counterparts. The regime also had temporarily closed two opposition periodicals, which soon reappeared with much the same critical stance toward the government as before.[66]

The approach of the U.S. government during this period has been described as "quite low-key."[67] In general terms, this seems to have been the case, perhaps because the government was in a transition from the Johnson to the Nixon administration, and no new bold initiatives or hard-line postures were advisable under those circumstances. This does not mean necessarily, however, that the United States was a passive bystander as events unfolded in Peru. According to George Philip in his study of the regime, the two main army opponents to Velasco within the cabinet were Minister of Finance General Angel Valdivia Morriberon and Minister of Development General Alberto Maldonado Yanez. Both were seen as supporters of the IPC position within the Council of Ministers and eager to take actions to avoid economic sanctions, and both appeared to have connections with U.S.-based business and government sectors. Valdivia, a strong proponent of fiscal austerity, was also the apparent choice of the U.S. government to succeed Velasco, who was scheduled for retirement from the army in January 1969.[68]

Philip's conclusions are based on journalistic sources and a Ph.D. dissertation wherein the author cites a contact in the U.S. embassy as having "persuaded Valdivia of the correctness of IPC's position."[69] There is nothing in the State Department records to substantiate these assertions. Moreover, in early December Valdivia issued a public warning to the United States not to apply undue economic pressure on Peru to advance IPC interests. The issue, he asserted, was an "internal matter" to be determined in the courts. As he put it, "We do not understand why Washington is upset because, first, I. P. C. is a Canadian company and, second, the charges against it would be valid in any country. Whether or not the Canadian company's

---

66. The outlines of these developments are provided in Pease García and Verme Insúa, *Perú, 1968–1973*, 1:35–52.
67. Goodsell, *American Corporations and Peruvian Politics*, 130.
68. Philip, *The Rise and Fall of the Peruvian Military Radicals, 1968–1976*, 90.
69. Ibid., 35n.

shareholders are American does not alter the situation. Peru does not interfere in the internal quarrels of other nations, and we expect the same consideration." On the internal front, Valdivia claimed great progress in collecting taxes, purging the bureaucracy of "corrupt or redundant civil servants," and reducing substantially the internal deficit. He reiterated the junta's claim that foreign investors were more than welcome in Peru as long as they played by the rules. Any threats by Washington to halt all aid to the nation under these circumstances, he concluded, would be "not only futile but dangerous to those concerned with the orderly pattern of trade and development. Peru will continue to make it profitable for foreign investors, but not outside the law."[70]

These remarks, at least on the surface, do not seem overly friendly either to the IPC or the U.S. government. They might, however, be interpreted as friendly advice to both the company and the government to follow a moderate course that would avoid undue confrontations. At any event, if Valdivia was involved in an internal power struggle within the regime to succeed Velasco, he ultimately failed, and in February 1969, along with Maldonado, was forced to resign his cabinet position.[71] Whatever efforts the United States might have made on Valdivia's behalf, therefore, proved to be unsuccessful.

On January 19, 1969, one day before the inauguration of Richard Nixon as president, Jones sent a confidential airgram to Washington summarizing the first one hundred days of the military regime. While tensions still existed within the junta, Jones wrote, Velasco for the moment still seemed to be in control and enjoying majority support among the population at large. The ideology of the regime remained "undefined and eclectic" and the future of its relations with the United States hinged, as so often had been the case with Belaúnde, on the resolution of the still pending IPC issue. Jones implied his own frustration with this matter, arguing that if it were not a factor then the regime could be expected to adopt a moderate reformist course and perhaps General Montagne, to his mind a more acceptable leader than Velasco, would take control. However, as long as the IPC matter festered, it would serve to strengthen the more nationalistic elements within the regime, now clearly led by Velasco. If the Hickenlooper amendment were enacted, that would only serve to bolster the nationalists' hand and might produce an even stronger anti-U.S. sentiment and accelerate the regime's move "to replace U.S. influence by European and possibly even Soviet Bloc influence." "An ironic aspect of this situation," Jones concluded,

---

70. *New York Times*, December 4, 1968, 46.
71. Philip, *The Rise and Fall of the Peruvian Military Radicals, 1968–1976*, 91–92.

"is that without the complicating factor of the IPC issue, the Military Government, especially once President Velasco left office, presumably in favor of General Montagne, might have had a good chance to achieve the economic, social and constitutional reforms which might, in the long run, have served to strengthen democratic institutions in Peru."[72]

There was something plaintive about Jones's musings over what "might have been." As he neared the end of his tenure as ambassador, his frustrations with the role the IPC issue had played in preventing his efforts to promote democracy in Peru were palpable. Perhaps, too, he was trying to suggest to the new Nixon administration that the kind of support the U.S. government had given to the company had proved counterproductive on a number of levels, and a new approach that downplayed the company's interests on behalf of the nation's greater policy objectives would produce better results. The prospects that a Republican administration even more closely tied to big business interests than its predecessors would adopt such a course, however, seemed unlikely.

72. "Confidential Airgram A-29 from Jones, January 19, 1969," USNA (1967–1969) (Box 2424, Folder 2), 9–10.

7

VELASCO AND THE NIXON ADMINISTRATION

Less than four months after he assumed power, General Juan Velasco found himself confronting a new administration in the United States. After eight years of Democratic presidents, the Republicans had returned to the White House with the election of Richard Nixon. Velasco would deal with the Nixon administration for most of his time in office, and while the two main protagonists never met, they established a relationship through various communications and intermediaries that allowed for the development of peaceful coexistence despite the numerous disagreements and tensions that marked U.S.-Peruvian relations in these years. In the first half of 1969, both sides tried to take the measure of the other. The United States had the greater challenge as it tried to come to grips with a Latin American military regime so different from the norm as well as to understand its often enigmatic leader.

Nixon and Latin America

Richard M. Nixon was inaugurated as the thirty-seventh president of the United States on January 20, 1969, capping one of the most incredible comebacks in U.S. political history. Packaging himself as the New Nixon, he had promised to end domestic disturbances at home with a policy of "law and order" and to end the conflict in Vietnam with a "secret plan." As with his predecessor, the Vietnam War absorbed much of his attention and energy during his first term. However, he also sought to establish new relationships with the Soviet Union and the People's Republic of China and to bring peace to the troubled Middle East.

Nixon considered himself an expert on foreign policy because of his past experiences as vice president and frequent travels around the world, and he planned to give foreign affairs top priority. Aiding him in this effort was his newly named national security advisor, Henry Kissinger. To carry out policy effectively, both thought it essential to center authority in the White House and to marginalize the State Department. From his experience as vice president, he felt that the foreign service was staffed with too many "liberals" who were disdainful of him.[1]

For Nixon, North-South issues involving Latin America were not high on his list of priorities. As he later told Special Assistant Donald Rumsfeld, "The only things that matter in the world are Japan and China, Russia and Europe. . . . Latin America doesn't matter. Long as we've been in it, people don't give one damn about Latin America."[2] His view of Latin America was undoubtedly part of his larger global vision, one shared by Kissinger.[3] It may also have been colored by his unhappy 1958 tour of the region. Certainly, he must not have had particularly fond memories of Peru despite his rather successful return there in the mid-1960s. Whatever the larger priorities, however, he and his administration would have to pay considerable attention to Peru in the months following the inauguration. A series of challenges, both old and new, complicated the relationship between the two nations. The actions of the new military government at this time made Peru the most important and problematic Latin American nation for Nixon and his foreign policy team until the election of Marxist Salvador Allende in Chile in late 1970 came to dominate U.S. concerns in the region.[4]

First Impressions

In Washington, a few days before Nixon's inauguration, embassy attaché Carlos Alzamora provided a preliminary assessment of the new administration's

1. Bundy, *A Tangled Web*, 54–59.
2. As quoted in Mann, *Rise of the Vulcans*, 16.
3. Kissinger was equally dismissive of the importance, or lack thereof, of Latin America. In a luncheon meeting with Chile's foreign minister, Gabriel Valdés, in June 1969 he asserted that "nothing important can come from the South." When Valdés replied that Kissinger knew nothing of the south, he reportedly responded, "And I don't care." As quoted in Dallek, *Nixon and Kissinger*, 228–29.
4. A Peruvian diplomat/historian, commenting on this period, perhaps with some exaggeration stated that "after Chile and Cuba, Peru has been the [Latin American] country that has caused the most headaches for the United States." Bákula, *Perú*, 1497.

likely policy toward Latin America. He noted Nixon's experiences in the region as Eisenhower's vice president and foresaw a replay of that administration's Latin American policy, one that focused on anticommunism and protection of U.S. economic interests over the promotion of programs like the Alliance for Progress. He predicted a reversal of the trend begun by presidents Kennedy and Johnson to name academics and career diplomats to important posts in the region and a return to the appointment of businessmen or their representatives as ambassadors. For the moment, he concluded, these were matters for speculation. While it seemed likely that traditional Republican support for big business would prevail, the New Nixon might also have a few surprises up his sleeve for Latin America.[5]

If Nixon did have any such surprises, they certainly were not revealed during his inaugural address. As Fernando Berckemeyer reported back to Lima, the new president's failure even to mention Latin America in his speech had caused considerable concern among the hemisphere's diplomatic community. The concern was assuaged somewhat when, a few days later, Nixon, along with Secretary of State William P. Rogers and Kissinger, met with Organization of American States secretary-general Galo Plaza of Ecuador to assure him of their continuing interest in the region.[6] Whatever these assurances, it remained clear that Latin America was still not high on the administration's agenda because it took Nixon several months to appoint a new assistant secretary of state for Inter-American Affairs to replace the departed Covey Oliver.

In Lima, U.S. ambassador John Wesley Jones continued to take the measure of the Velasco regime. In a communication on January 26, he reported that the regime seemed prepared to stay in power for the long haul and was committed to a nationalistic course. Just how "revolutionary" that course would be remained to be determined.[7] Jones met personally with Velasco on the following day. During the meeting, the Peruvian leader seemed "somewhat ill at ease and harassed." He complained to Jones of the "constant pressure of 'audiences' and the various meetings which he had going on in the Palace simultaneously." He also expressed his frustration at recent press treatment, which, on the one hand, accused him of being a "Communist," while, on the other, it claimed that he was closely tied to the interests of the oligarchy. With regard to the main purpose of the visit, to ascertain from Velasco any thoughts he might have on outstanding issues

---

5. *Correspondencia* (5–3/Y/2) (January 15, 1969), 1–5.
6. *Correspondencia* (5–3-Y/4) (January 23, 1969), 1.
7. "Confidential Air-Gram A-41 from Jones, January 26, 1969," USNA (1967–1969) (Box 2423, Folder 3), 8.

between Peru and the United States before Jones's return to Washington to consult with the new administration, the Peruvian president remained noncommittal except to assure Jones that "he would be delighted (*encantado*) to see me at any time."[8] A secret State Department intelligence note a few days later reaffirmed Jones's observations that the regime seemed firmly in control and dedicated to a nationalist course, which meant little possibility of a shift on the International Petroleum Company (IPC) dispute. "The situation," the note concluded, "promises to produce increasingly serious strains in US-Peruvian relations."[9]

Increasing Tensions

From the end of January to the middle of February, a series of dramatic events served to exacerbate these serious strains. First, the IPC issue remained a paramount concern. Earlier in January, the Empresa Petrolera Fiscal (EPF) had sent an invoice to the company for $14.4 million for costs of products drawn from the Talara refinery from October 9 to December 31, 1968. When the company refused to agree to this amount, the government ordered the EPF to take over the administration of the IPC. On January 28, army officers representing the state company occupied the IPC's Lima offices and ordered the company's personnel to leave. This action, according to one source, coincided with a decision by the Nixon administration to take a harder stance than had been the case previously, with a State Department spokesman affirming to the press on January 29 "that Peru would be subject to sanctions if IPC went uncompensated."[10] Despite the threat of sanctions, the move gained a considerable amount of support from all quarters of Peruvian society and from much of the rest of Latin America as well.[11]

A few days later, on February 1, Foreign Minister Edgardo Mercado Jarrín announced that Peru had established diplomatic relations with the Soviet Union. This came as little surprise to the United States as press reports and Mercado's own comments over the previous several weeks had indicated that such an action was in the works. While this was yet another step that implied confrontation with the United States, the State Department did

---

8. "Limited Official Use Air-Gram A-48 from Jones, January 29, 1969," USNA (1967–1969) (Box 2425, Folder 2), 1–2.
9. "Secret Intelligence Note 52, January 30, 1969," USNA (1967–1969) (Box 2424, Folder 2), 1.
10. Goodsell, *American Corporations and Peruvian Politics*, 130.
11. *New York Times*, January 31, 1969, 14.

not seem unduly alarmed by this turn of events. An intelligence note on February 4 predicted that the Soviets would move cautiously in Peru until the exact orientation of the military regime became clearer. They would provide some economic support, the note speculated, but would avoid becoming overextended in this regard and would "feel their way cautiously in what is still for them an unfamiliar—and not entirely comfortable [dealing with a Latin American military government]—situation."[12]

Less than three weeks after establishing diplomatic relations, Peru and the USSR announced the signing of a trade agreement that the Peruvians claimed would mean the end of that country's traditional economic dependence on the United States. Mercado trumpeted the agreement as "the opening of a new commercial front; the end of an era in which our trade was channeled in only one direction." This new step, he averred, would open up the markets of Eastern Europe to Peruvian exports and would mark the first step on the road to economic prosperity.[13]

While these developments were unfolding, there was renewed action on the IPC case. On February 6, Velasco announced the takeover of all the company's holdings in Peru. Underlying his move was the claim that the IPC owed the Peruvian government debts amounting to $690,524,283, debts that the company had consistently refused to recognize or to pay. Wrapping his statement in the usual nationalist rhetoric, he proclaimed that "the revolutionary Government announces to the Peruvian people, to its brother peoples in America, and to the whole world, that Peru has taken the final step to close definitely and forever this ignominious chapter in its history." Again, he reiterated that this was a "special and unique" case involving "the despoliation of the natural resources of a generous people," a "generous people," he reminded his audience both at home and abroad, "who have always offered, and continue to offer, guarantees of law to foreign investors who came, are coming and will come to live and work here honestly." He hoped that the "celebrated and profoundly sad" Hickenlooper amendment would not be applied in this case and, quoting John Kennedy, underscored the long-standing good relations between Peru and the United States.[14]

As could be expected, Velasco's action produced another general outpouring of public support and favorable press comment in Peru. His attempts to convince the United States that the IPC case was unique and that the

---

12. "Secret (No Foreign Dissemination) Intelligence Note from Thomas L. Hughes to the Secretary of State, February 4, 1969," USNA (1967–1969) (Box 2425, Folder 1), 1–8.

13. *New York Times*, February 18, 1969, 1.

14. *New York Times*, February 7, 1969, 10. The speech is also included in Velasco Alvarado, *La revolución*, 83–89.

Hickenlooper provisions should not be applied, however, were not successful. Initially, at least, the Nixon administration adopted a hard line in response to the February 6 takeover, asserting that the sanctions provided by the Hickenlooper amendment would be applied by April 9 if no compensation was provided for the expropriation.

The implications for Peru if the sanctions were applied were serious. Not only would the nation lose about $25 million in economic assistance but also a corresponding reduction of the sugar quota could mean an additional $65 million loss. Moreover, the effects on trade with the United States and the flow of foreign investment could be substantial. Overall, it was estimated that sanctions would cost Peru about $180 million.[15] It seemed highly unlikely that Soviet trade and assistance could make up for these losses.

As if the strains over the IPC matter were not enough, on February 14, there was another incident involving U.S. fishing vessels in what Peru claimed were its territorial waters. In this instance, Peruvian naval forces fired on one vessel, the *San Juan*, which had refused to be boarded. Fortunately, there were no injuries. Another vessel, the *Mariner*, was also fired on, boarded, escorted to the port of Talara, where the captain paid the assessed fine, and released. Both incidents produced a flurry of actions by the United States. In Washington, Secretary of State Rogers called in Berckemeyer for consultations and to express his "serious concern" over the incident. In Lima, Deputy Chief of Mission Ernest V. Siracusa (Jones was in Washington at the time) asked to meet with Mercado, presumably to register an official protest.[16] Industry leaders and various congressmen urged strong retaliatory action, including the use of the navy to protect U.S. fishermen.

According to Charles Goodsell, the administration already had taken action. On the day of the seizures, military sales to Peru were suspended in compliance with the Pelly amendment. Goodsell does not say which officials in which branch made this decision, which was to be an automatic consequence of attacks on U.S. fishing vessels, but observes that the decision was kept secret from the Peruvians until they were finally informed of the action almost three months later.[17]

While Goodsell is correct in asserting that a decision was made to sanction

---

15. Ingram, *Expropriation of U.S. Property in South America*, 64–65.
16. *New York Times*, February 15, 1969, 2.
17. Goodsell, *American Corporations and Peruvian Politics*, 133. Goodsell gives April 3 as the date when the United States informed Peru of the decision, but as later discussion will show it appeared not to have been revealed until early in May, although there is some confusion about when the Peruvian government was officially told, when it actually was known by the junta, and when the whole issue became public.

the Peruvians by halting military arms sales and that this was not revealed to them until later, it may not have been an immediate decision. A confidential memorandum from State Department officials Viron P. Vaky and Leonard C. Meeker to the secretary of state, dated February 19, five days after the incident, suggests that the matter of applying the statutory provisions was still being considered. The memo warned that such action could be counterproductive and not only lead to "a sharp deterioration in relations with Peru" but also "a confrontation between the U.S. and Latin America as a whole." Before sanctions were applied, they recommended that Nixon "designate and dispatch an emissary to Peru as soon as possible" to try to resolve outstanding disputes. While they were not particularly optimistic that the emissary would be able to achieve positive results, "the resulting confrontation would be no worse than that now anticipated, and the negotiating effort should significantly strengthen our position with other governments in the Hemisphere."[18]

Preparing for an Emissary

By the beginning of March, as Vaky and Meeker had recommended, the Nixon administration was ready to send a special envoy to Peru. In preparation, the State Department charged Jones to meet with Velasco to get his agreement to receive the emissary. He was to communicate to him the department's desire that everything be done to reach a solution on the IPC and fishing rights matters to avoid the application of sanctions.[19] As Jones was preparing to meet with Velasco, Peru came up during President Nixon's March 4 press conference. When a question was asked about the IPC takeover, Nixon responded that the Peruvian government had the right to expropriate but that they also "have the obligation to pay a fair amount for that expropriation." If such payment was not forthcoming, the administration would be obliged to invoke the Hickenlooper amendment, something he hoped could be avoided "because that would have a domino effect—if I can be permitted to use what is supposed to be an outworn term—a domino effect all over Latin America." He claimed that in his study of the matter it seemed that some progress was being made in terms of compensation to

---

18. "Confidential Memorandum from Viron P. Vaky and Leonard C. Meeker to the Secretary of State, February 19, 1969," USNA (1967–1969) (Box 2425, Folder 2), 8.

19. "Secret Outgoing Telegram from Department of State to Jones, March 3, 1969," USNA (1967–1969) (Box 2425, Folder 3), 1–5.

the IPC, which could lead to a satisfactory resolution of the matter, although he was not specific about the measures being taken.[20]

The following day, Jones reported back to Washington on his interview with Velasco. The president, he said, along with Foreign Minister Mercado, who was also present, had received the news of a special envoy with "apparent enthusiasm." During their forty-five-minute conversation, Velasco spoke of his "high regard" for the United States and the appreciation he had for a twenty-seven-day stay at Walter Reed Hospital for treatment that saved his life. Overall, Jones wrote, Velasco seemed "more relaxed and self-assured than [the] last time I called on him." That there was still some background tension was seen in Velasco's denial "that his government has left wing or had communist leanings or that he had communist advisors in the palace." He referred specifically to Alberto Ruiz Eldridge, president of the Peruvian Bar Association, who was described as a communist and who many saw as an important civilian advisor of the regime. Velasco claimed, however, that "he had consulted him [Ruiz Eldridge] only once on some law but had never seen him before or since."[21]

Certainly, one reason Jones found Velasco "more relaxed and self-assured" than previously was the cabinet changes he had made to consolidate his position. These included, as mentioned, the resignations of opponents Generals Alberto Maldonado Yanez and Angel Valdivia Morriberon. The U.S. embassy report on these changes, quoting a source within the military regime, said they meant that "the president has won again." The embassy lamented the resignation of Finance Minister Valdivia, "in that it removes . . . [a] technician and strong personality in favor of moderation." However, it found his replacement with General Francisco Morales Bermúdez "heartening since he also brings with him previous experience in this field [finance] as well as independence of thought and personal fortitude. Whether he will be as independent-minded on [the] IPC problem as was Valdivia, however, is not known."[22]

While behind-the-scenes negotiations proceeded in early March, an article in *Caretas* underscored the continued and growing tensions between the two nations. According to its sources, the U.S. embassy, located on Avenida Garcilaso de la Vega (in a sign of the symbolic nationalism associated with the military regime—and seen by many as clear evidence of growing anti-Americanism—the avenue, which originally had been named Avenida Wilson for the former U.S. president, had been renamed to commemorate the

20. *DOSB*, 60, 1552 (March 24, 1969), 245.
21. "Secret Telegram 1484 from Jones, March 5, 1969," USNA (1967–69) (Box 2421, Folder 7), 1.
22. "Limited Official Use Telegram No. 1381, March 3, 1969," USNA (1967–69) (Box 2421, Folder 7), 1.

renowned Peruvian colonial author), was preparing contingency plans to evacuate the nine to ten thousand American citizens living in Peru if conditions should worsen, particularly if the Hickenlooper provisions were applied. Although one unnamed advisor to the junta was quoted as saying that "the gringos would not dare to apply the amendment," *Caretas* was less confident and urged the regime to work with other Latin American nations to find a solution that would avoid such a confrontation.[23]

In the midst of these complications, President Nixon announced that Charles Meyer would fill the all-important post of assistant secretary for Inter-American Affairs in the State Department, a post that had gone vacant for several months. Meyer was a controversial choice. Although he was fluent in Spanish and had deep experience in Latin America, he had no background in diplomacy. Instead, his career was in business, notably as director of Latin American operations for Sears Roebuck. More serious, as far as his image in Latin America was concerned, was that he was a director of the United Fruit Company at the time of his appointment. No company had a worse reputation for arbitrary behavior in Latin America, particularly with regard to its labor practices. U.S. officials were quoted as being aware of these potential problems but felt that his "style" and his background in retailing rather than in mineral mining along with his "sense of humor and a wife and family who share his regard for the Latin American peoples" would be enough to overcome whatever doubts there were about his qualifications.[24] Commenting on the appointment, the *New York Times* observed that Meyer would have no honeymoon period once he assumed office and that the confrontation with Peru would be at the top of his agenda.[25]

Encouraging Signs

At the time the Meyer appointment was announced, the State Department saw some promising signs that the current crisis with Peru could be resolved. A March 11 intelligence note interpreted Ambassador Jones's report of his meeting with Velasco and the president's willingness to receive a special emissary and to begin negotiations as especially promising.[26] On the same day this note was written, President Nixon publicly announced the appointment

---

23. *Caretas*, 19, 390 (February 28–March 13, 1969), 16.
24. *New York Times* (March 7, 1969), 48, and (March 11, 1969), 30.
25. *New York Times* (March 10, 1969), 44.
26. "Secret Intelligence Note 163, Department of State, March 11, 1969," USNA (1967–69) (Box 2424, Folder 3), 1.

of John N. Irwin as his special emissary to Peru. Praising Irwin's "intelligence, candor, and ability," Nixon claimed that the emissary would engage in wide-ranging discussions and "explore with the Peruvian Government all factors that could lead to mutually agreeable resolution of differences that may have arisen over such current issues as the expropriation of the IPC and incidents connected with U.S. tuna boats fishing in international waters claimed by Peru."[27]

Irwin, a New York attorney, was a former assistant secretary of defense. He also had been involved in negotiations in Panama over a new canal treaty. One day before the official announcement of his appointment, William P. Stedman, director of the Office of Ecuadorean and Peruvian Affairs at the State Department, sent Jones a communication describing Irwin in some detail. Noting that Irwin preferred to be called "Jack," Stedman said that he was a "pleasant, unassuming, mild-mannered man" who was "polite in the extreme" and "totally unflappable." "Of course," Stedman added, "he speaks no Spanish" and would be depending heavily on the embassy for support and advice. With regard to the mission, he was under no illusions that finding a resolution of outstanding issues would be easy but "has a mandate to question anything and to try out anything new or old." While Irwin did not expect to reach a final agreement on this visit, he did hope to initiate a procedure by which such an end could be achieved.[28]

Before his arrival in Lima on March 14, Ambassador Jones urged the emissary to adopt a low-key approach, emphasizing the traditionally friendly relations between the United States and Peru and their mutual interests.[29] The following day, he informed Washington of his conversations with Mercado and other government officials on the upcoming visit, all of whom expressed optimism about the Irwin mission. Jones had responded to this reaction with caution, underscoring that much work remained to be done. He also suggested that the change of attitude from what, the previous week, had been "anguish and near panic" to one of "near euphoria" might simply be a negotiating ploy in response to pressure from moderates within the

---

27. *New York Times* (March 12, 1969), 19.

28. "Official-Informal-Personal letter from Stedman to Jones, March 10, 1969," Personal Papers of John Wesley Jones, Box 23, Folder 5, LBJ Library. In the same communication, Stedman also indicated that the State Department was doing all it could to assure that the IPC would receive some compensation. He ended the letter with the observation that in writing it "I am being very indiscreet" and that it was intended only for "you [Jones], Ernie [Siracusa] and the burn bag." Obviously, since it was included in Jones's personal papers, the ambassador did not follow the final suggestion.

29. "Confidential Telegram from Jones, March 12, 1969," USNA (1967–1969) (Box 2424, Folder 3), 1.

junta and what appeared to be little broader Latin American support for Peru's hard-line position.[30]

Irwin in Lima

Irwin initiated his talks with Velasco, Foreign Minister Mercado, and Prime Minister Ernesto Montagne on March 18. Fully aware of the April 9 deadline for the application of sanctions, Irwin met every day for three weeks with Peruvian officials. Throughout his discussions, which extended into early April, the emissary refrained from making any public statements on how the talks were proceeding. He finally broke his silence on April 3 before taking advantage of the Easter holiday to return to Washington for further consultations. At that time, he declared with regard to the negotiations that "I am not optimistic, but I refuse to be pessimistic until we have completed all our conversations." While Irwin refused to provide details, the *New York Times* reported that "it was reliably understood that virtually no progress has been made and Peru's position, if anything, is even harder than it was in the beginning."[31]

For his part, at a press conference on March 31, Velasco declared that the talks with Irwin had been "favorable" and claimed that "the problem of the IPC is resolved in accordance with our laws."[32] However, on that same day, the State Department issued a statement reaffirming that the Hickenlooper sanctions would be applied if "the Peruvian government does not show it is arriving to an agreement with the International Petroleum Company."[33] Clearly, from the U.S. government's point of view, the issue was far from resolved.

The view from the U.S. embassy at this time was not optimistic. Commenting on Velasco's press conference remarks, Ambassador Jones asserted that, according to one of his sources, the president "takes [a] considerably tougher view on [the] Irwin negotiations than his comments . . . would indicate," was prepared to take an "intransigent" line with regard to the "debts" the IPC owed, and believed that ultimately the United States would

---

30. "Confidential Telegram from Jones, March 13, 1969," USNA (1967–1969) (Box 2424, Folder 3), 1–3.
31. *New York Times*, April 4, 1969, 8. A detailed, almost blow-by-blow account of the Velasco-Irwin discussions was later published in Zimmermann, *El Plan Inca*, 221–80.
32. *El Comercio*, April 1, 1969, 1.
33. Pease García and Verme Insúa, *Perú, 1968–1973*, 1:78.

not apply sanctions and the Peruvian government would not have to pay compensation.[34]

On another level, however, Velasco continued to try to appear accommodating. In a secret letter dispatched to President Nixon on April 3, he expressed his high regard for Irwin and his appreciation for sending an envoy of "such high professional caliber." In their discussions, he told Nixon, the Peruvians had sought to represent their "just aspirations" in a way that would maintain at the highest level the friendship and the active and efficient cooperation between Peru and the United States." "Dr. Irwin's visit," Velasco concluded, "has led to a better understanding of the important matters we have discussed, and above all, in Peruvian opinion it has had the healthy effect of producing confidence in the friendly and cooperative way in which your excellency will deal with Latin American questions—confidence which I am sure will not be betrayed."[35] While there was little in the letter, wrapped in the usual diplomatic niceties, to indicate Velasco's "intransigence" on the IPC issue or to suggest a confrontational tone, it nonetheless implied that much of what happened in the future between the two countries depended on the U.S. reaction to the Irwin talks, with the ball placed in the Nixon administration's court not to betray Peruvian "confidence" that it would continue to deal with the country and the region in a "friendly and cooperative way."

The CIA Enters the Picture

While these developments were transpiring, an April 13 *New York Times* article reported on speculation that Velasco would soon be deposed by fellow officers. According to this account, there were a substantial number in the armed forces who felt Velasco had gone too far in his confrontation with the United States and that any sanctions applied as a result would do their institution and the nation real harm. They were also concerned about the establishment of ties with the Soviet Union and the apparent influence of certain left-wing civilians within the regime. To muddy the waters further, accusations had been made in several quarters that the CIA was involved in efforts to remove Velasco from power through the Aprista Party (APRA)

---

34. "Limited Official Use Telegram 2332 from Jones, April 1, 1969," USNA (1967–69) (Box 2421, Folder 7), 2.
35. "Secret Letter from Velasco to Nixon, April 3, 1969," USNA (1967–69) (Box 2424, Folder 3), 1.

and certain elements within the armed forces, accusations that Velasco said had no basis in fact.³⁶

Rumors of CIA involvement in Peruvian affairs were nothing new. Indeed, even before the accusations reported in the *Times* article, there had been an incident in Lima that raised the specter of agency activity. On March 4, agents of the Peruvian police (PIP) and the National Intelligence Service had occupied the offices of the Plant Protection Company on the seventeenth and eighteenth floors of the Anglo-Peruano Building on Plaza Grau and detained about a dozen of the company's employees. When asked what motivated the raid, the minister of the interior responded only that it was a "very delicate" matter involving "national security." The owner of the company, William D. Chappers, was a U.S. citizen born in Czechoslovakia, married to a Peruvian, who had arrived in Peru in 1951 and had built a successful business that provided private security to various domestic and foreign companies, including the Cerro de Pasco Copper Corporation. Given Chappers's well-known anticommunist attitudes, the kind of business in which he was engaged, and the contacts he had both inside and outside of Peru, there was considerable speculation that he had at the least connections with the CIA or the FBI. One theory held that he was working with U.S. and Peruvian interests on behalf of the CIA to help overthrow the current government and that this had led to his arrest.³⁷

Communications from the U.S. embassy at this time reveal no mention of the Chappers affair. However, they do make clear that contrary to the *Times* reporting, Velasco's position within the government by early April was stronger than ever. In an April 3 confidential telegram, Ambassador Jones reported that the radical elements within the regime were now ascendant and that the moderates had either been eliminated or "rendered impotent." Velasco had benefited from a new "organic" law issued by the junta that had concentrated even more power and authority into his hands. Jones also speculated that recent reports of a "CIA plot" involving APRA had been cleverly manufactured by the regime to serve as an excuse to crack down on that party if necessary.³⁸

On April 5, Ambassador Jones provided a summary evaluation of his impressions of the Velasco regime after its first six months in power, a regime that appeared "hell-bent on [a] collision course with [the] U.S." With

---

36. *New York Times*, April 3, 1969, 7.
37. *Caretas*, 19, 391 (March 14–27, 1969), 14–15.
38. "Confidential Telegram 2377 from Jones, April 3, 1969," USNA (1967–1969) (Box 2421, Folder 7), 1–2.

regard to its ideological orientation, Jones stated that aside from its ultra-nationalism the Velasco government seemed an odd mixture of various elements—leftist civilians, "reform-minded and quasi-technocratic military officers," and "certain traditional oligarchic interests (particularly the Prado family interests) which resent and feel threatened by foreign, especially American, industrial and financial competition." "These three principal governing groups," the ambassador asserted, "preside over a vast inert but frightened Peruvian bureaucracy which is moving slowly into ill-defined new paths laid out by [the] military government." While this was an eclectic regime, most of its elements could "with accuracy be described as ultra-nationalistic with strong statist tendencies apparently based on [a] humanist philosophy influenced to some extent by teachings of radical and reformist elements within the Roman Catholic Church." Finally, while Velasco proved pragmatic and flexible enough to appoint "ultra-conservative Berckemeyer as ambassador to the U.S.," Jones had it on "good authority" that the president depended almost exclusively on his more radical civilian advisors to craft his position on the IPC issue, advisors who "are hostile to U.S. backed reforms," and ignored the advice of "those legalists most expert in the field." In conclusion, Jones observed that while the Velasco regime had "gradually eliminated or rendered impotent his rivals," it was still somewhat insecure, "which leads it to take prompt coercive action against any who threaten or even criticize it."[39] In sum, while certain aspects of the Velasco regime remained opaque to Jones, he was beginning to have a much clearer picture of its composition and its aims than had been the case when it first took power. Moreover, most of his and the State Department's assumptions about the future course of affairs in Peru under the direction of the reformist military were increasingly accurate.

Sanctions Deferred

These communications from Lima arrived at a time when the Nixon administration was fast approaching the deadline for application of the Hickenlooper amendment. In a conversation on April 4 with two members of Congress, the recently returned Irwin reported "that there had been no meaningful progress" in his discussions with the Peruvians, who were maintaining an intransigent stance on the IPC issue. Irwin asserted that Velasco was

---

39. "Confidential Telegram 2415 from Jones, April 5, 1969," USNA (1967–1969) (Box 2421, Folder 7), 1–2.

not widely popular either among the public at large or among the military hierarchy and was using his hard line on the IPC matter primarily to strengthen his political position. He believed that "all nationalist elements" would rally behind Velasco if the United States were to invoke the Hickenlooper amendment and cut the Peruvian sugar quota.[40] This was probably the same information and interpretation that Irwin provided to the secretary of state and President Nixon.

The impact of Irwin's assessment on the State Department and the chief executive was unclear at the time. The message seemed to be that there was little hope of accommodation but that if the Hickenlooper sanctions were applied it would only serve to strengthen Velasco's hand, perhaps making future agreements even more difficult to achieve. At any rate, at a news conference on April 7, two days before the deadline, Secretary of State Rogers announced that sufficient progress had been made in the Irwin-Velasco negotiations to defer the application of the amendment's provisions. Irwin, who was on his way back to Lima after having consulted with the State Department and President Nixon in Key Biscayne, Florida, had reported that the Peruvian government was willing to allow the IPC to contest through the courts the $690 million debt it was alleged to owe Peru. This willingness, according to Rogers, constituted "appropriate steps" toward the resolution of the dispute and allowed for the deferral of the Hickenlooper provisions. "In these circumstances," he concluded, "we believe that our determination offers the best hope that the dispute between IPC and the Government of Peru can be resolved without injury to the tradition of close and friendly relations between the United States and Peru."[41]

The decision meant that for the moment an important bullet had been dodged. For Peru, it seemed a clear if perhaps temporary victory. The strategy employed by Velasco and Mercado had worked. As one U.S. official put it, "Maybe there was an element of brinkmanship in this whole situation . . . and if so, we blinked." However, from the U.S. perspective, the decision prevented a further worsening of relations between it and Peru and avoided the larger adverse reaction from much of the rest of Latin America if the sanctions had been applied.

On the same day as Rogers's announcement, Irwin informed Velasco personally of the decision. Velasco, in turn, expressed his pleasure and in a public statement said that it had served to improve relations between the

---

40. "Confidential Department of State Memorandum of Conversation, April 4, 1969," USNA (1967–1969) (Box 2424, Folder 7), 1.

41. *DOSB*, 60, 1557 (April 21, 1969), 357. See also Ingram, *Expropriation of U.S. Property in South America*, 65–66.

two countries. He also hoped that it meant that credits from U.S. banks, which had been withheld as a result of the standoff over the IPC matter, would soon be resumed. Velasco was not the only one pleased by the decision. Many U.S. citizens in Peru connected with business interests, in anticipation of a strong adverse reaction and possible violent demonstrations directed against them if the decision had been otherwise, had moved their families and possessions out of the country. While the dispute between Peru and the IPC was still far from being definitively resolved, at least some significant tension had been momentarily removed from the atmosphere. As one unnamed prominent U.S. businessman in Peru said, "Every United States businessman and investor in Peru is more relieved than I can possibly tell you. . . . I suppose the problem is not over, but any time we can buy is heaven-sent."[42]

Peruvian press reaction to the decision was predictably favorable if not outright triumphant. In its lead editorial on April 8, *El Comercio* called the decision not to apply sanctions "the correct measure for the United States" and "the first step on the road to good sense." If this road were followed, the paper claimed, the amendment would never be applied and Peruvian-U.S. relations would improve along "normal" lines. The accompanying cartoon showed President Nixon carrying a briefcase labeled "International Policies of the U.S." and carefully avoiding the banana peel (the Hickenlooper amendment) in his path.[43] In the United States, the *New York Times* hailed the Nixon administration's decision as the "Right Action on Peru."[44]

Actions of the Peruvian Embassy in Washington

Back in familiar surroundings in Washington, Ambassador Berckemeyer had been placed in a rather unique and difficult situation. First, rarely in recent years had relations between Peru and the United States been as strained as they were at the beginning of 1969. Second, he was representing a regime that in many ways was attacking the very oligarchy of which he was a proud member and on the surface could not have been more different from the previous administration—that of conservative president Manuel Prado—in which he had served. However, Ambassador Jones had mentioned that the Prado family was supportive of the Velasco government. Moreover, there

---

42. *New York Times*, April 8, 1969, 1.
43. *El Comercio*, April 8, 1969, 2.
44. *New York Times*, April 8, 1969, 46.

was a broad range of Peruvian opinion that backed the regime's position on the IPC and fishing rights issues and its overall defense of the nation's sovereign rights, a position with which Berckemeyer was entirely in agreement. Finally, Berckemeyer, whatever his political opinions, was a seasoned and experienced diplomat who approached his responsibilities in a professional and serious manner and who undoubtedly felt an obligation to justify the confidence placed in him by Mercado, who had appointed him to the most important and sensitive position in Peru's diplomatic service.

As had been established practice, both Berckemeyer and embassy official Alzamora directed a steady stream of correspondence to Lima concerning the general political situation in the United States as well as press and governmental attention to Peru, which at the beginning of 1969 was considerable. The major focus, of course, was on the IPC case and the possibility that the Hickenlooper amendment might be applied. On these matters, the embassy regularly sent clippings of articles and editorials from various publications presenting various points of view on this issue. Included among these were reports of efforts by various senators and representatives to enure that, at the least, the Hickenlooper amendment would not be applied to Peru.[45]

Responding to a request from the Foreign Ministry, Alzamora had forwarded to Lima the entire text of the Hickenlooper amendment in early March before Irwin was named as special emissary.[46] At about the same time, also in response to another Foreign Ministry request, he sent to Lima a detailed eighteen-page analysis of U.S. actions and attitudes with regard to past expropriations of U.S.-owned properties. Tracing these developments from the Mexican oil expropriation of 1938 through to the takeovers by Fidel Castro in Cuba, Alzamora provided both historical detail as well as a rather sophisticated insight into long-standing North American attitudes toward private property and protection of its interests abroad.[47] Although there is no evidence of what use the ministry made of this information, much of which was generally well known, it would nonetheless have been a useful guide as the Velasco regime entered into its talks with Irwin. Nine days later, Berckemeyer forwarded a complete copy of the two-volume allegation (*alegato*) that the IPC had prepared "to defend its position before the public opinion and official circles of this country." This information,

45. *Correspondencia* (5–3-Y/11) (March 18, 1969), 2.
46. *Correspondencia* (5–3-Y/7) (March 5, 1969), 1.
47. *Correspondencia* (5–3-Y/8) (March 10, 1969), 1.

in turn, was forwarded by order of Minister Mercado to the presidential palace.[48]

When the decision was announced on April 7 not to apply the Hickenlooper sanctions, Berckemeyer gave his and the embassy's efforts some of the credit for this outcome. From the beginning of his return to the post, he wrote, he and the embassy staff had pressed Peru's case, especially with sympathetic members of the media and with influential and mostly liberal congressmen and senators. Berckemeyer also claimed to have used "political and personal friends" to communicate the Peruvian government's views directly to President Nixon. He was also careful, however, to give the main credit to Mercado and Velasco for the final result. "The firmness of the Peruvian government's position, maintained throughout the process, but especially in the course of the conversations with Emissary Irwin," he wrote, "was the decisive factor that convinced the North American government of the uselessness and inconvenience of the application of the amendment and precipitated the announcement that postponed its application." General Latin American support for Peru's position, cultivated by Mercado, was another important factor in the overall successful strategy. At the moment, thanks in large measure to Peruvian actions, he judged the general political environment in Washington to be favorable to either a substantial revision or a complete revocation of the amendment. While many matters remained to be resolved, he concluded, he was optimistic that these now could be achieved in a mutually satisfactory manner.[49] As future developments would show, this optimism was premature.

Continued Confrontations

When Secretary of State Rogers announced on April 7 that the Hickenlooper sanctions would not be applied, President Velasco described it as a "Peruvian victory." However, he also warned that it was a "tactical" victory rather than a final solution and described the amendment as a "sword of Damocles" that still hung over the nation. While the mandatory six months had passed for the sanctions to be applied, there was a very real possibility, if no satisfactory solution were arrived at on the IPC matter, that a new deadline of August 9 would be imposed. Velasco noted that Peru still did not

---

48. *Correspondencia* (5–3-Y/10) (March 19, 1969), 1.
49. *Correspondencia* (5–3-Y/16) (April 17, 1969), 1–9.

have access to credits from international lending institutions because of the "veto" imposed by the United States.[50]

The man most responsible for trying to keep the sword from falling was Foreign Minister Mercado. Recognizing clearly the asymmetric relationship between Peru and the United States and to meet the challenge of sanctions, he developed a strategy of seeking broader Latin American assistance in confronting the "Colossus of the North."[51] He prevailed on his Chilean counterpart, Gabriel Valdés, to call a special meeting of the members of the Economic Commission for Latin America in Santiago between March 31 and April 8, at the time the Hickenlooper sanctions were about to be applied, a meeting to which, for the first time, the United States was not invited. The final resolutions generally followed Peruvian recommendations; the most significant one read: "No state can apply or employ coercive measures of an economic and political character to force its will over the sovereignty of another state. An action of this nature constitutes *economic aggression* [my emphasis]."[52] It did not take too much imagination to see this as a direct reference to any economic pressures applied by the United States on Peru—or any other Latin American country—by way of punitive amendments such as Hickenlooper and Pelly.

At a meeting of the United Nations Economic Commission for Latin America (CEPAL), held in Lima in mid-April, Mercado closed the six-day sessions with a call again for all Latin American nations to resist "economic aggression."[53] In response to these remarks, which were clearly aimed at current Nixon administration policies, the U.S. delegation considered walking out of the session before they were completed but ultimately decided to remain.[54] That the U.S. representatives could consider such an action to protest the remarks of a man who was seen as generally more moderate and more balanced in his approach than others in the Velasco regime was eloquent testimony to the continued strained relationships between the two nations.

From Washington, Ambassador Berckemeyer worked hard to play his

---

50. Pease García and Verme Insúa, *Perú, 1968–1973*, 1:79; and *El Comercio*, April 8, 1969, 1.

51. In an interview a few years later, Mercado, when asked what was the most difficult and "agitated" period of his tenure, pointed to the "dangerous" situation created by the confrontation with the United States over the IPC issue and the threat of the Hickenlooper amendment. Moreira, *Modelo Peruano*, 77–79.

52. República del Perú, Ministerio de Relaciones Exteriores, *El Perú y su política exterior: Recopilación de los principales discursos pronunciados por el Ministro de Relaciones Exteriores, General de División E. P. Edgardo Mercado Jarrín (Del 24 Nov. 1968 al 28 Abril 1971)*, 40.

53. República del Perú, *El Perú y su política exterior*, 59.

54. *New York Times*, April 26, 1969, 9.

role in Mercado's overall strategy. On April 15, he met with Assistant Secretary Meyer (probably for the first time) to discuss the delay in providing Peru with naval and air equipment because of the provisions of the Pelly amendment. Meyer promised to do all he could to resolve this matter, but he also underscored the restrictions that the amendment placed on his and the department's course of action. Berckemeyer, however, was little swayed and warned Meyer of the "unfavorable political repercussions" the delay would have in Peru, "especially at this moment."[55]

Two days later, Berckemeyer forwarded detailed accounts of congressional hearings on U.S.-Peruvian relations. These hearings, which lasted three days, had been called by Democratic Senator Frank Church of Idaho, who was concerned about the recent deterioration in Peruvian-U.S. relations. It featured academic experts, government officials, including Assistant Secretary Meyer, and the IPC president.[56]

In his comments on the hearings, which received extensive press coverage in Peru, Berckemeyer believed that despite IPC president Dean's best efforts to present a strong case, he had failed to convince most of the senators to agree with his interpretation of events or to support the company's position. He also found a general consensus among all participants, senators and witnesses alike, that the Hickenlooper amendment was in need either of significant modification or outright revocation. He concluded that he found it "improbable that the North American Congress will demand the application of sanctions on our country in conformity with the much criticized text of the amendment."[57]

There were other developments behind the scenes, however, which, if he had been aware of them, would have tempered his optimism. On April 22, National Security Advisor Kissinger sent a secret note to Secretary Rogers in which he said, "I thought you should know that in a handwritten note to me, the President indicated his support for the program of *economic pressures on Peru* [my emphasis], and indicated that he wanted a step-up in pressure, where possible. The President also indicated a desire for substantial reductions in the staffs of all U.S. agencies in Peru."[58] In an accompanying secret note, Richard Moose of the White House requested that the

---

55. *Correspondencia* (5–3-Y/14) (April 15, 1969), 1–2.
56. "United States Relations with Peru," United States Senate, *Hearings Before the Subcommittee on Western Hemisphere Affairs of the Committee on Foreign Relations, Ninety-First Congress (April 14, 16 and 17, 1969)* (Washington, D.C.: U.S. Government Printing Office, 1969).
57. *Correspondencia* (5–3-Y/17) (April 18, 1969), 3–4.
58. "Secret Note from Kissinger to Rogers, April 22, 1969," USNA (1967–1969) (Box 2424, Folder 3), 1.

State Department inform Kissinger, through a weekly report, of the status of the pressures placed on Peru and their effect.[59]

In memoirs published some ten years later, Kissinger claimed that the Nixon administration dealt with the expropriation of U.S. companies in both Chile and Peru with great equanimity and flexibility. With regard to Peru, he wrote, the administration "stretched our legislation almost to the breaking point" to achieve an equitable settlement of the IPC dispute without imposing congressional sanctions: "We repeatedly sought pretexts to postpone application of the Hickenlooper Amendment and made clear that we were prepared to accept a compensation payment for IPC of less than full values, so as to maintain friendly relations with an important country. . . . After patient and sustained efforts, we worked out a modus vivendi with the Peruvian government."[60]

While it is true that the Hickenlooper provisions were never applied, the covert policy of applying economic pressure by denying aid and restricting access to loans, which Kissinger did not mention in his memoirs, had much the same effect. This is a tactic that would be applied with a vengeance against the government of Chile's Salvador Allende the following year. For Peru, of course, Kissinger's and Nixon's policy of applying economic pressure was basically a continuation of the Mann Doctrine, with both sides aware of what was being done surreptitiously but saying little in public about it. It also underscored that despite the regime's assertion that the IPC case had been resolved definitively, the pattern of the United States withholding full assistance to the Peruvian government until some compensation was provided prevailed.

More Negotiations and Berckemeyer's Analysis

As part of the ongoing negotiations over the IPC case, a special four-man group from Peru arrived in Washington at the end of April to meet with Irwin and others to try to resolve the seemingly never-ending dispute. After three weeks of talks, little was accomplished, with both sides adhering to their respective positions. As these meetings proceeded, the Foreign Ministry in Lima sent an urgent request to Berckemeyer to provide an assessment of U.S. reaction. The ambassador responded with a detailed, twelve-page

---

59. "Secret from Richard Moose to John Walsh, April 22, 1969," USNA (1967–1969) (Box 2424, Folder 3), 1.

60. Kissinger, *White House Years*, 657.

document. He began with the most important actor, the White House, asserting that it had shown a "discreet preoccupation" with the issue, hoping to avoid a further deterioration of the "traditionally friendly relations" between the two countries and particularly desirous of avoiding any wider or deeper implications for its overall policy toward Latin America. He characterized Nixon's approach to the matter as one of "measured prudence." Clearly, at this point, he was unaware of the administration's tactic of applying economic pressures on the regime.

As far as the State Department was concerned, he believed that the several months gap between Oliver and Meyer had worked to Peru's advantage. With no one firmly in control of Latin American affairs, the department had taken a position of not pushing too hard for application of sanctions and continuing to work on negotiations. The picture in Congress was mixed, with conservatives generally favoring the company's position and liberals adopting a more accommodating posture. The initial reaction of "economic pressure groups" to the IPC takeover had now dissipated in light of recent announcements by other U.S. companies of either expanding or initiating investments in Peru. Intellectuals and "university sectors" in general seemed sympathetic to Peru's stance while labor unions, perhaps because the IPC employed relatively few North American workers, were relatively silent on the issue.

Underscoring the embassy's efforts in presenting the case from the Peruvian perspective, he again praised the "firm attitude" of the regime. While the future was difficult to predict, there were already signs of a return to "the normal course of the traditional relations of friendship and open collaboration between the two countries," although the possible application of the Hickenlooper sanctions still remained as a threat to this "normalization." In this continuing delicate situation, Berckemeyer also emphasized "the importance that there not develop in our country unnecessary manifestations of hostility towards the U.S.," manifestations that would undermine "our cause" and be "incompatible with the measured and mutual respect between two nations." Finally, he stated his view that the actions of the government to develop a sense of continental solidarity on this issue was a major foreign policy achievement and had placed the nation in a position of international leadership whatever the outcome of the dispute.[61] It is not known what impact this report had on the Foreign Ministry, but it was a reasonably accurate and comprehensive picture of where matters stood at the time.

61. *Correspondencia* (5–3-Y/21) (May 7, 1969), 1–12.

Increased Tensions

While it might not have counted, strictly speaking, as one of the "manifestations of hostility" against which Berckemeyer had warned, on May 16, the situation between Peru and the United States worsened when Peruvian forces once again detained and fined a U.S. fishing vessel operating without a license and within the 200-mile limit. Again, Congressman Pelly demanded a firm response, calling on President Nixon to provide Coast Guard protection for U.S. fishermen operating off the Peruvian coast.[62] Apparently as a result of these actions, on May 18, the State Department publicly announced the suspension of arms sales to Peru, a suspension that had become effective automatically three months earlier but, as mentioned, had been kept confidential.[63]

The general Peruvian reaction to the official announcement of the aid cutoff decision was uniformly negative. All media outlets roundly condemned the action. The Peruvian government responded by declaring that a scheduled visit by Nelson Rockefeller as part of a larger fact-finding tour of Latin America would now be "inopportune." Announcing what amounted to a withdrawn invitation in retaliation for the arms aid suspension, Foreign Minister Mercado claimed that "the indispensable conditions for Rockefeller's visit to Peru do not exist." He added, however, that "I do not think that the present situation will lead to a break in diplomatic relations."[64] At the same time, the government demanded that all U.S. military missions leave the country, ending for the moment decades of close cooperation between the armed forces of the two nations.[65]

In the eyes of the U.S. embassy, the military aid cutoff had provided yet another golden opportunity for the Velasco regime, as Jones put it, "to play the nationalist card" and further consolidate its position. Because Peruvian anti-American nationalism was now at a "fever pitch," the ambassador reported, "even those military officers friendly to us must now conform [to Velasco's actions] to support armed forces 'dignity.'"[66] Some two weeks later, another embassy telegram suggested that the regime had known all along about the arms cutoff decision and had cleverly waited until the United States made it public to turn it to its own purposes. Underscoring

---

62. *Congressional Record—House* (May 21, 1969), 13245.
63. *New York Times* (May 22, 1969), 17.
64. *New York Times* (May 24, 1969), 19.
65. Masterson, *Militarism and Politics in Latin America*, 258.
66. "Confidential Telegram 3675 from Jones, May 21, 1969," USNA (1967–1969) (Box 2419, Folder 1), 1–2.

the surprising diplomatic agility of the regime and the confusing situation in which the United States now found itself, the communication observed that "this whole incident . . . again demonstrated [the] difficulty of trying to judge whether Peruvians have these problems with us because they are genuinely difficult of solution or because it is politically useful to them to have these problems."67

Preparing to leave his post after six years of service, Ambassador Jones met with Mercado on May 27 to try to keep relations from worsening. The foreign minister was pessimistic, seeing little hope for improvement in the near future. The IPC matter was still pending with no resolution in sight, and he also mentioned a recent report that suggested the U.S. Agency for International Development (AID) mission in Peru was being cut in half. He presumed the Hickenlooper amendment was in effect since no loans or credits were available. Jones replied that the AID cuts were due to budgetary issues and made no reference to any specific policy by the United States to put an economic squeeze on Peru. (It was not clear whether Jones was aware of the Nixon-Kissinger policy in this regard.) On the IPC matter, the ambassador said certain specific proposals had emerged from the recent talks between the Peruvian delegation in Washington and Irwin, which apparently was a surprise to Mercado. Jones promised to provide him with further information as soon as possible.68

Jones's farewell meeting with Velasco offered few reasons to be optimistic. On the one hand, Velasco stressed the anticommunist and overall pro-U.S. position of the military government and expressed his "regret" at having to cancel the Rockefeller visit and expel the U.S. military missions. But on the IPC issue, he still saw a failure of the United States to understand fully the Peruvian side of the dispute. He said that Irwin would be welcome back to Lima to continue discussions, but it was his understanding that Irwin had demanded that compensation for the expropriated properties be provided and that under those conditions a resumption of talks was not possible. At the end of the meeting, Velasco expressed concern that no successor to Jones had yet been named, seeing this as a possible ominous development, and mentioned that there had been some pressure on him to recall Ambassador Berckemeyer to protest recent U.S. actions but that he had resisted to avoid a further deterioration in relations. Jones sought to assure the president that a successor would be named and that in the meantime

---

67. "Confidential Telegram 1975 from Lima, June 6, 1969," USNA (1967–1969) (Box 2420, Folder 1), 1.

68. "Confidential Telegram 3904 from Jones, May 27, 1969," USNA (1967–1969) (Box 2420, Folder 1), 1–2.

the embassy would be in "the capable hands" of Ernest Siracusa. The Peruvian leader assured Jones "of his personal friendship and esteem and offered to be of any help to me personally in the future."[69]

Velasco's final comments probably provided little solace. His conversations with the president and Mercado ended for Jones a frustrating tenure as U.S. ambassador to Peru, during which he had tried with apparent energy and good will to resolve some particularly difficult issues with, for the most part, little success. Sympathetic to Fernando Belaúnde Terry, he had been unable to convince Washington to lift restrictions on its assistance to that reformist and democratic regime or to foresee accurately or forestall the military coup that overthrew him. Despite his best efforts to resolve outstanding disputes with the new military regime, by the time he left Lima, relations between Peru and the United States were at a historic low point. As he recalled two decades later, "I tell my friends . . . that I stayed in Peru too long." If he had left before October 3, 1968, he might have exited in a blaze of glory on the heels of the Talara agreement, but the coup dashed those hopes. Afterward, he told his interviewer, thanks to Velasco's nationalistic policies, "my last year in Peru was a very sad one, diplomatically and professionally, because I spent most of my time carrying notes of protest to the Foreign Minister."[70] While he might not have put it in these terms, Jones seemed another victim of a U.S. policy that frequently seemed to put the interests of the IPC above those of an overall good relationship with Peru.

Signs of Progress

Temporarily in charge of the U.S. embassy until a new ambassador arrived, Ernest Siracusa provided a virtually seamless transition. Having served as Jones's chief deputy for most of his tenure in Peru, he knew the country and its leaders well and had relatively easy access to them. On June 11, while Mercado was in Argentina looking for more continental support, he met with Velasco for a lengthy discussion on pending disputes. The results were not particularly encouraging. While Velasco showed some flexibility on the fishing rights issue he remained adamant on the IPC matter. As Mercado had indicated to Jones, he also believed that the Hickenlooper provisions

---

69. "Confidential Telegram 3952 from Jones, May 29, 1969," USNA (1967–1969) (Box 2420, Folder 1), 1–3.

70. Oral Interview with John Wesley Jones, 1988, 19–20. Back in Washington, Jones was nominated by the State Department to be ambassador in Mexico, but the post went to a political appointee. Instead, he accepted an assignment to teach at the National War College.

were de facto in effect and, as a result, the United States had paralyzed Peru's economy. Siracusa also believed that Velasco was under considerable conflicting pressures, buffeted on one side by nationalists who demanded no give on the IPC case and on the other by pragmatists who were concerned that continued confrontation with the United States would do serious damage, especially on the economic front. These pressures could be seen in mood swings during his conversation when he would appear "almost pitiful in his protestations of friendship for the United States" and in the next moment "would suddenly become defiant and talk about dignity, sovereignty, refusal to accept any conditions whatsoever." While the meeting provided few signs of any significant change of course for the Peruvian leader, he did make clear that he wanted to keep lines of communications open with both the U.S. embassy and the State Department to avoid either a worsening of relations or even an outright break.[71]

Two weeks after this meeting, the Velasco government took another step that promised to complicate its relationship with the United States. On June 24, it announced one of the most sweeping agrarian reform programs in Latin American history, yet another way in which it distinguished itself so dramatically from its counterparts in the region. News of the announcement made the front page of the *New York Times*, which observed that some U.S. interests would be affected. These included holdings related to the Rockefeller family and most especially coastal properties owned by the W. R. Grace Company.[72] The following day the government announced that it had taken over the bank accounts of W. R. Grace and would begin to assume control of its operations.[73] The big losers, however, were the Peruvian oligarchs, who traditionally had owned most of these coastal properties. While various parties and individuals had talked for some time about the need for agrarian reform, and some modest efforts in that direction had been made under Belaúnde, the military government showed through this decree that it was sincerely prepared to carry out sweeping social and economic changes in Peru. The break from the conservatives in the country was now as clear as it could be.

Officially, both the White House and the State Department declined comment on the reform, seeking not to rock the boat at a time when chances for an improvement of relations with Peru seemed to be on the horizon. This opportunity arose primarily because the Peruvians and other interested

---

71. "Confidential from Siracusa to Meyer, June 12, 1969," USNA (1967–1969) (Box 2420, Folder 1), 1–3.
72. *New York Times*, June 25, 1969, 1, 2.
73. *New York Times*, June 27, 1969, 6.

parties had agreed to attend a four-party conference, including the United States, Chile, Ecuador, and Peru, to discuss fishing rights issues. This agreement, according to the *New York Times*, was due to "weeks of patient inter-American diplomacy" and pressure from Governor Rockefeller to lift the ban on arms sales that had led to the cancellation of his visit to Lima.[74] Also working behind the scenes was Ambassador Berckemeyer, who took advantage of a visit to the United States by Chilean Foreign Minister Gabriel Valdés to coordinate with him and the ambassador of Ecuador a common position on the meeting.[75] These developments were sufficient for Congressman Pelly to send a letter to President Nixon recommending that the sanctions on Peru required by his amendment be lifted.[76]

Although there were some in Congress who wanted to maintain pressure on Peru, especially after the agrarian reform decree threatened U.S. interests, the Nixon administration determined to follow Pelly's lead. On July 4, it announced that it had lifted the sanctions on Peru and would resume arms sales.[77] Five days later all parties announced that a meeting of representatives of the United States, Chile, Ecuador, and Peru would be held on July 30 in Buenos Aires to discuss the fishing problem. Two days later, Prime Minister Montagne declared that Nelson Rockefeller would be invited to visit Peru "as soon as representatives in Washington and Lima began conversations on the current problems between the two countries."[78]

These actions signaled that some of the ice between Peru and the United States had been broken. On July 7, Siracusa reported from Lima that Mercado had been unusually forthcoming and "very constructive in attitudes toward [the] fisheries conference and IPC." He found it particularly encouraging that Mercado had stated publicly that talks on the IPC matter could be resumed. Despite these positive developments, he warned, there were still many complications to be confronted and resolved. That most Peruvians attributed the recent favorable turn in relations to the United States having given ground on the arms sales ban "indicates that, as in [the] past, Peru will find it difficult, and may be unwilling, to make significant concessions on its own in seeking solutions to bilateral problems." However, "at the same time, it is apparent that while [the] new Peruvian nationalism demands that [the] government stand up to [the] U.S. over real or

---

74. *New York Times*, June 15, 1969), 1, 25.
75. *Correspondencia* (5-3-Y/24) (June 19, 1969), 1–3.
76. *Congressional Record—House* (June 23, 1969), 16865–66. The following day, Berckemeyer forwarded a copy of Pelly's remarks to Lima. *Correspondencia* (5-3-A/181) (June 24, 1969).
77. *New York Times*, July 4, 1969, 1, 5.
78. Pease García and Verme Insúa, *Perú, 1968–1973*, 1: 97–98.

imagined slights, there remains strong interest, and perhaps growing recognition, that Peru cannot afford to break completely with [the] U.S., and must do its part to preserve [the] basis for mutually beneficial bilateral relations."[79]

Future Prospects

At a lengthy State Department conference on U.S.-Peruvian relations following the cancellation of the Rockefeller visit, Secretary of State Rogers was reported to have complained, "How can such a little country produce such major headaches for the U.S.?"[80] Some of those headaches had been relieved with the decision to rescind the Pelly sanctions and the prospects for talks on the fishing rights issue. The United States could also hope that continuing to apply certain economic pressures would lead to some moderation in the regime's hard-line stance on the IPC matter and upcoming complications from the agrarian reform law.

From the Peruvian point of view, there were several potential problems for the Velasco regime on the horizon. First, under Belaúnde, an agreement had been reached with three U.S. copper companies to expand their operations in Peru at a cost of $520 million. However, almost two-thirds of the cost was to come from an Export-Import Bank loan, which, under present conditions, seemed unlikely to be approved. Second, while the Peruvian balance of payments and foreign exchange situation was currently healthy, payments on the nation's long-term debt would triple in 1970, placing a heavy burden on its reserves. Third, Velasco's new economic team had discarded the tax reforms enacted by the Belaúnde administration just before the coup and had embarked on spending policies that had undermined the confidence of both domestic and foreign investors. Fourth, given the growing uncertainties involving the regime's economic and social policies, private foreign banks in both the United States and Europe were holding back on loans until the situation was clarified.

In the last analysis, just how all of this would play out in terms of U.S.-Peruvian relations remained something of an enigma. Clearly, there were compelling practical reasons for both sides to agree. Most observers in the United States believed that the key element to achieving this was "the personality of the junta leader, General Juan Velasco Alvarado: Suspicious,

---

79. "Limited Official Use Telegram from Siracusa, July 7, 1969," USNA (1967–1969) (Box 2424, Folder 5), 1–2.
80. *New York Times*, June 8, 1969, sect. 4, 4.

ultra-nationalistic, rigid."[81] Also crucial, as it had been for years, was the ultimate resolution of the IPC matter and the still pending question of compensation. This issue as well as the fishing rights dispute and all the complications involved with them would be the main items on his agenda as a new U.S. ambassador took over for Jones in Lima.

81. Ibid.

FIG. 1 President Lyndon B. Johnson meets with Assistant Secretary of State for Inter-American Affairs Thomas Mann, who appears to be paying close attention, August 13, 1964.

FIG. 2 President Johnson, back to the camera, hosts a lunch on October 1, 1965, in the White House Fish Room with Latin American ambassadors. To President Johnson's immediate left at the table is Peruvian ambassador Celso Pastor de la Torre.

FIG. 3 President Johnson meets with his Latin American foreign policy team on February 3, 1966, before special advisor Walt Rostow's trip to Peru. From left to right, Robert Sayre (obscured), Walt Rostow, Lincoln Gordon, McGeorge Bundy, and President Johnson.

FIG. 4 President Johnson and Jack Hood Vaughn, director of the Peace Corps, July 18, 1966.

FIG. 5 President Johnson meeting with U.S. Ambassador John Wesley Jones and Covey T. Oliver (back to the camera) to discuss the situation in Peru, November 8, 1967.

FIG. 6 President Johnson and Assistant Secretary Oliver in the Oval Office, November 8, 1967.

FIG. 7 President Johnson and Ambassador Jones in the Oval Office, November 8, 1967.

FIG. 8 Fernando Berckemeyer, Peruvian ambassador to the United States, 1960–1963, 1968–1974.

FIG. 9 Fernando Belaúnde Terry, president of Peru, 1963–1968, 1980–1985.

FIG. 10 General Edgardo Mercado Jarrín, foreign minister of Peru, 1968–1972.

FIG. 11 Celso Pastor de la Torre, Peruvian ambassador to the United States, 1963–1968.

FIG. 12 General Miguel Angel de la Flor, foreign minister of Peru, 1972–1974.

FIG. 13 General Juan Velasco Alvarado, president of Peru, 1968–1975.

FIG. 14 President Richard M. Nixon speaking to the Organization of American States at the Pan American Conference, APRIL 14, 1969.

FIG. 15 President Nixon (center front) with his cabinet, June 16, 1972. Secretary of State William P. Rogers is to Nixon's immediate left.

8

PUBLIC AND PRIVATE NEGOTIATIONS

Relations between Peru and the United States remained contentious and complicated for the remainder of 1969. There was little real movement on the main issues, especially the International Petroleum Company (IPC) matter, as the Velasco government adhered to a strong nationalist line and extended its expropriation policies to include other U.S. companies. Internationally, the regime continued to seek to establish new alliances with Asia, the Soviet bloc, and within the hemisphere to counter the weight and influence of the United States. The United States continued to pursue negotiations on the major issues of dispute between the two nations and determined once again not to apply the Hickenlooper sanctions on Peru while at the same time pursuing policies that had nearly the same effect. Meanwhile, behind the scenes, there were developments to indicate that the relationship was not as tense and as confrontational as it might seem on the surface.

A New U.S. Ambassador Arrives

In yet another sign of how different the Peruvian military government was from the norm in Latin America, in mid-July, its reformist actions received the qualified endorsement of Cuban leader Fidel Castro. In his first public comment on the Velasco regime, he described many of its measures, especially the nationalization of IPC and the agrarian reform, as undoubtedly "revolutionary." He promised that "if in Peru a true revolution ensues—and it does not matter who has initiated it—our people will be at the side of that revolution, at the side of the Peruvian people."[1] Two weeks later, in his July 28 address to the nation to commemorate Peruvian independence, General Juan Velasco Alvarado reiterated that his regime indeed was revolutionary and pointed to the same measures mentioned by Castro, agrarian reform and nationalization of the IPC, as the primary accomplishments of his first ten months in power. He also promised more reforms to ensure social justice and to change the status quo in a profound manner, but at the same time, he stressed that his regime was not Marxist but rather "nationalistic." For many, this may have appeared a distinction without much of a difference.[2]

Velasco's disavowal of the regime's "socialist" character was founded on the junta's image of itself and how it viewed its particular character. Indeed, the revolution they were attempting to carry out was in many ways designed to preempt the possibility of a more radical, Castro-style solution to the nation's many problems. However, his remarks might also have been intended to reassure those members of his regime who were anti-Cuban as well as to address some of the concerns of the United States on this score. Nonetheless, while Velasco promised that Peru would not become another Cuba, he and members of his regime were talking about breaking the U.S.-imposed isolation of the communist island and reestablishing relations with the pariah nation. Ministry of Energy and Mines General Jorge Fernández Maldonado, in an interview in Paris, suggested the possibility of such a step provided that the Castro regime promised not "to export its violence" to other countries. As *Oiga* put it, such a step "would imply that Peru is not disposed to follow submissively the line imposed by the U.S. in the OAS and that, instead, to take pride in an action that shows its independence with regard to its international decisions."[3]

Pride, however, was one thing, reality another. While a connection with Cuba might have a certain symbolic significance, normal relations with the United States were still fundamentally important to the regime, no matter how "revolutionary" and "nationalistic." Not only was U.S. private investment and public economic assistance vital to the overall well-being of the Peruvian economy but so, too, was the dominant role the United States played in international lending institutions. If financing from these institutions was not forthcoming, there were few alternative sources on which the regime could draw. Meeting with a high-government official in mid-July to

1. *New York Times*, July 15, 1969, 5.
2. *New York Times*, July 29, 1969, 7.
3. *Oiga*, 7, 336 (August 8, 1969), 9.

discuss the upcoming fisheries conference, Acting Chief of Mission Ernest Siracusa reported being told by him that the "greatest contribution President Nixon could make to improve relations" would be "reopening international credit to Peru." The repeated insistence on this point, Siracusa observed, "is further evidence of [the] degree to which [the] GOP is feeling the pinch."[4]

At about the time of Siracusa's report, the State Department announced that Taylor G. Belcher would be the new U.S. ambassador to Peru. Born in New York in 1920, Belcher had graduated from Brown University in 1941, had managed a coal company for a brief period, and then enrolled in the navy, serving as a lieutenant from 1942 to 1945. At the end of the war, he joined the Foreign Service and steadily worked his way up the ranks. Most of his experience had been in Europe, including a stint as chargé d'affaires in Nicosia and as ambassador to Cyprus in the early 1960s. In Washington, he had worked on Latin American affairs before his nomination to the Lima post.[5]

Once the announcement had been made, Siracusa reported a generally favorable reaction from the Peruvian press to the news, which emphasized the proposed ambassador's Latin American experience.[6] After Belcher had been confirmed by the Senate (August 13) and then sworn in officially as the new ambassador, Fernando Berckemeyer wrote that the envoy seemed to enjoy considerable prestige among his peers given the number of high officials who attended his swearing-in. He noted as well that Belcher had promised to work "indefatigably" to strengthen "the traditionally friendly relations between Peru and the United States."[7] That Belcher would face some daunting challenges in fulfilling that pledge was indicated by an accompanying communication from Berckemeyer, who informed Lima that the original choice to replace Jones, Charles W. Adair, had instead elected to be named ambassador to Uruguay, a choice dictated by "personal reasons" and his desire to serve in a post "surrounded by fewer tensions." At any rate, he added, Belcher was a "functionary of recognized prestige."[8]

Before his confirmation, Belcher had met with Secretary of State William P. Rogers and the desk officer for Peru to discuss current and future policies.

---

4. "Confidential Telegram from Siracusa to State, July 15, 1969," USNA (1967–1969) (Box 2424, Folder 5), 1.

5. U.S. Department of State, *The Biographic Register, July 1970*, 26.

6. "Limited Official Use Telegram from Siracusa, July 14, 1969," USNA (1967–1969) (Box 2424, Folder 5), 1.

7. *Correspondencia* (5–3-A/252) (August 22, 1969), 1.

8. *Correspondencia* (5–3-A/253 [D]) (August 22, 1969), 2. Adair's choice turned out to be rather ironic in that he landed in a country in the throes of a virtual civil war involving the government and the revolutionary urban guerrilla group the Tupamaros. Nonetheless, that he would choose Uruguay over Peru for the reasons Berckemeyer suggested indicates how important and how contentious U.S.-Peruvian relations were at this time.

In Belcher's view, even if the major bilateral problems between the two nations—presumably the IPC compensation matter and the fishing dispute—were resolved, there would continue to be long-term difficulties based on the slowdown of foreign investment, inflation, and the withholding of credits. Rogers agreed but also thought that this might not be an entirely bad thing from the U.S. point of view. It disturbed him, he said, when governments "like the present one in Lima continually use the United States as a whipping boy and scapegoat for its self-created problems." He told Belcher that "we should maintain a firm position with the Government of Peru in order to gain the respect of other Latin American countries." When Belcher pointed out that "our present policy of economic pressure" might allow the current regime to blame us for its domestic troubles, Rogers also agreed but again added that "he was not sure it was a bad idea for it to be known that we have the capability of hurting Peru when it does not conduct its relations with us in accord with international law." Rogers added, however, that he did not think the Hickenlooper amendment, which necessitated "a very heavy-handed approach," was a very "effective tool of U.S. policy."[9] In a conversation with under-secretary for political affairs, U. Alexis Johnson two days later, Belcher heard the same low opinion of the Hickenlooper amendment but also Johnson's prediction that if compensation were not provided to the IPC the application of sanctions was "virtually inevitable," and he instructed Belcher to make the Peruvians aware of this fact.[10]

The following day, July 25, Berckemeyer met at the State Department with an unnamed official to discuss the results of his most recent trip back to Lima. The conversation seemed to promise some breakthrough on the IPC case. The ambassador reported that Velasco was putting the finishing touches on a personal letter to President Nixon in which, reading between the lines, the regime was showing some new flexibility on the matter of compensation and displaying awareness that it was necessary to be "sensible" about the problem. He also relayed the regime's wish that John N. Irwin return to Lima in September to resume negotiations on the matter. The department representative told Berckemeyer that once this wish was made known officially there would be little difficulty in approving the envoy's return, which indeed was announced on August 7.[11]

---

9. "Confidential Memorandum, Department of Sate, July 22, 1969," USNA (1967–1969) (Box 2420, Folder 1), 1.

10. "Confidential Memorandum, Department of State, July 24, 1969," USNA (1967–1969) (Box 2420, Folder 1), 1–2.

11. "Confidential Telegram 124087 from the Department of State to Lima, July 25, 1969," USNA (1967–1969) (Box 2419, Folder 1), 1.

Berckemeyer's visit appeared to promise an improvement in the overall environment between the two nations before Belcher's arrival. Another opportunity seemed to present itself a few days later, on July 30, when the planned four-party talks among Chile, Ecuador, Peru, and the United States over the fishing dispute began in Buenos Aires. At the end of the talks, a joint declaration rather optimistically concluded that as a result of the conversations "the four delegations arrived at a better understanding and appreciation of the points of view of their respective countries" and promised to meet again in Buenos Aires later in the year.[12] Little real progress was made at this meeting as participating South American nations refused to cede any ground on their claim to sovereign rights to the 200-mile limit. As *Oiga* put it, Edgardo Mercado Jarrín's firm insistence on this point signaled "another reverse for the U.S. Department of State's policy."[13]

Further complications soon arose. First, on August 6, President Velasco announced that the IPC had been denied its request for him to reconsider his decision that it should begin to pay off its alleged $690 million debt, leaving the company no other recourse than to submit the matter to the judicial system. Then, on August 22, government officials assumed control of the W. R. Grace paper and chemical complex about two hundred miles north of Lima, claiming that the facility was included in the agrarian reform decree. A spokesman for Grace, the only U.S. property holder affected by the reform with about twenty-five thousand acres in sugar land taken over by the government, protested that its industrial activities were exempt from the law.[14] The following day the government agreed with the company's claim and withdrew its officials from its facility. However, at the same time, it announced that it was taking control of the IPC's Lima headquarters office and its retail outlets and vehicles, presumably because the company had failed to begin to pay off its debts. Just why this move was made three days before the return of the Irwin mission was not entirely clear, but it seemed part of the elaborate chess game with the U.S. government over this issue in which both the Belaúnde and Velasco regimes had been involved for some time.[15]

Against this background, recently arrived Ambassador Belcher met with the Foreign Ministry's chief of protocol and then with Mercado on August 25. As he reported, he was received "cordially" by both, who, along with Belcher, promised to dedicate themselves to maintain "the friendly relations

12. *DOSB*, 61, 1576 (September 8, 1969), 216–17.
13. *Oiga*, 7, 331 (July 11, 1969), 9, 50.
14. *New York Times*, August 23, 1969, 1.
15. *New York Times*, August 24, 1969, 22.

which have traditionally existed between Peru and and [the] U.S." Both officials also spoke of the work of Belcher's predecessors, John Wesley Jones and Siracusa, in "warm and friendly terms." For his part, Mercado took pains to emphasize the immense social problems that afflicted Peru, most notably the widespread poverty, and the efforts of the current regime to address these, "which if successful would preclude a more drastic revolution at a later date." He also repeated previous claims that the IPC case was "exceptional and unique" and that the regime "wanted and needed the friendship of the U.S. and foreign investment which would enjoy fullest guarantees. He said one billion dollars was needed for investment alone."[16]

Despite these conciliatory exchanges and reports of improved relations, Belcher and Irwin had arrived in Peru at a time when nationalist sentiments, often translated into anti-American feelings, seemed to be at a peak. An unexpected string of soccer victories, culminating in a match late in August that ousted Argentina from the South American cup playoffs and guaranteed the Peruvian team a spot, set off a joyous and raucous street demonstration in Lima. Addressing a crowd that had gathered in front of his home, Velasco sought to reap the political benefit from the triumph by claiming that previous administrations had resulted in unsuccessful soccer teams, but under his administration, the Peruvians had produced a victory that "had 'the odor of agrarian reform and petroleum.'" Reporting on the demonstration, the *New York Times* saw the soccer celebration, combined with the recent agrarian reform decree and what appeared to be Peruvian success in confronting the United States over the IPC and fishing matters, as producing "the most intense wave of nationalism in the recent history of Peru." It quoted one Peruvian as saying to an acquaintance from the United States, "We beat you Gringos fair and square, and now we can be friends."[17]

The Peruvian magazine *Caretas* adopted a similar celebratory tone. According to its interpretation, relations between Peru and the United States had now entered a "new stage." The arrival of Belcher and the return of Irwin, it claimed, marked its formal initiation.[18] The leftist *Oiga* agreed. Reporting on Irwin's renewed mission, it claimed that the envoy had more or less given up on the IPC compensation question and was now working to normalize relations so that future foreign investment, especially in the mining sector, would be forthcoming. In that effort, he was undertaking

---

16. "Confidential Telegram from Belcher, August 25, 1969," USNA (1967–1969) (Box 2424, Folder 5), 1.
17. *New York Times*, September 5, 1969, 5.
18. *Caretas*, 19, 401 (August 28–September 11, 1969), 15.

a kind of "charm" offensive, including a willingness to participate in the Andean *huaino* dance at one of the official luncheons he attended. The Nixon administration had still not formulated a clear-cut policy with regard to Latin America but obviously wanted to avoid further confrontations with Peru. It gave much of the credit for this new stage to the firm position of the revolutionary government on the IPC matter and the skillful direction of the nation's foreign policy by General Mercado and urged the regime to continue to pursue these same policies in future dealings with the United States.[19]

Developments Behind the Scenes

Oiga's assessment of Irwin's mission was close to the mark but was not the whole story either. On August 29, in his first meeting with Irwin upon the negotiator's return to Lima, Velasco, in the company of Prime Minister Ernesto Montagne and Mercado, received the envoy warmly and thanked him for "defending Peru's interests" before the U.S. government at critical moments. He also assured Irwin of the regime's commitment to restoring relations with the United States to a "friendly basis" and that his regime "was not communist, as some had charged." He also presented Irwin with a copy of the agrarian reform law and a recording of his July 28 address to the nation.[20]

A little more than a week later, Mercado arranged a party for Irwin attended by Velasco. The Peruvian leader used the occasion to impress on Irwin that the social goals of his government aimed to improve the lot of the nation's people and again emphasized the noncommunist nature of his regime. He also reiterated his and Mercado's own pro-U.S. sentiments and his belief that "the USG would not apply the Hickenlooper Amendment, [and] in fact that he was willing to bet on it." Irwin responded that while his current conversations had been helpful in delineating differences between the two sides nothing had been resolved on the IPC matter or anything else. He agreed that it was unlikely that the Hickenlooper sanctions, with the August deadline for their implementation already passed, would be applied, but that focusing on the amendment missed the point. Until the IPC matter was resolved, the U.S. government would have "great difficulty"

---

19. *Oiga*, 7, 341 (September 12, 1969), 8–9.
20. "Confidential Telegram 6090 from Lima, August 29, 1969," USNA (1967–1969) (Box 2419, Folder 3), 1.

in helping Peru "positively" in terms of providing badly needed economic and financial assistance. As Belcher noted in his report of the meeting, it was not apparent that the Peruvian officials had clearly understood this point—or perhaps had chosen to ignore it.[21] *Oiga*'s assertion notwithstanding, then, Irwin had not abandoned trying to resolve the still outstanding IPC dispute and to ensure that the company received some compensation.

During his conversation with Irwin, Velasco had repeated his appreciation for the medical treatment he had previously received at Walter Reed Hospital in Washington, treatment, he claimed, that had saved his life. A few days earlier, on September 4, Ambassador Fernando Berckemeyer had approached the State Department to inquire whether Mrs. Velasco could also receive treatment for an undisclosed condition at that same hospital. On September 5, the department informed Belcher that such an admission for Mrs. Velasco had been approved, although it was "a rare exception" to the general rules for the use of the hospital and it was an exception that would receive no publicity in the United States.[22] About a month later, Belcher recommended to the State Department that all efforts be made to ensure that Mrs. Velasco not be presented with a bill upon her release from Walter Reed as that would vitiate "a good deal of the benefit which we trust will derive from this gesture" and that the U.S. government cover all costs. If the Department of the Army, which spent a million dollars a year in helping to train the Peruvian military to create "a more effective fighting force but also to make and hold friends within those services," would not agree, Belcher suggested that the State Department use some of its confidential funds for this purpose.[23]

While there is no indication in the State Department files about whether Mrs. Velasco received a bill, the result appeared to be quite beneficial for U.S. interests in Peru. On October 29, Berckemeyer sent a letter to Rogers expressing the Velascos' "warmest appreciation" for the department's assistance in arranging for her recent stay at Walter Reed, where "all members

---

21. "Confidential Telegram 6280 from Lima, September 9, 1969," USNA (1967–1969) (Box 2419, Folder 3), 1–2. While it is not clear just where this party was held, it seems likely that it was in Mercado's home. When I interviewed the former foreign minister, he made it a point to show me a wall that contained the signatures of various distinguished guests, among which was Irwin's. According to Mercado, Irwin had enjoyed himself immensely as his guest, dancing and drinking in a convivial atmosphere and assuring him that the Hickenlooper amendment would not be applied. Interview with Edgardo Mercado Jarrín, Lima (July 18, 2003).

22. "Limited Official Use Telegram 150047 from Department of State to Lima, September 5, 1969," USNA (1967–1969) (Box 2419, Folder 3), 1.

23. "Confidential Telegram 6278 from Lima, October 1, 1969," USNA (1967–1969) (Box 2419, Folder 3), 1–2.

of the staff . . . were most kind and attentive and did everything possible to make Mrs. Velasco comfortable."[24] Whatever the public difficulties between Peru and the United States, and Velasco's frequent use of anti-American sentiment to burnish his nationalist credentials, on a personal level, as he often reiterated in private conversations, the regime's revolutionary leader had a much different and much more sympathetic attitude toward the "Colossus of the North."

Mercado in the United States and Belcher in Lima

Foreign Minister Mercado made his first official visit to the United States in September. He presented a major address to the United Nations General Assembly on September 19 and took the occasion to meet with Rogers and Charles Meyer. In his UN address, Mercado repeated many of the themes that he and Velasco had been emphasizing since they took power. There were, he said, major inequalities and injustices in Peru, which the revolutionary and nationalist new government was committed to erasing. This experiment, he argued, was unique and "completely differs from the models, patterns, and schemes of the past." It was a Peruvian approach to Peruvian problems. He also strongly defended the agrarian reform as integral to the process of bringing greater social justice to the nation and laid out the main points of Peru's "independent" foreign policy and its position on global issues such as world peace and security, international cooperation, and respect for human rights.[25]

After his return from the United States, Mercado met with Belcher to discuss his conversations with Secretary Rogers in New York. From Mercado's point of view, these had not been very satisfactory. While he expressed his appreciation for the time the secretary had given him, he regretted that the sole topic of conversation had been the IPC matter, which Rogers seemed to see as the "central factor" in U.S.-Peruvian relations. Belcher then observed that the secretary of state's concerns about the IPC "undoubtedly" were a reflection of similar concerns of the State Department, the Congress, and financial interests in the United States. Clearly, whatever the Peruvian press and the Velasco regime might say to the contrary, in the eyes of the Nixon administration, the IPC matter was still far from resolved.

---

24. "Berckemeyer to Rogers, October 29, 1969," USNA (1967–1969) (Box 2419, Folder 3).
25. For excerpts from the speech and an interview with Mercado before his departure to New York, see *Oiga*, 7, 342 (September 19, 1969), 8–11, 40.

While the IPC dispute retained its primacy, there were other related issues pending. One had to do with government efforts to nationalize the holdings of the International Telephone and Telegraph Company in Peru and the other involved providing compensation for the properties taken from the W. R. Grace Company. Belcher urged Mercado to influence the regime to move to a favorable resolution on these two matters to show that it was not unremittingly hostile to foreign investment and to give evidence that the IPC matter "was indeed a special case." In a closing comment, Belcher observed that "throughout [the] meeting Mercado could not have been more cordial. His pleas for understanding and help certainly seemed sincere and I think perhaps reflected a growing conviction that [the] GOP has painted itself into a difficult corner by ill-considered actions in connection [with] certain aspects [of the] IPC case. Incidentally, he again made [a] plea for IPC recurrence to courts, to which I have given him no encouragement."[26]

Not long after he met with Mercado, Belcher sent a secret telegram to Washington laying out what he saw as the current situation regarding the Velasco regime and its future prospects. He repeated the common view that the military government seemed caught in a contradictory bind of pursuing nationalistic policies on the one hand while trying to attract foreign investment on the other, leading at the moment to "economic depression," with little likelihood of immediate improvement and possible increased social agitation. On the domestic front, the regime's allies remained firm. These included the Prado interests, for whom the influential Alberto Ruiz Eldridge was a legal advisor, and the Miro Quesada family and others involved in urban real estate. Domestic industrialists, whose interests were benefiting directly from Velasco's policies, also generally favored the regime as did nouveau riche promoters. The general public also saw the government as less corrupt than many of its predecessors. Even with some of the contradictions and economic difficulties, the ambassador argued, the regime seemed fairly well established, and there was little likelihood of any dramatic changes in its hold on power in the immediate future. If such change were to occur, he speculated, it would come from within the military and result in a more extreme junta of a leftist or rightist persuasion, depending on which faction prevailed.

With regard to the future of U.S.-Peruvian relations, the ambassador was hopeful that "needless conflicts . . . will be avoided." However, this would be difficult if further nationalizations without compensation were to occur.

---

26. "Confidential Telegram 6764 from Belcher, October 3, 1969," USNA (1967–1969) (Box 2420, Folder 1), 1.

Also, he and the embassy staff "were not sanguine" about any quick resolution of the IPC matter or the fisheries question. "In short," he concluded, "we feel that [the military government] is beginning to learn to live with contradictions inherent [in] its policies. We hope it will be possible for US policies to be sufficiently flexible to permit our accommodations to them also."[27]

Some Signs of Accommodation

Not long after Belcher sent his secret telegram, there were signs of some flexibility and accommodation, at least on the Peruvian side. In early August, Under-Secretary Alexis Johnson had sent a telegram to Lima expressing the State Department's concern that the regime might be planning nationalist moves against U.S. mining interests along the lines of its actions against the IPC. Such actions, he noted, "could have serious adverse effects not only on U.S. investors but also on overall U.S.-Peruvian relations."[28] In his speech at the United Nations, however, Mercado reassured investors in this sector, both present and potential, that their presence in Peru was more than welcome as long as they operated within the laws of the country. Referring to the great mineral wealth of Peru, he claimed that "in the mining sector, we offer to investors possibilities that are without doubt the most important that they could hope to find."[29] Later, Belcher noted that the government was "exerting [the] strongest possible pressures on US mining companies to make multi-million dollar investments."[30] Ambassador Berckemeyer complemented these efforts in early October with an invited address to representatives of U.S. mining interests in New York, emphasizing once again the "uniqueness" of the action against IPC and claiming that the Peruvians welcomed foreign investment in all sectors. There were some in the audience, however, who expressed concerns that the terms of concessions in Peru were not yet clearly spelled out. There was also a general unease over actions taken by the Frei government in Chile to exert greater national control over the U.S.-dominated copper mining industry, something that was seen to have connections with actions by the Velasco regime.[31]

---

27. "Secret Telegram 6794 from Belcher, October 4, 1969," USNA (1967–1969) (Box 2419, Folder 3), 1–5.
28. "Limited Official Use Telegram from Johnson to Lima, August 5, 1969," USNA (1967–1969) (Box 2424, Folder 5), 1.
29. República del Perú, Ministerio de Relaciones Exteriores, *El Perú y su política exterior*, 94.
30. "Secret Telegram 6794 from Belcher, October 4, 1969," USNA (1967–1969) (Box 2419, Folder 3), 3.
31. *New York Times*, October 4, 1969, 49, 53. The Peruvian embassy in Washington forwarded to Lima a copy of Berckemeyer's speech that appeared in a trade publication, the *American Metal Market*, on October 6. *Correspondencia* (5-3-A/327) (October 7, 1969).

In Lima, Velasco tried to reassure foreign investors. In his address to the nation on October 3 to commemorate the first year of the regime, he reiterated that both domestic and foreign investments were more than welcome and would receive certain guarantees as long as they operated within the established legal framework. The conditions existed, he claimed, for all to invest in Peru "with confidence."[32] Two days later, in a sign that Washington was loosening some of the screws on credit to Peru, Finance Minister Francisco Morales Bermúdez announced a new agreement with the Inter-American Development Bank for project funding and a standby agreement with the International Monetary Fund to help maintain an equilibrium in its balance of payments.[33]

By the end of the month, after extensive negotiations, the government also came to agreements with two major U.S. investors. First, in late October, the government and the IT&T issued a joint statement laying out the details of a new accord, whereby the government would assume greater control of the company's assets and operations in return for "fair and just value" for the company's equity. IT&T would continue to perform services, including parts manufacturing, in a joint venture. As part of the compensation package, the company was given some prime land downtown to construct a modern Sheraton Hotel (the hotel chain was a subsidiary of IT&T) to be designed by a Peruvian architect, a project that was completed in 1973. Both sides seemed to agree that the arrangement was mutually beneficial.[34]

The second agreement was more complex and more controversial. At about the time the IT&T accord was announced, the government also reported that negotiations with the U.S.-owned Southern Peru Copper Corporation to expand its operations at the Cuajone mining complex were nearing completion. The final agreement, announced in late December, seemed to guarantee a future investment by the company of between $355 million and $550 million. Later, in paid advertisements in the *New York Times*, the government hailed this agreement as "one of the greatest investments ever made in the world by a single corporation . . . [and proof that] to invest money in Peru does not mean taking a risk . . . [and] between the [*sic*] foreign capital and the nationalist way of the Peruvian revolution an understanding is possible."[35]

32. Pease García and Verme Insúa, *Perú, 1968–1973*, 1:111.
33. Ibid., 113.
34. Goodsell, *American Corporations and Peruvian Politics*, 151.
35. Ibid., 159; and *New York Times*, March 22, 1970, sect. E, 4. For more on these negotiations, see Goodsell, *American Corporations and Peruvian Politics*, 152–59, and Ingram, *Expropriation of U.S. Property in South America*, 72–74.

Reaction to this agreement was mixed. While the government trumpeted it as a major accomplishment, leftist critics claimed that it was a measure "applauded on the right" and one that posed the danger of "privileged" control of Peru's most valuable resource by a North American monopoly.[36] This was a concern apparently shared privately by elements within the regime.[37] From the viewpoint of U.S. interests, the "sharp contrast" between the current strategy of the Velasco regime to negotiate differences and the more radical measures against IPC and W. R. Grace earlier was a welcome development. There were, however, continued matters of concern. In September, for example, the government told all foreign mining companies that they had to submit detailed plans for the development of unworked concessions or face losing them. While the companies filed more than nine hundred such plans, most were declared inadequate and their concessions lapsed without compensation. Among the losers were multinational giants Anaconda, Cerro, and even Southern Peru. Moreover, the fanfare over the Cuajone contract notwithstanding, Southern Peru found it very difficult to find financing for its commitment and little actual expansion of its Cuajone operation occurred over the next few years.[38]

The basis for much of the shift in regime tactics on investment matters at this time stemmed from a poor economic performance. Unemployment had increased by 34 percent over the previous year, and the country was stalled in a recession. Underscoring Velasco's concern with this matter, he addressed a meeting of Peruvian businessmen late in October and reiterated once again that the regime was "not going to establish a Communist society" and called on the "patriotic and loyal cooperation of the business sector" in the government's efforts both to change Peru and to cope with the current economic crisis.[39]

Privately, Velasco met on October 30 with Belcher to push his case. The successful resolution of the IT&T and Cuajone matters, he asserted, represented a "turning point for the revolution." He hoped these agreements would dispel certain "misunderstandings" between Peru and the United States and show that the IPC matter indeed was a "special case arising out of very special circumstances and did not represent [a] pattern for [the] future." He said, too, that early conclusion of contracts with Anaconda and the Northern Peru Copper Company would provide further evidence that U.S. firms could do business with the new regime. He also told Belcher that

36. Pease García and Verme Insúa, *Perú, 1968–1973*, 1:117–18.
37. Ingram, *Expropriation of U.S. Property in South America*, 73.
38. Goodsell, *American Corporations and Peruvian Politics*, 157–59.
39. *New York Times*, October 30, 1969, 4.

leftist claims that these contracts represented "sell-outs" should be expected but, he implied, also ignored. Finally, he expressed his hope that in light of these positive developments on other fronts, the IPC matter could now be put to rest. Belcher responded that while he and the United States applauded the regime's recent efforts at accommodation, the IPC matter "was still a question affected by U.S. law, and we could not just put it to one side." This disappointing response notwithstanding, Velasco closed the discussion with renewed "hope that [the] new climate produced by many agreements would be reflected in USG attitudes."[40]

The Rumor Mill

While the Peruvian government was engaged in various negotiations with U.S.-based multinationals and worked to keep its relations with the Nixon administration on as even a keel as possible, there were new reports in the press and elsewhere that the CIA was working to destabilize the regime. Earlier in the year, Mercado was called to an urgent cabinet meeting to discuss reports that there was a plot emanating from the U.S. embassy to assassinate Velasco while he was traveling from his home to the presidential palace on the Paseo de la República, popularly known as the *Zanjón*, or Big Ditch. Allegedly involved were Deputy Chief of Mission Ernest Siracusa and political officer Frank Ortiz, both reported to have connections with the CIA.[41] Mercado, for his part, did not place much credence in the report, believing that it was a maneuver by certain (unnamed by him) elements on the left to provoke further confrontations and a break with the United States. He contacted Ambassador Jones about the matter and then delayed any action until the whole incident blew over.[42]

Perhaps of more substance was the ongoing matter of U.S. businessman William D. Chappers and his Plant Protection company. On October 17,

---

40. "Confidential Telegram 7310 from Lima, October 31, 1969," USNA (1967–1969) (Box 2419, Folder 3), 1–3.

41. Journalist Augusto Zimmerman, for example, said that the Velasco regime considered Frank Ortiz "as a politically active diplomat, very well versed on national affairs, and suspected of belonging to the Central Intelligence Agency." Zimmermann Zavala, *El Plan Inca*, 220. Late in the year, reporting on an attempted coup in Chile against the Frei government, *Oiga* claimed that Siracusa, now U.S. ambassador in Bolivia, was "head of the C. I. A. in Latin America." *Oiga*, 7, 354 (December 12, 1969), 22–24. In his memoirs, published in 2005, Ortiz described the charges against him as totally unfounded and labeled them "a bizarre accusation." Ortiz, *Ambassador Ortiz*, 95–104.

42. Interview with General Edgardo Mercado Jarrín, Lima, July 18, 2003. There is no mention of this matter in the State Department records.

the Peruvian police arrested Chappers on his return from a vacation in the United States, following up on their earlier raid of his company offices. Chappers was held incommunicado, with no U.S. embassy official able to speak with him; according to a government spokesman, the investigation into his activities involved "national security." Chappers's Peruvian-born wife identified her husband as a former agent of the U.S. Federal Bureau of Investigation but denied that he had anything to do with the CIA.[43] *Oiga*, however, suggested that Plant Protection was connected to the CIA and had worked closely with the Apristas and others to foment labor unrest. It reported that the investigating officers had located at the company's headquarters secret files on more than fifty thousand Peruvians "at all levels, not only with information as to their religious and political beliefs, but also of their 'human weaknesses,' of which the organization could take advantage in pursuing its activities." It compared the company and its operations in Peru with other U.S.-sponsored intelligence-gathering and destabilizing efforts such as the failed Project Camelot in Chile.[44]

Whatever the truth of these rumors and speculations, they served as a further indication, if any was needed, of the complicated environment in which Peruvian and U.S. officials operated. In general terms, of course, there was nothing unique to Peru about this. Many of the same dynamics operated in the rest of Latin America, including neighbors such as Bolivia and Chile where the role—or alleged role—of the CIA in the internal affairs of those nations was a constant theme of discussion and preoccupation. Again, what seemed to set the Peruvian case apart from many others was the speculation that the CIA might be trying to undermine a military regime when the general trend was for the United States and its agencies to provide such regimes with support and encouragement.

Berckemeyer's Actions

In Washington, Berckemeyer and his staff continued to be active participants in Mercado's larger strategy in dealing with the United States. In late August, the ambassador optimistically reported that the embassy's efforts had played a role in producing a decidedly favorable shift in U.S. press coverage

---

43. *New York Times*, November 2, 1969, 22.
44. *Oiga*, 7, 347 (October 24, 1969), 9–10. Again, there was no mention that I could find of these matters in the official State Department records. Given that Chappers was a U.S. citizen being detained by a foreign government and that his case had received some international press coverage, such an omission does seem peculiar.

of developments in Peru. He noted the generally positive reception to the agrarian reform program and the renewed efforts to settle the IPC issue through the Irwin negotiations. The Hickenlooper amendment, he observed, was now hardly mentioned.[45] The work of the government and the embassy to restore investor confidence in Peru also seemed to be bearing some fruit. He pointed as evidence of this to recent articles in the *Wall Street Journal*, "which have been very favorable to our cause and disseminated with approval within the economic and financial circles of the U.S."[46] Also important in this regard was the previously mentioned address by Berckemeyer to U.S. mining officials in New York in early October.

In late October, Berckemeyer was able to report that since the Pelly amendment was in abeyance a Peruvian army purchase from the Pentagon of twenty-six trucks for carrying water had been approved and should be delivered soon. At the same time, however, he notified Lima that there was evidence that the Chilean military was in the process of acquiring equipment from both the United States and Europe that would "constitute a rupture of the equilibrium in Latin America and promote an arms race in the region." In light of this information, he had instructed the air, naval, and air force attachés of the embassy to express "discretely but firmly" to their contacts at the Pentagon the danger that these Chilean purchases posed to hemispheric stability. For his own part, he would continue to work with Congress and the State Department to inform them of the possible serious repercussions for Latin America of the Chilean arms purchases.[47]

While Berckemeyer's communication on this issue stressed the implications for Latin America in general, it was clear that a strengthening of the Chilean military that would alter the balance in the region would have special implications for Peru, given their shared border and long-standing rivalries and suspicions. Therefore, while President Eduardo Frei's foreign minister, Gabriel Valdés, had publicly stated his nation's "solidarity" with the Peruvians on such matters as the nationalization of the IPC and the establishment of a 200-mile limit for fishing, more traditional geostrategic concerns lay not too far under the surface. The same could be said with regard to Peru's relations with its northern neighbor Ecuador, a participant, along with Chile, in the ongoing four-party talks over fishing rights.

In terms of how the embassy reported to Lima, there was fundamentally

---

45. On August 14, Berckemeyer forwarded an article from the *Washington Evening Star* that claimed the Hickenlooper amendment was "dead" and "destined for the diplomatic garbage dump" and at best a "paper tiger." *Correspondencia* (5–3-A/244) (August 14, 1969), 1.

46. *Correspondencia* (5–3-Y/42) (August 29, 1969), 2–3.

47. *Correspondencia* (5–3-Y/57) (December 4, 1969), 1.

little difference in the items forwarded. However, beginning in late July and as a result of Mercado's efforts to reorganize the Foreign Ministry, Berckemeyer was asked to provide a detailed weekly summary of developments in the United States, both with regard to domestic and foreign affairs. Given the complexity of summarizing the week's events, these reports often reached twenty pages in length and covered a wide variety of matters, ranging from observations on possible Democratic challengers to Nixon in 1972 to the administration's failure to secure approval for the Supreme Court nomination of Clement Haynsworth, "the first major defeat for the administration in Congress," to the mounting intensity of the domestic opposition to the Vietnam War.[48]

At the end of the year, Berckemeyer sent to Lima copies of articles by José Yglesias in the *New York Times* and John M. Goshko in the *Washington Post* on the particular nature of the military government in Peru.[49] Both were generally positive and underscored the unique nature of a reformist military seeking to bring about fundamental change in a Latin American country. Goshko saw the major internal struggle within the regime as between "moderates" and "hard-liners," with the former in the ascendancy. If the internal situation were to deteriorate, however, in his view, it seemed likely that the more radical elements would come to the fore and that would mean new attacks on U.S. interests and further complications in the relationship. Berckemeyer described the articles as on the whole balanced and objective and said that they indicated the interest that the Peruvian experiment had aroused not only in Latin America but also in the United States. He thought the most important message that came through in them was the emphasis on the special nature of the Peruvian Revolution, which had "placed our nation in a situation of pre-eminence in Latin America."[50]

A Mixed Picture

In early November, Berckemeyer had sent to the Foreign Ministry a clipping from *BusinessWeek*, a publication he described as "an influential weekly." The article in question suggested that the Nixon administration was encouraged that some of Latin America's "hot spots," most notably Bolivia

---

48. *Correspondencia* (5-3-A/260) (August 25, 1969), 3; (5-3-A/372), 1–8; and (5-3-A/379) (November 26, 1969), 1–3.
49. Yglesias, "Report from Peru," 56+. Goshko's articles were inserted into the *Congressional Record* on December 18, 1969 (40074–81), by Senator Frank Church.
50. *Correspondencia* (5-3-A/395) (December 19, 1969), 5–6.

and Peru, were beginning to "cool off." This upbeat assessment merited a special red-pencil notation by the ministry.[51]

Not all the signs, however, were rosy. An article in *Caretas* at about the same time underscored the many challenges facing Foreign Minister Mercado and the regime, including the still pending matter of the IPC compensation. With regard to the Nixon administration, "it appeared to be smiling on the one hand and applying pressures on the other. Given the phenomenal economic weight of this country, the conflict [over the IPC] will have clear consequences for our economy." In the face of these challenges, it urged Mercado to intensify his efforts to pursue further economic integration with the Andean Pact nations.[52]

From the U.S. point of view, in addition to concerns over nationalizations and the fishing dispute, there was a persistent preoccupation with Peru's newly established relationship with the Soviet Union. Some of these concerns had been assuaged when Javier Pérez de Cuellar was named as Peru's ambassador to Moscow in March. At the time of the appointment, then-ambassador Jones informed Washington that the new envoy was "sufficiently sophisticated to understand that Soviet policy toward Peru will be motivated entirely by self-interest" and would at the same time recognize the need "to continue traditional cooperation with us." From the U.S. standpoint, he concluded, "he is an excellent choice to represent Peru initially in the USSR."[53]

When the appointment was announced, the Soviets still seemed to be taking the measure of the Velasco regime, probably because of a combination of its unique nature and wariness about acquiring what might be another dependent client state like Cuba. As one Soviet official informed the U.S. embassy in Moscow in March, the USSR "will not under any circumstances buy Peruvian sugar."[54] By midyear, however, some of the caution was gone. The Soviets responded favorably to the agrarian reform law, and there were reports that Velasco and Mercado had been invited to make an official visit to the USSR. If accepted, this would be the first such visit from any Latin American head of state (except Fidel Castro) to the Soviet Union.[55]

---

51. *Correspondencia* (5–3/A/355) (November 7, 1969), 1.
52. *Caretas*, 19, 405 (October 27—November 7, 1969), 10–11.
53. "Confidential Telegram from Jones, April 30, 1969," USNA (1967–1969) (Box 2425, Folder 1), 1–2.
54. "Limited Official Use Telegram from Moscow, March 11, 1969," USNA (1967–1969) (Box 2425, Folder 1), 1–2.
55. "Limited Official Use Airgram A-781 from Moscow, July 10, 1969," 1; and "Secret Intelligence Note 536, July 16, 1969 to the Secretary of State," 1, USNA (1967–1969) (Box 2425, Folder 1).

In October, a Soviet publication was effusive in its praise for the Peruvian experiment as a model for the rest of Latin America to follow.[56] The enthusiasm was tempered somewhat, however, when later in the year, the official press organ TASS reported on the arrangement worked out with the Southern Peru Copper Company and the regime's attempts to entice foreign investment. Such "apparent backsliding," the U.S. embassy reported, "will not go unnoticed, and could form the basis for future Soviet criticism."[57]

By the end of 1969, relations between the United States and Peru remained in flux. During a visit to the southern city of Arequipa on December 20, Mercado had claimed that relations between the two nations "had notably improved" since the deterioration caused by the IPC nationalization and the fishing-boat seizures. As evidence, he pointed out that the Hickenlooper and Pelly sanctions had not been applied. That indeed was the case as the deadline for the Hickenlooper sanction application had passed in August with no fanfare and no announcement, and the Pelly amendment had become pretty much a dead letter as the four-party talks on the 200-mile limit proceeded. The Sword of Damocles, while not totally lifted, did not seem as close to falling as it had earlier in the year.

Despite these optimistic remarks, there was much that remained to be resolved. As the U.S. embassy noted when commenting on Mercado's statements, the foreign minister was "one of the leading moderates" in the regime and "increasingly has become identified with this line." Therefore, his "statements, encouraging as they may be, probably should be interpreted more as [a] reflection of [the] views of moderate elements than as [an] indication of [the] prevailing attitude across the board."[58] As Goshko had reported, the struggle between moderates and hard-liners for the heart of President Velasco and control of the regime continued, with considerable implications for the U.S. position in Peru. Just how this struggle would be resolved remained to be seen.

---

56. "Limited Official Use Airgram A-1303 from Moscow, October 23, 1969," USNA (1967–1969) (Box 2425, Folder 1), 2.

57. "Limited Official Use Airgram A-1601 from Moscow, n.d.," USNA (1967–1969) (Box 2425, Folder 1), 1.

58. "Limited Official Use Airgram A-480 from Lima, December 31, 1969," USNA (1967–1969) (Box 2424, Folder 5), 1.

9

CONTINUITY AND SOME CHANGE

Over the next two years, there were few fundamental changes in the Peruvian-U.S. relationship. The same problems involving the regime's nationalistic stance on the International Petroleum Company (IPC) and other companies along with the 200-mile-limit dispute persisted without any major breakthroughs. The Nixon administration still seemed somewhat puzzled by the behavior of the Velasco government and often appeared somewhat unsure about how to respond to the various twists and turns that it took. An opportunity to improve relations occurred in early June 1970 when a serious earthquake hit the Andean highlands. The United States responded immediately with assistance, and First Lady Patricia Nixon personally visited the affected area. The good will generated by this humanitarian effort did much to improve the overall image of the United States in the eyes of most Peruvians. However, it did little to alter the course of relations or to defuse the most controversial issues over which they clashed. The election of Marxist Salvador Allende to the presidency in neighboring Chile in 1970 also sent shockwaves through the hemisphere and had significant implications for U.S. policy in the region. The Peruvian leadership did its best to take advantage of the opportunity this election presented to position itself as an acceptable reformist alternative while still pursuing a basically independent foreign policy that saw it continue to establish relations with nations often at odds with the United States.

Little Change in the Status Quo

Ambassador Taylor Belcher's first reports from Lima at the beginning of 1970 provided scant room for optimism that major disputes would be resolved anytime soon. He saw little movement on these issues, and while moderates seemed to prevail within the regime for the moment, he expressed concerns that a U.S. hard line could strengthen the hand of the radicals. He suggested a reconsideration of the policy of "non-overt financial pressures," a policy that could backfire if it played to the regime's nationalism, and instead recommended a policy that would provide greater flexibility and allow the United States to respond to developments in Peru on an ad hoc basis as circumstances dictated.[1] In a subsequent communication, he urged the State Department to do all it could to dissuade U.S. fishing vessels from operating in Peru's claimed territorial waters to avoid further complications and opportunities to stoke Peruvian nationalism.[2]

Apparently taking his cue from Belcher's reports, Secretary of State William P. Rogers forwarded a confidential memorandum to President Nixon on January 16 concerning the current state of U.S. policy toward Peru. In essence, he recommended that the administration adopt the flexible "wait and see" approach the ambassador had suggested. This meant, for the moment, deferring any application of the Hickenlooper amendment for the next few months but also "maintaining non-overt economic pressures." These policies could change, of course, depending on future developments. If the Hickenlooper provisions were applied, Rogers advocated reactivating the Irwin mission as a way to defer nationalist reaction. He also expressed concerns about the current plans for U.S. mining companies to sign contracts with the Peruvian government, making such investments, as with the petroleum sector, susceptible to nationalist pressures and creating "the potential for another Hickenlooper situation down the road."[3]

Belcher's warnings notwithstanding, at the end of February, Peru apprehended and fined another U.S. tuna vessel operating off its coast. The seizure, along with a similar action by Ecuador, led to the usual reaction from Congressman Pelly, who, in this instance, proposed a rider to the next foreign aid bill that would withhold funds for State Department salaries until

---

1. "Confidential Limited Distribution Telegram 26 from Belcher to Meyer, January 2, 1970," USNA (1970–1973) (Box 2544, Folder 5), 1–3.
2. "Confidential Telegram 258 from Belcher, January 16, 1970," USNA (1970–1973) (Box 2543, Folder 7), 1–3.
3. "Confidential Memorandum from Rogers to Nixon, January 16, 1970," USNA (1970–1973) (Box 2544, Folder 5), 1–2.

the department upheld the provision that deducted "the amounts of these illegal fines."[4]

The Peruvian embassy in Washington kept Lima abreast of Pelly's actions. On March 6, chargé Luis Marchand forwarded copies of the *Congressional Record* that included the congressman's speeches on the subject. He stated that Pelly was a primary political spokesman for the fishing interests and was seeking "to stir the waters with the winds of his showy interventions" to appeal to and rally support from the conservative and reactionary sectors of North American opinion. According to Marchand's interpretation, Pelly had been frustrated by the lack of progress at the Buenos Aires conference and by the firm stance taken by the Peruvians in defense of their national interests. He suggested that an upcoming visit to Lima by Assistant Secretary Charles Meyer would allow the Foreign Ministry, in the person of Edgardo Mercado Jarrín, to discuss the fishing problem in a clear and frank manner and to seek a solution to "problems that distant and particular interests often distort." He also indicated his belief that State Department officials were trying to avoid the hard line on this matter and seek a more flexible approach. He concluded that Mercado's personal relationship with Meyer should be helpful.[5]

In his lengthy review of the embassy's activities for 1969, Ambassador Fernando Berckemeyer made many of these same points. He also gave Chile some credit for acting as a useful intermediary in the negotiations and, like Marchand, saw the State Department as trying to avoid a hard line on this issue. The department, he concluded, "is apparently inclined to maintain a constant dialogue on pragmatic and reciprocally flexible bases that will lead to a satisfactory solution to the problem, which will permit it to reject the local demands of a radical nature."[6] Whether such optimism was justified, of course, would have to be confirmed by future developments. At the time of the evaluation, however, it did not seem off the mark.

Assistant Secretary Meyer made his first visit to Peru in mid-March. Upon his arrival, he asserted that Peru and the United States were "natural partners," that the various punitive amendments were of little value, and that he was coming to Lima "to learn." Upon his departure, he stated that relations between the two nations were at a "high level." It did not seem, however, that his stay had produced any of the breakthroughs that Marchand had predicted. The weekly *Unidad* claimed that the Meyer visit was only a

4. *Congressional Record—House* (March 2, 1970), 5, 463.
5. *Correspondencia* (5–3-Y/6) (March 6, 1970), 9–10.
6. *Correspondencia* (5–3-Y/7) (April 10, 1970), 2–6.

prelude to some unnamed "new aggression against Latin America."⁷ *Oiga* stated that little had changed or been accomplished during the visit and that Mercado had underscored Peru's "unbreakable" (*inquebrantable*) position with regard to the 200-mile-limit issue. Mercado was also cited as saying that, despite Meyer's claim of good relations between the two nations, such an assertion ran contrary to the facts. As he pointed out, "The credits from the international organizations that the United States controls are not forthcoming, nor are investments, and the promises that Nixon has made on preferential tariffs for primary products from Latin America in the North American market have not been realized."⁸

From the perspective of at least one influential U.S. newspaper, however, the Meyer visit was seen more positively. In an article in the March 30 edition of the *New York Times*, Joseph Novitski claimed that there had recently been some significant easing of the tensions between Peru and the United States. These he traced to a shift in the Nixon administration's policy away from confrontation and toward cooperation, in the Peruvian case seen most clearly in the continued postponement of the sanctions of the Hickenlooper amendment. This policy, in turn, was based on points made by President Nixon in a major address on Latin America delivered in Washington on October 31, 1969. In these remarks, he reaffirmed the importance of the region to the United States and his administration's commitment to accommodate to the forces of change, including growing nationalism, in a spirit of partnership and multilateral as opposed to unilateral efforts to achieve improvements. Future actions would emphasize shared responsibility for social and economic development, expanded trade, lifting restrictions on AID assistance, support for regional integration, and easing of debt burdens.⁹ These policies, Novitski wrote, reflected an overall commitment for the United States no longer to be "an overwhelming presence in the Western Hemisphere." Meyer's recent visit to Lima, he speculated, "must have reinforced this impression," given that Velasco, following his meeting with the assistant secretary, had declared himself "satisfied with relations between the United States and Peru." Moreover, it now appeared that the Nixon administration was more willing to accept certain kinds of regimes, ranging from the repressive military dictatorship in Brazil to the possibility of a socialist president in Chile to the now apparently left-leaning nationalist regime of Peru, than might have been the case with previous administrations.¹⁰

---

7. Pease García and Verme Insúa, *Perú, 1968–1973*, 1:153.
8. *Oiga*, 8, 366 (March 20, 1970), 36. The cover of this edition features Meyer in silhouette.
9. *DOSB*, 61, 1586 (November 17, 1969), 409.
10. *New York Times*, March 26, 1970, 8.

The situation behind the scenes was more complex. On April 1, Meyer spoke with IPC president James Dean concerning his recent discussions with Velasco and Mercado during his visit to Lima. Meyer reported that these discussions were "frank" and did not evoke "an emotional reaction" as he tried to clarify the administration's position on compensation. The message he delivered, he told Dean, was that the lack of a resolution of this matter was "a primary obstacle to improving bilateral relations and increasing the flow of foreign capital to Peru," indicating that the United States was somewhat less accommodating to the "new realities" in that nation than the Novitski article suggested. For his part, Dean left Meyer with the company's annual report and its assessment of the book value of its holdings in Peru along with a calculation of recent losses due to the Velasco regime's actions. He also informed Meyer that his sources in Peru had informed him that the regime was preparing a new set of regulations for petroleum investment and operation that would be "much less attractive to foreign investors than previous codes."[11]

Trying to Clarify the Course of the Revolution

What appeared to be more bad news for foreign investors in Peru came a few days later. Addressing the Latin American Congress of Industrialists meeting in Lima, Velasco underscored the importance of diversified economies and diversified industrialization as major tools to address the problems of "under-development and dependency" in Latin America. Referring specifically to Peru, he then suggested new rules and regulations for foreign investment, arguing that while companies' rights, including the rights to fair profits, had to be respected, so too must the interests and rights of the host nations. Once a certain level of profit had been achieved, he argued, such investments should revert to the state. The solution to Peru's many problems had to be found through measures that were based primarily on the nation's realities, drawing on but not blindly imitating ideas and methods created elsewhere. Quoting the nation's best-known Marxist thinker, José Carlos Mariátegui, he concluded that such solutions would begin to emerge when "we Peruvians 'Peruvianize' Peru."[12]

The Peruvian press reaction to the address was almost uniformly enthusiastic. The reaction in the United States, naturally, was much less favorable as stock prices for some major U.S. companies operating in Peru, especially

---

11. "Confidential Telegram 52088 from the Department of State to Lima, April 9, 1970," USNA (1970–1973) (Box 1514, Folder 4), 1–2.

12. Pease García and Verme Insúa, *Perú, 1968–1973*, 1:158–59.

mining companies, immediately fell in response to Velasco's remarks, which seemed to portend future expropriations. Ambassador Berckemeyer tried to calm matters by calling Velasco's observations "casual remarks," a choice of words that got him in some hot water back home, and asserting that Peru "welcomes foreign investment."[13]

Responding to the adverse reaction to Velasco's remarks and U.S. concerns about what appeared to be an increasingly leftward trend, the regime began to take some steps to reassure constituencies at home and abroad about its noncommunist nature and to deny any Marxist influence. On April 15, Energy and Mines Minister Fernández Maldonado, in a public address on the new mining law, underscored the government's guarantee that investors could "recuperate their capital" from their enterprises in Peru. Five days later, the interior minister, General Armando Artolo, in a press conference denied emphatically that there existed "communist infiltration" in the government. The following day, in an address to some one thousand former soldiers who had returned to civilian life, Velasco affirmed that the regime would support "organizations that support the revolution," which was interpreted as government backing for the Committees for the Defense of the Revolution, organizations that seemed to be similar to those that existed in Cuba.[14] Ambassador Belcher saw this as a positive development in that Velasco was making clear that the government would exercise control over these committees and not allow the Communist Party of Peru to do so.[15]

Somewhat less reassuring were remarks the following day by Minister of the Economy Morales Bermúdez. Speaking at the tenth anniversary meeting of the Inter-American Development Bank in Punta del Este, Uruguay, he urged greater state control over economies in general and greater regulation of foreign aid and investment to ensure the achievement of national goals. Repeating a familiar theme of the Velasco government, the minister criticized both communist and capitalist economic and political formulas, arguing that neither one would ensure the "economic independence" of Latin American nations. Reporting on the speech, the *New York Times* emphasized that the Peruvian military government's nationalization of U.S. companies and its confrontation with the United States "has captured the imagination of many Latin American military and civilian economists and social thinkers and leaders."[16]

---

13. *Wall Street Journal*, April 8, 1970, 16.
14. Pease García and Verme Insúa, *Perú, 1968–1973*, 1:161–63.
15. "Limited Official Use Telegram 1951 from Belcher to Department of State, April 22, 1970," USNA (1970–1973) (Box 2543, Folder 7), 2.
16. *New York Times*, April 23, 1970, 55.

The apparent growing attractiveness of the Peruvian model for the rest of Latin America could not have been very good news for U.S. policymakers. To alleviate some of these concerns and to defuse the adverse reaction to a new press law that had closed down some antiregime publications, Foreign Minister Mercado took the novel and innovative step of arranging a series of lectures by government officials for the diplomatic corps based in Lima. Inaugurating these meetings at the Torre Tagle Palace on May 11, Mercado spent much of his opening address justifying and reaffirming Peru's position on the 200-mile limit. He also repeated arguments that the Peruvian Revolution was a distinct break from the past, was inspired by a "true nationalism," and aimed for improvements that would create a society based on "liberty and justice."[17]

The second part of this strategy was to use the second annual meeting of Peru's ambassadors in the hemisphere to consider ways to counter "the alleged campaign against Peru."[18] In his closing remarks to this group, Mercado instructed his charges to carry forward a message that Peru was not pretending to be a "model of development" for the rest of Latin America but was embarked on a "revolutionary" course, and the nation's diplomatic representatives should do all they could to counter any "distortions or lies" directed against it.[19]

In a related move, in early June the chairman of the national oil company, Petroperú, and the head of the National Planning Institute traveled to New York to assure U.S. businessmen that Peru welcomed investment, especially in oil and mineral development and light industry. They claimed that the government was "reasonable" and "not blindly dogmatic" and would approach foreign investors in a "business-like fashion" and would stand by all agreements. They also promised that investors could expect "reasonable profits and reasonable repatriation of these profits."[20] Whether this charm offensive was sufficient to produce a major shift in U.S. policy toward the regime, however, was a matter yet to be determined.

The Earthquake and Its Aftermath

Tragic circumstances soon provided an opportunity for an improvement in U.S.-Peruvian relations. On May 31, a massive earthquake with its epicenter

---

17. República del Perú, Ministerio de Relaciones Exteriories, *El Perú y su política exterior*, 205–6.
18. *New York Times*, May 24, 1970, 30.
19. República del Perú, Ministerio de Relaciones Exteriores, *El Perú y su política exterior*, 221. See also *Caretas*, 20, 416 (May 26–June 12, 1970), 13.
20. *New York Times*, June 3, 1970, 68.

in the beautiful Andean valley of the Callejón de Huaylas in the Department of Ancash some 150 miles north of Lima struck with devastating force, setting off avalanches of mud and ice that covered the town of Yungay, taking twenty thousand lives and causing massive destruction throughout the region. The resultant dust made the district invisible from the air for two days. While later estimates would vary, the overall death toll was set at approximately sixty thousand with hundreds of thousands injured and left homeless. Up to that point, it was the greatest known natural disaster in Western Hemisphere history.[21]

Ignoring, for the moment, strains over other issues, the United States responded to the disaster with immediate relief assistance. President Nixon quickly pledged $10 million in a special grant for Peru with more to follow. U.S. military helicopters, in somewhat short supply due to the demands of the Vietnam War, were dispatched to Peru to assist with airlifting of relief supplies, assistance that was especially welcome given the destruction of so many access roads into the area. In Congress, disputes over fishing rights and what many considered the more extreme measures of the Velasco regime were momentarily put aside as various congressmen and senators introduced resolutions officially expressing condolences for the loss of life and property caused by the disaster and applauding U.S. efforts to assist the affected and the Peruvian government's positive response to these efforts.[22]

The strongest signal of U.S. concern was Mrs. Nixon's visit to Peru in late June. Accompanying her were two large jet transport planes loaded with clothing, blankets, and other privately donated goods, along with cash and checks, some of which reportedly came from White House staffers. Before her departure, President Nixon stated that it was better that his wife make the trip rather than he as it implied a more personal as opposed to official concern. Mrs. Nixon said that the disaster had affected her deeply "because that's the type [of] citizen I am." When questioned if she were nervous going on her first foreign trip of this type on her own, she responded that she felt at home "in any part of the world" and viewed foreign travel as "always a pleasure and never a problem." Despite a public impression of shyness, she added, "I am anything but that. I make friends instantly, and have a warm personality."[23]

While not everyone might have agreed with her own assessment of her

---

21. For a detailed analysis of the earthquake and the disaster relief efforts that followed, see Patch, "The Peruvian Earthquake of 1970," 18, 6–9.

22. For example, a resolution along these lines was introduced by Representative Richard T. Hanna, Democrat of California, on June 22. *Congressional Record—House* (June 22, 1970), 20843.

23. *New York Times*, June 29, 1970, 1.

personality, Mrs. Nixon made a uniformly favorable impression in Peru. Touring the hardest-hit areas in the company of Mrs. Velasco, she also established a close personal relationship with the Peruvian first lady that at least on that level seemed to smooth over some of the larger difficulties between the two countries. The contrast between the warm and appreciative reception she received in Lima and elsewhere and that accorded to her husband some thirteen years earlier, albeit under quite different circumstances, could not have been starker.

In addition to official aid and Mrs. Nixon's visit, U.S. companies operating in Peru pitched in generously in the relief effort. The Southern Peru Copper Company and the Cerro Corporation provided equipment to reopen blocked roads; Sears Roebuck (Assistant Secretary Meyer's old company) and other U.S. businesses donated clothing and money; and Braniff Airways ferried relief supplies free of charge from the United States. "Even the International Petroleum Company," President Velasco acknowledged at a press conference, "sent money."[24] Whether these efforts would translate into a softening of the government's nationalist line, of course, would have to await future developments. But, at least for the moment, some of the prevailing tension and anger on both sides seemed to have diminished.

While the United States provided the great bulk of relief aid, other nations also provided assistance. Although they were not the largest donor, the contributions of the Cubans were probably among the most notable. This aid came primarily in the form of medical supplies and volunteer medical personnel to help out in the earthquake zone. It was reported that one shipment of blood had come directly from Fidel Castro and was used in a transfusion for a Peruvian child.[25] Cuban supplies that landed in Lima were mingled with those of other nations and airlifted by U.S. planes to the affected area. As one U.S. Air Force pilot admitted, "Sure we carry Cuban supplies. A lot of it is from the Russians and Red Chinese. But our attitude is when the Peruvians call, we haul."[26] Again, at least for the moment, the magnitude of the Peruvian disaster had even managed to overcome deep-seated Cold War hostilities.

Despite the momentary good will created by the U.S. response to the earthquake, the Velasco regime showed few signs of making fundamental shifts in its basic course of action. On June 22, the *New York Times* reported that the regime was planning dramatic changes in its economic laws dealing with mining, manufacturing, banking, and commerce, calling them "the

24. *New York Times*, June 15, 1970, 14.
25. *New York Times*, June 7, 1970, 31.
26. *New York Times*, June 15, 1970, 14.

most radical measures taken in Latin America since the Castro take-over in Cuba." They would include mandatory profit sharing in all enterprises by workers and eventual nationalization of various foreign-owned enterprises after a yet-to-be-determined period of time. To lessen the blow, and to repeat points made earlier in the month by the regime's representatives in New York, it was also reported that the government was planning to assure foreign investors a reasonable repatriation of profits, and the deadline for turning assets over to the state would be in the range of some fifteen years from the date of the decree.[27]

In late June, Foreign Minister Mercado met with top State Department and White House officials in Washington before the General Assembly meeting of the Organization of American States. In his meeting with Meyer and White House counselor Robert Finch, he thanked the United States for its post-earthquake aid but also pushed hard for further assistance, especially in providing funds for the purchase of helicopters, earth-moving equipment, and transport aircraft. While the meeting was described as "cordial," Mercado also expressed his disappointment that further promises of aid were not forthcoming.[28]

At a meeting with Secretary of State Rogers on June 26, in the company of Berckemeyer and other Peruvian officials, Mercado repeated these requests, especially asking for U.S. help in getting the World Bank to approve emergency relief loans. Rogers promised that the administration would give the problem "very close attention" and do what it could to help. The secretary also conveyed to Mercado that U.S. earthquake support "was not the product of an automatic response by the Government but rather reflected the personal interest and involvement of President Nixon." He cited the appointment of counselor Finch to coordinate the relief effort and Mrs. Nixon's trip to Peru as evidence of this interest. Mercado expressed his appreciation for these efforts but also persisted in pushing for more money to meet the nation's needs following this unprecedented disaster.[29] A few days later, the State Department notified Lima that it had put Mercado in touch with representatives of the Lockheed Aircraft Company regarding the purchase of transport planes but noted that the demands of the Vietnam War made the acquisition of helicopters problematic. The department had also contacted the Caterpillar Tractor Company to investigate the possibility

27. *New York Times*, June 22, 1970, 57.
28. "Limited Official Use Telegram 103011 from Department of State to Lima, June 28, 1970," USNA (1970–1973) (Box 2542, Folder 3), 1–4.
29. "Memorandum of Conversation (Limited Official Use), June 26, 1970," USNA (1970–1973) (Box 2544, Folder 6), 1–2.

of purchasing earth-moving equipment pursuant to the foreign minister's request.[30]

The continued repercussions of the earthquake and the outside assistance provided could be seen in Velasco's July 28 Independence Day address to the nation. He made a special point to thank the various nations that had aided in the relief effort and particularly "the beautiful message of solidarity from the people of the United States that was symbolized by the visit of Mrs. Patricia Nixon." But he also underscored that the revolutionary government would continue to pursue its goals of fundamental change at home and independent foreign policy abroad. He then reviewed what he considered some of the major accomplishments of the regime over the past year and then announced the promulgation of a new industrial law that would ensure greater profits for workers and greater worker control. With regard to foreign companies, the law reiterated earlier promises to guarantee "reasonable" profits but also added that after a certain time they had to sell at least 51 percent of their capital to Peruvian interests. He described this measure as a "truly revolutionary instrument" that would "stimulate the development of a truly dynamic national industrial sector." While the measure did not call for the immediate nationalization of foreign-owned industries, the long-term implications for U.S. interests were clear.[31]

Another issue of concern to the United States was the possibility of closer relations between the Soviet Union and Peru due to earthquake relief efforts. The situation, from the U.S. point of view, seemed mixed. When the earthquake hit, the Soviets had promised sixty-five planeloads of supplies, but logistical problems reduced the number to twenty-one, many of which flew only half full. U.S. officials saw this result as strategically significant in that it underscored problems the Soviets would have to overcome if they were to establish a greater presence on the Pacific Coast of South America. But while the total of goods delivered to Peru might have been less than promised, the closer relationship between the two nations that had begun early in the Velasco regime showed no signs of lessening. On August 25, an agreement was signed in Moscow between the Soviet Deputy Minister for Foreign Trade and Ambassador Pérez de Cuellar to provide Peru with a $30 million credit to purchase Soviet equipment at a low rate of interest and

---

30. "Outgoing Limited Official Use Telegram 105324 from Department of State to Lima, July 2, 1970," USNA (1970–1973) (Box 2542, Folder 3), 1–2.

31. The full text of the speech can be found in Velasco, *La revolución peruana*, 90–126. See also *New York Times*, July 29, 1970, 9.

with the option to pay the ten-year loan off at least in part through the importation of manufactured goods.[32]

At about the same time this agreement was announced, and perhaps not coincidentally, there were some signs that Mercado's efforts in Washington to get emergency funding were beginning to bear fruit. On August 16, the World Bank announced that it would consider a $30 million loan for road construction in the earthquake zone, which was agreed to on September 11.[33] On August 17, Berckemeyer forwarded to Lima the details of a contract he had signed on August 13 with the Inter-American Development Bank for a $23 million loan, and on August 25, it was announced that a contract had been signed between the Peruvian government and the Inter-American Development Bank for another $35 million, earmarked for reconstruction in the areas affected by the earthquake.[34] While these developments might have been due to the special circumstances of the earthquake and in response to Soviet assistance, they nonetheless suggested some loosening of the Nixon administration's policy of denying financial assistance to the Velasco regime. Whether further changes were in store remained to be seen.

Reporting on Domestic Politics and the Election of Allende

From Washington, in an apparent response to the reorganization and reorientation of the foreign service set in motion by Mercado, the Peruvian embassy provided more detailed and comprehensive coverage and reports on developments in the United States than had been previously provided. Considerable attention, naturally, was given to matters of particular interest to Peru, such as debates over coastal limits and fishing rights. Dispatches in the second half of the year also focused on what both Berckemeyer and chargé Marchand perceived to be a weakening U.S. position on the Soviet Union, observations that might well have had an impact on the larger Peruvian foreign policy. On October 26, for example, Marchand sent a detailed report on a recent meeting between Secretary of State Rogers and Soviet Foreign Minister Andrei Gromyko. He observed that for the past twenty-five years the United States had enjoyed a clear military superiority over the Soviets but that "now things have been transformed." Nixon, he wrote,

---

32. *New York Times*, August 26, 1970, 11:1; and Pease García and Verme Insúa, *Perú, 1968–1973*, 1:196.
33. Pease García and Verme Insúa, *Perú, 1968–1973*, 1:193, 1:203.
34. *Correspondencia* (5-3-A/305) (August 17, 1970), 1; and Pease García and Verme Insúa, *Perú, 1968–1973*, 1:195–96.

had assumed office "in a period in which North American military power is declining in relation to growing Soviet military power and the men of the Kremlin are dedicating themselves to exploiting this new situation: They had done so or are beginning to do so in Egypt and Cuba; in sum, all reflects a determination on the part of the Kremlin to improve their position with regard to the United States, for so long the dominant power."[35] At the end of the year, a report from Berckemeyer suggested that the administration's failure to take a more aggressive posture on Soviet naval activities in the Caribbean, or to do much about rumors the Soviets were constructing a submarine base in Cuba in violation of the agreements reached after the missile crisis of 1962, was further evidence of the shift in strategic power.[36]

On the foreign policy front, the most important development as far as Peru was concerned was the election of Salvador Allende as president of Chile and the U.S. response to it. In mid- and late September, Berckemeyer forwarded numerous clippings from various newspapers on the reaction to the election as "evidence of the deep U.S. interest in and concern with the first time a Marxist leader assumes power by democratic means."[37] Several days after Allende was inaugurated, Berckemeyer sent on additional material concerning the U.S. reaction and in a classic understatement reported that the United States found the "spectacle of the installation of a Marxist government in Santiago far from agreeable." Washington's frustration, he noted, was exacerbated because it had so strongly supported the reformist efforts of the Frei regime to little avail. Up to now, he reported, the Nixon administration had remained relatively silent on these developments, perhaps recognizing that the "days of the Monroe Doctrine" and unilateral intervention were over and that Washington's options in this case were limited.[38] Behind the scenes, however, and unbeknown to Berckemeyer and others, the administration was already laying plans to undermine the new Marxist government and to show that in many ways the Monroe Doctrine, at least from the U.S. point of view, was far from dead.

The election of Allende posed possible future complications for Peru. After some initial concerns over perceived Argentine influence in the military coup of October 1968, the Christian Democratic government of Eduardo Frei had established a solid and supportive relationship with its historic rival during the first two years of the Velasco regime. In particular,

---

35. *Correspondencia* (5–3-A/432) (October 26, 1970), 4–5.
36. *Correspondencia* (5–3-A/550) (December 21, 1970), 4.
37. *Correspondencia* (5–3-A/373) (September 21, 1970), 1.
38. *Correspondencia* (5–3-Y/39) (November 9, 1970), 3.

foreign ministers Mercado and Valdés had worked closely and cooperatively together on such matters as the 200-mile-limit issue. Whether that close and mutually supportive relationship would continue under the more radical government of Allende and with his more dogmatic and outspoken foreign minister, Socialist firebrand Clodomiro Almeyda, remained to be seen.

On the surface at least, it would seem that there would be a general coincidence of interests between the Allende and Velasco regimes. The new Chilean government planned to pursue an agenda in areas of agrarian reform, economic nationalism, and social justice that were not far removed from the policies that the Peruvian military regime had put into place, albeit in their case under civilian control, retaining democratic institutions, and excluding the armed forces from any significant participation in the changes implemented. The Peruvian experience could be seen as both a forerunner and a kind of model for what the Allende government might try to do. However, soon after Allende's election, there were some White House officials who argued that the influence might work in the opposite direction. When certain unnamed administration spokesmen speculated that the election in Chile might lead to communist governments in neighboring Argentina, Bolivia, and Peru, diplomats representing those three countries quickly discounted this possibility and attributed such speculation to a lack of understanding of the particular features of each of the nations involved. Soon after the election, Peruvian spokesmen yet again had been quick to reaffirm the noncommunist and indeed anticommunist nature of the military government.[39]

As the Chilean Congress prepared to confirm Allende's victory at the end of October, spokesmen for the Velasco regime followed up these earlier assertions by using the occasion to argue that the measures they had implemented to date had served to prevent the "Marxist solution" that had emerged in their southern neighbor. They hoped that the more radical nature of the Chilean alternative would cause the U.S. government and investors to lessen pressure on Peru and resume assistance and investments. However, they were also concerned that the more extreme measures taken by the Allende government would stimulate the Peruvian left to push for equally radical steps and perhaps awaken an internal threat that had been relatively quiet since the ouster of Belaúnde. On a strategic level, they were also concerned that Allende might seek to pacify the Chilean military by permitting them to purchase more modern equipment, thus touching off an arms race to which Peru would have to respond. They also feared that

39. *New York Times*, September 23, 1970, 13.

events in Chile might have repercussions in Argentina, helping to undermine the military government there, allowing the Chileans then to divert more of their strategic attention northward.[40]

Only time would tell whether all of these calculations and concerns would play out as the Peruvian leaders envisioned. One thing did seem clear at this point, however. The reality of a full-fledged Marxist government in Chile would force the United States to refocus its attention, at least to some extent, away from a preoccupation with Peru and to the more serious threat to its interests from the neighbor to the south. This refocusing could well work to the advantage of the Velasco regime.

New Year Assessments and Initiatives

While the Velasco regime's nationalist moves did not sit well with all Peruvian and foreign investors, the economy in general seemed to be in reasonably good shape at the beginning of 1971. An increase in purchasing power among the top third of the nation's income earners (a third strengthened by the increase in government jobs as a result of various nationalization measures), in part fueled by the forced conversion of dollars into soles, had produced something of a boom in retail sales and "a massive spending spree." The intrusion of the state into the economy was highlighted by the nationalization of the country's second-largest bank, the Banco Popular, as well as the government's purchase of Banco Continental, a branch of Chase Manhattan. Major foreign businesses had mixed reactions to the restrictive measures put in place by the regime with General Motors and Ford announcing plans to cease their operations in Peru despite increasing sales while Chrysler and American Motors, along with Volkswagen and Japanese automakers, determined to stay. In the all-important mining sector, Cerro and Anaconda had returned some unworked concessions to the state but had yet to give up their main operations.[41]

Within the context of these developments, in late January the U.S. embassy submitted a lengthy secret assessment of the regime and its possible future to the State Department. It began by asserting that it was important to U.S. interests that the reform efforts of the Velasco government, "*misguided and inept though its leaders may prove to be*" (emphasis mine), not fail in that the U.S. could well be held responsible if they did. From a national security angle, efforts should be made to prevent a too close alliance between

---

40. *New York Times*, October 23, 1970, 2.
41. *New York Times*, January 25, 1971, 58.

Peru and the Soviet Union or Communist China. The emergence of a Marxist regime in Chile gave "particular urgency to the need for preventing a hostile relationship from developing between our two countries." Events in Chile could cut various ways. Signs of success for Allende's reform program might well push Peruvian leftists to encourage even more radical changes. However, a close alliance between Chile and the Soviet Union and Cuba could lead the Peruvian military to see the Marxist regime as a serious strategic threat and lead to a military build-up. This eventuality, the report stated, could work to the advantage of the United States. However, the report warned, "we must bear in mind that U.S. Government reactions and countermoves against Chilean actions affecting U.S. private economic interests will have a significant effect on our position in Peru. This factor must be kept in mind as we consider and develop our policy vis-à-vis the Chilean challenge." The linkage between developments in Chile and Peru would remain as a constant policy concern for the United States over the next several years.

On the domestic front, the report urged U.S. support for Peruvian economic development and for the regime's goals of achieving social justice. The interests of private companies like IPC should not be allowed to overshadow larger national interests. The good feelings following the earthquake relief effort should be followed with new initiatives, although the months ahead might be fraught with complexities and difficulties. While the economy was generally strong at the moment, the report predicted that over the next few months a decline of export prices and foreign investment could well produce the kind of crisis that would put larger U.S. aims at risk.

In conclusion, the report recommended a continuation of attempts to settle outstanding issues "without forcing the pace." It was hoped that "provocative" incidents could be avoided. On the IPC matter, the Velasco regime saw it as closed, and prospects of any settlement in the near future were "unlikely in terms of our reading of the Peruvian environment." Repeating suggestions from Belcher earlier the embassy called for a "flexible" and "pragmatic" policy toward Peru in the years ahead.[42]

Public and Private Diplomacy

The glow and good feelings from Mrs. Nixon's visit to Peru following the earthquake of 1970 persisted into the following year. In his report to

---

42. "Secret Air-Gram A-22 from Lima to Washington, January 28, 1971," USNA (1970–1973) (Box 2544, Folder 4).

Congress on February 22 laying out "U.S. Foreign Policy for the 1970s," President Nixon reiterated the basic themes for the Western Hemisphere—a mutuality of interests, shared responsibility, partnership, and friendship. With regard specifically to Peru, the president mentioned his wife's visit and asserted that "her warm reception was tribute to the profound ties between the peoples of Peru and the United States."[43] As a further sign of these "profound ties," on June 29 Mrs. Velasco recognized Mrs. Nixon for her relief efforts at a ceremony at the Peruvian embassy in Washington by presenting her with the Grand Cross of the Order of the Sun, the nation's highest honor. In his remarks, Ambassador Berckemeyer claimed that the "people of Peru from one end to the other of the nation have happy memories of your visit to our country in a time of sorrow."[44]

The ceremony in Washington was part of a larger three-week tour of the United States by Mrs. Velasco at the invitation of Mrs. Nixon. When she returned to Lima, she was greeted at the airport by her husband and the entire cabinet. President Velasco declared the visit "a great success" and expressed to a U.S. embassy official his appreciation for the warm reception accorded to his wife by President and Mrs. Nixon.[45] In an interview soon after her return, Mrs. Velasco claimed not to know much about an invitation extended to her husband also to visit the United States but reported that President Nixon "told me to convey to the Peruvian president that they were expecting him soon."[46] According to one source, Mrs. Velasco also told her husband in private that President Nixon had assured her that "as long as I am the president no harm will come to Peru," adding that he, like Velasco, did "not come from the oligarchy; I, too had to elbow my way up."[47] As it happened, apparently under pressure from the radical elements within the regime, Velasco decided not to accept the invitation to follow in his wife's footsteps. Left up in the air was the possibility of a visit later in the year, one that ultimately never took place.

For Ambassador Belcher, who had delivered the invitation for President Velasco's visit, the negative decision left him, as he reported, "somewhat relieved." At that time, the regime was running into difficulties with the financial and business community, and the proposed visit to the United States

---

43. *DOSB*, 64, 1656 (March 22, 1971), 362.
44. *New York Times*, June 30, 1971, 37.
45. "Limited Official Use Telegram 4170 from Edward Clark to Department of State, July 22, 1971," USNA (1970–1973) (Box 2542, Folder 3), 1.
46. "Unclassified Telegram 4255 from the U.S. Embassy in Lima to State, July 23, 1971," USNA (1970–1973) (Box 2542, Folder 3), 1.
47. Kruijt, *Revolution by Decree*, 105.

would have served to bolster his prestige and position. Belcher was clearly ambivalent. On the one hand, he did not want the Peruvian experiment to fail as it might lead to more radical consequences, but on the other hand, he was personally not particularly sympathetic either to Velasco or the regime. He concluded that "it is perhaps better to leave well enough alone and see what Peru's future has in store for this *impetuous and outspoken little man* [emphasis mine]."[48]

"Tacit Bargaining" and an Improved Atmosphere

According to Charles Goodsell, the Velasco regime and foreign investors began to develop a new modus vivendi over the course of 1971 through a process he described as "tacit bargaining." Up to the beginning of the year, new foreign investment in Peru had come to a virtual halt in the face of the regime's radical measures. In June, however, Petroperú, the new state oil company, signed a contract with the Occidental Petroleum Corporation for exploration, an agreement that was followed by similar deals with other companies. Investments by foreign concerns in mining and industrial activities increased during the second half of the year. Agreements were also signed with U.S. chains and Braniff Airways by the state tourist company to construct six new hotels.[49]

Goodsell traced this change to several interrelated factors. First, and perhaps most important, as the U.S. embassy had predicted, the economy performed poorly in the first half of the year. Profits from mining operations were affected by numerous strikes and the government's mishandling of its fish meal resources, over which it had assumed control, had led to a significant decline in foreign-exchange earnings.[50] Second, the economic decline probably had an important role in a cabinet shake-up in late April when a moderate replaced radical Admiral Jorge Dellepiane, who had drafted the new industrial law and "was strongly disliked by business leaders," as minister of industry and commerce.[51] This action suggested that Velasco and his top advisors were aware that a more flexible and accommodating stance with regard to foreign investment was necessary, given the new economic realities they faced. Third, there was a growing acceptance by the

---

48. "Confidential Telegram 2714 from Belcher to Department of State, May 13, 1971," USNA (1970–1973) (Box 2542, Folder 3), 1–2.
49. Goodsell, *American Corporations and Peruvian Politics*, 162–63.
50. Some of these problems are described in *New York Times*, July 12, 1971, 39.
51. Goodsell, *American Corporations and Peruvian Politics*, 162–63; and Philip, *The Rise and Fall of the Peruvian Military Radicals, 1968–1976*, 124.

foreign business community of the new "rules of the game" established by the regime that seemed firmly in control and offered a certain amount of stability and predictability. Moreover, Goodsell added, these "'rules' did not look so bad by comparison to what was by now going on in the Marxist regime of Chile."[52]

Mercado Goes to Washington and Beyond

Nearing the end of his term as foreign minister, General Mercado prepared for his last official visit to the United States, scheduled for the end of September. In early August, he had spearheaded an initiative to establish diplomatic relations with the People's Republic of China (PRC) as part of his pursuit of an independent foreign policy and announced that the government was also considering restoring relations with Cuba. In a lengthy interview with *Oiga*, Mercado observed that Peru had been the first nation in the Americas to recommend that the PRC be admitted into the United Nations. While there were obvious points of tension with the United States, he also provided an upbeat assessment of relations with that nation. He noted in particular that in a recent dispute over cutting the nation's sugar quota in retaliation for expropriation of W. R. Grace properties, the State Department had "vigorously" defended the Peruvian position and "had categorically opposed" the proposed punitive measure.[53]

Arriving in Washington at the end of September, Mercado held meetings with most of the important U.S. officials who had a say in relations toward his country, with the exception of President Nixon. In his meetings with his old friend John Irwin, now an under-secretary of state, and Assistant Secretary Meyer, he expressed his appreciation for the department's efforts with regard to the sugar quota. He then brought up his main concern—Peru's continued lack of access to international credit, specifically from the World Bank. The Velasco regime, he noted, had been in power for almost three years and had, he claimed, brought stability, social peace, and economic improvement to Peru. Foreign investors, including U.S. oil companies, had begun to recognize these facts and were increasing their involvement in the country. Other nations had recognized the regime's accomplishments and had accepted its "revolutionary process" as a way to eliminate inequality and injustice. Contrasting the Peruvian experiment in

52. Goodsell, *American Corporations and Peruvian Politics*, 163.
53. *Oiga*, 9, 435 (August 6, 1971), 40.

reform with the Chilean, he argued that the Peruvian Revolution offered a "non-Marxist model for change to other Latin American nations." Accordingly, while he knew that the department was constrained from pressing the World Bank directly, he hoped that it could use whatever influence it had on his nation's behalf. Irwin responded that, while he sympathized with much that Mercado had to say, he and the Velasco regime had to recognize that its expropriations had complicated matters and that the subject of compensation still remained to be resolved. Until this was done, he implied, access to credit would be difficult.[54]

Mercado made many of these same points in subsequent meetings with Secretary of State Rogers and Henry Kissinger. In his discussions with Kissinger, the most important figure in U.S. foreign policy-making besides President Nixon, Mercado reemphasized the noncommunist nature of the Peruvian Revolution and its accomplishments, which had kept the basic capitalist structure of the nation intact and had continued to value private initiative and private enterprise. He made a strong contrast between the Velasco and Allende governments and said that Peru "viewed with concern the emergence of a Marxist regime in Chile arising from outside influences." He also argued that if the socialist experiment in Chile were successful, it would have "a powerful demonstration effect on Latin America." In this light, therefore, the success of the Peruvian experiment was in the United States' best interests and the best support the United States could provide would be to refrain from placing obstacles in the way of Peru receiving loans from international financial organizations.

Kissinger seemed to agree with Mercado's arguments. He assured his visitor that the United States was "interested in the success of the Peruvian revolution—both for its own sake and as a non-Marxist alternative to the Chilean experience in Latin America." He also hoped that the complications arising from the Velasco regime's expropriation policies could be resolved amicably and asserted that the Nixon administration "was not placing obstacles in the way of granting new credits to Peru, at least so far as he was aware," a claim that, given his earlier policy recommendations in this regard, might have been more than a little disingenuous. He promised Mercado he would personally look into this matter to ensure that this was not the case.[55]

54. "Confidential Department of State Memorandum of Conversation, September 27, 1971," USNA (1970–1973) (Box 2542, Folder 1), 1–4. Belcher was informed of these discussions in "Confidential Outgoing Telegram 178667 from the Department of State, September 28, 1971," USNA (1970–1973) (Box 2544, Folder 6), 1–3.

55. "Confidential NODIS Memorandum of Meeting, September 29, 1971," USNA (1970–1973) (Box 2544, Folder 6), 1–3.

In an address to the UN a few days later, Mercado pulled no punches in stating Peru's position on a number of contentious issues. He denounced what he called the "daily aggressions" carried out by the industrialized countries against the third world, defended the 200-mile-limit thesis, demanded the participation of the less-developed nations in making international monetary policy, and proposed the admission of the PRC into the UN and the reincorporation of Cuba into the OAS.[56] He then embarked on a tour of several European nations with an important stop in Yugoslavia, a nation that was seen as a major player in the nonaligned movement and whose path of independent development within the Soviet bloc had provided something of a model for the Peruvian military regime. Writing to Washington before Mercado's departure from Lima, Ambassador Belcher had pointed out the importance of the Yugoslav model for Peru and its relationship to the creation of an "independent" foreign policy. Mercado, he observed, was the chief architect of that policy and "will no doubt benefit personally" from the prestige of an official visit to that nation.[57]

Mercado's efforts soon began to produce results. His visit to Yugoslavia reinforced Peru's role in the nonaligned movement and gained the support of that government for the 200-mile-limit claim.[58] In early November, the PRC government announced it was establishing formal diplomatic relations with Peru and reiterated its support for the 200-mile limit.[59] On November 12, special presidential advisor Robert Finch, who was initiating a six-nation Latin American fact-finding tour on behalf of President Nixon, signed a $31 million loan agreement in Lima with Mercado to provide for rebuilding housing and supporting community development in the earthquake zone. At the signing ceremony, Finch claimed that the loan agreement provided "another example of the continuing cooperation between Peru and the United States." Moreover, Finch, in the company of Meyer, met for an hour with Velasco to discuss the possibility of new four-party talks on the fishing rights issue. While there were no official communications, the implication was that both sides were showing some new flexibility on this matter.[60] Two weeks later, it was announced that the PRC would provide Peru with a $42 million interest-free loan and promise to buy $100 million

---

56. Pease García and Verme Insúa, *Perú, 1968–1973*, 1:317.
57. "Confidential Air-Gram A-285 from Belcher to Department of State, September 18, 1971," USNA (1970–1973) (Box 2542, Folder 3), 3–4.
58. "Unclassified Air-Gram A-474 from U.S. Embassy in Belgrade to Department of State, October 4, 1971," USNA (1970–1973) (Box 2542, Folder 1), 1.
59. *New York Times*, November 3, 1971, 9.
60. *New York Times*, November 13, 1971, 3.

worth of Peruvian mineral products. While it was Energy and Mines Minister Fernández Maldonado who negotiated the deal, it was also the result of Mercado's overall efforts and strategy.[61] Finally, at the end of the year, the Inter-American Development Bank agreed to provide a loan of 470 million soles to support the agrarian reform program.[62]

On the heels of the Finch visit, Ambassador Belcher sought to follow up with Mercado the possibility of efforts to resume constructive negotiations on the fishing rights dispute. Immediately after the visit, he met with him at the foreign minister's beach house and pressed him on the issue, encouraging him to do what he could to restrain the regime from any further seizures that might complicate matters. For his part, Mercado said he would do what he could to push for such restraint while at the same time pressing for the United States to lift its ban on military sales to Peru.[63] At the same time, Belcher, in a revealing comment, suggested to Washington that if Under-Secretary John Irwin could be included in discussions with Mercado on this matter "it would immensely flatter *his considerable ego* [emphasis mine]."[64] While this suggestion went unheeded, there were no major incidents over U.S. fishing vessels at the end of the year, aided in great part by the migration of tuna out of these waters. However, there were no significant breakthroughs on the underlying problem of the 200-mile limit, a matter that would need to be addressed by Mercado's successor.

Embassy Views

The most important development on the domestic front in Peru during the year was the creation of the Sistema Nacional de Apoyo a la Movilización Social (National System of Support for Social Mobilization). Announced on June 24 by Velasco, *Sinamos* (Without Masters), as it was known, was designed to encourage the development of autonomous institutions that would increase citizen participation in the social, economic, and political life of the country, accelerating a "revolution from the top down."[65] The U.S. embassy had relatively little to say about this new organization upon

61. Pease García and Verme Insúa, *Perú, 1968–1973*, 1:338; and *New York Times*, December 13, 1971, 5.
62. Pease García and Verme Insúa, *Perú, 1968–1973*, 1:348.
63. Various aspects of the ongoing negotiations among the United States, Peru, and Ecuador, and Mercado's position in these, were described in "Secret Department of State Telegram 209805 to Lima, November 18, 1971," USNA (1970–1973) (Box 2544, Folder 1), 1–2.
64. "Confidential Telegram 6867 from Belcher to Department of State, November 18, 1971," USNA (1970–1973) (Box 2544, Folder 1), 1.
65. Werlich, *Peru*, 347.

its creation, but in October described it for Washington as a program staffed by "Communists, Trotskyists [*sic*], and other leftist ideologues and opportunists," perhaps either as an initial move to creating an official party or as a way to ward off pressure for elections.[66]

At the end of the year, Belcher submitted a thorough review of the situation in Peru and its implications for U.S. policy. The "Country Analysis and Strategy Paper (CASP) for Fiscal Year 1973" was intended to suggest guidelines for policy over the next two and half years based on current circumstances and likely future trends.[67] In essence, it repeated arguments made in earlier assessments; namely, that greater flexibility in policy had to be achieved and the IPC case should not be allowed to predominate over broader national interests. Improved relations with Peru were vital, it argued, because the Velasco regime offered an important contrast with Marxist Chile and because the military reformers were an attractive model for other developing nations. The armed forces, it predicted, would hold on to power for some time and with time the more moderate elements would come to prevail. The "cooperative aspects" of the relationship between the two countries should be emphasized "to reestablish the mutual trust and respect that will permit us to pursue our larger interests." More specifically, efforts should be made to make credit and financing from international lending institutions more available to Peru, to resume the Foreign Military Sales program, and to show greater flexibility on the fishing rights issue.[68] Whether these recommendations would be followed remained to be seen.

Belcher's Peruvian counterpart in Washington continued to inform Lima of domestic developments in the United States with implications for Peru. Many of Berckemeyer's dispatches in these months had to do with fishing questions, including more information on the activities of Pelly and others and the Nixon administration's own efforts to formalize some sort of international agreement on rights to the seas questions.[69]

---

66. "Confidential Telegram 5893 from Belcher to Department of State, October 7, 1971," USNA (1970–1973) (Box 2543, Folder 6), 1–4.

67. The CASP was prepared by the ambassador and his "country team" and was reviewed at various levels of the State Department. These documents were designed "to delineate, both generally and specifically, major U.S. policy objectives" and to serve as the basic document for funding requests from Congress. Their use was explained in more detail in "United States Foreign Policy As to Latin America," an address by Covey T. Oliver to the Council on Foreign Relations, New York, May 22, 1968. Personal Papers of Covey T. Oliver, Box 1, LBJ Library.

68. "Secret National Security Council Interdepartmental Group for Inter-American Affairs Decision Memorandum 25, December 28, 1971," USNA (1970–1973) (Box 2544, Folder 4), 1–3. Also included in this file was the CASP for 1973.

69. In August, John R. Stevenson, a legal advisor in the State Department, submitted the U.S. proposal for an international agreement on fishing and ocean use rights submitted to a UN Committee

In early August, Berckemeyer, in the company of his air attaché, met with the State Department's Hugh Crimmins to push for the resumption of arms sales to Peru. His main request was to replace certain older aircraft, furnished under the Bilateral Military Assistance Agreement, with newer models. Berckemeyer claimed that the Peruvians had been having difficulty in purchasing military equipment from the United States, presumably because of the constraints of the Pelly amendment, although this was not mentioned specifically. Crimmins responded that, at least as far as he was concerned, no such requests had passed his desk and seemed to indicate that if they had they would have been considered. However, he also told the ambassador that Peru's apparent move toward reestablishing relations with Cuba, and particularly Foreign Minister Mercado's recent remarks, could well complicate matters. The department was also considering a waiver for Peru on the sale of commodities under the Food for Peace program, waivers that were rare and hard to come by, and once again any resumption of relations with Cuba could dim the chances that the waiver would be approved. Crimmins made it clear "that the U.S. position on Cuba had not changed and that the U.S. had seen no indication that Castro is willing to moderate his policies in order to re-join the inter-American family." He asked Berckemeyer, who was scheduled to return to Lima soon on personal business, to communicate these concerns directly to Mercado, something the ambassador promised to do.[70]

No record to indicate the results of these instructions could be found. It seems likely that Berckemeyer communicated Crimmin's concerns directly to Mercado and that, given the Foreign Ministry's continued pursuit of ties with Cuba, they had little effect. On December 5, returning from a lengthy visit to Chile, Fidel Castro had a five-hour airport interview with Velasco in which he reiterated his support for the Peruvian revolutionary process and said that to do otherwise would be to surrender to "imperialism."[71]

Returning to Washington, Berckemeyer reported in mid-September that the Nixon administration seemed to have adopted a "hard line" toward "some Latin American countries of a nationalist tendency." Such a policy presumably would include Peru, although it was Allende's Chile that seemed the principal target. He claimed that the main actor in this policy was Treasury Secretary John Connally, a rising star in the administration, "in opposition

---

dealing with the issue in Geneva. The U.S. proposal included an article that set a twelve-mile limit for fishing rights. *DOSB*, 65, 1680 (September 6, 1971), 261–68.

70. "Confidential Department of State Memorandum of Conversation, August 6, 1971," USNA (1970–1973) (Box 1781, Folder 4), 1–4.

71. Pease García and Verme Insúa, *Perú, 1968–1973*, 1:342.

to the more flexible attitude of the Department of State." Under Connally, he wrote, "many believe that the Treasury Department is gradually acquiring more strength in the decisions on international commerce, investments, and foreign aid" and using that strength to reward "friends" and punish "enemies."[72] Berckemeyer followed up these observations with another communication on October 29 that described in some detail the testimony of an under-secretary of the treasury before the House Sub-Committee on International Finance and Banking in which the official stated that the United States would cut off aid to countries that expropriated U.S. investments without compensation. Again, the main target was Chile, but the implications for Peru also seemed clear.[73]

Summary

During 1970 and 1971, relations between Peru and the United States showed some improvements. Mrs. Nixon's visit had helped defuse some of the hostility between the two nations; U.S. investors had learned to live with the new rules and regulations imposed by the military government and come to appreciate the stability and predictability it provided; and there were some indications of a loosening of the financial purse strings from international institutions under Washington's sway. Despite President Nixon's personal assurances that "no harm" would come to Peru, Ambassador Berckemeyer's dispatches indicated that Peruvian attempts to establish closer relations with Cuba did not sit well with U.S. officials and that the still unresolved compensation issues posed a major obstacle to restoring full U.S. funding and assistance to the Velasco regime. For his part, Ambassador Belcher, despite what appeared to be his distaste for the military government and the low regard in which he held some of its members (apparently including its leader), called for greater flexibility in dealing with the regime. The administration's new hard line toward nationalist governments that Berckemeyer had reported at the end of 1971, particularly seen in the actions and attitudes of Treasury Secretary Connally, raised questions, however, about whether these calls would be heeded in the months to follow.

72. *Correspondencia* (5–3-Y/84) (September 14, 1971), 3.
73. *Correspondencia* (5–3-Y/93) (October 29, 1971), 2.

10

CHANGE, CRISIS, AND CONTINUITY

Over the next two years, both Nixon and Velasco experienced some major ups and downs. Nixon won reelection in November 1972 by a sweeping majority, but several months later the unfolding Watergate scandal began to undermine both his authority and influence. General Juan Velasco Alvarado continued to hold onto power, successfully manipulating the radicals and moderates within the regime and continuing to adhere to his nationalist agenda. In early 1973, however, he suffered a major health crisis, from which he was able to recover but which had long-term consequences for his hold on power. There were major changes in the foreign policy personnel on both sides. However, these had little effect on the continuing fundamental disagreements between the two nations. At the end of 1973, it seemed that the long-standing issue of compensation for expropriation of U.S.-owned properties would be resolved, while, at the same time, Velasco took aim at the holdings of the powerful Cerro de Pasco Corporation's mining operations. From the Peruvian side, too, its relations with its neighbors, especially Brazil and Chile, persisted as a major concern.

A Changing of the Guard

On January 4, 1972, Brigadier General Miguel Angel de la Flor Valle officially replaced Mercado Jarrín as Peru's foreign minister. Born in Peru's northern coastal department of Lambayeque on March 11, 1924, he had graduated from the Escuela Militar in Chorrillos in 1945 and subsequently pursued studies at the Escuela Superior de Guerra and in France in the late 1950s. He was one of a small group of colonels who helped the October 3 coup and from that time served as a close advisor to Velasco as a member of the Comité de Asesoramiento de la Presidencia (COAP) from 1968 to 1969, as president of the Peruvian Telephone Company, and as commandant of the Centro de Instrucción Militar del Perú (Center of Military Instruction of Peru, or CIMP).[1]

In her study of the military regime's leadership, Liisa North located de la Flor in the small but influential Progressive faction (she placed Mercado in the Centre). That faction was mostly made up of officers like de la Flor—and like Velasco—who were mostly from the provincial lower and lower-middle classes, held key positions within the regime, and pushed for the most radical reforms and changes. In summarizing their position, she argued that they sought to address "the worst forms of mass poverty," encourage income redistribution, and promote full employment. In pursuing these goals, the Progressives were not necessarily wedded to retaining capitalism. They also found the Cuban Revolutionary model attractive, particularly its emphasis on promoting mass participation in bringing about social and economic change and its "courageous nationalism," as most clearly seen in its willingness to confront the United States.[2]

In his first press conference, de la Flor emphasized that he would continue the basic policies crafted by his predecessor. These included giving priority to the development of the Andean Pact, showing continued solidarity with the third world, and vigorously defending the 200-mile-limit claim. He announced plans to expand the nation's contact with socialist nations, initiating relations with North Korea and East Germany. On the question of relations with Cuba, he observed that it seemed anomalous that Peru and most other nations had normal relations with Chile, now under a Marxist government, but not with Cuba. He promised to pursue this matter through the Organization of American States (OAS) and in consultation with other American nations.[3] Reporting back to Washington, Ambassador Taylor Belcher stressed the continuity between Mercado and de la Flor and saw this as a trend that would likely continue over the near future. However, he found it "significant that [the] foreign minister reaffirmed that

---

1. Foster, *Latin American Government Leaders*, 105.
2. North and Korovkin, *The Peruvian Revolution and the Officers in Power, 1967–1976*, 50–54.
3. *Oiga*, 11, 457 (January 14, 1972), 18–19.

[the] GOP intends to pursue [the] lifting of sanctions on Cuba within [the] OAS framework."[4]

Rumblings from Washington

Not long after de La Flor's appointment, a potential new challenge to Peru came from Washington. On January 19, President Nixon sent to Congress a policy statement regarding economic assistance to developing nations in which he took a more explicit hard-line stance with regard to the linkage between assistance and expropriation of U.S.-owned properties. Claiming that international law and practice demanded compensation for such acts, he declared that when a country expropriated U.S.-owned properties without compensation, "the United States will not extend new bilateral economic benefits to the expropriating country unless and until it is determined that the country is taking reasonable steps to provide adequate compensation *or that there are major factors affecting U.S. interests which require continuance of all or part of these benefits* [emphasis mine]." In these cases as well, the United States would "withhold its support from loans under consideration in multilateral development banks."[5]

This new policy, in effect, replaced the Hickenlooper amendment with provisions that allowed the president greater flexibility in determining whether to apply punitive sanctions. That amendment by now had lost much of its force with the Nixon administration's failure to apply sanctions on Peru following the International Petroleum Company (IPC) takeover, although de facto assistance had been withheld and obstacles placed in the way of multilateral loans. The main target of the current policy, however, was the Allende regime in Chile, which had nationalized U.S. copper companies and so far had rejected any claim for compensation.[6]

The newly announced policy apparently was of little consequence to Velasco. At about the time it was announced, Ambassador Belcher met with the Peruvian leader to inform him of President Nixon's forthcoming trips to Peking and Moscow. During their conversation, Velasco told Belcher that about a year earlier he and his advisors had feared some sort of coup against the regime that included CIA involvement. The government had broken

---

4. "Limited Official Use Telegram 132 from Belcher to Department of State, January 10, 1972," USNA (1970–1973) (Box 2543, Folder 5), 2–3.
5. *DOSB*, lxvi, 1702 (February 7, 1972), 154.
6. *Latin America*, 6, 4 (January 28, 1972), 29–30.

off official liaison with U.S. intelligence agencies. Since then, Velasco said, such fears had receded and overall relations with the United States had, in his judgment, "improved greatly." Therefore, he would soon recommend that contacts with these agencies be resumed. He also believed that by now the United States had recognized that the Peruvian regime was clearly noncommunist and that it represented "a reasonable alternative to communist Chile and Cuba and that, therefore, it is in the interest of the United States to collaborate more closely with it." Belcher also reported that the Peruvian government was concerned that, if Soviet weapons were supplied to Chile, that "could only be a danger to Peru."

Belcher concluded from this conversation that Peruvian suspicions of the United States seemed to have been allayed and that there were opportunities for cooperation on the intelligence front.[7] However, Velasco would continue to seek an improved relationship with Cuba and to take the lead in trying to reintegrate the island nation into the formal hemispheric community. And, while the long-standing suspicions between Chile and Peru persisted, the Velasco regime's relations with the Allende government gradually improved over the course of the year. The Chilean leader had visited Peru in early September 1971 and had assuaged many of the concerns of some of the anti-Marxist military leaders.[8] During his welcoming speech, Velasco had underscored the common "dominance of foreign investment" over the two nations and their shared "anti-imperialist struggle."[9] During 1972 and 1973, relations between the two nations were "most cordial" and Foreign Minister de la Flor and his Chilean counterpart "became fast friends and held many views in common."[10]

Differences over Cuba

In early April, Foreign Minister de la Flor made his first official visit to the United States to attend the General Assembly meeting of the OAS. He openly clashed with Secretary of State William P. Rogers by advocating a lifting of sanctions on Cuba. Two months later, at a special session of the

7. "Secret Department of State Memorandum for Henry Kissinger from Theodore L. Eliot, Executive Secretary, January 21, 1972," USNA (1970–1973) (Box 2544, Folder 5), 2.

8. According to one source, "Allende's visit to Lima signaled a turnabout in the hitherto tense relations between the two states. The reception committee was much impressed and somewhat afraid of Allende; in preparation of his arrival his collection of suits and his eating habits were carefully noted." Kruijt, *Revolution by Decree*, 106.

9. Pease García and Verme Insúa, *Perú, 1968–1973*, 1:305.

10. Kruijt, *Revolution by Decree*, 106.

OAS, the Peruvians followed this up with an official call for normalization of relations with Castro's regime. This proposal, strongly opposed by the United States, was soundly defeated. Not to be deterred, on June 20, President Velasco announced that as part of his nation's "independent foreign policy" it was negotiating with the Cuban government to reestablish the diplomatic relations that had been broken under the Prado administration. As a precedent, he pointed to the recent overtures from the Nixon administration to China and the Soviet Union, despite their "distinct political and ideological positions." He was also careful, however, to indicate that the normalization did not mean that his regime shared the same "political-ideological position" as Castro's and that the "revolutionary government of Peru follows a path distinct from that of Cuba."[11]

On July 9, both governments signed documents formally reestablishing diplomatic relations and exchanging ambassadors. At the ceremony in the Torre Tagle palace, Foreign Minister de la Flor called the moment of "transcendental historical importance" and asserted that it represented "an authentic sense of sovereignty and of our recuperated independence." He also claimed, in a not-so-veiled reference to the United States, that it marked the beginning of the end of the "ancient hegemonies" that had previously governed diplomatic relations among American states.[12] For its part, the State Department issued a public statement expressing dissatisfaction with the Peruvian decision, arguing that the resumption of relations with Castro's government should result only from a collective OAS decision "that Cuba is no longer a threat to the peace and security of the hemisphere."[13]

Following the decision, the Peruvian embassy forwarded to Lima information on the U.S. congressional reaction to it. In response, the Foreign Ministry emphasized to the embassy the "transcendental" significance of the renewal of relations with Cuba and requested that it pay particular attention to informing Lima of other aspects of the U.S. reaction to the move and any possible changes in U.S. policy toward the Castro regime.[14] In compliance, on July 12, Manuel A. Roca Zela, second-in-command at the embassy, sent on a detailed description of the State Department announcement as well as other material related to the official U.S. reaction.[15] Subsequently, throughout the rest of the year, the embassy reported on any possible changes in the U.S. position toward Castro, speculating that regardless of

11. *Oiga*, 11, 480 (June 23, 1972), 14.
12. *Oiga*, 11, 483 (July 14, 1972), 11–12.
13. *Washington Post*, July 7, 1972, A4:6.
14. *Correspondencia (Salidas)* (5-3-Y/32) (June 22, 1972), 1.
15. *Correspondencia* (5-3-Y/75) (July 12, 1972), 1–2.

the outcome of the upcoming presidential election some new accommodation might be likely. They judged that the Democratic presidential candidate, South Dakota Senator George McGovern, would be more likely to be flexible in dealing with the Castro regime, while Nixon, the incumbent seeking reelection, following his opening to China, might pursue the same policy with regard to Cuba. Following Nixon's smashing victory, however, Berckemeyer reported back at the end of the year that there seemed little likelihood that U.S.-Cuban relations would improve unless Castro made the first move, something he showed no signs of doing.[16] Indeed, in one of his final dispatches of the year, Berckemeyer noted that the Cuban leader had made it abundantly clear that there would be no rapprochement with the United States as long as the economic blockade of the island continued and the United States "follows its hostile policy towards Chile and Peru."[17] One can only guess at what the strongly anti-Castro and anticommunist Berckemeyer felt in drafting a report that underscored the strong rhetorical support Cuba was providing to the government he represented.

The Connally Visit

While Peru's decisions to reestablish relations with Cuba promised to complicate its relations with the United States, Berckemeyer saw certain personnel shifts at the highest levels of the Nixon administration as potentially hopeful. In particular, he pointed to the replacement of John Connally with George Shultz as secretary of the treasury. Connally, he argued, had been a principal figure in denying assistance to Peru, and his departure from the treasury post "we ought to see with moderate optimism" in that his successor, Shultz, was "non-partisan" and "balanced." He predicted that Shultz's "line of conduct will not reach the disoriented and impulsive tendency that Connally sometimes imposed." The "moderate optimism," however, might be tempered by the fact that some were talking about Connally, clearly a favorite of President Nixon, as the next secretary of state and one who "will continue to play an important role in the foreign policy of the United States."[18]

Connally had an opportunity to confirm or to dispel some of these notions when he visited Lima briefly on June 13 as part of a whirlwind

---

16. *Correspondencia* (5–3-Y/169) (December 11, 1972), 2.
17. *Correspondencia* (5–3-Y/172) (December 21, 1972), 2.
18. *Correspondencia* (5–3-Y/47) (May 19, 1972), 2.

six-nation Latin American tour as special envoy for President Nixon. Following meetings with Velasco, De La Flor, and Economy Minister Francisco Morales Bermúdez, he had relatively little to say to the press other than to emphasize that the United States was opposed to the 200-mile territorial sea claim.[19] When asked by a reporter from *Oiga* point-blank whether the IPC case had affected Peruvian-U.S. relations, Connally responded that he considered such relations "excellent." Questioned by the same reporter about whether the United States was blocking aid to Peru in the Inter-American Development Bank and other multinational institutions, he responded disingenuously that "the United States does not control these international institutions. . . . My country has always provided the required aid, as in the case of the earthquake that struck Peru. Always we have aided."[20]

Writing to Lima on July 24, Roca Zela commented on the results of Connally's tour. As he reported, Connally generally reinforced the hard line with which he was associated, letting most of those he visited in the third world know that foreign assistance was a "tough sell" in the U.S. Congress and would be limited in the near future. With regard to the domestic political front, he wrote that Connally was very well regarded by Nixon, for both "political and personal" reasons, was one of the president's "closest collaborators," and would play a major role in the president's reelection effort. However, he downplayed speculation that Connally would replace Rogers as secretary of state. Up to now, the dominant figure in the administration's foreign policy apparatus was Henry Kissinger. While Rogers was de jure secretary of state, it seemed that Kissinger was de facto secretary of state, an arrangement that the mild-mannered and low-key Rogers seemed to accept.[21] It appeared quite unlikely that Connally, himself a formidable personality, if he became secretary of state, would agree to a similar arrangement. Therefore, Roca Zela speculated, it was most probable that Kissinger would prevail, perhaps naming his former patron Nelson Rockefeller as secretary of state, thus ensuring that he had a "natural ally" in that position rather than a "natural rival" such as Connally.[22] While the ultimate results would be a bit different, Roca Zela's speculations, at least as far as Connally's appointment as secretary of state were concerned, proved to be generally on target. However, these personnel shifts, both real and imagined, had little real effect for the moment on U.S. policy toward Peru.

19. *Caretas*, 22, 459 (June 22–July 6, 1972), 12.
20. *Oiga*, 11, 479 (June 16, 1972), 12–13.
21. While Rogers might have been "agreeable," his relationship with Kissinger was often bitter and antagonistic. For more, see Dallek, *Nixon and Kissinger*.
22. *Correspondencia* (5-3-Y/85) (July 24, 1972), 2–3.

Belcher's Activities

While Connally's tough stance seemed to dominate much of the Peruvian-U.S. relationship at this time, Ambassador Belcher did his best to deal with local sensitivities and to improve the relationship on a range of issues. From the beginning of the year, he pressed the State Department to do what it could to resume military sales to Peru, with the sanctions of the Pelly amendment due to expire at the end of March. If such assistance were not resumed, he informed Assistant Secretary Meyer in February, the U.S. relationship with the military government would deteriorate even further.[23]

Apparently in response to Belcher's urging, in April the State Department recommended to the Pentagon prompt attention to the Peruvian requests for military purchases.[24] And on May 1, the embassy reported to Lima that the Defense Department had approved Peru's request for the purchase of equipment from the U.S. Navy. At the same time, it also provided general information on overall U.S. military aid to Latin America, figures that the Peruvian Foreign Ministry highlighted in red in the margins.[25] Perhaps in reaction to this information, de la Flor, meeting with Belcher in mid-May, complained that on the matter of military assistance, the United States seemed to be favoring Chile to the detriment of Peru, another indication of "a prejudiced attitude" on the part of the United States. Belcher did his best to disabuse him of this notion, pointing out that over the past ten years Peru had actually received more U.S. military assistance than had its southern neighbor. He also observed that Peru's recent requests for assistance were substantial and that it was unrealistic to expect that the full amount would be approved, something that de la Flor seemed to accept.[26]

In June, Belcher met again with de la Flor to try to calm him on other sensitive matters. These included concerns over yet another punitive amendment from the U.S. Congress, which was introduced by Democratic Representative Henry Gonzalez of Texas. This amendment had gone into effect on March 10 and instructed U.S. representatives to international banks to vote against loans to "offending nations." While this would have implications for Peru, Belcher told the foreign minister that the executive branch still had considerable discretion in this matter. On a related matter, de la

---

23. "Confidential Letter from Belcher to Meyer, February 17, 1972," USNA (1970–73) (Box 1781, Folder 4), 1–3.
24. *Correspondencia* (5-3-Y/27 [D] [H] [PL]), April 10, 1972, 1.
25. *Correspondencia* (5-3-Y/33 [D] [H] [PL]), May 1, 1972, 1.
26. "Confidential Telegram 2839 from Belcher to Department of State, May 13, 1972," USNA (1970–1973) (Box 1781, Folder 5), 1–2.

Flor was particularly incensed by the actions and attitude of Treasury Department officials, who in recent meetings seemed to reinforce their former boss's obdurate position on loans to Peru. While the ambassador did his best to reassure the foreign minister that there was more flexibility on loan issues than these developments suggested, his efforts seemed to have little effect.[27]

In late June, the State Department instructed Belcher to meet with Velasco to try to defuse some of the recent tensions that had developed between the two nations. First, he was to inform him that the United States had granted Peru humanitarian loans to be used for disaster relief. Second, the ambassador should ask the president and other government officials to tone down some of the anti-imperialist rhetoric directed not so subtly at the United States. Belcher should impress on Velasco that the loans being granted "demonstrate the effort of the USG to do what it . . . can within the various constraints created by unresolved problems between us, and remarks such as those . . . do not make the effort any easier." Finally, he should be told that while the United States does not believe Velasco intends a direct confrontation by these statements, "the U.S. Government has been concerned and disturbed by them."[28]

On July 26, at an elaborate ceremony in the Torre Tagle Palace, Belcher and de la Flor signed the promised loan agreements. A total of $27.6 million, provided and administered by the Agency for International Development, was slated for earthquake and flood relief.[29] Meeting privately with Velasco that same day, Belcher told the president that it was more than a little ironic that having just finished signing the loan agreements Peru and the United States remained, while not in a state of outright confrontation, caught in what seemed a vicious circle. Following his instructions, Belcher brought up the harsh words often uttered by leading figures in the regime (not explicitly referring to Velasco in this regard), words that "were not at all helpful to those in Washington who were doing as much as they could within the law to be cooperative with the revolutionary government." He pointed in particular to recent comments by Minister of Energy and Mines Jorge Fernández Maldonado, who had a well-known friendship with the Soviet ambassador and who had seemed to imply that the CIA was actively plotting against the government. Velasco made no direct response on this point but assured Belcher that he would find nothing objectionable in his

---

27. "Confidential Telegram 3340 from Belcher to Department of State, June 22, 1972," USNA (1970–73) (Box 1781, Folder 5), 1970–73, 1–2.

28. "Confidential Telegram 116002 from the Department of State to Belcher, June 27, 1972," USNA (1970–1973) (Box 2544, Folder 6), 1.

29. *Oiga*, 11, 485 (July 27, 1972), 40–41.

upcoming July 28 address to the nation. The ambassador concluded his report on this meeting by noting that he had reiterated to Velasco the importance of toning down the heated rhetoric. "I reminded him again," Belcher wrote, "of the reservoir of good will which exists in Washington and I said I hoped that this could be taken advantage of in the future rather than see it dissipated as a result of statements made here by government officials perhaps for internal political reasons but which had adverse repercussions in my country."[30] In a follow-up telegram on July 29, Belcher seemed pleased to report that, true to his word, Velasco's Independence Day speech not only contained "no new startling announcing of new revolutionary measures nor [any] statement which might be considered anti-American."[31]

Future Prospects

As the four-year anniversary of the military coup against Belaúnde neared, articles in the U.S. press and reports from some U.S. embassy officials were critical of both the slow pace of reform and some of the authoritarian actions the regime took against its opponents.[32] Whatever the growing criticisms of the regime, however, the embassy's own review of the military government's four-year anniversary saw little reason to expect major changes in the near future. The primary reason to forecast continued military control, the review argued, was the unity of the armed forces and the advantages and benefits for the officer corps, particularly in terms of the power and prestige that they accrued from being in command of the government. High-ranking military men who formerly had been consigned to routine duties "now have exciting work; and in place of being snubbed by upper class civilians, the officers and their wives are persons whose influence is worth seeking in many ways." While perhaps somewhat less susceptible to bribery than their predecessors, "within limits they can get jobs for their relatives, settle problems for old and new friends, and fix their enemies."

Other factors arguing for continued military rule included what the report called the "massive passivity" of most of the population. Except for some student and labor groups, there was little active resistance to the

---

30. "Confidential Telegram 4660 from Belcher to Department of State, July 27, 1972," USNA (1970–73) (Box 2544, Folder 6), 1–2.

31. "Limited Official Use Telegram 4678 from Belcher to Department of State, July 29, 1973," USNA (1970–73) (Box 2543, Folder 4), 1.

32. For example, *New York Times*, May 3, 1972, 4:3, and October 5, 1972, 16:1. Both these articles provoked a response from Peruvian officials in the U.S. objecting to their tone and accuracy.

regime. Included among the passive were major political figures and groups, apparently willing to bide their time until some point of crisis emerged as well as withstand intimidation by the regime and its repressive measures. There also was some fear, apparently, that even though the regime had failed to develop real popular support, replacing a *cholo* (mestizo) like Velasco with a lighter-skinned leader might provoke massive retaliation from the darker-skinned Peruvian majority. Moreover, the absence of any guerrilla movement and the regime's efforts to bring about substantial social and economic change had co-opted many opposition arguments. While certain circumstances might arise to threaten the regime in the future, the report concluded, "We see no inexorable forces pushing the government to its downfall."[33]

Apparently taking its cue from the embassy report, the State Department's Bureau of Intelligence and Research's study of the outlook for Peru over the next two years saw little real threat to the stability of the Velasco regime and predicted the military would "probably remain in control at least for the next several years." In terms of its foreign relations, it saw the regime as "not basically hostile to the United States" and, its independent position notwithstanding, in need of economic and military assistance. No matter what the needs, however, "the military will not back off from its public stance on the IPC expropriation case—the symbol of its call for a revolution in the first place." In the immediate future, the study concluded, Peru "will continue to make an issue of its requests for large-scale financial assistance in an effort to pressure the United States into relaxing its opposition to public international financing."[34]

At about the time this study was released, Velasco made a change in his governing team that might have implications for these predictions. In late October, he announced that former foreign minister Mercado would replace General Ernesto Montagne Sánchez as prime minister and minister of defense at the beginning of the next year. Reporting to Washington on this development, an embassy political officer predicted that Mercado would "undoubtedly wield much greater influence in the Military Government than did his predecessor." He would bring to the post the international stature and prestige that his predecessor lacked. Moreover, "his manner is urbane and his style is elegant—in marked contrast to the barracks traits of the present Chief of State." In addition, while serving as commander in

---

33. "Confidential Air-Gram A-368 from U.S. Embassy in Lima to Department of State, October 6, 1972," USNA (1970–1973) (Box 2543, Folder 7), 1–9.

34. "Peru: Political and Economic Outlook Through Mid-1974, Confidential/No Foreign Dissemination Study of Bureau of Intelligence and Research, Department of State, October 18, 1972," USNA (1970–1973) (Box 2544, Folder 6), 1–2.

chief of the army, he had developed a base of loyalty among the regional commanders that could stand him in good stead in future power struggles within the regime. Unlike his predecessor, too, he was "clearly ambitious and undoubtedly sees himself (and now with greater reason) as the logical successor to Velasco." Given these ambitions, Mercado's relationship with the president might produce certain tensions, but up to this point, he "has been a loyal member of the team" and would most likely continue to maintain that loyalty.

With regard to the regime's foreign policy, Mercado was seen as friendlier to the United States than Velasco although he had exhibited "some exasperation with U.S. policies." Few major shifts, however, could be expected. Mercado would stick to the 200-mile-limit position, push for Peru's leadership within the third world movement, and continue to reach out to other nations regardless of their ideological orientation.[35] Indeed, when it was announced that he would become prime minister he was on a visit to China.[36]

End-of-the-Year Ambiguities

In a general review of U.S.-Latin American relations at the end of the year, the London-based publication *Latin America* wrote that "relations with Peru are much improved and United States capital is flowing in again."[37] A sign of the alleged improvement was an apparent breakthrough on the negotiations between the government and W. R. Grace over compensation for the expropriation of that company's properties. After an entire year of extended discussions, both sides had concluded their respective valuations of the property, and it was hoped that an arrangement for compensation could be reached by mid-1973.[38]

If things seemed to be improving on the investment front, they were far from settled with regard to another persistent irritant between the United States and Peru. On October 27, just a few days before the national election, President Nixon signed an amendment to the fisheries protection law

---

35. "Confidential Air-Gram A-390 from González to Department of State, October 31, 1972," USNA (1970–1973) (Box 2543, Folder 4), 1–4.

36. Returning from that visit, Mercado reported his very favorable impression of Chinese leader Chou-En-Lai and claimed that the Chinese "admire our position of independence with respect to other countries and are disposed to collaborate with us, supporting resolutely our doctrine with regard to the 200-mile limit." *Oiga*, 11, 500 (November 10, 1972), 16–18.

37. *Latin America*, 6, 52 (December 29, 1972), 413.

38. *Andean Air Mail and Peruvian Times*, 32, 1662 (November 17, 1972), 5–6.

that seemed to reaffirm provisions that deducted fines levied on U.S. fishing vessels for fishing within the 200-mile limit from any aid earmarked for the offending country. Not surprisingly, the announcement produced a firestorm of protest in Peru. Minister of Energy and Mines Fernández Maldonado labeled the action as "flagrant imperialist aggression." Fisheries Minister Javier Tantaleán Vianini, who had recently returned from an unsatisfactory visit to the United States to find aid for the distressed Peruvian fishing industry severely affected by a dramatic decrease in the quantity of the small sardine-like *anchovetas* that sustained the fish meal industry, claimed that the U.S. had "no right" to formulate such a measure. "We must prepare ourselves for bad times," he stated. "The danger has not yet begun."[39]

The Peruvian press joined the chorus. *Oiga* described the action as one more example of the "arrogant super-imperialism of the United States," and *Caretas* argued that, by signing this law, Nixon had added "a new affront (*baldón*) to his Latin American policy."[40] In its report back to Lima, the Peruvian embassy interpreted Nixon's actions as a preelection maneuver to gain votes in California.[41] According to one unnamed senior U.S. official speaking privately, the controversy over Nixon's action had placed relations with Peru "at their lowest ebb since 1969."[42]

These reactions, especially on the part of government officials, may well have been calculated. As U.S. officials were quick to note, the measure that Nixon signed was not a new law but rather an amendment to existing legislation. Instead of reflecting a hard line, it actually increased presidential discretion in terms of applying sanctions. The main purpose, they argued, was to speed reimbursements from the U.S. Treasury to affected fishermen. Whatever the reality and the fine print, officials in Peru and other affected Latin American countries took advantage of the measure to restate their commitment to the 200-mile principle in anticipation of a United Nations–sponsored conference on the law of the sea to be held in Geneva the following year. In the meantime, Ecuador continued to capture U.S. tuna boats operating in its claimed waters, and in mid-December the Peruvian navy did the same with the *Blue Meridian*, found operating twenty-five miles offshore. After being escorted to Talara, the vessel was fined $10,000 and the captain obligated to purchase a $500 fishing license.[43]

---

39. Ibid.
40. *Oiga*, 11, 499 (November 3, 1972), 9; and *Caretas*, 22, 467 (November 10–23, 1972), 8–9.
41. *Correspondencia* (5-3-Y/146) (November 6, 1972), 5.
42. *Andean Air Mail and Peruvian Times* (November 17, 1972), 5.
43. *Andean Air Mail and Peruvian Times*, 32, 1667 (December 22, 1972), 4.

Actions of the Peruvian Embassy

Over the course of the year, the Peruvian embassy in Washington significantly increased the frequency, quantity, and quality of its reports back to Lima. By the end of the year, it had become common for the embassy to forward a weekly report on developments in the United States that ran to forty single-spaced pages. Considerable attention was given to domestic political developments, but sections also covered U.S. relations with other nations, economic and cultural affairs, and matters of particular interest to Peru. As usual, these were often buttressed with newspaper and magazine clippings, official U.S. government reports, and pages from the *Congressional Record*.

From July to November, many of these summaries focused on the presidential race. As with most observers, Berckemeyer thought the chances that Democratic candidate George McGovern would defeat the incumbent and perhaps initiate a change in policies toward Latin America were "remote."[44] A week after Nixon's smashing triumph, he reported on Secretary Rogers's address to the OAS ambassadors in which he promised that the changes initiated by the administration to "modernize" relations with Latin America would continue. The ambassador took these promises with a grain of salt. He pointed out that, given the Nixon administration's policy of reducing economic assistance to the region, its apparent support for various punitive amendments, and the Republican platform that barely mentioned Latin America, Rogers's comments were no more than diplomatic niceties (*simples palabras de occasión*). In the same communication, however, he also reported that, in his conversations with State Department officials, he had been reassured that the policy of threatening but not actually applying the punitive aspects of the Pelly and Gonzalez amendments would continue. He feared, nonetheless, that such amendments would encourage "new acts of provocation on the part of North American fishermen."[45]

In subsequent reports, Berckemeyer provided information on the personnel changes in the administration. Contrary to speculation, there were no appointments for Connally or Rockefeller, and both Rogers and Shultz remained in their posts. In the State Department, Kenneth Rush replaced Irwin as under-secretary, removing at least one high-level official with whom the Peruvians were familiar and with whom they had worked cooperatively in the past.[46] Near the end of December, the ambassador forwarded

---

44. *Correspondencia* (5–3-Y/111) (September 11, 1972), 1.
45. *Correspondencia* (5–3-Y/159) (November 20, 1972), 1.
46. *Correspondencia* (5–3-Y/164) (December 4, 1972), 6. Berckemeyer provided no commentary on these developments.

a statement from the White House Press Office about the administration's accomplishments over the past four years and its plans for the next four. He observed that the document said relatively little about Latin America other than making some of the usual promises, "many times repeated and which up to date have not been fulfilled." Preoccupied with the Soviet Union, China, Japan, and Europe, he concluded, the United States had placed "at a clearly secondary level its relations with the Latin American nations."[47]

Fishing Disputes Again and Velasco's State of Mind

At the beginning of 1973, the tuna returned to Peruvian waters as did U.S. fishermen. Whether emboldened by the Gonzalez and Pelly amendments to "new acts of provocation," as Berckemeyer reported might happen, or simply by the renewed abundance of tuna, a substantial increase in the number of North American tuna boats were detected in January. Twenty-two boats were seized by the Peruvian navy for fishing in claimed territorial waters. Owners of four of the mostly California-based boats paid $500 licenses and were soon released. The rest paid penalties of up to $95,180, later to be reimbursed by the U.S. government. The official response from Washington was muted, and one unnamed diplomat said that the United States was "keeping things cool" and seeking to avoid confrontation until the matter of limits could be discussed at an international meeting.[48]

In Lima, President Velasco strongly defended the tuna boat seizures and a recent decision to purchase arms from the Soviet Union. With regard to the arms purchases, a State Department intelligence note at the end of 1972 had mentioned the possibility that the Peruvian air force might soon buy four Soviet helicopters, representing the "first significant sale of military equipment [by them] to any of the hemisphere's armed forces." Nonetheless, the report concluded that the army was unlikely to follow the same course and allow "air and naval appetites for equipment [to] dominate policy decisions."[49] Despite these reassurances, in late January 1973, Ambassador Belcher reported on a conversation with Mercado, now the defense minister, who stated that the Peruvian government preferred to buy army tanks from the United States but because of the furor caused by the tuna boat

47. *Correspondencia* (5-3-Y/175) (December 21, 1972), 2.
48. *Andean Air Mail and Peruvian Times*, 33, 1672 (January 26, 1973), 1, and *Washington Post*, January 20, 1973, A12:7.
49. "Confidential Intelligence Note RAAN-56, Bureau of Intelligence and Research," USNA (1970–73) (Box 1781, Folder 1), 1–4.

seizures might be forced to retaliate by purchasing tanks from the Soviet Union.[50] Concerns about the Peruvians' pursuit of Soviet arms would soon lead the Nixon administration to shift course in its position on military assistance to the Velasco regime.

On the fishing dispute, de la Flor and the Foreign Ministry were working hard to line up other nations in support of the 200-mile-limit claim. The Peruvian position got a significant boost when the fisheries minister of the Soviet Union, who had sided previously with the United States on recognizing only a twelve-mile limit, assured his Peruvian counterpart, Minister Tantaleán, during a visit to Lima, that his nation and its fishermen would respect the Peruvian claim. That support aside, the Peruvians were unsure of having enough allies on the matter for the international meeting scheduled for Geneva later in the year, which they tried to postpone. The United States government was beginning to feel that the tide was turning against it and was seeking some sort of compromise.[51]

As the resolution of these and other matters remained pending, officials in Washington sought to gauge the strength of Velasco's position and the direction he might take the nation. In early February, a State Department official forwarded a memo to Hugh Crimmins, head of the American Republics Division, of a conversation he had had with the manager of International Affairs at the Dow Chemical Company, who, along with other business representatives, had met with the Peruvian leader on January 25. Velasco expressed again his appreciation for the United States, noting that if it had not been for the treatment he received at Walter Reed he would have no stomach; he nonetheless claimed that the United States was *"Muy Duro Con Todos Paises* [very harsh with all countries]," including Peru. He could not understand how the Nixon administration could open up to China and the Soviet Union while still withholding military sales and other forms of assistance to his country. He also expressed some concern with what seemed to be an administration tilt toward Brazil, describing that nation, historically a geostrategic concern for Peru, as "frightening and dangerous in its bursting growth, expansion and power."

On the domestic front, Velasco admitted that the workers were not yet with the regime, attributing this to a failure for them to understand fully what the military government was doing for them. The *campesinos*, however, were solidly behind the government's efforts and could be mobilized

---

50. "Confidential Telegram 579, 1–2573, from Belcher to the Department of State, January 26, 1973," USNA (1970–73) (Box 2544, Folder 6), 1.

51. *Latin America*, 7, 5 (February 2, 1973), 34.

easily to provide mass support, or so he believed. He also stated that certain publications like *El Comercio, La Prensa, Correo*, and *Ultima Hora* were "getting on his nerves" and might have to be closed. In a postscript, the Dow representative related that while the U.S. government and multilateral lending institutions "had their purses closed" in terms of loans to Peru, this was not true of "U.S. commercial bankers and Europeans who were in Lima fingering their checkbooks and anxious to lend."[52] As if to underscore this point, during a trip to San Francisco in January, Ambassador Berckemeyer thanked the Wells Fargo Group for the $40 million loan it had approved for Peru and was informed that Wells Fargo was also considering another $75 million loan.[53]

On February 7, Ambassador Belcher forwarded to Washington the embassy's annual "Country Analysis and Strategy Paper" for the next two fiscal years. He argued for the importance of Peru to overall U.S. interests in Latin America, particularly as a contrast to "Marxist" Chile. He saw the possibility of cooperation on various issues and pleaded for "pragmatism" and "flexibility." Sounding much like his predecessor, John Wesley Jones, he asserted that the policy of withholding loans to Peru had achieved "few positive results" and instead had made things more difficult for the embassy. As in the past, holding firm on the IPC compensation matter led Peruvians to believe—and not without reason—that the U.S. government was more concerned with protecting a private company than furthering the common good. While not abandoning efforts to get compensation for expropriated properties, Belcher concluded, it was now time "for a change and a new approach" to avoid future confrontations.[54]

The State of Velasco's Health

Any possible changes in U.S. policy toward Peru because of Belcher's advice were immediately overshadowed by a major domestic crisis. In late February, the government announced that President Velasco was gravely ill and close to death. He had suffered a stroke; however, his life was saved with emergency surgery that ultimately required the amputation of his right leg. During this period, both Cuba and the United States sent medical personnel to Peru to provide assistance. In his weekly report to the Foreign Ministry,

---

52. "Limited Official Use Memo to Crimmins from Willis C. Armstrong, February 5, 1973," USNA (1970–1973) (Box 2544, Folder 6), 1–3.

53. *Correspondencia* (5-3-Y/12) (January 22, 1973), 1.

54. "Country Analysis and Strategy Paper, FY 74 & 75, Peru," included in "Secret Air-Gram A-32, February 7, 1973," USNA (1970–1973) (Box 2544, Folder 3), 1–14.

chargé Roca Zela took pains to laud the efforts of the State Department in easing the way for a Peruvian and three U.S. specialists to get to Lima quickly to aid in the treatment of the ailing president.[55]

In Washington, both Kissinger and Nixon were advised of Velasco's illness on February 26. Two days later, President and Mrs. Nixon sent a message to Velasco in which they expressed their hopes for a successful surgery and a speedy recovery and assured him that he was in their "thoughts and prayers."[56] At the same time, Belcher reported back to Washington on the political implications of the crisis. While the power struggle going on within the regime was played out mostly behind the scenes, the general speculation, which Belcher shared, was that former foreign minister Mercado Jarrín, who had assumed the post of prime minister and defense minister on February 1, would succeed Velasco if the president either expired or failed to recover sufficiently to resume his full duties. The embassy's assessment of the consequences of that result was that there would be little change in the regime's basic foreign and domestic policies but that the "emphasis might shift and the tone and style would be different."[57]

On March 7, Belcher reported that Velasco's health seemed to be much improved (although this was before the amputation of his right leg due to gangrene), but it would still likely be months before he could resume office. In the meantime, Mercado continued as the dominant figure. There was some talk, however, that General Arturo Cavero Calixto, head of the Joint Command of the Armed Forces and an important advisor to Velasco, also might be a contender to succeed him.[58] According to Belcher, "U.S. interests would best be served if Cavero were to be the successor," but he revealingly observed that "either Mercado or Cavero would be better than what we have had," presumably meaning Velasco.[59] Another communication two days later saw the power struggle within the regime as between "good guys," including Mercado and Cavero, and the "bad guys," or more radical members of the ruling junta, including Generals José Graham Hurtado and Fernández Maldonado. "Our money," he concluded, "is still on some combination of the Mercado-Cavero forces."[60]

---

55. *Correspondencia* (5–3-Y/34) (March 5, 1973), 1.
56. "Rush Message, Department of State, February 28,1973," USNA (1970–1973) (Box 2543, Folder 4), 1.
57. "Confidential Telegram 1259 from Belcher to State, February 28, 1973," USNA (1970–1973) (Box 2543, Folder 4), 1–2.
58. For more on Cavero Calixto, see Frost, ed., *Latin American Government Leaders*, 104–5.
59. "Confidential Telegram 1452 from Belcher to State, March 7, 1973," USNA (1970–1973) (Box 2543, Folder 4), 1–2.
60. "Confidential Telegram 1533, from Belcher to State, March 9, 1973," USNA (1970–1973) (Box 2543, Folder 4), 2.

A few days later, Belcher informed Washington that Velasco had begun "what appears to be [a] one-in-million recovery but one that can never be complete." Perhaps somewhat grudgingly, he also observed that "thus [it] appears this remarkably tough and determined individual will continue as president somewhat longer, until service policies combine to determine [a] graceful exit."[61]

Belcher's final report on the crisis came on April 2. In a confidential telegram, he reported that Mercado had stepped down as provisional president and that Velasco had resumed his official duties. He added that various sources questioned whether the president would be "able to exert effective control" and that the next few weeks would be crucial in terms of determining the course of the regime. If Velasco did not "exert effective control," the power struggles that had taken place during his illness would continue. Mercado, now apparently backed by Cavero, would seem the most likely successor, "but other actors could figure in [an] attempt to fill [the] power vacuum."[62]

Whatever Belcher's sources were for this information, they were not all that accurate or reliable. During the crisis, strains between Velasco and Mercado emerged, with the president angered and disturbed by the prime minister's assumption of the presidential duties and the message he seemed to communicate that his interim status would inevitably become permanent. Once Velasco resumed office, the personal relationship between the two men cooled. Moreover, weary of the speculation concerning the matter of succession, Velasco henceforth downgraded the influence of the prime minister and assigned many of that position's tasks to COAP leader Graham. While Mercado resigned himself to this situation, this did not mean that Graham and the radicals had triumphed. Indeed, the individual who emerged as increasingly important within the cabinet and increasingly influential with Velasco was Minister of Economy and Finance General Francisco Morales Bermúdez. In the end, even though it was not clear at the time, from the viewpoint of U.S. interests, the ascendancy of the moderate and pragmatic Morales Bermúdez augured well for improved relations between the two nations.[63]

---

61. "Confidential Telegram 1614 from Belcher to State, March 13, 1973," USNA (1970–1973) (Box 2543, Folder 4), 1.

62. "Confidential Telegram 2105 from Belcher to State, April 2, 1973," USNA (1970–1973) (Box 2543, Folder 4), 3.

63. For more on the internal power struggles during the crisis and their results, see Kruijt, *Revolution by Decree*, 139–46.

Berckemeyer's View of Changes in Washington

While the behind-the-scenes power struggle played out in Lima, Ambassador Berckemeyer kept tabs on changes in the State Department that might affect Peru. Following an announcement by Charles Meyer that he would step down as assistant secretary for Inter-American Affairs, the ambassador's speculation about a successor focused on Hugh Crimmins of the State Department, who had stepped into the post temporarily, or John Hennesy, an official in the Treasury Department with whom the Peruvians had had some disagreements.[64] In mid-March, however, he wrote Lima that Jack B. Kubisch had been chosen for the post. Kubisch had been an attaché in the U.S. embassy in Paris, where he aided Kissinger in the peace talks with North Vietnam. He had previously served in Mexico and Brazil. Because he was fluent in Spanish, French, and Portuguese, Kubisch had been considered during his posting to Rio de Janeiro in 1963 as *muito amigo* (very much a friend) of Brazil.[65]

In a lengthier communication to Lima on the nomination, Berckemeyer argued that Kubisch's close links to Brazil were especially significant. That nation, now firmly under right-wing military control, was, he argued, "openly playing a preponderant (sub-imperial) role in promoting and advancing the interests of the United States in our region." The nominee was also a specialist in economic affairs, as the ambassador described it, "within the neo-colonialist orbit of the much criticized AID." Moreover, while it was still too early to tell with certainty, if there were to be any positive shifts in U.S. policy towards Latin America, "Mr. Kubisch would not appear to be the appropriate official to encourage a fuller opening of this country towards our region." Finally, Kubisch's role in assisting Kissinger in Paris indicated the United States' preoccupation with other areas of the world, relegating Latin America far down the list of the nation's foreign policy priorities. Nevertheless, Berckemeyer concluded, it was worth noting that Kubisch would be the first career diplomat since Thomas Mann to hold the assistant secretary position.[66]

In subsequent, increasingly detailed reports, Berckemeyer covered a wide range of items. These included Senate hearings into the possible involvement

---

64. *Correspondencia* (5–3-Y/39) (March 12, 1973), 11.
65. *Correspondencia* (5–3-Y/44) (March 19, 1973), 1.
66. *Correspondencia* (5–3-Y/48) (March 12, 1973), 1–2. Reporting on the nomination, *Latin America* agreed with Berckemeyer that the more nationalistic, Spanish-speaking nations of the region were unlikely to be "overjoyed" by the choice and to be confirmed in their belief "that Brazil is to be the United States's Trojan horse in Latin America." *Latin America*, 7, 13 (March 30, 1973), 100–101.

of the International Telephone and Telegraph Company (IT&T) in the internal affairs of Chile as well as some of the early developments of the evolving Watergate scandal.⁶⁷ He also forwarded information on proposals by some Republican congressmen to extend the U.S. fishing zone to two hundred miles, proposals that ran counter to the administration's own position.⁶⁸ When the OAS met in Washington in early April, Peru's ambassador informed Lima that he was not much impressed by Nixon's promise that "the days of paternalism [with regard to Latin America] have ended."⁶⁹ These and other promises of cooperation, in his view, were simply the same pious statements that had been made since 1969, with few concrete measures taken to back them up. He also observed that Nixon's absence from Washington during what he had labeled a "historic assembly" and that his remarks were read by someone else reflected further on the lack of seriousness on the administration's part in following through on its promises. Secretary of State Rogers's speech, while delivered directly, only "reiterated concepts and/or wishes still not put into practice."⁷⁰

Peru was represented at the OAS assembly by Foreign Minister de la Flor. De la Flor again took a confrontational stance regarding the United States. Sitting next to Secretary Rogers, he accused the United States of dominating the OAS and argued that Latin America needed a common front to oppose "imperialism, which was still present in America in both its old and new manifestations." Among the reforms he suggested was to move the headquarters of the organization from Washington to Panama, thus putting it closer to "the realities of Latin America" and farther removed from "the capital of the country which has the strongest political influence" in the organization.⁷¹

De la Flor's opposition to U.S. policies, however, did not prevent him from following the course of several of his military colleagues when it came to matters of personal health. Before his departure for the OAS meeting, he had requested through Belcher that a physical examination be arranged for him at Walter Reed Hospital. Belcher relayed the request with his recommendation that it be approved as it was "in the national interest."⁷² The State Department responded quickly, informing Belcher that the request

67. *Correspondencia* (5-3-Y/49) (March 26, 1973), 1–33.
68. *Correspondencia* (5-3-Y/58) (March 27, 1973), 4.
69. *DOSB*, lxviii, 1770 (May 28, 1973), 675–83.
70. *Correspondencia* (5-3-Y/63) (April 9, 1973), 1.
71. *Washington Post* (April 6, 1973), A4:2, and *Oiga*, 12, 521 (April 19, 1973), 18–20.
72. "Limited Official Use Telegram from Belcher to State, March 26, 1973," USNA (1970–1973) (Box 2542, Folder 1), 1.

had been approved but that de la Flor would be expected to reimburse Walter Reed for the expenses incurred.[73] Returning to Lima after the OAS meeting, de la Flor asked Belcher to let the staff at Walter Reed know of his "most sincere appreciation for the excellent treatment he received."[74]

Midcourse Corrections

Reporting on the OAS meeting, *Caretas* observed that "the image of the United States of Richard Nixon in Latin America is today at its lowest point," as evidenced by the confrontations with Peru and others in recent international gatherings.[75] An April 18 article in the *New York Times* reported that both Peruvians and U.S. businessmen operating in the country were growing weary of the U.S. government's policy of trying to force the Velasco regime to compensate IPC by withholding economic assistance. Most saw the policy as counterproductive and one that had become "a major annoyance in Peruvian-American relations."[76]

Behind the scenes, top Nixon administration officials were also expressing their private concerns about what appeared to be a recent deterioration in relations with Peru. On the same day the *Times* article appeared, Secretary of Defense Elliot Richardson sent a secret memo to Secretary of State Rogers with a copy to Kissinger suggesting some shift in the policy of denying military assistance to Peru to avoid that nation's increasing reliance on the Soviet Union for arms purchases.[77] A communication from Belcher on April 23, relaying the details of a conversation with Prime Minister Mercado, added some urgency. In that report, the generally moderate and pro-U.S. Mercado complained bitterly that the United States was providing the military of "Marxist" Chile with arms and assistance while denying the same to Peru.[78]

In an apparent response to these concerns, on April 25 Rogers sent a memorandum to President Nixon recommending that he issue a special waiver to allow the resumption of military sales to Peru. While such an action

73. "State Department Response, March 28, 1973," USNA (1970–1973) (Box 2542, Folder 1), 1.
74. "Limited Official Use Telegram from Belcher to State, April 10, 1973," USNA (Box 2542, Folder 1), 1.
75. *Caretas*, 23, 482 (August 15–29, 1973), 26, 28.
76. *New York Times* (April 18, 1973), 8:1.
77. "Secret Memorandum 7307449 from Richardson to Rogers and Kissinger, April 18, 1973," USNA (1970–1973) (Box 2544, Folder 6), 1–2.
78. "Confidential Telegram 2545 from Belcher to State, April 23, 1973," USNA (1970–1973) (Box 2544, Folder 6), 1–3.

might cause problems with congressmen pushing for sanctions on the fishing issue, larger Cold War concerns should prevail and the Soviets should not be allowed to establish a military relationship with Peru and potentially other Latin American countries "through our default."[79] Apparently convinced by Rogers's arguments, Nixon signed the waiver on May 14, determining that it was "important to the security of the United States" to do so.[80]

A few weeks earlier, there had been more good news for Peru, also indicating some positive changes in U.S. policy. On April 25, as Berckemeyer reported to Lima, the directors of the Inter-American Development Bank had voted to approve a $6 million loan for Peru. All the directors had voted in favor while the U.S. representative had abstained. This abstention was seen by the directors and by Berckemeyer as positive since, according to the Gonzalez amendment, the U.S. representative should have voted against the loan. Moreover, on this occasion that representative had expressed an inclination to reach "reasonable agreements" with Peru and had not reiterated the official thesis of the Nixon administration of the need for "swift, adequate, and effective compensation" for expropriated property. The ambassador interpreted this as "the first step in the search for solutions and as a sign of good will."[81] A week later, Berckemeyer informed Lima of World Bank President Robert MacNamara's announced intention to consider a $25 million loan to Peru for agricultural credits. The ambassador saw this as part of a "thawing" of the Peruvian situation at the bank.[82]

Mr. Rogers Visits the Neighborhood

There were further opportunities to improve the U.S.-Peruvian relationship when in mid-May Secretary of State Rogers undertook an eight-nation tour of Latin America. The purpose of the trip was to pave the way for a planned visit to the region by President Nixon later in the year (ultimately postponed because of the Watergate crisis) to show that the United States was not neglecting the hemisphere, as many had charged, and to show that the United States appreciated and was prepared to deal with the diversity of regimes that had appeared over the past few years.

---

79. "Confidential Memorandum 7307009 from Rogers to Nixon, April 25, 1973," USNA (1970–1973) (Box 1781, Folder 1), 1–5.
80. "Unclassified Letter from Marshall Wright, Assistant Secretary for Congressional Relations," USNA (1970–1973) (Box 1781, Folder 1), 2–3.
  81. *Correspondencia* (5–3-Y/82) (April 30, 1973), 2–3.
  82. *Correspondencia* (5–3-Y/89) (May 7, 1973), 7.

Certainly among the most diverse of these regimes was Peru's. During his thirty-six-hour stopover in Lima, Rogers had an unannounced two-hour meeting with a still recuperating Velasco in his weekend home in Chaclacayo on the outskirts of Lima, a meeting that was described as "very friendly."[83] In these and other talks, there was apparently a frank exchange of views in which the Peruvian military leaders communicated to the secretary the sincerity of their efforts to accelerate social and economic development and some of the obstacles they were encountering. Rogers reportedly came away from these discussions "highly impressed by the country's ruling generals." On his departure, he told Foreign Minister de la Flor that he now had a much clearer picture of the government's efforts "to improve the lives of the people of Peru" and promised to inform President Nixon of the regime's "dynamism." In later interviews, he also stated that the administration generally favored efforts of regional cooperation like the Andean Pact and, while the United States still stood firm in demanding compensation for expropriated properties, indicated some flexibility in its overall stance on this issue and a greater understanding than heretofore of the nationalist pressures and dynamics that led to such takeovers.[84]

Peruvian press coverage of the visit was generally positive. On a personal level, *Oiga*, for example, favorably contrasted the "suave and discreet" Rogers with the last important U.S. visitor to Peru, John Connally. It also reported that the conversations the secretary had with Mercado and de la Flor had been particularly productive in explaining clearly to the secretary the goals of the government. According to its report, the IPC matter did not come up for discussion because, in Mercado's words, "that is a matter that is over so far as Peru is concerned."[85] Back in Washington, Rogers observed in a press conference in early June that relations with Peru were "definitely improving" and that negotiations over compensation for expropriated companies with both Peru and Chile were showing some positive signs.[86]

Despite Rogers's upbeat assessment, there still remained many obstacles to a better relationship between the United States and Peru. On May 8, the Peruvians had nationalized the fish meal industry, a move that affected five U.S. firms. While a formula for compensation was provided, it did not satisfy the parties involved.[87] Then, over the next few months, there were delays in approving and delivering promised military equipment to Peru

---

83. *New York Times*, May 17, 1973, 12:5.
84. *Washington Post*, May 20, 1973, A4:1.
85. *Oiga*, 12, 525 (May 18, 1973), 9–12.
86. *Washington Post*, June 6, 1973, A4:7.
87. *New York Times*, May 13, 1973, 15:1.

and little progress on the fishing rights dispute. Finally, contrary to Peruvian embassy predictions, in late July the U.S. Congress, instead of revising or eliminating various punitive amendments, voted to keep them in force. Writing to Lima in early August, chargé Roca Zela traced these problems to the growing weakness of Nixon due to the Watergate scandal, the continuing power of the U.S. fishing lobby, and the weakness and ineffectiveness of the State Department in confronting private interests. "Given these circumstances," he concluded, "it should be noted, with melancholy objectivity, that the trip of [Secretary] Rogers to Peru, instead of being, as many had remarked, a chance to make up for lost time, is on the verge of being a waste of time."[88]

Signs of a Breakthrough and Further Complications

Further strains were put on the relations between the two countries when the Velasco regime began to criticize the operations of another major U.S. corporation, the Cerro de Pasco Company. In June, Minister of Mining and Energy Fernández Maldonado accused the company of violating regulations to provide adequate housing for its workers and claimed that some $58 million in investment was required to meet these needs.[89] The company sought to cut back its operations in Peru and was negotiating with the government to acquire some or all of its holdings, not including its share in the Cuajone project.[90] In his July 28 Independence Day address, Velasco referred to these negotiations without going into detail. These details were important in that the company claimed that its assets in Peru were worth some $174 million for which, according to some reports, the government was only prepared to offer a payment of $12 million. Foreign Minister de la Flor tried to deflect concerns about a possible confrontation over this issue by noting that satisfactory compensation agreements had been reached with other U.S. concerns, including IT&T and Southern Copper, and the same could well occur with Cerro.[91]

As this new complication arose, on August 9 both governments simultaneously announced the appointment of a new U.S. special envoy to try to resolve some of the outstanding issues between the two countries. Following in the footsteps of John Irwin was James Greene, a vice president

---

88. *Correspondencia* (5-3-Y/151) (August 2, 1973), 1–2.
89. *Wall Street Journal*, June 20, 1973, 20:3.
90. *Wall Street Journal*, July 6, 1973, 12:2.
91. *Washington Post*, August 16, 1973, G13:2.

of Manufacturers Hanover Trust. In making the announcement, the State Department clarified that the ongoing matter of the IPC compensation would not be on the table for discussion.[92] Most observers, however, believed that, while the IPC issue might not be on the agenda, the Cerro de Pasco matter certainly would be.[93]

That the Greene mission might be complicated soon became apparent. The special envoy arrived in Lima in mid-August and met with the Peruvian team headed by Prime Minister Mercado and four ministers. While the Cerro de Pasco issue did not come up during this visit, it was slated for future discussion. Shortly thereafter, at a press conference on August 29, Velasco, to the surprise of some, announced that, if some sort of accommodation with the company were not reached, the government would take over its properties directly, "by force if necessary." He added that the decision to take a harder line resulted from the company's failure to respond more quickly to demands that it improve workers' housing. Some interpreted this new stance as a negotiating ploy to get Cerro to lower its asking price. The company seemed taken aback, responding that official negotiations were slated to begin on September 10 and that the company had drafted a plan to address the housing issue.[94]

Despite Velasco's tough words, in early September, the United States determined to adopt a more conciliatory approach to Peru. In what the *Washington Post* described as a "major policy turnabout," the Nixon administration agreed to allow its representatives to vote favorably on loans to Peru from the World Bank and the Inter-American Development Bank. The reversal was attributed to the fact that negotiations on compensation matters had been undertaken by the Greene mission, the positive impression that Secretary Rogers had gained of the regime during his visit to Peru, and the "long pleading [for greater flexibility]" by Ambassador Belcher.[95] As a follow-up to this decision, on September 20 President Nixon notified Congress, by way of a presidential determination, that the extension of credit to Peru to purchase F-5 military aircraft had his approval since to do so was "important to the national security of the United States."[96]

Against the backdrop of these developments, negotiations between the Velasco government and the Cerro de Pasco Corporation commenced in

---

92. *DOSB*, lxix, 1783 (August 27, 1973), 310.
93. *Oiga*, 12, 538 (August 17, 1973), 9–10; and *Wall Street Journal*, August 21, 1973, 4:3.
94. Excerpts from Velasco's press conference can be found in Pease García and Verme Insúa, *Perú, 1968–1973*, 2:590–91. See also *Wall Street Journal*, August 30, 1973, 24.
95. *Washington Post*, September 20, 1973, A21:1.
96. *DOSB*, lxix, 1793 (November 5, 1973), 572.

mid-September. As the talks began, the company seemed prepared to surrender its Peruvian holdings but not without some fair compensation. Velasco appeared determined to walk a thin line between not alienating foreign investors in general while retaining his nationalist credentials. The different agendas put the company and the government on a collision course. On September 24, Cerro president C. Gordon Murphy announced that the company was pulling out of the negotiations, accusing the Peruvian government of bad faith. According to his interpretation, the regime was applying undue pressure through legal harassment and other tactics, including "public vilification," to force the company to accept a minimal amount, reportedly again of about $12 million, for properties it estimated to be worth $175 million. Murphy mentioned that the company had contacted both the Treasury and State departments, presumably to intercede on its behalf, and made reference to the provisions of the Gonzalez amendment, implying that they should be applied if the company's properties were nationalized without compensation.[97]

Naturally, Peruvians saw things differently. One official charged Cerro with behaving in "an anti-social, arrogant, and imperial manner, which the Peruvian government is disinclined to tolerate under any circumstances."[98] In a press conference soon after Cerro withdrew from the negotiations, Velasco was more circumspect but promised that the regime would adhere to its revolutionary and nationalistic course on this matter. While he blamed Cerro for the breakdown in the negotiations and indicated little give in the government's own conditions, he did not foreclose the possibility of future talks.[99] The war of words continued, however, making any outcome satisfactory to both sides increasingly unlikely.

The View from Washington

From Washington, the Peruvian embassy continued to keep Lima closely advised of developments there. Among these was the replacement of William Rogers as secretary of state by Henry Kissinger. Writing on August 23, Roca Zela noted, in a classic understatement, that Kissinger "does not appear to be a person with great affection for our continent," but that given current circumstances would be forced to deal with it. He correctly expected

---

97. *Wall Street Journal*, September 25, 1973, 12:3, and *Washington Post*, September 25, 1973, D10:5.
98. Pease García and Verme Insúa, *Perú, 1968–1973*, 2:617–18.
99. Ibid., 2:620–21.

the new secretary to have considerably more influence than his predecessor and to provide more cohesion and imagination in crafting and implementing foreign policy. He also saw the prior naming of Kubisch to the assistant secretary's position as part of Kissinger's pattern of surrounding himself with like-minded colleagues.[100]

On September 12, Berckemeyer forwarded his thoughts on the military coup the previous day that had overthrown the Allende regime in Chile. As he saw it, the United States was undoubtedly involved in some way in the events that led up to the overthrow, but in his view, its role should not be exaggerated in that he judged Chilean issues to be paramount in what happened there. Much of his attention was focused on Kissinger, whose extensive involvement in undermining the Allende government was not yet known. Instead, the ambassador focused on the new secretary of state's testimony before the Senate on the Law of the Seas treaty wherein he seemed to show little familiarity with a matter of great concern to Peru.[101] In a later communication, however, he reported on Kissinger's proposal to make a "great effort" to reinvigorate U.S. policy toward Latin America and to come up with new hemisphere initiatives. In pursuit of that effort, Kissinger planned to reorganize the State Department, putting Peruvian affairs under the direction of career diplomat Harry Schlaudeman.[102]

When talks with the Cerro de Pasco Corporation broke down, Peruvian officials in Washington worked energetically to bolster the government's case. Under explicit instructions from de la Flor, the embassy made known the Peruvian position on the matter to the State and Treasury departments, the U.S. Congress, and various international lending institutions. Foreign ministry and embassy officials met on several occasions with Assistant Secretary Kubisch and others in the State Department not only to explain their position but also to gauge the U.S. stance and possible reaction if the company's assets were to be nationalized. In one such meeting late in October, Roca Zela and Carlos García Bedoya of the Foreign Ministry told Kubisch that Peru was "prepared to be reasonable" in upcoming discussions on the matter. Kubisch said that he found little to object to in Velasco's recent comments on the company's actions and that the government's reaction to the company's communiqué breaking off the talks had been "restrained." García Bedoya agreed, noting that the company's remarks had severely hurt Peru's "nationalistic feelings," but that the "restrained" response indicated a

100. *Correspondencia* (5–3-Y/170) (August 23, 1973), 2.
101. *Correspondencia* (5–3-Y/184) (September 12, 1972), 1.
102. *Correspondencia* (5–3-Y/191) (September 20, 1973), 1–3.

willingness to find a negotiated settlement.¹⁰³ While Kubisch's remarks may have been for diplomatic discussion, they also suggest that the State Department had learned from the IPC dispute not to go too far out on a limb to protect the interests of a private company, particularly one with a somewhat tarnished image as an enterprise that acted like an autonomous entity that exploited its workforce and contaminated the surrounding environment.

While the Cerro conflict was the dominant theme of most embassy reports, Peruvian representatives also kept Lima up to date on President Nixon's deepening troubles because of the Watergate scandal. In early November, Roca Zela wrote that the administration was "close to collapse" and the possibility of impeachment was real.¹⁰⁴ Whatever Nixon's weakened position, he still had enough authority to override congressional pressures and in late December determined not to apply the punitive sanctions of the Pelly amendment to either Ecuador or Peru. The State Department informed the embassy that this was yet another demonstration of "good will" toward Peru on the part of the administration and showed that some accommodation on the 200-mile-limit dispute was possible "within the same conciliatory spirit that inspired the U.S.-Peruvian conversations through Mr. Greene."¹⁰⁵

In his end-of-the-year summary report, Ambassador Berckemeyer provided a rather hopeful assessment of the relationship with the United States. Peru, he began, had assumed a certain importance in the eyes of the United States over the past year, given its leadership role in the nonaligned movement and in pushing for reform of the OAS, forcing the Nixon administration to pay more attention to it in 1973 than it had in 1972. A positive sign of this new attention was Nixon's decision not to apply the punitive amendments. Crucial in this decision, Berckemeyer said, were State Department efforts in this direction, the Rogers visit, a Kissinger-inspired policy of a "new dialogue" with Latin America, and the Greene mission. Not to be forgotten, he added, were the continued efforts of the embassy "in defense of our national interests" as seen through the many contacts and discussions the ambassador and his staff had had with high administration officials, with important sectors of the international financial community, and with John Greene.

There were elements within political and diplomatic circles, Berckemeyer

---

103. *Correspondencia* (5-3-Y/219) (November 1, 1973), 6–8; and "Secret/No Distribution Department of State Memorandum of Conversation, October 29, 1973," USNA (1970–1973) (Box 2544, Folder 6), 3–4. There are no major differences or disagreements between these respective reports.

104. *Correspondencia* (5-3-Y/219) (November 1, 1973), 1.

105. *Correspondencia* (5-3-Y/245) (December 20, 1973), 6.

continued, who had their reservations about the Velasco regime and the direction it was taking the country—skeptical of the "neither capitalist nor communist" formula. Nevertheless, the Nixon administration seemed to have realized that the revolutionary government was not Marxist and did not represent a threat to hemispheric security. It also seemed to have accepted Peru's resumption of relations with Cuba within those same parameters. The potential resumption of arms sales, the easier access to loans from multilateral institutions, and the lack of any serious administration effort to discourage the flow of private investment into Peru were all seen as encouraging signs. Berckemeyer emphasized that, while Nixon had remained firm in his position that the expropriation of U.S. property required compensation, the administration had also indicated a greater tendency toward flexibility than had been apparent in the past.

A year that had begun with Peru defending its 200-mile claim with the capture of U.S. fishing vessels and ended with a threatened expropriation of the Cerro de Pasco holdings, had been clearly marked by the regime's firmness in upholding its own revolutionary and nationalistic principles. This firmness, he concluded, had convinced the United States that the best course to resolving disputes with Peru was through negotiation, not through coercion. As a result, the bilateral relationship had experienced "a perceptible improvement in relation to the four previous years."[106] Whether this would continue, of course, depended on the ultimate results of the Greene-Mercado discussions.

---

106. *Correspondencia* (5-3-Y/251) (December 31, 1973), 1–6.

11

NIXON AND VELASCO EXIT THE SCENE

Over the next two years, Peruvian-U.S. relations followed familiar patterns but also entered into a transition that reflected larger domestic developments. In August 1974, President Nixon was forced to resign his office as a result of the Watergate scandal. He was replaced by Vice President Gerald Ford. By retaining Henry Kissinger as his secretary of state, Ford's overall foreign policies differed little from his predecessor's. A year later, continued health problems and a deteriorating national and international situation forced General Velasco to surrender his post to General Francisco Morales Bermúdez Cerrutti, who abandoned much of the radical rhetoric and actions of the regime and took Peru in a more moderate direction, including in its relationship with the United States. During this period, the two men who had represented their respective nations as ambassadors since 1969, Taylor Belcher for the United States in Lima and Fernando Berckemeyer for Peru in Washington, were replaced. During the two final years of the Velasco regime, the course of the Peruvian-U.S. relationship continued to be occasionally confrontational followed by attempts at compromise and reconciliation.

The Cerro de Pasco Expropriation

On New Year's Eve of 1973, General Velasco announced the long-expected expropriation of the Cerro de Pasco mining operations. In his remarks to the nation, he underscored the benefits that would accrue to the country and particularly to the workers of the corporation from this new action by the revolutionary government. Cerro, he claimed, had represented "the most authentic symbol of the imperialist presence in Perú."[1]

From the Velasco regime's viewpoint, the Cerro de Pasco expropriation was an important event, which reinforced its nationalist credentials and which enjoyed clear popular support. Cerro had been operating in Peru since 1902, twenty years before the International Petroleum Company (IPC), and was much more vital to the overall Peruvian economy than the oil company. The expropriation, however, was less of a blow to the company than the regime's rhetoric suggested. The company's highland operations had become increasingly antiquated and would require considerable investment to update. Now this would be the Peruvian government's responsibility. In addition, its 20 percent investment in the Cuajone project, which was still ongoing and which had not been affected by the expropriation decree, was "worth more than all the assets of Cerro de Pasco put together."[2] Finally, the government had proceeded cautiously in preparing the groundwork for this takeover, not wanting to provoke another confrontation with the United States, which had occurred with the IPC takeover, and not wanting to scare off future foreign investors. An important ingredient in this process was the ongoing discussion with Nixon's special representative, John Greene, in trying to arrange compensation for nationalized U.S. properties with the Cerro de Pasco matter implicitly included in these.[3]

While the Cerro expropriation burnished the Velasco regime's nationalist credentials, robust economic growth at the beginning of the year fortified its overall position. There were, however, some clouds on the horizon. On the continental front, Peru faced the danger of increasing isolation. The military government of General Augusto Pinochet was now fully in charge in Chile, the government of Juan Perón in Argentina had taken a rightward turn, as had that of neighboring Uruguay, and the Acción Democrática Party, no friend of the Velasco government, had won recent elections in Venezuela. In addition, the right-wing military remained firmly in control on Brazil. Particularly worrisome were recent arms build-ups in Chile and Ecuador. Presidential advisor General José Graham Hurtado tried to put a positive spin on these developments, claiming that "things may look grim, but we know there are many military men who think like us in Chile, Bolivia,

---

1. *Oiga*, 13, 557 (January 11, 1974), 13–15, 19–23, 41.
2. *Latin America*, 8, 1 (January 4, 1974), 1–2.
3. *Peruvian Times*, 33, 1,721 (January 4, 1974), 3–4; and *Wall Street Journal*, January 2, 1974, 4.

Brazil and Argentina, men who believe in social change and are not with the imperialists." While this may have been true, it was not clear that these men were currently those who were ascendant in these regimes. Finally, growing opposition to the regime's policies among some sectors of the working and middle classes posed perhaps the most serious threat to the government's position.[4]

The Greene Negotiations

At the end of January, Ambassador Belcher reported what he considered good news with regard to progress on the Greene mission negotiations. On January 30, the Velasco regime announced a panel of civilian experts to advise the government on the details of these talks, particularly details regarding the appropriate compensation for the properties expropriated.[5] As the negotiations proceeded, the position of Prime Minister Edgardo Mercado Jarrín, who chaired the interministerial committee, appeared to have weakened. At the end of 1973, Velasco had appointed General Francisco Morales Bermúdez to be the new army chief of staff and next in line to replace Mercado as minister of defense and prime minister. Nonetheless, Mercado achieved an important victory when he announced on February 19 that the Greene negotiations had been concluded successfully. While both sides could claim satisfaction, it appeared that the major advantages accrued to Peru. Although the exact numbers remained to be determined, it was announced that Peru would pay compensation to five expropriated U.S. companies—Cerro de Pasco, W. R. Grace, Star-Kist, Gold-Kist, and Cargill—for about $150 million, with about half of that provided through remittances from the U.S. government. The final agreement, signed by Mercado and Miguel Angel de la Flor Valle for Peru and Greene and Belcher for the United States, specifically excluded any compensation for IPC, which, the text of the agreement clearly stated, was "a matter which has been definitively resolved." Moreover, the text also averred that the agreement represented "a total and definitive solution" to the problems of compensation and was intended to prevent any future claims by the companies involved.[6]

---

4. *New York Times*, January 15, 1974, 2.
5. The message from Belcher is "Confidential Telegram 0857 from Lima, January 31, 1974," from *Declassified Documents Released by the US Department of State EO Systematic Review 30 JUN 2005* and available on the National Archives Web site for Central Foreign Policy Files, hereafter cited as *EO Review*.
6. The full text of the agreement can be found in *Peruvian Times*, 33, 1,728 (February 22, 1974), 3–5.

The agreement was significant enough to warrant a press release from President Nixon, who expressed his satisfaction with the final resolution of a long-standing dispute and suggested that it could provide a pattern for a new approach to similar confrontations elsewhere in Latin America.[7] The response of representatives of the various companies involved was mixed. C. Gordon Murphy, president of Cerro, the company most affected by the agreement, complained that the compensation received was much less than the total value of assets seized. Nevertheless, it would continue its other operations in Peru.[8] Spokesmen for W. R. Grace and Star-Kist expressed cautious optimism about the results of the negotiations and called the settlement "reasonable" under current conditions. Most seemed willing to accept the outcome as "the best of a bad bargain."[9]

The Peruvian response to the accord was clearly more enthusiastic. At the signing ceremony, Prime Minister Mercado hailed the act as reflecting "an understanding and a respect among states that has prevailed over private interests. For this reason, it marks, clearly, a significant milestone in the process of relations between Peru and the United States."[10] *Oiga* described the agreement as a "clear triumph" for Peruvian diplomacy and "has opened the possibility of greater technological aid and economic collaboration with the United States."[11] In an informal sampling of public opinion a few weeks later, *Oiga* found general satisfaction with the agreement and a belief that it had worked to Peru's advantage. A number of those interviewed, however, just as with U.S. business representatives, had reservations. A labor leader warned that the agreement did not mean that "imperialism has been definitely defeated" and that the government had to continue to pursue its revolutionary and nationalistic path. A white-collar employee echoed these sentiments and argued that the regime had to be vigilant in dealing with "the voracious Yankee octopus." A university student agreed and predicted that the agreement "will not end the imperialistic exploitation of our country." Finally, a construction worker saw the accord as having little direct influence on his life, especially in the face of a rising cost of living and stagnant salaries. The government, he recommended, should spend less time on measures like the Greene agreement, which only served to "enhance its

---

7. *DOSB*, 70, 1812 (March 18, 1974), 272–73.
8. *Wall Street Journal*, February 20, 1974, 4, and *Washington Post*, February 20, 1974, A03.
9. *New York Times*, February 20, 1974, 11.
10. *Caretas*, 24, 494 (February 21–March 7, 1974), 6. In his interview with me almost thirty years later, Mercado still evinced a sense of pride in having accomplished the Greene agreement, which he saw as clearly beneficial to Peru and the result of his own policies and practices.
11. *Oiga*, 8, 563 (February 22, 1974), 9.

image" and more on addressing the fundamental social and economic conditions of the poor.[12]

As these judgments were expressed in the Peruvian press, U.S. Ambassador Belcher, who had played a major role in facilitating the Greene mission negotiations, sent an extensive telegram to Washington explaining in some detail how they had come to fruition. Internal dynamics, he argued, were important. On February 21, 1973, Greene had met secretly with Velasco, carrying a private message from President Nixon suggesting that the two governments once again try to resolve outstanding issues on compensation for expropriated U.S. properties. By this time, unlike the case with the earlier Irwin mission, Velasco was well established in power and feeling fairly confident in the regime's status and progress. Much of the revolutionary program had been implemented, prices for mineral exports were high, and Peru had little difficulty in getting credits and loans from international banks. While the visit of Secretary of State William P. Rogers had certain positive repercussions, the regime, especially through Mercado and de la Flor, continued to take a rather strident anti-U.S. stance in various international meetings.

Greene's next visits in June and August did not find the internal climate much changed and little headway was made. During his next trip in late September, however, a number of developments had occurred to change the tenor and direction of the talks. Internal dissent from both peasants and workers had shaken the regime. The conservative navy had not been happy with the nationalization of the fish meal industry and a crackdown on the press. There was also some concern within the regime to counterbalance what appeared to be the growing influence of Soviet arms purchases. The economy began to stagger with the worldwide energy crisis, the need to import more oil, and increasing balance-of-payments problems. Other than the Cuajone project, there had been almost no new foreign investment over the past several years. Another factor may have been the desire of Velasco, who was reported again to be in poor health, to leave a legacy with an agreement with the United States that "would place a welcome stamp of respectability and even of acceptance on the Peruvian revolution." Finally, according to Belcher, of great influence was the overthrow of the Allende regime in Chile, serving both to contribute to the diplomatic isolation of the Velasco government and as a warning about the consequences of an intransigent position on compensation for nationalization.

With the impetus provided by these developments, by early February

---

12. *Oiga*, 8, 564 (March 1, 1974), 4–5, 46.

1974 the regime was ready to accept the agreed-upon conditions. At a cabinet meeting on February 12, the vote was 9 to 4 in favor, with Foreign Minister de la Flor and Minister of Mines and Energy Fernández Maldonado opposed. After what Belcher described as "a frenzied week of activity," the final details of the complicated package were hammered out and the accord signed on February 21.

Whatever the reasons for the ultimate resolution, the agreement was, in Belcher's terms, "a significant achievement" from the U.S. point of view: "It serves to reaffirm the principle of adequate compensation for expropriated properties. It removes a major irritant in relations with Peru, one of the hemisphere's shrillest and most persistent U.S. critics. As an accommodation with a sometime antagonist, it is consistent with the fresh start the U.S. is seeking to make in Latin America." However, he warned, the United States should not be sanguine about the prospects for an overall rapprochement with the Velasco government, which more than likely would continue to adhere to its independent and nationalist course.[13]

Belcher Departs

For Belcher personally, the Greene agreement was the high point of his mission to Peru. As he prepared to leave his post in March, he told *Caretas* that he considered the agreement not only to have eased certain tensions between the United States and Peru but also "to have initiated a new step in inter-American relations" as evidenced by Secretary of State Kissinger's renewed emphasis on a "new dialogue" with Latin America at the recent Mexico City assembly of foreign ministers. These remarks came following a farewell luncheon for the ambassador hosted by Foreign Minister de la Flor at the Torre Tagle Palace, where he was called by the minister "a good friend of Peru and of the Revolutionary Government of the Armed Forces, as well as a lucid and effective diplomat and a loyal and intelligent servant of the interests of his country."[14] Even the leftist *Oiga*, which had featured Belcher's predecessor Jones as the "Ambassador of the IPC" on one of its covers, had generally kind words for the departing diplomat. In what it described as a "cordial interview," Belcher told *Oiga* that he had learned much about Peru and about Latin America during his mission and had been profoundly affected by his tours of the *pueblos jovenes* (urban shantytowns) and the poverty he witnessed there. With the recent Greene accord,

---

13. "Confidential Telegram 1798 from Belcher to DOS, March 7, 1974," *EO Review*, 1–5.
14. *Caretas*, 24, 497 (April 4–18, 1974), 11.

he concluded, some of the loans that the United States had previously withheld had begun to arrive. While he could not guarantee the resumption of substantial foreign investment, he thought that the agreement had at least provided "a more welcoming environment" than had been the case before the accord.[15]

In an interview with the *Washington Post* after his return to the United States, Belcher showed a considerable amount of sympathy for the efforts of the Velasco government to bring fundamental change to Peru. Over the past fifteen years, he observed, the United States had been urging Latin Americans to change the inequitable land-owning patterns that characterized much of the region and with little success. Peruvian efforts in this regard, however, had begun to produce notable changes. Programs to increase and improve public housing, reduce illiteracy, and attack poverty in both urban areas and in the sierra had been implemented although they still had a long way to go to achieve significant results. In carrying out these programs, Belcher noted, certain "vested interests," some of which were North American, were affected. "We had to find a way to live with it, so that we could get into a position to cooperate with the Peruvian government in its effort to improve the lot of millions of Peruvians living in relative poverty for centuries." That way, he implied, was the Greene agreement. Finally, with regard to the future of the military regime, he concluded, "They have a sense of mission and they have no intention of turning over to others what they regard as their duty to renovate, strengthen, and unite the nation."[16]

Dean Takes Over

Belcher's successor was fifty-four-year-old Robert W. Dean, who arrived in Lima to assume his post on April 22. A career diplomat since 1950, he had served previously in various posts in Latin America, including Brazil, Chile, and Mexico. He was fluent in Spanish and was married with four children. His wife, the former Doris May Wilkins, was a student of colonial Latin American history and was writing a thesis on indigenous uprisings in Peru and Mexico. Dean was reported to be informal, preferring to be called "Bob," as well as a being a golf and tennis enthusiast.[17]

---

15. *Oiga*, 8, 565 (March 8, 1974), 14–15, 39.
16. *Washington Post*, June 2, 1974, L2. Belcher's actions, the *Post* observed, "left the two nations at their best level of understanding since President Juan Velasco Alvarado took power."
17. *Oiga*, 8, 571 (April 19, 1974), 8; and *Peruvian Times*, 24, 1737 (April 26, 1974), 16. Dean had been Deputy Chief of Mission in Santiago, Chile, from 1965 to 1968 and had held the same post in Mexico City prior to his appointment to Peru. U.S. Department of State, *The Biographic Register, 1974*, 81.

Dean took over the embassy at a propitious moment. The Greene agreement seemed to have broken the logjam for international credit to flow to Peru. In mid-April, the Export-Import Bank approved a $55 million loan to the Southern Peru Copper Corporation to complete the financing of the Cuajone project. This loan was a direct result of the Greene accords.[18] Later in the month, the World Bank authorized a $26 million loan for highway construction in the sierra.[19] The State Department had also informed the Velasco government in March that it was pursuing efforts to have Congress approve the sale to Peru of twenty-four A-37B trainer aircraft.[20] In late April, Nixon's special representative on trade issues, William D. Eberle, met with the junta and while no specific agreements were reached, the United States showed a willingness to be more flexible on certain issues involving tariffs on and quotas for Peruvian exports than previously had been the case. Despite continuing disagreements over the punitive measures such as the Gonzalez amendment, Eberle concluded that the overall tone of his meeting was "positive."[21]

Ambassador Dean reported that embassy officials had received indications from a Peruvian Foreign Ministry source that the regime was more willing to show flexibility on the 200-mile limit.[22] In addition, perhaps trying to reinforce what seemed to be a more cordial relationship between the two nations, Dean also recommended that military assistance, particularly supplying the Peruvian army with armored personnel carriers, be approved. Aware of State Department concerns with fueling an arms race in Latin America, he argued that "U.S. security assistance to Peru helps to dispose this militarily ruled country more favorably to our overall interests, *notably access to natural resources* [my emphasis], and it reduces what is obtained from communist sources."[23]

Dean's recommendation came on the heels of growing U.S. concern about previous Peruvian arms purchases from the Soviet Union. A *Washington Post* article in late December 1973 highlighted that the delivery of Soviet helicopters and tanks to the Velasco regime had been the first of such sales in Latin America and represented what could be the beginning of a troubling trend of increased Soviet influence in the hemisphere.[24] These

18. *Peruvian Times*, 24, 1736 (April 19, 1974), 3.
19. *Wall Street Journal*, April 26, 1974, 6.
20. "Confidential Telegram 053025 from State to Lima, March 16, 1974," *EO Review*, 1–3.
21. "Limited Official Use Telegram 089566 from State to all American Republic Diplomatic Posts, May 1, 1974," *EO Review*, 1–5.
22. "Confidential Telegram 04042 from Lima to State Department, May 23, 1974," *EO Review*, 1–3.
23. "Secret Telegram 05010 from Dean to State, June 21, 1974," *EO Review*, 1–3.
24. *Washington Post*, December 18, 1973, A13.

fears were echoed by Republican Congressman Floyd Spence of South Carolina, who on March 7, 1974, read into the *Congressional Record* a newspaper article on the danger such purchases posed in helping to stimulate an unhealthy arms race in Latin America.[25] At this time, however, the U.S. embassy in Lima downplayed the significance of these purchases, arguing in a March dispatch that Velasco had probably agreed to them as a way to mollify the leftist elements within his regime while simultaneously moving forward on such matters as the Greene negotiations to improve relations with the United States and thereby assuage the concerns of the more moderate members of his governing team.[26]

In another communication two months later, the embassy was a bit more alarmist. It observed that the Soviets had made a "significant entry into Peru through its tank sales and military advisers" and argued that, to counter these influences, Peruvian requests for military equipment from the United States be granted.[27] This was followed shortly by Dean's favorable recommendation. In August, the ambassador reported that the Peruvians appeared not to be pursuing further Soviet arms because of the unfavorable terms imposed. He also suggested a cooling in the overall relationship, with the Soviets somewhat baffled by "Peru's repeated denunciations of communism as a way of organizing society." He also recognized, however, that the military equipment the Velasco regime had received from the USSR had tipped the balance in Peru's favor when it came to any possible confrontation with Chile, a possibility that was of some concern by the end of the year. Accordingly, he recommended that the United States maintain "an even handed approach" in providing security assistance to both nations to prevent any "further imbalance."[28]

Twists, Turns, and Tensions

While the Greene agreement appeared to have improved Peruvian-U.S. relations in general and could be heralded by the Velasco regime as a triumph for its nationalist and revolutionary orientation and policies, there remained important internal strains within the government. Many of these were related to Velasco's illness, the maneuvers that had occurred to replace him

---

25. *Congressional Record—House* (March 7, 1974), 5843.
26. "Confidential Report 01798 from the U.S. Embassy, Lima to DOS, March 7, 1974," *EO Review*, 1–5.
27. "Confidential Report 04055 from the U.S. Embassy, Lima to DOS, May 24, 1974," *EO Review*, 1–4.
28. "Secret Telegram 06418 from Dean to DOS, August 5, 1974," *EO Review*, 1–3.

while he was incapacitated, and his own estrangement from elements within the armed forces, his principal base of his support, along with certain key civilian advisors and the populace at large. Although his physical and mental toughness had enabled him to survive the amputation of his leg, a continued deterioration in his overall condition exacerbated his political difficulties.[29]

These internal tensions became public in early June when Velasco forced the resignation of the naval minister, Admiral Luis E. Vargas Caballero, who had become something of a rallying figure for the more conservative elements of the regime and the public. Rear Admiral José Arce Larco, who had been Peru's naval attaché in Washington, was recalled to Lima to replace Vargas. Shortly thereafter, two other admirals resigned their cabinet positions. The U.S. embassy had reported on strains within the cabinet earlier, noting in particular that the navy had been upset by the nationalization of the fish meal industry and the regime's attacks on the freedom of the press.[30] In early June, Velasco announced that members of former president Fernando Belaúnde Terry's Acción Popular Party, who had been among the regime's severest critics, had been conspiring with the Brazilian government in a "counter-revolutionary plot" aimed to undermine the government. As a result, the party's offices were closed and its secretary-general, Javier Alva Orlandini, sent into exile.[31]

In late July, Velasco began a campaign either to take over directly or to shut down most of the major newspapers and magazines in Peru, claiming that they represented only the "privileged" sectors of society and were more responsive to their wealthy owners than to the people of the country. Perhaps most notable was the takeover of *El Comercio*, the nation's oldest and most prestigious daily, long owned and edited by the Miro Quesada family. *El Comercio*, despite its conservative bent, had been a longtime champion of nationalizing the IPC holdings and had lauded the Velasco government's actions in that regard. Over time, however, it had become more critical. To ensure more favorable coverage and opinion, the regime turned the paper over to the Christian Democrats under the editorial direction of party leader Héctor Cornejo Chávez.[32] Over the next few months, the crackdown led to the closure of magazines that generally had been supportive of the regime, such as *Oiga* and, at least temporarily, *Caretas* and even extended to a nonpartisan and limited distribution publication, the *Peruvian Times*.

29. For a good summary of these developments, see Kruijt, *Revolution by Decree*, 142–47.
30. "Confidential Telegram 01798 from the U.S. Embassy, Lima to DOS, March 7, 1974," *EO Review*, 3.
31. *Latin America*, 8, 22 (June 7, 1974), 170; and *Peruvian Times*, 24, 1,743 (June 7, 1974), 3.
32. *Latin America*, 8, 30 (August 2, 1974), 233–34; and *Peruvian Times*, 24, 1,751 (August 2, 1974), 4–6.

The newspaper takeover initially prompted little immediate domestic response. However, combined with the official visit by Cuban war minister Raúl Castro to observe the July 28 military parade along with public disclosure of the "Plan Inca," which laid out the radical aspirations of the regime and which was the major subject of Velasco's Independence Day speech, it did produce some street demonstrations, especially in the upscale suburbs of Miraflores and San Isidro.[33] In the United States, the most extensive coverage of the press crackdown came from the *New York Times*, which published two editorials critical of these measures.[34] The second of these, "Reign of Silence," prompted a strongly worded letter from Berckemeyer, objecting to what he considered an unjustified "personal attack" on President Velasco.[35]

In Lima, Ambassador Dean, still relatively new in his post, found himself caught up in what threatened to be a new crisis in the Peruvian-U.S. relationship. On August 6, he informed Washington that he was alert to the new situation and had already made his concerns with regard to the changes in the press known to the regime. In particular, he had relayed to high officials his objections to charges made by Hugo Neira, the recently appointed director of *Correo*, that the United States was somehow encouraging an arms race that would lead to a conflict between Peru and Chile.[36]

A few days later, Dean followed up with a more extensive review of developments in Peru over the past three months and their implications for U.S. policy. These developments, especially revelation of the details of the "Plan Inca," seemed to indicate that the more radical forces within the regime were now in control. Some, he said, were calling these events a "Marxist Putsch." The main thrust of the recent changes seemed to be toward complete state and worker control of all economic enterprises. "The new Peru," he wrote, "will apparently be a uniquely Peruvian military-dominated, corporate-Marxist model." Embassy hopes that Morales Bermúdez, still slated to assume the prime minister's post in February of the following year, might swing the regime in a more moderate direction, had now dimmed. Morales Bermúdez was not "Velasco's close revolutionary associate," and there was speculation that he would soon be replaced by someone who was. All of these developments, he concluded, did not bode well for the future relationship between the two countries. "In short, Peru will continue to be a very testy state with which to deal, both bilaterally and in multinational

---

33. *Latin America*, 8, 31 (August 9, 1974), 247.
34. The two editorials appeared in the editions of June 19, 1974 (44), and July 30, 1974 (32).
35. *New York Times*, August 6, 1974, 32.
36. "Confidential Telegram 06519 from Dean to DOS, August 6, 1974," *EO Review*, 1–2.

fora."³⁷ While not all of these predictions, especially regarding the fate of Morales-Bermúdez, would prove accurate, on the whole, they were generally on target.

In another report one week later, Dean commented on possible discontent with Velasco from within the armed forces. Having stated earlier that the removal of Vargas Caballero, "the one service commander whom he had not been able to bend to his will," had made Velasco "stronger than ever in power," Dean amended that assessment to suggest that enmity toward the regime still persisted within the navy, especially among its "junior and middle grade ranks." While some of this discontent was also evident within the air force, the army, "the service that counts," still seemed solidly behind the president and, the ambassador concluded, "what dissatisfaction now exists does not so far appear serious enough to threaten him [Velasco]."³⁸

A further ingredient in the mix for evaluating the regime's course and prospects was the state of the economy. In early September, Dean reported that the agricultural sector, largely as a result of problems with agrarian reform measures, had performed poorly over the past year or so and a lack of private investment had combined to produce a shortage of consumer goods, leading to growing popular discontent. Adding to the discontent was a projected 25 percent increase in the inflation rate. The overall management of the economy had done little to inspire confidence and many skilled managers and technical personnel were leaving the country to pursue other opportunities. Moreover, it seemed unlikely that new petroleum resources would become available in the foreseeable future. To add to these woes, the regime was facing balance-of-payments problems and a growing internal deficit. On the plus side, the nation's international credit position was still strong, and foreign investors continued to show confidence and interest in the nation's prospects. Despite some ongoing difficulties, it seemed as though the Cuajone project would proceed soon. "On balance," the embassy concluded, "the government will not find it necessary to modify the basic direction of its reforms nor will it encounter sufficient public discontent to threaten the stability of the government itself."³⁹

Further insight into the state of the regime came in a report Dean provided of a private meeting with Velasco on September 23. The meeting began on a less than promising note. Dean said that he found the president "unusually quiet, cold and uncommunicative." The first part of the conversation

---

37. "Confidential Telegram 06692 from Dean to DOS, August 13, 1974," *EO Review*, 1–9.
38. "Confidential Telegram 06933 from Dean to DOS, August 20, 1974," *EO Review*, 1–2.
39. "Confidential Telegram 07508 from Dean to DOS, September 7, 1974," *EO Review*, 1–7.

was a Velasco monologue on alleged CIA and Peace Corps involvement in the nation's internal affairs and a supposed U.S. bias in favor of Brazil and Chile as opposed to the interests of Peru. In response, Dean sought to assure the Peruvian leader that the United States was trying to achieve a balanced and evenhanded policy with all three nations, especially regarding military assistance. He pointed out that the State Department had recommended some $20 million of assistance to both Chile and Peru for fiscal year 1975, and if any congressional cuts in these proposals were to be made, they would come in the funding for Chile because of concerns over human rights violations. He also went over familiar ground in describing how particular requests for equipment and aid took time as they worked their way through the bureaucratic process. Velasco seemed little convinced by these assertions, telling Dean point-blank that he believed that "you [the U.S.] are both feeding and arming Chile."

As the conversation proceeded, Velasco provided a strong defense of his recent measures. The "Plan Inca," he claimed, "was not a communist but a national revolutionary effort." The press law, he asserted, "is designed to achieve objectives of the revolution, and to bring into the main stream certain classes or groups of Peruvians." Reciting a familiar refrain, he assured Dean that the government was neither Marxist nor procommunist and "that neither the Soviets nor the Cubans nor any others are going to dominate Peru." In response, Dean took pains to emphasize that the United States did not consider his regime to be communist and to repeat again that it was not favoring Chile over Peru.

In concluding his report, Dean observed that Velasco "thawed" during their conversation, which "may have cleared the air somewhat." "We can certainly expect," he observed, "the Peruvians to be alert both here and in Washington to any signs of discriminatory treatment favoring Chile over Peru." With regard to internal dynamics within the regime, he emphasized the continued division between the "moderates," who were the majority, and the "hard-liners," who, while in the minority, for the moment seemed to be ascendant. That situation could change at the end of the year when important command and ministerial appointments were to be made. In the meantime, he believed, Velasco "is still in very firm control—but these manifestations of domestic opposition add to his suspicions and concerns."[40]

Although it received little attention at the time, another important issue arose to bedevil Peruvian-U.S. relations. From midyear onward, for the first but certainly not the last time, embassy dispatches from Lima reported on

---

40. "Secret Telegram 08043 from Dean to DOS, September 24, 1974," *EO Review*, 1–7.

joint efforts by both countries to stem the growing tide of drug trafficking from South America to the United States. Peru's role consisted primarily in producing the raw coca leaf, mostly grown on the eastern slopes of the Andes, which was then shipped to Ecuador and Colombia for processing and shipment. There had been some success in apprehending carriers at Jorge Chávez airport; however, control in Peru was complicated because there was no major cartel in charge of the trafficking but rather it was in the hands of many small-time dealers, making enforcement extremely difficult. Nonetheless, on May 31, 1974, the two governments had signed an agreement whereby the United States would provide a grant of $235,208 to the Peruvian Investigation Police (PIP) for counternarcotic efforts. As time would show, this was only a small down payment on what would become an increasingly expensive—and increasingly frustrating—campaign. Unlike on many other issues involving the two nations, however, the embassy reported that on this matter "the relations enjoyed by the DEA [Drug Enforcement Agency] office with the PIP narcotics division have been excellent."[41] For the moment, on at least this subject, both governments seemed to agree.[42]

Change and Continuity in Washington

While Velasco's actions in Peru signaled certain shifts in tactics, more fundamental and spectacular changes occurred in the United States. In early August, faced with the possibility of impeachment because of the Watergate scandal, Richard Nixon became the first president in U.S. history to resign his office, turning the presidency over to Vice President Gerald Ford. Somewhat ironically, given what its own fate would be in the not-too-distant future, *Oiga* heralded the resignation as a triumph for a free press, given the important role newspapers such as the *Washington Post* played in Nixon's downfall.[43]

In a dispatch on August 12, Ambassador Berckemeyer provided considerable detail on Nixon's resignation and its possible consequences. While this was clearly an unprecedented event in U.S. history, he predicted that it would have little effect on foreign policy, especially since Ford had determined to keep Secretary of State Kissinger, who had avoided the fallout from Watergate. Therefore, the foreign policies championed by Nixon, which many, he noted, saw as the disgraced ex-president's most important legacy,

    41. "Confidential Telegram 05825 from Dean to DOS, July 17, 1974," *EO Review*, 1–5.
    42. For a more thorough study of this issue, which remains a main focus of U.S.-Peruvian relations up to the present, see Cotler, *Drogas y política en el Perú*.
    43. *Oiga*, 8, 588 (August 16, 1974), 18–20.

would continue. Soon after the resignation, all the chiefs of missions had been called to a special meeting at the State Department to confirm this continuity.[44] In subsequent communications, he reported on speculation that Ford would name either Nelson Rockefeller or George H. W. Bush as vice president and relayed in some detail the adverse reaction to the new president's pardon of Nixon.[45]

On October 21, Berckemeyer reported that William D. Rogers had been named as the new assistant secretary of state for Inter-American Affairs. Rogers was a forty-seven-year-old attorney from the prestigious Washington law firm Arnold and Porter and had served in the 1960s as a program coordinator for the Alliance for Progress and as an administrator in AID. From 1966 to 1970, he had been president of the Center for Inter-American Relations in New York, and he still served on its board of directors. Berckemeyer described Rogers as a "Kennedy Liberal," who had written a book favorable to the Alliance for Progress and who "knew profoundly the problems of our region" and was considered an expert in hemisphere affairs.[46]

In his confirmation hearings, Rogers claimed that over the past several years the OAS had served as a forum for confrontation between Latin America and the United States but that a different and more positive spirit had evolved because of Kissinger's proposed "new dialogue." After assuming his post, Rogers assured Latin American diplomats that, while the region might have been overlooked somewhat during the Nixon presidency, "it is now included in the list of the ten major policy preoccupations of the United States." Rogers also underscored his opposition to any interventionist actions by the United States in the region, particularly along the lines of alleged CIA involvement in the overthrow of the Allende regime in Chile. Berckemeyer observed that he found these assurances "attractive" (*aliciente*), but that "we shall see if the theory is confirmed in practice." Kissinger's decision not to attend a meeting of hemisphere foreign ministers in Quito, for example, seemed to belie the assertion that Latin America was a priority for the administration. He also described U.S. actions in the OAS as "not very constructive." Despite these reservations, Berckemeyer found Rogers's appointment overall as encouraging and hoped that it would lead to productive bilateral conversations in the future.[47]

---

44. *Correspondencia* (5-3-A/922) (August 12, 1974), 4.

45. *Correspondencia* (5-3-A/964) (August 19, 1974), 1; and *Correspondencia* (5-3-A/1024) (September 9, 1972), 2.

46. Rogers's book on the Alliance was entitled *The Twilight Struggle* and had a foreword by Senator Robert F. Kennedy.

47. *Correspondencia* (5-3-Y/188) (October 21, 1974), 1–4.

There were some signs that such hopes might be realized. On October 10, the State Department had instructed the embassy in Lima to deliver to Foreign Minister de la Flor a "Dear Miguel Angel" letter from Kissinger, suggesting that the two nations engage in talks involving small working groups of senior officials to discuss outstanding issues such as the restructuring of the OAS. These talks, Kissinger said, would be undertaken in the spirit of the "new dialogue" and that "Assistant Secretary William Rogers and I feel these consultations would help us to clarify the issues we face, identify opportunities for improved bilateral cooperation, and generally pave the way for our personal deliberations [which would take place at the Quito meeting scheduled for mid-November]."[48] In addition to this attempt to reach out to the Peruvian regime, Rogers sought to assure Berckemeyer at an October 18 meeting that he and the State Department were doing all that they could to respond positively to Peru's requests for military assistance and equipment and assured him that "we are not footdragging" but rather were working on the various "bureaucratic problems" that were slowing delivery.[49] In what could be interpreted as another positive sign, Dean reported on October 24 that he and Special Ambassador Sheldon Vance had had a productive meeting with Interior Minister General Pedro Richter Prada over ways to deal with the growing narcotics problem. While Richter complained of the lack of cooperation of "neighboring countries" in dealing with the issue, he was complimentary about DEA efforts to assist the Peruvian police. As a result of their conversations, Dean and Vance recommended bolstering the DEA staff in Lima, but they also warned that a too visible presence could be counterproductive "in this volatile and sensitive environment," where "nationalistic hackles" and "exaggerated charges of [a] CIA presence in this country" could easily be raised.[50]

A Tense Two Months

It did not take long for these nationalistic hackles and exaggerated charges to surface. On November 2, Dean reported to Washington that the Velasco regime would soon ask the United States to withdraw all Peace Corps volunteers from Peru, alleging that they were involved in espionage activities

---

48. "Confidential Telegram 223426 from DOS to Lima, October 10, 1974," *EO Review*, 1–3. For more on Kissinger's Latin American initiatives at this time, see *Latin America*, 8, 44 (November 8, 1974), 345–46.

49. "Confidential Telegram 230826 from DOS to Lima, October 20, 1974," *EO Review*, 1–2.

50. "Confidential Telegram 09039 from Dean to DOS, October 24, 1974," *EO Review*, 1–3.

and were performing duties, particularly in the agricultural sector, that could be better served by Peruvian government agencies. Before the departure, the government was planning to request the transfer of all volunteers from the southern region, presumably because they represented a threat if a war with Chile broke out. This decision, Dean argued, was the culmination of a recent steady drumbeat of allegations in the government-controlled press, now reflecting the views of leftist elements within the regime, that the Peace Corps volunteers were in league with the CIA to undermine the government.[51] Despite Dean's assurances to Velasco, de la Flor, and Richter that the volunteers and AID officials were not engaged in intelligence-gathering activities, he was unable to overcome what he described as their "paranoid concern" over CIA involvement in the country.[52] In response, the State Department advised Dean to inform the Peruvian government that, if it no longer wanted the Peace Corps, the volunteers would depart. At the same time, the ambassador was advised to reject categorically any implications that the volunteers were engaged in intelligence activities.[53]

Dean's assurances had little effect. At a press conference on November 13, President Velasco announced that the 137 Peace Corps volunteers currently within Peru were to leave the country within three months. Although this had been expected, what was unexpected was an accompanying statement that, at the beginning of the military government, the regime had asked for the expulsion of former Deputy Chief of Mission Ernesto Siracusa, political officer Frank Ortiz, and an unnamed third individual, alleging that they were CIA agents working against the interests of the junta. While these men were long gone, Velasco apparently intended to link them and the CIA, which, he claimed, "can turn up anywhere," with his decision on the Peace Corps.[54]

Dean responded quickly to these charges. He met with Foreign Minister de la Flor upon his return from a trip to Quito to attend a gathering of hemisphere foreign ministers at the Lima airport at 2:30 A.M. on the morning of November 15 to assure him that "there is no truth whatever to allegations that Ambassador Siracusa or Mr. Ortiz were affiliated any time in any way with [the CIA]."[55]

---

51. For a good review of these developments, see Ameringer, *U.S. Foreign Intelligence*, especially chap. 24.
52. "Confidential Telegram 09257 from Dean to DOS, November 2, 1974," *EO Review*, 1–3.
53. "Confidential Telegram 244713 from DOS to Dean, November 6, 1974," *EO Review*, 1–2.
54. *El Comercio* (November 14, 1974), 1, and "Limited Official Use Telegram 09655 from Dean to DOS, November 14, 1974," *EO Review*, 1–4.
55. "Confidential Telegram 09685 from Dean to DOS, November 15, 1974," *EO Review*, 1–2.

After hearing the allegations, Siracusa, serving as the U.S. ambassador to Uruguay, informed Washington that he had "always [been] on good personal terms" with Velasco, Mercado, and others and that "at no time ever did the government of Peru request my expulsion from the country." He did recognize that what he called "slanderous lies associating me with the CIA . . . were invented and given currency by *Oiga* magazine several months after my departure from the country" but that these accusations were without foundation. Siracusa urged the State Department to do what it could "promptly and officially to correct President Velasco's misinformation on this matter" and "also to see that the public record is correct as well," noting that obviously such accusations could have a serious negative effect on his duties in Uruguay.[56]

On November 20, the State Department ordered Dean to meet as soon as possible with Velasco to clear the air. First, he was to inform him that the United States was deeply concerned about the "totally unfounded allegations" against two senior officers of the State Department. Second, these allegations threatened to jeopardize bilateral relations at an "important and delicate juncture" and "work at cross purposes with the mutually shared objective of furthering a constructive dialogue between our governments." Third, the U.S. government planned to withhold any immediate public comment on the matter, giving the Peruvians time "to correct the error."[57]

While there is no record of Dean's conversation with Velasco on these matters, on November 22 *El Comercio* published the ambassador's statement on the Peace Corps' removal. In it, he strongly defended the actions of the volunteers in Peru, noting that they had acted in collaboration with the Peruvian government, and denied any involvement by the volunteers in internal political affairs, something strictly prohibited by the government of the United States. Nonetheless, the United States would "respect the decision of the revolutionary government of Perú, and will continue to cooperate with the government and the people of this country."[58]

While the expulsion of the Peace Corps volunteers from Peru was not totally unprecedented, it was unusual.[59] It received a certain amount of press

---

56. "Limited Official Use Telegram 03357 from Siracusa to DOS, November 16, 1974," *EO Review*, 1–2.

57. "Secret Telegram 252482 from Kissinger to Dean, November 20, 1974," *EO Review*, 1–2.

58. *El Comercio* (November 22, 1974), 4.

59. Writing in 1985, Gerard T. Rice noted that "of the eighty-eight countries in which the Peace Corps has operated, it has asked or been asked to leave forty. The Peace Corps has subsequently re-entered eleven of these countries." See Rice, *The Bold Experiment*, 304n5.

coverage in the United States that was limited primarily to the facts of the case.⁶⁰ Speaking in the U.S. Senate, Democrat Frank Church of Idaho, who was leading a committee investigating the actions of the CIA in Latin America and elsewhere, traced the expulsion to that agency's activities, especially in Chile. "Since they could not find the CIA and kick it out, the military government of Peru fastened on the Peace Corps instead." This was a shame, he argued, because the volunteers in Peru had been performing ably and constructively. As far as he was concerned, "no convincing evidence has yet been uncovered that the Peace Corps has ever been involved in the gathering of intelligence, or in any covert action conducted by the CIA in any foreign country."⁶¹

Whatever the reality, the perception in Peru was different. The press mostly shared and supported the government's decision. These attitudes represented a marked shift in press opinion of the Peace Corps from the mid-1960s, when all but far-left publications had a positive view of the volunteers' contributions.⁶² Since then there had been many more revelations about CIA actions in the region, and by this time, too, much of the press was now under firm government control. Moreover, at the end of the year, this control was increased when the *Peruvian Times* and *Oiga* were also closed down because of alleged critical comments of the regime's policies. This left *Caretas*, shut down in midyear and allowed to reappear in September, as the only independent magazine in Peru.⁶³ These closures led the Inter-American Press Association to accuse the Velasco regime of "totalitarian methods to sweep away the last vestiges of freedom of expression" in the country.⁶⁴

Whatever pressure *Caretas* was under, it did not prevent the magazine from providing extensive coverage of one of the more spectacular episodes of the Velasco years that provided further public evidence of some of the tensions within the junta. Near midnight on December 1, several shots were fired into the automobile carrying Prime Minister Mercado, Minister of Fisheries Javier Tantaleán Vianini, and Tantaleán's brother-in-law, General Guillermo Arbulu. Mercado and his brother-in-law, Guillermo Newman, escaped unscathed but Tantaleán suffered a wound in the elbow and Arbulu was

---

60. *New York Times*, November 16, 1974, 10; and *Washington Post*, November 15, 1974, A11.
61. *Congressional Record—Senate* (December 13, 1974), 39, 706–39, 707. For more, see Rice, *The Bold Experiment*, 132–36.
62. Dobyns, Doughty, and Holmberg, *Peace Corps Program Impact in the Peruvian Andes*, 202–27.
63. *New York Times*, November 21, 1974, 8; *Latin America*, 8, 46 (November 22, 1974), 366–67; *Washington Post*, November 22, 1974, A14.
64. *New York Times*, November 21, 1974, 8.

shot in the chest. Both the wounded men recovered, with Tantaleán later sent to Walter Reed Hospital for further treatment. Despite police roadblocks and an extensive manhunt, the perpetrators of this attack, the first on cabinet ministers since the 1968 coup, were never found. Within official circles, there were accusations of possible CIA involvement in the attack, which, given Mercado's moderate position and close contacts with the United States, seemed unlikely. Rumors also circulated that perhaps persons affiliated with the Naval Intelligence Service, angered by that branch's marginalization within the regime, had been involved. That organization allegedly did have close links to the CIA, which helped to supply it with up-to-date equipment.[65] In an interview several years later, Mercado speculated that the assault could have come from the extreme right but that the investigation, under the responsibility of the police and not the armed forces, had never located the perpetrators.[66]

Caretas pointed out the attack on Mercado and others was only the latest in a spate of violent incidents in Lima. Labeling this kind of terrorism as a "repudiated form of criminality," it asked rhetorically whether perhaps questions of a more equitable distribution of wealth or the lack of political participation might lay behind these acts.[67] The government attributed these episodes to right-wing counterrevolutionaries. However, some of the targets—a Sears Roebuck store and the Sheraton Hotel—seemed to suggest leftist origins or at least to produce the appearance of such origins. Whatever the source, these incidents provided the regime with the excuse to increase its crackdown on dissidents, including ever more militant rural peasant unions, of both the left and the right.[68]

It was within this increasingly tense atmosphere that Assistant Secretary of State Rogers arrived as the official U.S. representative to the celebration to commemorate the climactic 1824 battle of independence from Spain in Ayacucho.[69] Received by high-ranking Peruvian officials on December 6, he issued remarks intended, at least publicly, to reassure the regime. While observing that the two nations had had and continued to have their differences, he was confident that these would be overcome through diplomacy and dialogue and that "our friendship will be strengthened as a result." He also assured Peruvians that "the policy of the United States towards Peru is

---

65. *Caretas*, 24, 506 (December 4–18, 1974), 10–11. For the possible role of the CIA and naval intelligence, see Kruijt, *Revolution by Decree*, 146.
66. *Caretas*, 40, 622 (November 3, 1980), 30.
67. *Caretas*, 24, 506 (December 4–18, 1974), 11.
68. *Latin America*, 8, 49 (December 13, 1974), 389–90.
69. This important commemorative event was attended by most Latin American presidents. Notably absent was Chilean leader Augusto Pinochet.

one of cooperation: cooperation *without intervention* [my emphasis] and with total respect for the sovereignty and national dignity of this country."[70]

Whatever good feelings emanated from these assurances, they were soon overshadowed by the opening of an old wound. In mid-December, the State Department announced a decision to use $22 million of the Greene agreement funds to compensate Standard Oil (ESSO) for the IPC expropriation. As expected, the Peruvian government and press produced a strong negative reaction. On December 18, Secretary-General García Bedoya of the Foreign Ministry called Malcolm R. Barnebey, deputy chief of mission at the U.S. embassy, to the ministry to discuss the matter. While the secretary-general's own reaction was more muted than Velasco's and de la Flor's, he still expressed frustration at both the timing and the substance of the announcement that such compensation would be paid. However, Barnebey observed, the Peruvians did not challenge the right of the U.S. government, under the terms of the Greene agreement, to make such a payment.[71] That same night, the ministry, on behalf of the revolutionary government, returned to the embassy a memorandum announcing the payment, calling it "unacceptable" and in "violation of the spirit" of the Greene agreement.[72] These comments were followed by several additional high-level meetings between officials in both Lima and Washington. By the end of the year, however, there had been no real change in the State Department's decision to provide the IPC some compensation from the Greene agreement.

On December 11, Ambassador Dean sent an extensive secret telegram to the State Department assessing the position of the regime at the end of the year. He judged Velasco, his health issues aside, still firmly in control and becoming more "arbitrary and radical" and inclined to blame the United States and the CIA for many of his troubles. The pace of expropriations, he predicted, might accelerate, but he believed that accommodations could be reached given the government's pressing needs for foreign investment. There was little prospect that the armed forces would surrender power anytime soon, and in the meantime the United States should carry out a "damage-limiting operation" and maintain good links with the military by providing it with needed assistance. As had been the case from the beginning, he concluded, U.S. policy toward this perplexing and often enigmatic regime and its leader would require a delicate balancing act that mixed both firmness and flexibility.[73]

70. *El Comercio*, December 7, 1974, 1.
71. "Confidential Telegram 10690 from Barnebey to DOS, December 19, 1974," *EO Review*, 1–3.
72. *El Comercio*, December 19, 1974, 1.
73. "Secret Telegram 10425 from Dean to DOS, December 11, 1974," *EO Review*, 1–12.

Personnel Changes and Domestic Crisis

At the end of the year and in the first months of 1975, there were reports in Washington that Peru was preparing to go to war with Chile.[74] Many of Berckemeyer's reports to Lima at this time dealt with the war rumors and his and the embassy's efforts to calm the waters. These would be among his last dispatches. In March, he was replaced as ambassador by Admiral José Arce Larco. Born in 1917 and married with five children, Arce had graduated from the Escuela Naval in 1939 and had worked his way up the ranks to rear admiral by 1969 and vice admiral by 1974. Like many in the Velasco regime, he had studied at the Centro de Altos Estudios Militares. In May 1974, he was named minister of the navy before his ambassadorial appointment. His credentials for his new post included serving as naval attaché to the United States and the OAS and as a Peruvian naval delegate to the Inter-American Defense Board.[75] Within the regime, he was identified as belonging to the "radical" faction.[76]

In early January, the "radical" group to which the new ambassador-designate belonged was seen as firmly in control, following several months of internal maneuvering and infighting within the regime. This shift would seem to portend further difficulties for U.S.-Peruvian relations, especially given that the generally sympathetic Mercado Jarrín was scheduled to retire as prime minister at the end of the month. His replacement, however, was former finance minister Morales Bermúdez, long well regarded by the United States and described as "moderately more progressive" than his predecessor while at the same time enjoying "the confidence of the military radicals."[77]

Morales Bermúdez, who was also minister of war and commander-in-chief of the army, got off to a rocky start in his new position. On February 3, a strike for higher wages by the Lima police left the city virtually unprotected. A delay in responding led to widespread looting and destruction, producing the worst domestic crisis in six years for the Velasco regime. When the army finally responded on February 5, considerable force was required to quell this major urban disturbance, resulting in 86 civilian deaths and 155 wounded as well as tens of millions of dollars in damages. Most analysts traced the roots of the riots to continued problems of inflation and

---

74. Adding fuel to this speculation was an article in the December 2, 1974, edition of *Aviation Week and Space Technology* that described in some detail a Peruvian military buildup along the border with its southern neighbor. The Peruvian embassy forwarded a copy of this article without comment to Lima.
75. Frost, *Latin American Government Leaders*, 101–2.
76. *Latin America*, 9, 26 (July 4, 1975), 205–6.
77. *Latin America*, 9, 2 (January 10, 1975), 13–14.

unemployment. Student groups had also been active in the protests, reflecting middle-class resentment of the authoritarian features of the regime.[78] The crisis also overshadowed a major breakthrough on the impasse over financing from the United States with the announcement earlier in the year that various lending institutions, including the Export-Import Bank, would be providing funding for the Southern Peru Cuajone project.[79]

As the riots reached their peak, the now government-controlled *La Prensa*, in a front-page editorial, blamed them on "the forces of imperialism and their right arm, the CIA." Allegedly, it charged, the United States was trying to effect a "Chilean-style" disruption aimed to undermine the Velasco regime by promoting the disturbances. At the same time, Foreign Ministry spokesman Oscar Faura, when asked if he believed in such involvement, responded that he could not comment officially but that personally "it could well be, on the basis of what's happened in other countries of Latin America."[80] Foreign Minister de la Flor alleged a connection between the Aprista Party (APRA) and the CIA in the riots and claimed, without proof or specifics, that the disturbances had been "carefully planned by specialists from abroad."[81]

Washington responded quickly and forcefully to these accusations. On February 7, Assistant Secretary Rogers called in Roca Zela of the Peruvian embassy and told him that "there was absolutely no foundation to suggestions of CIA involvement" in the recent disturbances, nor were former embassy officials Frank Ortiz and Ernest Siracusa, as previously charged, acting for the agency, and urged the Peruvian government to "make every effort to avoid giving currency to such impressions in [the] future."[82] In Lima, Ambassador Dean issued a public statement denying the accusations and reported to Washington that the government apparently had told its press organs "to lay off charges against [the] CIA."[83]

On February 17, following department instructions, Dean met with de la Flor to express the United States' "deep concern" over the recent charges of CIA involvement and to assure him "that the USG is not intervening in

---

78. *Latin America*, 9, 7 (February 14, 1975), 49–50. The strike also reached the front page of the *New York Times*, February 6, 1975, 1–2. For a good review of the strike and the role of the Aprista Party in it, see Graham, *Peru's APRA*, 57–60. For Morales Bermúdez's reflections on his own actions, or inactions, during the crisis, see Prieto Celi, *Regreso a la democracia*, 143–47.
79. *Wall Street Journal*, January 6, 1975, 7.
80. *Washington Post*, February 7, 1975, A11.
81. *Latin America*, 9, 8 (February 21, 1975), 60.
82. "Limited Official Use Telegram From Secretary of State Kissinger to Lima Embassy, February 8, 1975," *EO Review*, 1–2.
83. "Confidential Telegram from Dean to Secretary of State, February 10, 1975," *EO Review*, 1–3.

Peru's internal political affairs and has no intention of doing so." He also reaffirmed that the CIA had no presence, as some had charged, in the AID mission or the Peace Corps. The foreign minister responded that the government had not charged the Peace Corps with a CIA connection and that it had been expelled from Peru for other reasons. As far as Faura's comments on possible CIA intervention were concerned, he attributed these to the spokesman's being caught off guard when the question came up and admitted that someone with "all of his experience should have been more careful."[84]

By the end of the month, the debate over a possible role of the CIA in the Lima riots seemed to have died down. In all likelihood, the regime had floated the accusation as a time-honored tactic to divert attention away from its own failings and the internal dynamics that led to the disturbances. But, as both Roca Zela and de la Flor pointed out in their discussions with Rogers and Dean, there was considerable press coverage of CIA actions around the world and Peru was especially sensitive to the possibility of "economic destabilization" as had occurred in Chile. Over the next several months, Ambassador Arce kept Lima well informed about the hearings conducted by Idaho Senator Frank Church into CIA actions to destabilize hostile regimes and to order assassinations of foreign leaders, with a particular focus on its activities in Chile. Finally, although the regime could provide no concrete evidence to support its claims, an editorial in the government-controlled *La Crónica* stated that there was CIA infiltration of the Peruvian police, suggesting a direct link to the riots. Subsequently, the newspaper reversed itself and said that such an assertion was a "misprint."[85] Recently, however, it has been shown that the CIA had influence within various police forces around the world, including in Peru.[86] Whether, in the last analysis, the CIA had anything to do with the riots remains speculative but seems unlikely. Nonetheless, the aura of suspicion that the United States might resort to covert means to destabilize a government with which it had many disagreements still lingered.

Repercussions, "Air Wars," and Other Matters

The February disturbances had several important repercussions. The government responded immediately by creating a new cabinet-level committee

---

84. "Confidential Telegram from Dean to Secretary of State, February 21, 1975," *EO Review*, 1–4.
85. As reported in "Dean to Secretary of State, February 10, 1975," 2.
86. Weiner, *A Legacy of Ashes*, 279.

to organize a political movement to back the regime. Recognizing that *Sinamos* had failed to achieve the goal of mobilizing popular support, the committee was charged with what, by this time, was an impossible mission of cultivating grassroots enthusiasm from the top down.[87] On another front, the regime recognized that APRA had shown in the recent disturbances that it had considerable popular backing of its own, some of which extended into the ranks of the military.[88] To meet this challenge, the regime began to adopt in fits and starts a policy of accommodation with its longtime nemesis.[89] At the same time, it continued to crack down on the press, shutting down *Caretas*, and forcing opposition journalists and politicians into exile.

While harassment of the press and of political opponents would continue throughout much of the rest of the year, for many the clearest result of the February crisis was that Velasco's days as the leader of Peru were numbered. A combination of his own declining health, continued economic difficulties, growing opposition, and a realization that the changes he had set in motion had failed to reach the majority of the population all spelled serious trouble for him. In late March, the *Washington Post* reported that "most Peruvians" believed that it would not be too long before the president surrendered control to Prime Minister Morales Bermúdez, "a man considered particularly talented" to manage the nation's many problems.[90]

Whatever Velasco's weakened position, his government continued to confront the United States aggressively on a number of issues. These involved, for the most part, a continuation of the nationalist posture with regard to foreign enterprises operating in Peru that had characterized the regime from the beginning.

The first involved international air travel. In February 1974, the Peruvian government cancelled the existing operating permit of Braniff airlines and issued a new permit that cut its flights to Lima by more than half, from thirty-four a week to sixteen to level the playing field for the new national airline, Aeroperú, now embarking on international service of its own. In response, early in 1975 the Civil Aeronautics Board had threatened to cancel all landing rights for Aeroperú in the United States, a threat that was only forestalled by direct intervention from President Ford.[91] In the meantime, there were intense negotiations between representatives of Braniff and the Peruvian government in Lima to try to reach a negotiated solution.

---

87. *Latin America*, 9, 9 (February 28, 1975), 66–68.
88. Graham, *Peru's APRA*, 59.
89. Philip, *The Rise and Fall of the Peruvian Military Radicals, 1968–1976*, 156–57.
90. *Washington Post*, March 24, 1975, A02.
91. *Miami Herald*, April 14, 1975.

Ambassador Dean met on several occasions with Foreign Minister de la Flor and Secretary-General García Bedoya and kept Washington closely informed of how the talks were proceeding.[92] The intense negotiations produced a satisfactory result. On July 8, the State Department announced that de la Flor and Dean had signed an agreement that allowed Braniff to operate fifteen flights a week for three years between Lima and various points in the United States. In return, Aeroperú would be permitted to operate between Lima and Los Angeles, Miami, and New York "at certain specified frequency levels."[93] This crisis was resolved, although it would crop up again from time to time in future years.

The second issue involved a decision by the Velasco regime in late July to take over the holdings of the Marcona Mining Company. This action followed a by now familiar story line. Marcona was jointly owned by the U.S.-based Cyprus Mines Corporation and Utah International, Inc. It had been operating a major iron mine in southern Peru for about twenty years under a concession due to expire in 1982. Most of its output went to Japan. When the government imposed the new industrial law in the early 1970s, the company had originally gone along with it, but as the profits from iron mining declined over the next three years, it abandoned plans to expand its operation and began to diversify into shipping and undertook negotiations to sell its subsidiaries to the Velasco government.[94]

These negotiations did not go well. On April 30, Ambassador Dean reported that embassy officials had met with Marcona's managing director in Peru, who told them that the five recent meetings with the government board appointed to carry out the negotiations had been unsatisfactory, that the company was being subjected to a "vicious" government-sponsored press campaign, and that the regime was repeating an argument made in the IPC case, namely, that the company actually owed Peru money, in this case some $37 million in back taxes. The company feared, with some justification, that the regime was preparing for outright expropriation without compensation. In response, Dean recommended that Assistant Secretary of Rogers meet with the Peruvian minister of commerce, who was due to visit Washington in late May, and to thoroughly discuss the "Marcona situation" with him.[95]

---

92. For example, in a communication in late May, Dean reported that de la Flor seemed amenable to a negotiated solution to the impasse. "Confidential Telegram from Dean to Secretary of State, May 23, 1975," *EO Review*, 1–3.
93. *DOSB*, 73, 1883 (July 28, 1975), 147.
94. For more, see Guasti, "The Peruvian Military Government and the International Corporations," in McClintock and Lowenthal, *The Peruvian Experiment Reconsidered*, 189–90.
95. "Confidential Telegram 3623 from Dean to Secretary of State, May 22, 1975," *EO Review*, 1–7.

Whatever Rogers's or the embassy's efforts on the company's behalf, they had little effect. When Minister of Mines and Energy Fernández Maldonado announced the expropriation, he claimed that the company had done "serious damage to our country by actions typical of the immoral conduct that the great multinational consortiums traditionally exercise." Among these immoral actions were tax evasion and hidden profits. A company officer heatedly denied these charges and claimed that Marcona had always conducted itself "legally in Peru, and any allegation to the contrary is unfounded."[96] Whatever the truth of these charges, they created an atmosphere that made an agreement on compensation unlikely.

Arce in Action

In Washington, Peru's new ambassador to the United States followed a path of action that did not deviate much from his predecessor's. In his early dispatches, Arce kept Lima abreast of the Ford administration's plans for military and economic assistance to Latin America and congressional investigations into the activities of the CIA in Chile. In April, he wrote a letter to the *New York Times* responding to an advertisement that had appeared on April 15 implying that Peru was "A New Soviet Beachhead" in the Americas, pointing to the presence of Cuban and Soviet military advisors, the Soviet-provided military equipment, and "a consistent preparation on the part of the Peruvian government for hostilities against Chile."[97] Arce called these charges "absurd" and argued that the unique nature of "the humanitarian philosophy guiding the Government's actions" meant that Peru "could never be a 'beachhead of the Soviet Union' or of any other foreign country."[98] In his report to Lima on his letter, he noted that the ad had been placed by an organization called the American Security Council, which, he alleged, was of the "extreme right" with links to anti-Castro Cuban exiles and groups such as the infamous AAA (Argentine Anti-Communist Alliance) of Argentina. He promised that the embassy would be particularly attentive to efforts by such groups, including "Chilean interests," which in the future might seek "to tarnish the always growing prestige of Perú and its Government."[99]

---

96. *Wall Street Journal*, July 28, 1975, 11. Guasti suggests that the government's charges had merit, writing that "Marcona engaged in illegal behavior perceived as a direct challenge to the government's legal sovereignty." See Guasti, "The Peruvian Military Government and the International Corporations," 190.
97. *New York Times*, April 15, 1975, 27.
98. *New York Times*, April 29, 1975, 32.
99. *Correspondencia* (5–3-Y/41) (April 21, 1975), 3.

Over the next few months, Arce was active on a number of fronts. With regard to the Braniff-Aeroperú dispute, he claimed that the embassy played only a collateral role as most of the major negotiations took place in Lima. However, he also provided a detailed summary of its activities in Washington during the dispute, suggesting that it had exerted some influence on Ford's decision not to apply the Civil Aeronautics Board sanctions and through its various interactions with State Department officials had been instrumental in the final successful resolution.[100] He also reported possible good news on the fishing rights issue, with the House of Representatives considering new legislation that would establish a 200-mile limit for the United States, thereby recognizing the same for other countries.[101]

On the Marcona issue, Arce told Lima that aside from the *Wall Street Journal* and *American Metal Market*, both specializing in economic news, the press in the United States had generally ignored the takeover.[102] At the same time, he met with State Department officials to discuss the matter more fully. As expected, these officials expressed a desire to maintain "friendly" relations with Peru while working out some fair compensation for Marcona. For his part, Arce promised to inform Lima of the gist of the conversation and then proceeded to give an extensive exposition of the reasons behind the expropriation, underscoring the "infractions and grave irregularities carried out by Marcona Mining in an affront to Perú, such as avoiding taxes, irrational [*sic*] exploitation of its mines, etc."[103] Whether Arce sincerely believed these charges or was simply repeating the official line cannot be determined. Again, however, it did little to promote a climate conducive to compromise.

In Arce's final dispatch to Lima before the change from Velasco to Morales Bermúdez, he reported in detail on the revelation of the so-called Track II efforts to prevent the ascension of Salvador Allende to Chile's presidency along with Kissinger's denial of any involvement in CIA-sponsored assassination plots. As he saw it, these plans followed a common pattern of U.S. interventionism, evidenced in its most blatant form in the 1965 intervention in the Dominican Republic. The difference in the Chilean case was that the "intervention was more camouflaged and carried out by other means." Again, he promised that the embassy would be alert to whatever else might be revealed. What had been discovered so far, he concluded, "shows once

---

100. *Correspondencia* (5-3-Y/72) (June 3, 1975), 1–5; (5-3-Y/77) (June 14, 1975), 1–2; and (5-3-Y/95) (July 11, 1975), 1–2.
101. *Correspondencia* (5-3-Y/110) (July 18, 1975), 1.
102. *Correspondencia* (5-3-Y/119) (August 1, 1975), 1–2.
103. *Correspondencia* (5-3-Y/122) (August 8, 1975), 1–2.

again that the United States has not ceased to attack by diverse means—subtle or not—the countries that it considers under its aegis."[104]

The End of the Velasco Regime

Although General Velasco might have had some suspicions to the contrary, there is no evidence that the United States had anything directly to do with his removal from power. On August 26, Dean sent a communication to the State Department reporting on stalled negotiations over the Marcona compensation matter because of the United States' decision to take a hard line and refuse credits to Peru until an accommodation was reached. Referring to conversations between embassy officials and Peruvians in the ministry of economy and finance, he told Washington of the regime's concerns over this confrontation and the desire of some to reach an accord. For the moment, however, Prime Minister Morales Bermúdez, apparently sympathetic to a compromise, did not have "sufficient 'ammunition' to confront Velasco and his radical advisers who apparently support a nationalistic position of no retreat on Marcona." For this reason, Morales Bermúdez had thus far refused to meet with Dean to discuss the matter.[105] At no place in this communication is there any indication of a dramatic change in Peru's leadership in the near future.

On August 29, three days later, the armed forces removed Velasco from the presidency and replaced him with Morales Bermúdez. While the move was not totally unexpected, the timing was a bit peculiar in that it coincided with a weeklong meeting in Lima of the conference of nonaligned nations. Like the coup that removed Belaúnde, it was planned by a relatively small group of officers and was carried out quickly and efficiently. Velasco, weakened politically and physically, offered no resistance. Commentators at the time traced the change to tensions within the armed forces, especially involving the always more conservative navy, and the apparent grip that radicals had over Velasco, as seen in increased crackdowns on the press and the deportation of various intellectual and political opponents of the regime in recent months. Immediately after the coup, the new leadership promised to do away with all "personality cults," apparently referring to "Velasco's tendency toward one-man autocratic rule."[106] Continuing economic difficulties,

---

104. *Correspondencia* (5–5-Y/139) (August 18, 1975), 2.
105. "Confidential Telegram 6489 from Dean to Secretary of State, August 26, 1975," *EO Review*, 1–5.
106. *New York Times*, August 30, 1975, 18.

including persistent inflation, like those that had triggered the February riots, also played a role. While the new leaders promised to continue the revolutionary path begun in October 1968, most predicted that Morales Bermúdez would take Peru in a more moderate and pragmatic direction.[107] In its "Daily Activity Reports from the Bureaus" for August 30, the State Department informed Secretary Kissinger of the developments in Peru and in its preliminary analysis stated that there probably would be no immediate changes in the regime's policies or programs but that "we do estimate that Morales will be easier to deal with than the mercurial Velasco."[108] While this was an easy prediction to make, unlike more than a few others the State Department had made about Peru over the years, this one proved quite accurate.

In an interview with *Caretas* a year and a half later, Velasco was asked what had been "the real objective" of his government. His response was that it was to make Peru a truly "independent and sovereign nation" no longer forced "to live on its knees." Crucial to attaining that goal was to free the country from subordination to the United States. Perhaps with some exaggeration, "Here the United States ambassador ruled! When I was president, he had to request an audience with me and maintain a distance of six steps. I harassed them. I kicked out the American military mission. Before, they used to have 50 to 60 officers and the Peruvian government had to pay their salaries and even the travel expenses for the kittens that came with the family. And they formed part of the information network for the CIA. We did not need them."[109]

While the statement contained its share of bombast and bluster, it was also revealing. From the beginning, Velasco believed that real change could come to Peru only by following a nationalistic and independent course. His policy toward the United States, while perhaps not as confrontational under the surface as it seemed, was nonetheless an important ingredient in achieving his long-term goals. While the changes were not as profound or as lasting as he might have liked or envisioned, they were significant. The agrarian reform had long-term effects as did certain aspects of his nationalization

---

107. For U.S. press coverage of the coup, see *New York Times*, August 30, 1975, 1, 6, and *Washington Post*, August 30, 1975, A01, A08. For Morales Bermúdez's recollections of his actions at this time, see Prieto Celi, *Regreso a la democracia*, 159–65.

108. "Daily Activity Reports from the Bureaus, August 29, 1975," in Secret State 207030 to SecI00333, August 30, 1975, *EO Review*, 4.

109. The interview was with well-known journalist César Hildebrandt. *Caretas*, 27, 512 (February 3, 1977), 30–35. It is also referred to, with a somewhat different translation, in McClintock, "Velasco, Officers, and Citizens: The Politics of Stealth," in McClintock and Lowenthal, *The Peruvian Experiment Reconsidered*, 282–83.

program. He also introduced elements of social justice and racial equality that echo down to the present day. With regard to foreign policy, his regime also was something of a trendsetter, early on confronting the United States on a variety of issues, establishing relations with communist nations, and playing a leading role in the nonaligned movement.

For the United States, the Velasco regime represented a puzzle and a challenge. Its expropriation of U.S.-owned companies, even when tempered with pragmatism, was not what Washington expected of a military regime. The same held for its sweeping agrarian reform program, its attempts to give workers greater control of the enterprises that employed them, and a foreign policy that reached out to China, Cuba, and the Soviet Union. Often, these were the kinds of steps in the 1960s and 1970s that led to U.S. intervention either to change the course of an "unfriendly" regime or to have it replaced altogether with one that was more accommodating. The Peruvian case posed a dilemma. The alternative of choice in changing regimes was the armed forces, as in Brazil and Chile. In Peru, however, that alternative was foreclosed. Encouraging the Apristas, with whom the U.S. embassy always maintained close contact, was a possibility, but under what circumstances could they replace the military?

In essence, the Nixon policies toward Peru and Velasco were not much different from those of Johnson toward Belaúnde. In response to the Velasco regime's expropriations, the United States withheld economic assistance and discouraged multinational lending organizations from extending financing. As with Johnson, this was not a clearly enunciated policy, but it was one that both sides seemed to understand. In the face of various provocations, the Nixon administration often expressed its displeasure but usually reacted with relative restraint. The Velasco government probably benefited as well from the fact that the priorities of U.S. foreign policy in these years were usually elsewhere. The one instance when Nixon and Kissinger did focus on Latin America, the election of Allende and the subsequent coup, served in some measure to isolate the Velasco regime, caught after 1973 between right-wing governments to its south in Chile and to its east in Brazil. At the least, these developments dampened any aspirations the Peruvian military regime might have had to lead an anti-U.S.–Latin American bloc. Finally, the combination of internal and external developments and pressures led to a change in Peru in 1975 that augured an end to the difficult and often contentious relationship that had bedeviled the United States for more than a decade.

CONCLUSION

As predicted, relations between the United States and Peru improved considerably under the Morales Bermúdez administration (1975–80). In 1976, an agreement was arrived at to compensate the Marcona mining interests for their expropriation, and this helped open the way for the regime to receive external financing from U.S. and multilateral agencies. A visit by First Lady Rosalynn Carter in 1977 also helped to improve the atmosphere. That same year Francisco Morales Bermúdez became the first Peruvian president since Prado seventeen years earlier to visit the United States and to be received by President Jimmy Carter. The regime also significantly slowed the pace of nationalization, welcomed foreign investment, and generally abandoned the militant "third world" and confrontational foreign policy of the Velasco years. Human rights issues, of major concern to the Carter administration, were not paramount at this stage in Peru's political history. Carter's policies, too, encouraged the gradual transition to democratic government that occurred in the late 1970s.[1]

Implementing much of this change was a new foreign minister, José de la Puente Radbill, who served in the post from 1976 to 1979. In a 2003 interview, Radbill claimed that he was chosen as a compromise choice more

---

1. For a careful examination of the first three years of the Morales Bermúdez regime, with comments on its improved relations with the United States, see Pease García, *Los caminos del poder*. See also McClintock and Vallas, *La democracia negociada*, 68–70. For Morales Bermúdez's own observations on his foreign policy and the men who helped him make it, see Prieto Celi, *Regreso a la democracia*, 175–205, 207–9.

attuned to the pro-U.S. Peruvian navy than was the army's candidate. His mother was North American, and he had served in the Peruvian embassy in Washington in the 1950s and knew the United States well. His mandate was to move the nation's foreign policy away from the nonaligned posture of Miguel Angel de la Flor Valle and toward a more pro-Western orientation, a mandate he did his best to fulfill. He recalled that the visit of Mrs. Carter had produced favorable impressions on both sides and led to cordial relations between him and the first lady as well as between Peru and the United States over the next few years. Unlike his predecessors, he remarked, he did not have to deal with many conflictive issues involving the United States.[2]

The normalization of relations continued during the second administration of Fernando Belaúnde Terry, elected by a substantial margin in 1980. Ironically, given the strong ties the United States had established in the 1960s and 1970s with the Aprista Party, some serious tensions arose during the term of the first ever Aprista president, Alan García Pérez (1985–1980), around such issues as terrorism, drug trafficking, and a decision to use only a certain percentage of export earnings to pay off Peru's growing foreign debt. In addition, statist policies that included nationalizing private banks in 1987 did not sit well with the U.S. government or U.S. investors. As a result, there was something of a reprise of the credit squeeze that had characterized policies used against Juan Velasco Alvarado and Belaúnde during his first term. Within the larger Latin American context, however, U.S. concerns with García took a definite back seat to the Reagan administration's almost single-minded focus on Central America in these years.

The subsequent administration of Alberto Fujimori (1990–2000) posed some complex challenges for the United States. Elected by a substantial margin over his main rival, the internationally acclaimed writer Mario Vargas Llosa, the virtually unknown Fujimori moved aggressively to attack Peru's hyperinflation and the growing strength of the revolutionary Sendero Luminoso. He enjoyed considerable success on both fronts, imposing "shock treatment" economic policies, and, in September 1992, his security forces captured Abimael Guzmán, the "maximum leader" of Sendero Luminoso, fatally crippling that organization. To achieve these results, however, he had employed authoritarian methods, including, in alliance with the armed forces, a "self-coup" in April 1992 that dissolved the Congress and allowed him to rule virtually by decree. In addition, there were numerous human

---

2. Interview with José de la Puente Radbill, Lima, Peru, July 24, 2003. For favorable coverage of Rosalynn Carter's visit to Peru, see *Caretas*, 520 (June 9, 1977), 16–17.

rights abuses committed by the army and the police in the antiterror campaign. However, Fujimori cooperated with the United States to crack down on coca cultivation and drug trafficking, and his "neoliberal" economic policies met with the approval of the Clinton administration and produced substantial and sustained growth throughout most of the decade.

Fujimori's government came to an ignominious end in 2000 when he embarked on a third term under charges of corruption and electoral manipulation, leading to his resignation. A brief caretaker government provided for a transition to new elections won by Alejandro Toledo, a Stanford-trained economist from a poor, indigenous background. Toledo's five years in office (2001–6) were marked by continued economic growth based primarily on mineral exports and fueled by substantial foreign investment but marred by charges of corruption in his regime and a dramatic decline in the president's popularity and approval ratings. While most Peruvians disapproved of George W. Bush's policies, particularly his intervention in Iraq, relations at the executive level remained good and progress was made on a free-trade agreement between Peru and the United States.

Within this framework, the period under study, especially the years from 1963 to 1975, still stands out as somewhat anomalous in the overall picture of U.S.-Peruvian relations. The failure to support adequately the reform-minded Belaúnde led directly to the many challenges and complexities of the Velasco regime, dominated by the ongoing dispute over the status of the International Petroleum Company (IPC). Throughout this period, too, Peru was a fairly prominent priority for the United States within the larger Latin American context.

The role of the respective ambassadors, notably John Wesley Jones and Taylor Belcher for the United States and Fernando Berckemeyer and Celso Pastor de la Torre for Peru, was important. As accomplished professionals, they did an able job of both representing their countries' interests and reporting back to their respective home governments in some detail developments of importance to each. They all seemed to have established good relationships with the principal foreign policy players. This, of course, was notably easier for Jones and Belcher, representatives of the most powerful and important foreign nation for Peru, allowing them to have frequent access to that nation's president, foreign minister, and other influential officials. Berckemeyer and Pastor, however, represented a medium-sized Latin American country in a capital city chock-full of embassies of great and small powers, all clamoring for Washington's attention. As a result, they rarely met with the U.S. president and met only a bit more frequently with the secretary of state. They did, however, seem to have fairly easy access to State

Department officials and to enjoy good, professional relations with them. Personal relationships among the ambassadors and top officials on both sides were clearly important as they allowed each nation's representatives to maintain lines of communication even when strains developed.

In diplomacy, personal chemistry among the participants is frequently significant for successfully resolving outstanding disputes, and U.S.-Peruvian relations between 1960 and 1975 are no exception. The results, however, were often mixed. Ambassador Pastor's friendship with and favorable impression of Thomas Mann might have obscured the particulars and an appreciation of the intensity of the assistant secretary's policy of using the withholding of aid from Peru to foster a favorable settlement of the IPC dispute, thereby making his reporting to Lima on this matter less clear, precise, and accurate than it might have been. The good relationship established between special advisor Walt Rostow and President Belaúnde helped produce something of a breakthrough on the IPC issue and apparently had some influence on Rostow as he and Johnson considered policy options for Peru. Ambassador Jones also had a good relationship with Belaúnde, compensating to some extent for President Johnson's low opinion of the Peruvian leader, and this undoubtedly helped in his efforts to achieve what both hoped would be final resolution of the IPC dispute in late 1968. These efforts, however, were not sufficient to keep Belaúnde in office. The U.S. ambassadors' personal relations with Velasco were less warm and sometimes tense despite the general often expressing his appreciation for the medical assistance he and his wife had received at Walter Reed Hospital. Their relations with Edgardo Mercado Jarrín, however, both as foreign minister and prime minister, remained good and helped to smooth some of the rough edges. Finally, the bonds between Mrs. Nixon and Mrs. Velasco, forged during the earthquake relief effort, helped to improve substantially the overall atmosphere between the two nations but did little to affect fundamental policy differences.

While diplomats are often criticized for living in splendid isolation that makes them insensitive to the culture and conditions of the nations to which they were assigned, that did not seem to be true in this case. All of the ambassadors and their aides on both sides seemed to have a firm grasp of the domestic political situations in their respective nations and their implications for foreign policy matters. Their reports, mostly, were thorough, balanced, and informative, not to say that they were necessarily always on-target. Overall, however, the diplomatic representatives of both sides seemed to understand and to appreciate the culture and political realities of the other.

Writing in the early 1970s, Herbert Goldhamer singled out the United States, because of its influence and prominence in the region, as behaving with "tutelary spirit," presuming to know what was best for its neighbors to the south. This position and attitude, he argued, was so deeply ingrained in U.S. officials that often they were not consciously aware of it and failed to appreciate how it could "irritate and aggravate relations."[3] Jones and Belcher probably shared this attitude to a certain extent, but how much it affected their effectiveness is difficult to measure.

In retrospect, the greatest failure of U.S. policy-makers with regard to Peru was to underestimate the powerful role nationalism played in such issues as the IPC dispute and the 200-mile-limit fight. In the context of the Cold War, nationalism was too often conjoined with communism, ignoring the broad appeal of the former and the limited appeal of the latter. By being present on the ground, Jones and Belcher had a greater understanding of the powerfulness of this nationalist sentiment and how it could complicate any attempts to resolve outstanding disputes. Nonetheless, their efforts to urge Washington to adopt more "pragmatic and flexible" approaches to Peru were often frustrated.

From the Peruvian point of view, there was considerable perplexity and frustration to reach some sort of agreement over these issues, reinforcing their interpretation that the U.S. government was too often beholden to private special interests—in these instances, a powerful oil company and west coast fishermen. The situation, of course, was more complex. At play were more than special interests. Although the much-reviled Hickenlooper amendment proved to be more of a hindrance than a help in formulating and implementing U.S. policies toward Peru and other nations embarked on a nationalistic course, it was not without some merit. Wholesale expropriations of private properties without compensation seemed not only unfair, whatever the past and present alleged abuses of companies operating abroad, but also a significant disincentive to future investments with possible benefits for both sides. However, the Hickenlooper and other punitive amendments proved to be too heavy-handed to be useful and indeed were rarely applied or enforced.[4] One State Department official likened them to nuclear weapons that were useful as deterrents but would have devastating consequences if used and therefore rarely were. As Jones and others pointed out, politically their existence was often counterproductive, serving only to enhance extreme nationalistic positions as convenient whipping boys.

---

3. Goldhamer, *The Foreign Powers in Latin America*, 206–10.

4. In the first eight years after its enactment, the amendment was only applied once, to Ceylon in 1963. Goldhamer, *The Foreign Powers in Latin America*, 74.

The role of the CIA in Peru during these years was murky, as was often the case. The agency appeared to have some sources able to report on the inner workings of the various revolutionary organizations of the 1960s and Philip Agee wrote of his activities in trying to counter their influence. However, it seems unlikely that the agency had anything to do directly with the counterguerrilla operations carried out by the armed forces in 1965 and 1966. Moreover, it failed to predict the coup of October 3, 1968, and its intelligence reports were often muddled and inaccurate. While there were frequent charges from the Velasco government of CIA meddling and attempts to weaken or to overthrow it, accentuated by growing revelations of agency involvement elsewhere in the late 1960s and early 1970s, especially in Chile, as far as the available evidence suggests, there was little substance to these and more often than not they were used as diversions from other issues.

While ambassadors, secret agents, and high-ranking government officials on both sides made and implemented policy, less official and perhaps more lasting and more influential relationships between the two countries were constructed at other levels. As in much of Latin America, and indeed, in the rest of the world, U.S. popular culture had an enormous effect on Peru in these years. The entertainment pages of even high-minded publications such as *El Comercio* and *La Prensa* as well as the always lively *Caretas* carried numerous stories almost daily of the lives and loves of U.S. celebrities. Hollywood films, present in Peru since the 1920s, continued to dominate the local market although the comeback of the European cinema in the postwar years added spice to the competition. The growth of television, with much of the programming consisting of reruns of popular U.S. shows, added to the cultural mix and helped create or perpetuate visions, both good and bad, of life north of the Rio Grande. Increasingly, rock and roll and North American popular music in general joined jazz as a major U.S. export to the rest of the world, even if sometimes by way of Great Britain.

On a somewhat loftier plane, over 50 percent of the books, periodicals, and newspapers imported into Peru in the early 1960s came from the United States.[5] Many of these were Spanish translations of major U.S. authors such as William Faulkner, Ernest Hemingway (who had fished off the coast of northern Peru in the 1950s), and John Steinbeck. *Time* magazine was available in both English and Spanish. English was the most popular foreign language of study in Peru, and the Peruvian–North American Cultural Institute in downtown Lima, with a branch in Miraflores, cosponsored by American residents and Peruvian nationals, housed a library of English-language

---

5. Ibid., 152.

books and offered English-language lessons at minimal cost. In addition, the United States Information Agency established a library in Lima and offered language lessons with the aim, in general, of furthering U.S. foreign policy objectives by "influencing public attitudes in other nations."[6]

In addition to the exchange of ideas and images, an increasing number of Peruvians began to visit the United States and vice versa. Despite the dispute between Braniff and Aeroperú, the introduction of jet air travel and the growing number of flights made it increasingly possible for Peruvians, even of the middle class, to visit the United States for family visits or on vacation. In turn, Peru increasingly became a popular tourist destination for North Americans, especially those who wanted to see the Inca ruins at Machu Pichu. Exhibitions of Peruvian art arranged by Ambassadors Berckemeyer and Pastor de la Torre helped to whet the interest of the U.S. public in the country they represented. Anthropologists from Cornell University, in collaboration with the Indigenous Institute of Peru and with the backing of the Peruvian government, in 1952 initiated a pilot program of community development in Vicos in the Callejón de Huaylas. The changes brought about through this joint project helped provide a model for later efforts in the highlands by Peace Corps volunteers.[7]

The presence of the Peace Corps in Peru, at least until its expulsion in 1974, was substantial. Hundreds of volunteers made their mark as educators, as community developers, and as experts in various technical fields. As important as their effect on Peru was the imprint that the experience had on them as they returned to the United States to engage in a variety of careers, some involving higher education and public service.

The role of the Peace Corps in Peru was not without its controversies and critics. So, too, were the activities of Protestant missionaries from the United States who began to expand their efforts in Peru in the postwar years. The most prominent were those associated with the Summer Institute of Linguistics, who set up camp in the Amazon in the 1940s under the guidance of William Cameron Townsend intending to teach "the natives" English so that they could better understand missionary sermons, read the Bible, and ensure their religious conversion. These efforts received considerable support from the Peruvian government, especially under President Manuel Odría. By the mid-1970s, the missionaries had established a thriving center at Yarinacocha near Pucallpa in the far-eastern Amazon, where they operated an extensive radio operation and had six planes to help them

---

6. Ibid., 148.
7. For more, see Holmberg, "Changing Community Attitudes and Values in Peru," 63–107.

reach even more remote locations. Some anthropologists criticized their efforts as undermining Indian culture and imposing a sense of cultural superiority, while leftists accused them of being agents of imperialism bent on extending capitalist enterprises into the hinterland.[8] Still, the Velasco government depended on the missionaries to translate to the indigenous population the consequences of new decrees that guaranteed their rights to property and citizenship.[9]

A steady stream of distinguished U.S. citizens (although no sitting president) visited Peru during this period, visits that received considerable and mostly favorable attention in the Peruvian press. Already mentioned were the well-received trips of Robert Kennedy and Richard Nixon in the 1960s and Mrs. Nixon's visit to earthquake-ravaged Peru in 1970. The chief justice of the U.S. Supreme Court, Earl Warren, also visited during this period as did Charles Lindbergh, who met with Belaúnde to discuss a ban on the killing of blue and humpbacked whales.[10] U.S. astronauts of the Apollo missions visited Peru as part of larger Latin American tours and were warmly received, as were various others of the academic, entertainment, and sports world. U.S. college basketball teams, for example, played exhibition matches with their Peruvian counterparts before enthusiastic audiences.

A variety of exchange programs between Peru and the United States were either created or greatly expanded in these years. One of the most controversial was associated with the American Institute for Free Labor Development (AIFLD), created in the early 1960s as part of the Alliance for Progress effort to achieve reform through democratic means and to counter communist influence within Latin American labor organizations. Part of the AIFLD's activities included bringing Latin American labor leaders to the United States to expose them to various aspects of North American life, with the idea and the hope that they would return to their home countries with a greater appreciation of the "Colossus of the North" and work to promote "free labor development." By the mid-1960s, several hundred Latin Americans had taken classes at the AIFLD residential institute at Front Royal, Virginia, and of the twenty-seven Peruvians among the first graduates, seventeen became general secretaries of their unions.[11] By the early 1970s, however, charges of CIA use of the AIFLD to interfere in domestic political affairs

---

8. For more, see Stoll, *Fishers of Men or Founders of Empire?* 98–211.

9. *New York Times*, February 19, 1975, 2.

10. Some details on these visits, including discussion of a confrontation between Warren and some U.S. exchange students during an embassy reception, can be found in the Personal Papers of John Wesley Jones, LBJ Library, Box 23.

11. Romualdi, *Presidents and Peons*, 429.

had seriously damaged the program's effectiveness. In 1971, the Velasco government requested that the U.S. government terminate the program in Peru. While the United States acceded to this request, it still maintained a presence in the country at a much lower profile and under careful embassy supervision. By early 1975, Ambassador Robert Dean determined that even this reduced presence was doing more harm than good in the supercharged atmosphere following the February riots and recommended that the office be closed down altogether while still encouraging nongovernmental union-to-union contacts and visitor exchange programs.[12]

Throughout this period, the number of Peruvians studying in U.S. universities, many at the graduate level, increased steadily, from 464 in 1963 to 1,474 in 1975.[13] Thanks in some measure to the impetus of the Alliance for Progress, there was also a significant expansion of international educational exchange programs that allowed Peruvian students and professors to study and teach in the United States with their North American counterparts doing the same in Peru.[14] While the numbers of Peruvians who received academic training in the United States was small, they were often influential figures in business and government. This was already evident in the Belaúnde administration and would become increasingly the case in subsequent civilian administrations.[15]

In the United States, as part of the post–Cuban Revolution boom in Latin American studies, there was increasing academic interest in Peru. Throughout the 1960s and into the 1970s, economists, sociologists, historians, and political scientists joined the anthropologists who had long found the indigenous cultures of Peru a rich field for study. The military regime, in particular, with its often contradictory but almost always dramatic features, stimulated a substantial number of monographs, articles, essays, and collected works, many of which are cited in this study. There were also collaborative efforts, such as the study of U.S.-Peruvian relations edited by Daniel Sharp and published in 1972, which emerged out of a conference at the Adlai Stevenson Institute in Chicago and which included Peruvian participants.

Another important link between the two nations was strengthened in these years when thousands of Peruvians settled permanently in the United States. At first, members of the upper class and middle-class professionals predominated, some motivated to leave by what they perceived to be the

---

12. "Confidential Telegram 2231 from Dean to Department of State, March 18, 1975," *EO Review*, 1–3.
13. United Nations, *UNESCO Statistical Yearbook: 1975*, 356.
14. For more on the general pattern, see Goldhamer, *The Foreign Powers in Latin America*, 150.
15. Contreras and Cueto, *Historia del Perú contemporáneo*, 350.

radical policies of the Velasco regime. Later, however, the deteriorating economic conditions of the late 1970s led Peruvians from the lower classes to find a better life in the north. The combination of economic catastrophe and terrorism in the 1980s turned the trickle of emigrants into a steady stream, and while the diaspora was widespread into Europe and other Latin American countries, the United States remained the favored destination. Between 1960 and 1980, the number of Peruvians in the United States grew from 7,102 to 55,496.[16] As Peruvians prospered in the United States and became a significant presence within the Hispanic American communities of certain major cities, they often retained their ties, especially their family ties, and their remittances home helped many in Peru to survive the economic difficulties of the late twentieth century.[17]

The most important ties between Peru and the United States throughout the period under study and beyond remained economic. Whatever the ups and downs at the diplomatic level and the disputes over expropriations and compensations—and whatever the attempts by Peru to look for other sources for its products and its commercial relationships—the United States remained by far Peru's main trading partner, usually absorbing one-third of its exports and providing one-third of its imports, easily outdistancing major competitors Germany and Japan.[18] U.S. private investment in Peru also predominated in these years and despite the various difficulties with the Belaúnde and Velasco governments grew steadily from $446 million in 1960 to over $1.2 billion in 1975, with more than half of that in the mining sector.[19] During the 1960s, U.S. investors had focused on the manufacturing sector in Peru to the point where it was estimated that by 1968 foreigners were providing some 80 percent of the total.[20]

While the U.S. business community in Peru, based primarily in Lima, was relatively small, it was visible and influential. It was represented by various associations and until 1974 there was a publication, the *Andean Times*,

16. United States Department of Commerce, U.S. Census Bureau, "Table 3: Region of Country of Area of Birth of the Foreign-Born Population: 1960 to 1990," Internet release date: March 9, 1999, 7.
17. For more, see Altamirano, *Los que se fueron*.
18. In 1972, for example, the United States bought 30.7 percent of Peru's exports and provided 33.5 percent of the nation's imports. For Germany in that same year, the figures were 10.5 percent of exports and 9.6 for imports. Japan, a growing market for Peruvian goods, absorbed 15.3 percent of exports but provided at that time only 8.1 percent of imports. Ruddle and Barrows, *Statistical Abstract of Latin America, 1972*, 502. By the turn of the twenty-first century, while China had become an increasingly important trade partner, the United States still enjoyed the same predominance at about the same levels as in the 1970s. Contreras and Cueto, *Historia del Perú contemporáneo*, 403.
19. Wilkie, *Statistical Abstract of Latin America*, 427. See also Pike, *The United States and the Andean Republics*, 346–47.
20. Pike, *The United States and the Andean Republics*, 331.

that catered to its interests. Another visible sign of U.S. influence was the effect of American-made products on the growing mass consumer-oriented market, especially pronounced among upper- and middle-class Peruvians.

Interactions between Peru and the United States in the 1960s and 1970s, then, operated at various levels. In this study, the main focus has been on the respective ambassadors and their roles in helping to forge and implement the foreign policies of their respective nations during a period of turmoil and challenge. While they were not the only players in the story, an examination of their views and their actions provides a fuller picture of the relationship between the two nations and its often complex and complicated nature. A closer look at how both sides viewed and interacted with each other may also offer useful lessons and insights if new challenges emerge in the future to threaten the traditionally "warm and friendly" relations between Peru and the United States.

BIBLIOGRAPHY

GOVERNMENT PUBLICATIONS

Association for Diplomatic Studies and Training. "Interview with John Wesley Jones, May 11, 1988." The Foreign Affairs Oral History Collection (http://memory.loc.gov/cgi-bin/query/D?mfdip:1:/temp/~ammem_LOco::).
Lyndon B. Johnson Presidential Library, Austin, TX.
    Administrative History, United States Department of State
    National Intelligence Estimates
    National Security Files
    Oral History Interview with Lincoln Gordon
    Oral History Interview with Thomas C. Mann
    Personal Papers of Covey Oliver
    Personal Papers of John Wesley Jones
    Personal Papers of Walt W. Rostow
    United States Central Intelligence Agency, Secret Intelligence Cables from Peru, 1964
República del Perú. Ministerio de Relaciones Exteriores, Archivo Central Raúl Porras Barrenechea. *Correspondencia desde la embajada del Perú en Washington, D.C., al Ministro de Relaciones Exteriores.* Lima, 1960–1975.
———. Ministerio de Relaciones Exteriores. *El Perú y su política exterior: Recopilación de los principales discursos pronunciados por el Ministro de Relaciones Exteriores General de División E. P. Edgardo Mercado Jarrín (Del 24 Nov. 1968 al 28 Abril 1971).* Lima: Empresa Editora del Diario Oficial "El Peruano," 1971.
United States Congress. *Congressional Record—House.* Washington, D.C.: Government Printing Office, 1960–1975.
———. *Congressional Record—Senate.* Washington, D.C.: Government Printing Office, 1960–1975.
United States Department of Commerce. U.S. Census Bureau. "Table 3: Region and Country or Area of Birth of the Foreign-Born Population: 1960 to 1990." Internet Release Date: March 9, 1999 (http://www.census.gov/population/www/documentation/twps0029/tab03.html).
United States Department of State. *The Biographic Register.* Washington, D.C.: Government Printing Office, 1960–1975.
———. *Declassified Documents Released by the U.S. Department of State EO Systematic Review. Telegrams from the U.S. Embassy in Lima, Peru, 1974 and 1975.* Available on the U.S. National Archives Web site, Central Foreign Policy Files.
———. *Department of State Bulletin.* Washington, D.C.: Government Printing Office, 1960–1975.
———. *Foreign Service List.* Washington, D.C., April 1963.

———. Keefer, Edward C., et. al. *Foreign Relations of the United States, 1961–1963*. Vol. 12, *American Republics*. Washington, D.C.: Government Printing Office, 1996.
———. Keefer, Edward, ed. *Foreign Relations of the United States, 1964–1968*. Vol. 31, *South and Central America; Mexico*. Washington, D.C.: Government Printing Office, 2004.
———. *Records of the Department of State Relating to Internal Affairs of Peru*. Record Group 59 (1964–1966) (1967–1969) (1970–1973). National Archives Building, College Park, MD.
United States Senate. "Rockefeller Report on Latin America." *Hearing Before the Subcommittee on Western Hemisphere Affairs of the Committee on Foreign Relations, Ninety-First Congress, First Session, November 20, 1969*. Washington, D.C.: Government Printing Office, 1970.
———. "United States Relations with Peru." *Hearings Before the Subcommittee on Western Hemisphere Affairs of the Committee on Foreign Relations, Ninety-First Congress (April 14, 16 and 17, 1969)*. Washington, D.C.: Government Printing Office, 1969.

MAGAZINES AND NEWSPAPERS

Andean Air Mail and Peruvian Times (Lima), 1972–1974.
Caretas (Lima), 1960–1975.
El Comercio (Lima), 1960–1975.
Latin America (London), 1972–1975.
La Prensa (Lima), 1960–1968.
La Tribuna (Lima), 1960–1968.
New York Times, 1960–1975.
Oiga (Lima), 1960–1975.
Wall Street Journal, 1971–1975.
Washington Post, 1972–1975.

BOOKS AND ARTICLES

Agee, Philip. *Inside the Company: CIA Diary*. New York: Stonehill, 1975.
Altamirano, Teofilo. *Los que se fueron: Peruanos en Estados Unidos*. Lima: Pontificia Universidad Católica del Perú, Fondo Editorial, 1990.
Ameringer, Charles D. *U.S. Foreign Intelligence: The Secret Side of American History*. Lexington, MA: D. C. Heath and Company, Lexington Books, 1990.
Arnove, Robert F. "Promoters of the U.S. Model in Latin American Universities: International Exchange Programs and the Peace Corps." In *Universities in Transition: The U.S. Presence in Latin American Higher Education*, edited by Richard R. Renner, 96–109. Gainesville: Center for Latin American Studies, University of Florida, 1973.
Astiz, Carlos A. *Pressure Groups and Power Elites in Peruvian Politics*. Ithaca: Cornell University Press, 1969.
Bákula, Juan Miguel. *Perú: Entre la realidad y la utopía; 180 años de política exterior*. 2 vols. Lima: Fondo de Cultura Económica y Fundación Academia Diplomática del Perú, 2002.
Barber, Willard F., and C. Neale Ronning. *Internal Security and Military Power: Counter-Insurgency and Civic Action in Latin America*. Columbus: Ohio State University Press, 1966.

Beals, Carleton. *Latin America: World in Revolution.* New York: Abelard-Schuman, 1963.
Béjar, Héctor. *Peru 1965: Notes on a Guerrilla Experience.* New York: Monthly Review Press, 1969.
Belaúnde Terry, Fernando. *Peru's Own Conquest.* Lima: American Studies Press, S.A., 1965.
Bernstein, Marvin D. *Foreign Investment in Latin America: Cases and Attitudes.* New York: Alfred A. Knopf, 1966.
Blasier, Cole. *The Hovering Giant: U.S. Responses to Revolutionary Change in Latin America.* Pittsburgh: Pittsburgh University Press, 1976.
Blum, William. *The CIA: A Forgotten History; U.S. Global Interventions Since World War 2.* London: Zed Books, 1986.
Bourricaud, Francois. *Power and Society in Contemporary Peru.* New York: Praeger, 1970.
Brown, Michael F., and Eduardo Fernández. *War of Shadows: The Struggle for Utopia in the Peruvian Amazon.* Berkeley and Los Angeles: University of California Press, 1991.
Brownlow, Cecil. "Peru Military Buildup Worries Neighbors." *Aviation Week and Space Technology,* December 2, 1974, 21–22.
Bundy, William. *A Tangled Web: The Making of Foreign Policy in the Nixon Presidency.* New York: Hill and Wang, 1998.
Cahn, Patricia. "Washington Hostesses Serve Their National Specialties as Diplomatic Delicacies." *Saturday Evening Post,* March 26, 1962.
Campbell, Leon G. "The Historiography of the Peruvian Guerrilla Movement, 1960–1965." *Latin American Research Review* 8, no. 1 (1973): 45–70.
Carey, James C. *Peru and the United States, 1900–1962.* Notre Dame: University of Notre Dame Press, 1964.
———. "Peru: Encouraging New Spirit." *Current History* 49, no. 292 (1965): 323–27.
Childs, Marquis. "Peru and Poverty, Oil and a Road." *Washington Post,* August 15, 1965.
Clayton, Lawrence A. *W. R. Grace and Co: The Formative Years, 1850–1930.* Ottawa, IL: Jameson Books, 1985.
Contreras, Carlos, and Marcos Cueto. *Historia del Perú contemporáneo.* 4th ed. Lima: Instituto de Estudios Peruanos, 2007.
Cotler, Julio. *Drogas y política en el Perú: La conexión norteamericana.* Lima: Instituto de Estudios Peruanos, 1999.
Cotler, Julio, and Richard R. Fagen, eds. *Latin America and the United States: The Changing Political Realities.* Stanford: Stanford University Press, 1974.
Dallek, Robert. *Nixon and Kissinger: Partners in Power.* New York: HarperCollins, 2007.
Dobyns, Henry F., Paul L. Doughty, and Allan R. Holmberg. *Peace Corps Program Impact in the Peruvian Andes: Final Report.* Ithaca, NY: Cornell Peru Project, Department of Anthropology, Cornell University, n.d.
Einaudi, Luigi. "U.S. Relations with the Peruvian Military." In Sharp, *U.S. Foreign Policy and Peru,* 15–48.
Frost, David William, ed. *Latin American Government Leaders.* 2nd ed. Tempe: Center for Latin American Studies, Arizona State University, 1975.
Gall, Norman. "Letter from Peru." *Commentary* 37 (June 1964): 64–69.
Geyelin, Philip. *Lyndon B. Johnson and the World.* New York: Praeger, 1966.
Goldhamer, Herbert. *The Foreign Powers in Latin America.* Princeton: Princeton University Press, 1972.
Goodsell, Charles T. *American Corporations and Peruvian Politics.* Cambridge: Harvard University Press, 1974.
———. "That Confounding Revolution in Peru." *Current History* 68 (January 1975): 20–23.

Goodwin, Richard N. "Letter from Peru." *The New Yorker*, April 26, 1969, 41–109.
———. *Remembering America: A Voice from the Sixties.* Boston: Little, Brown, 1988.
Gott, Richard. *Guerrilla Movements in Latin America.* Garden City, NY: Anchor Books, 1972.
Graham, Carol. *Peru's APRA: Parties, Politics and the Elusive Quest for Democracy.* Boulder, CO: Lynne Rienner, 1992.
Guasti, Laura. "The Peruvian Military Government and the International Corporations." In McClintock and Lowenthal, *The Peruvian Experiment Reconsidered,* 189–90.
Hayter, Teresa. *Aid as Imperialism.* Baltimore: Penguin Books, 1971.
Hoff, Joan. *Nixon Reconsidered.* New York: Basic Books, 1994.
Holmberg, Allan R. "Changing Community Attitudes and Values in Peru: A Case Study in Guided Change." In *Social Change in Latin America Today: Its Implications for U.S. Policy,* edited by Richard N. Adams, et al. New York: Vintage Books, 1960.
Hoyos Osores, Guillermo. "Crisis de la democracia en el Perú: Causas de su quebranto y condiciones para su recuperación." *Cuadernos Americanos* 1, no. 162 (1969): 7–31.
Hudson, Rex A. *Peru: A Country Study.* Washington, D.C.: Federal Research Division, Library of Congress, 1993.
Ingram, George M. *Expropriation of U.S. Property in South America: Nationalization of Oil and Copper Companies in Peru, Bolivia, and Chile.* New York: Praeger, 1974.
Jaquette, Jane S. *The Politics of Development in Peru.* Ithaca, NY: Latin American Studies Program, Cornell University, Dissertation Series, June 1971.
Kissinger, Henry. *White House Years.* Boston: Little, Brown, 1979.
Klaren, Peter. *Modernization, Dislocation, and Aprismo: Origins of the Peruvian Aprista Party, 1870–1932.* Austin: University of Texas Press, 1971.
Kruijt, Dirk. *Revolution by Decree: Peru, 1968–1975.* Amsterdam: Thela, 1994.
Kuczynski, Pedro-Paul. *Peruvian Democracy Under Economic Stress: An Account of the Belaúnde Administration, 1963–1968.* Princeton: Princeton University Press, 1977.
LaFeber, Walter. "Latin American Policy." In *Exploring the Johnson Years,* edited by Robert A. Divine, 63–89. Austin: University of Texas Press, 1981.
———. "Thomas C. Mann and the Devolution of Latin American Policy: From the Good Neighbor to Military Intervention." In *Behind the Throne: Servants of Power to Imperial Presidents, 1898–1968,* edited by Thomas J. McCormick and Walter LaFeber, 166–86. Madison: University of Wisconsin Press, 1993.
Lernoux, Penny. "Peruvian Adventure: Generals as Revolutionaries." *Nation,* October 19, 1974, 360–63.
Levinson, Jerome, and Juan de Onis. *The Alliance That Lost Its Way: A Critical Report on the Alliance for Progress.* Chicago: Quadrangle Books, 1970.
Linowitz, Sol M. *The Making of a Public Man: A Memoir.* Boston: Little, Brown, 1985.
Loeb, James I. "Irony in Peru." *New Republic,* February 9, 1974, 8–9.
Loring, David C. "The Fisheries Dispute." In Sharp, *U.S. Foreign Policy and Peru,* 57–124.
Lowenthal, Abraham F. "Peru's Ambiguous Revolution." *Foreign Affairs,* July 1974, 799–817.
Mann, James. *Rise of the Vulcans: The History of Bush's War Cabinet.* New York: Viking Press, 2004.
Marchetti, Victor, and John D. Marks. *The CIA and the Cult of Intelligence.* New York: Dell, 1974.
Marett, Sir Robert. *Peru.* New York: Praeger, 1969.
Martin, Edwin McCammon. *Kennedy and Latin America.* Latham, MD: University Press of America, 1994.

Masterson, Daniel M. *Militarism and Politics in Latin America: Peru from Sánchez Cerro to Sendero Luminoso.* New York: Greenwood Press, 1991.

———. "Peru's Military Junta at the Crossroads." *Christian Century*, November 27, 1974, 1127–28.

McClintock, Cynthia. "Velasco, Officers, and Citizens: The Politics of Stealth." In McClintock and Lowenthal, *The Peruvian Experiment Reconsidered*, 282–83.

McClintock, Cynthia, and Abraham F. Lowenthal, eds. *The Peruvian Experiment Reconsidered.* Princeton: Princeton University Press, 1983.

McClintock, Cynthia, and Fabián Vallas T. *La democracia negociada: Las relaciones Perú-Estados Unidos (1980–2000).* Lima: Instituto de Estudios Peruanos, 2005.

Mercado, Rogger. *Las guerrillas del Perú y la Revolución de Trujillo.* 2nd ed. Lima: Editorial de Cultura Popular, 1982.

———. *Las guerrillas en el Perú.* Lima: Fondo de Cultura Popular, 1967.

Moreira, Neiva. *Modelo peruano.* Buenos Aires: Editorial La Línea, 1974.

Nixon, Richard M. *Six Crises.* Garden City, NY: Doubleday, 1962.

North, Liisa, and Tanya Korovkin. *The Peruvian Revolution and the Officers in Power.* Montreal: McGill University, Centre for Developing-Area Studies, 1981.

Nunn, Frederick M. *The Time of the Generals: Latin American Professional Militarism in World Perspective.* Lincoln: University of Nebraska Press, 1992.

Ortiz, Frank J. *Ambassador Ortiz: Lessons from a Life of Service.* Edited by Don Usner. Albuquerque: University of New Mexico Press, 2005.

Packenham, Robert A. *Liberal America and the Third World: Political Development Ideas in Foreign Aid and Social Science.* Princeton: Princeton University Press, 1973.

Parker, Phyllis R. *Brazil and the Quiet Intervention, 1964.* Austin: University of Texas Press, 1979.

Parodi Trece, Carlos. *Perú 1960–2000: Políticas económicas y sociales en entornos cambiantes.* Lima: Universidad del Pacífico, 2000.

Patch, Richard W. "The Peruvian Earthquake of 1970." *American Universities Field Staff Reports: West Coast South American Series.* Nos. 6–9. New York: American Universities Field Staff, 1971.

Pease García, Henry. *Los caminos del poder: Tres años de crisis en la escena política.* 2nd ed. Lima: Centro de Estudios y Promoción del Desarrollo, 1981.

Pease García, Henry, and Olga Verme Insúa. *Perú, 1968–1973: Cronología política.* 2 vols. Lima: Centro de Estudios y Promoción de Desarrollo, Area de Estudios Políticos, 1974.

Peeler, John Allen. "The Politics of the Alliance for Progress in Peru." PhD diss., University of North Carolina, Chapel Hill, 1968.

"Peru: The New Conquest." *Time*, March 12, 1965, 32–42.

Petras, James. "Revolution and Guerrilla Movements in Latin America: Venezuela, Colombia, Guatemala, and Peru." In *Latin America: Reform or Revolution?* edited by James Petras and Maurice Zeitlin. Greenwich, CT: Fawcett, 1968.

Philip, George D. E. *The Rise and Fall of the Peruvian Military Radicals, 1968–1976.* London: Athlone Press, 1978.

Pike, Fredrick B. *The United States and the Andean Republics: Peru, Bolivia, and Ecuador.* Cambridge: Harvard University Press, 1977.

Pinelo, Adalberto. *The Multinational Corporation as a Force in Latin American Politics: A Case Study of the International Petroleum Company.* New York: Praeger, 1973.

Prieto Celi, Federico. *Regreso a la democracia: Entrevista biográfica al General Francisco Morales Bermúdez Cedrrutti, President del Perú (1975–1980).* Lima: Realidades, S.A., 1996.

Rabe, Stephen G. *Eisenhower and Latin America: The Foreign Policy of Anticommunism.* Chapel Hill: University of North Carolina Press, 1988.
———. *The Most Dangerous Area of the World: John F. Kennedy Confronts Communist Revolution in Latin America.* Chapel Hill: University of North Carolina Press, 1999.
Reyes Flores, Alejandro. "San Marcos y Richard Nixon, 8 de mayo de 1958." Lima: Programas Académicos de Ciencia Social, 1983.
Rice, Gerald T. *The Bold Experiment: JFK's Peace Corps.* Notre Dame: University of Notre Dame Press, 1985.
Rockefeller, Nelson A. *Quality of Life in the Americas.* Washington, D.C.: Government Printing Office, August 30, 1969.
Rodman, Selden. "Peruvian Politics Stalls Belaúnde's Reforms." *The Reporter,* July 14, 1966, 37–40.
Rogers, William D. *The Twilight Struggle: The Alliance for Progress and the Politics of Development in Latin America.* New York: Random House, 1967.
Romualdi, Serafino. *Presidents and Peons: Recollections of a Labor Ambassador in Latin America.* New York: Funk and Wagnalls, 1967.
Ruddle, Kenneth, and Kathleen Barrows, eds. *Statistical Abstract of Latin America, 1972.* Los Angeles: Latin American Center, University of California at Los Angeles, January 1974.
Rusk, Dean. *As I Saw It* (as told to Richard Rusk). Edited by Daniel S. Papp. New York: W. W. Norton, 1990.
Schlesinger, Arthur M., Jr. *A Thousand Days: John F. Kennedy in the White House.* Boston: Houghton Mifflin, 1965.
Shafer, D. Michael. *Deadly Paradigms: The Failure of U.S. Counterinsurgency Policy.* Princeton: Princeton University Press, 1988.
Sharp, Daniel A., ed. *U.S. Foreign Policy and Peru.* Austin: University of Texas Press, 1972.
Smith, Tony. "The Alliance for Progress." In *Exporting Democracy: The United States and Latin America,* edited by Abraham Lowenthal, 71–89. Baltimore: Johns Hopkins University Press, 1991.
St. John, Ronald Bruce. *The Foreign Policy of Peru.* Boulder, CO: Lynne Reinner, 1994.
Stoll, David. *Fishers of Men or Founders of Empire? The Wycliffe Bible Translators in Latin America.* London: Zed Press, 1982.
Tamariz Lúcar, Domingo. *Historia del poder: Elecciones y golpes de estado en el Perú.* Lima: Jaime Campodonico, Editor, 1995.
Tulchin, Joseph S. "The Promise of Progress: U.S. Relations with Latin America During the Administration of Lyndon B. Johnson." In *Lyndon Johnson Confronts the World: American Foreign Policy, 1963–1968,* edited by Warren Cohen and Nancy Bernkopf Tucker, 211–43. New York: Cambridge University Press, 1994.
Umeres Alvarez, Humberto. *Carlos García Bedoya y la Teoría de las Relaciones Internacionales.* Lima: Fondo Editorial, Fundación Academia Diplomática del Perú, 2000.
United Nations, *UNESCO Statistical Yearbook: 1975.* Paris, 1977.
Velasco Alvarado, Juan. *La revolución peruana.* Buenos Aires: Editorial Universitaria de Buenos Aires, 1973.
Villanueva, Víctor. *Ejército Peruano: Del caudillaje anárquico al militarismo reformista.* Lima: Libreria-Editorial Juan Mejía Baca, 1973.
Walker, William O., III. "Mixing the Sweet with the Sour: Kennedy, Johnson, and Latin America." In *The Diplomacy of the Crucial Decade: American Foreign Relations During the 1960s,* edited by Diane B. Kuntz, 42–69. New York: Columbia University Press, 1994.

Walters, Vernon A. *Silent Missions.* Garden City, NY: Doubleday, 1978.
Weiner, Tim. *A Legacy of Ashes: The History of the CIA.* New York: Doubleday, 2007.
Weis, W. Michael. *Cold Warriors and Coups d'État: Brazilian-American Relations, 1943–1964.* Albuquerque: University of New Mexico Press, 1993.
Werlich, David P. *Peru: A Short History.* Carbondale: Southern Illinois University Press, 1978.
Wilkie, James, ed. *Statistical Abstract of Latin America, 1977.* Los Angeles: Latin American Center, University of California at Los Angeles, 1977.
Wise, Carol. *Reinventing the State: Economic Strategy and Institutional Change in Peru.* Ann Arbor: University of Michigan Press, 2003.
Wise, David, and Thomas B. Ross. *The Invisible Government.* New York: Random House, 1964.
Yglesias, José. "Report from Peru: The Reformers in Brass Hats." *New York Times Magazine*, December 14, 1969, 58ff.
Zimmermann Zavala, Augusto. *El Plan Inca. Objetivo: Revolución Peruna.* Lima: Empresa Editorial del Diario Oficial "El Peruano," 1974.

INDEX

Acción Popular, 11, 16, 29–30, 44, 52, 57, 103, 126, 128, 288; divisions in, 114, 140; and IPC, 103
Acción Democrática, 280
Adair, Charles W., 207
Adlai Stevenson Institute, 318
Aeroperú, 303–4, 306, 316
Agency for International Development (AID), 24, 32, 45–47, 76, 83, 100, 125–26, 136, 191, 257, 302; complaints about, 97, 268; and fishing rights, 95; and Office of Public Safety, 36, 75
airports, 52, 99
Allende, Salvador, 169, 188, 224, 236–38, 306
Alliance for Progress, 6, 15, 17–19, 21–22, 25, 29–30, 35, 64, 80, 84, 88, 107, 139–40, 317; announcement of, 6–7, 12; criticisms of, 48, 55, 64, 68, 81, 104, 106, 159; and Johnson, 39–40, 44, 46, 49–50, 91; and military government, 146, 156; and Nixon, 159; reception of, in Peru, 12–13, 36, 59, 121
Almeyda, Clodomiro, 237
Alva Orlandini, Javier, 288
Alvarado Garrido, Luis, 9
Alzamora, Carlos, 158–60, 169–70, 184–85
American Institute for Free Labor Development, 317–18
American Security Council, 305
Americans for Democratic Action, 13
Anaconda, 217, 238
Aprista Party (APRA), 11, 16–18, 21, 23–24, 29–31, 126, 128, 303, 311; and CIA, 179, 219, 301; and guerrillas, 69; and IPC, 79, 102–3, 135; and military, 123–24, 143–44, 179–80; as opposition, 30–31, 52–53, 56, 59, 66, 71, 140; and protests, 97, 301
Arbulu, Guillermo, 297–98
Arce Larco, José, 3, 288, 300, 302, 305–7
Arequipa, 28, 54, 90, 223
Argentina, 18, 20, 29, 65, 162–63, 165, 237, 280–81; and military coup, 146–48
Argentine Anti-Communist Alliance, 305

Arsomena, Otto, 110
Artolo, Armando, 229
Ayacucho, 54, 57, 70–71, 79, 298

Ball, George, 19, 50–51
Banco Continental, 238
Banco Popular, 238
Barnebey, Malcolm R., 95, 299
Bedoya Reyes, Luis, 52
Béjar, Héctor, 69, 71–72
Belaúnde Terry, Fernando: and 1962 election, 16–17; and 1963 election, 28–30; background of, 30; and guerrillas, 68–75, 78–79; and IPC dispute, 31–34, 37–38, 42–43, 55–61, 79, 82, 87–89, 101–6, 112–19, 127–37, 141, 313; and Mann, 58–61; policies of, 31, 52–53, 59, 62, 94, 134; and military coup, 137–39; relations of, with United States, 31–32, 38, 48, 56–58, 63, 81–83, 89–92, 97–102, 109–11, 139; second presidency of, 311
Belaúnde, Víctor Andrés, 35, 98 n. 37
Belcher, Taylor, 3, 34, 44, 47, 225, 246; appointment of, 207–8; background of, 207; and IPC dispute, 210, 214; and Mercado, 209–10, 214; and military government, 240–41, 251–52, 256–58, 312, 314; replacement of, 279, 284–85
Belco, 148
Beltrán, Pedro, 11
Berckemeyer, Fernando, 3, 8–10, 14–15, 207, 316; appointment of, by military government, 158, 160, 163, 181; background of, 7–8; and communism, 9–10; and fishing rights, 173, 194; and IPC dispute, 187, 208; and Kennedy administration, 11, 23–29, 32; and Peruvian politics, 29–30; relations of, with United States, 183–85, 188–89, 219–21, 229, 262–63, 268–69, 292–94, 312–13; replacement of, 279; resignation of, 34; and Soviet Union, 235–36
Betancourt, Rómulo, 19, 21, 24
Bilateral Military Assistance Agreement, 247

Blanco, Hugo, 70
Bloomfield, Richard J., 108, 118, 122
Bolivia, 80, 219, 221–22, 237
Bowdler, William, 110
Braniff Airways, 232, 241, 303–4, 306, 316
Brazil, 20, 24, 29, 39, 49–50, 163, 264, 165, 268, 281, 288, 309; and United States, 42, 60, 77
Bundy, McGeorge, 45
Bush, George H. W., 293
Bush, George W., 312
Busumberg, Robert, 47

Carey, James C., 63–64
Cargill, 281
carretera marginal (marginal highway), 30, 59, 62, 111, 141
Carriquiry, Pablo, 126, 134–35
Carter, Jimmy, 310
Carter, Rosalynn, 310–11
Castro, Fidel, 13–14, 222, 247, 253–54; and expropriation, 33, 184; and Peru, 9, 53, 205–6, 232, 253
Castro, Raúl, 289
Cavaro Calixto, Arturo, 266–67
Center for Inter-American Relations, 293
Central Intelligence Agency (CIA): and Chile, 58; and coups in Latin America, 154; and Peru, 4, 17, 54, 72, 77, 143, 179–81, 218–19, 295–98, 301–2, 315
Centro de Instrucción Militar del Perú (CIMP), 138, 157, 250
Cerro de Pasco Mining Company, 27, 83–84, 148, 164, 180, 217, 232, 238, 249, 273–76, 278; compensation for, 281–82; expropriation of, 279–81
Chappers, William D., 180, 218–19
Chase Manhattan, 85, 238
Chile, 48, 50, 58, 65, 121–22, 169, 194, 209, 215, 220, 246, 248, 269, 276, 300; and Allende government, 236–39, 242–43, 251–52, 265, 283; and cotton, 15; and coup in Peru, 147–48; and United States, 42, 60, 77, 80, 104, 219, 293, 306, 309
China, People's Republic of, 1, 54, 169, 239, 242, 244, 264, 309
Christian Democrats, 28, 30, 52, 56–57, 60, 66, 79, 112, 140, 288; in Chile, 58; and IPC dispute, 79, 102–3
Church, Frank, 187, 297, 302
Colombia, 50, 80, 104, 121, 147
Comité de Asesoramiento de la Presidencia (COAP), 161, 250

communism; in Latin America, 9, 82–83, 237, 305; in Peru, 17, 20, 32, 54, 56–57, 59, 69, 90
Communist Party, 53, 229
Connally, John, 247–48, 254–55, 262, 272
Conte, Silvio, 108
Conte-Long Amendment, 108, 124, 126
Cooperación Popular, 52, 92
copper, 93, 148–49, 195, 215
Cornejo Chávez, Héctor, 79, 125, 288
Costa Mendez, Nicanor, 147
Costa Rica, 21, 24, 121
cotton, 14–15, 83
Crimmins, Hugh, 247, 264, 268
Cuba, 1, 222, 244; and Bay of Pigs, 14; and Chile, 239; and Cuban Missile Crisis, 25–26; and Cuban Revolution, 9; and expropriation, 33, 184; and Peru, 9, 13–14, 69, 82, 165, 205–6, 232, 242, 247, 250, 252–54, 309; and United States, 35–36, 39, 91, 252–54, 278
Czechoslovakia, 165

Dean, James, 127–29, 131, 149–50, 153–54, 187, 228
Dean, Robert, 3, 304, 318; appointment of, 285–86; background of, 285; and military government, 289–92, 294–96, 299, 301, 307; and Soviet Union, 286–87
De la Flor Valle, Miguel Angel: and air travel, 304; background of, 249–50; and Chile, 252; and Cuba, 252–54; and expropriation, 273, 281, 284; policies of, 250–51; and United States, 250–51, 255, 294, 301–2, 311
De la Puente Uceda, Luis, 54, 69, 71
Delgado Odría, María, 52
Dellepiane, Jorge, 241
Dianderas, Roberto, 126
Doig Sánchez, Julio, 123–24
Dominican Republic, 19, 23, 42, 66, 84, 306
drug trafficking, 291–92, 294, 312
Duncan, John C., 15
Dungan, Ralph, 31

East Germany, 250
Eberle, William D., 286
Ecuador, 67, 80, 96, 121–22, 147, 194, 209, 220, 280; and border conflict with Peru, 8–9, 14; coup in, 23; and fishing rights, 225–26, 261, 277
Eisenhower, Dwight, 110
Eisenhower, Milton, 110
Elijaldo, Eduardo, 149
El Salvador, 121
Empresa Petrolera Fiscal (EPF), 115–19, 128–29, 131–33, 135, 150, 171

Espinosa, Fernando J., 80, 106, 119, 129–32, 134–35
Export-Import Bank, 195, 286, 301
expropriation, 1, 4, 26, 33, 58, 83, 85–86, 125, 184, 188, 205, 243, 248–51, 272, 309. *See also* Cerro de Pasco; Hickenlooper Amendment; International Petroleum Company

Faura, Oscar, 301–2
Federico Villareal University, 97
Fernández Maldonado, Jorge, 206, 229, 245, 257, 261, 266, 273, 284, 305
Ferrero, Raúl, 112, 116, 119, 125
Figueres, José, 21, 24
Finch, Robert, 233, 244
Fishermen's Protective Act, 95–96
fishing rights, 1, 38, 89, 121–22, 133–34, 173, 190, 192–93, 244–45, 264–65, 277–78, 286; and four-party talks, 194–95, 209, 244; and U.S. policies, 4, 67–68, 91, 94–98, 225–26, 260–63, 272–73, 306
Ford, Gerald, 1, 292–93, 303, 306
Foreign Assistance Act, 26, 67, 120
Foreign Military Sales Act of 1968, 96
Foreign Service Institute, 49
Fowler, Henry, 155, 159
Franco, Francisco, 8
Frei, Eduardo, 42, 58, 90, 99 n. 41, 236
Frente de Izquierda Revolucionaria (FIR), 53
Frente de Liberación Nacional (FLN), 53
Frondizi, Arturo, 18
Fujimori, Alberto, 311–12
Fulbright, William, 67

Gagliardi, José, 137, 139
Gall, Norman, 48–49
García, Arturo, 15, 29–30, 34–35, 44
García Bedoya, Carlos, 276, 299, 304
García Pérez, Alan, 311
Gerberding, Carlos, 92
Goldwater, Barry, 20, 40
Gonzalez, Henry B., 50, 256
Gonzalez Amendment, 262–63, 271, 286, 314
Gold-Kist, 281
Goodwin, Richard, 33–34, 85
Gordon, Lincoln, 92, 111 n. 77
Grace, Peter, 8
Graham Hurtado, José, 266–67, 280
Greene, James, 273–74, 277–78, 280–84
Greuning, Ernest, 145, 159
Gromyko, Andrei, 235
Guatemala, 23
Guzmán, Abimael, 311

Haahr, James, 53
Haya de la Torre, Víctor Raúl, 16–20, 22–24, 26, 28–30, 53, 128, 139–40
Helms, Richard, 154
Hennesy, John, 268
Hercelles, Oswaldo, 126–27, 132, 134, 137
Hickenlooper, Bourke, 26, 159
Hickenlooper Amendment: criticisms of, 208; passage of, 26; under Johnson, 42–43, 45–47, 55, 81, 93, 116, 119, 150–51, 155; under Kennedy, 33; under Nixon, 166, 172–74, 176, 178, 181–82, 184–87, 191, 205, 211, 220, 223, 225, 227; replacement of, 251; utility of, 314
Honduras, 23
Hughes, Harold E., 159
Humphrey, Hubert, 32, 64, 159

Illia, Arturo, 146
Inter-American Affairs, assistant secretary of state for, 2–3, 14, 40, 65, 189, 268, 293
Inter-American Development Bank, 14, 25, 88, 100, 120, 126, 216, 235, 245, 255, 271, 274
Inter-American Press Association, 297
Inter-American Social and Economic Council, 58
International Monetary Fund, 100–101, 127, 159, 216
International Petroleum Company (IPC), 1, 3, 13, 312–13; and Belaúnde government, 31–35, 37, 44, 48, 55–61, 79–81, 87–89, 92–93, 101, 103–5, 112–19, 127–37, 141; and U.S. policy, 3–4, 45–47, 50, 83–86, 178, 188, 218, 270; and Velasco government, 144–45, 148–51, 165–66, 171–74, 181–82, 184, 191, 209, 239, 299
International Telephone and Telegraph (IT&T), 57–58, 105, 214, 216, 268–69, 273
Irwin, John N.: appointment of, 176–77; departure of, 262; negotiations of, 178–79, 181–82, 188–91, 208, 210–12, 242–43, 245

Johnson, Lyndon B.: and 1968 election, 86, 120–21, 159; background of, 39; and Belaúnde government, 38, 46, 82–83, 90–91, 94, 99, 109–11, 309; and IPC dispute, 1, 34, 42–43, 132, 313; and Latin America, 36–37, 39–40, 49–51, 90–91, 98; and military coup, 151–52, 154–55; perception of, in Peru, 84
Johnson, U. Alexis, 208, 215
Jones, John Wesley, 3, 26–28, 55, 312; and 1968 military coup, 143–44, 148, 152, 163–64, 166–67; appointment of, 26–29; and Belaúnde government, 53, 73, 89–91, 102, 105–6, 108–9, 111, 126, 137–38, 140, 192, 314; and fishing

Jones, John Wesley (continued)
  rights, 95, 97–98; and IPC dispute, 33–34, 59, 85, 103–5, 112–15, 117–18, 127–31, 134–36, 191–92; and Irwin mission, 177–79; and guerrillas, 73, 77–78; and Velasco government, 162–64, 170–71, 175, 180–81, 190–93
Jorge Chávez airport, 99, 138, 292

Katzenbach, Nicholas, 120–21
Kauffmann, Howard, 116–18, 127–29
Kennedy, Edward, 45, 67
Kennedy, John F., 1, 6, 10–11, 14, 18–23, 35; Latin American policies of, 11–12, 22–23, 35–37
Kennedy, Robert F., 84–86, 92, 317
Khrushchev, Nikita, 11
Kissinger, Henry, 169, 255, 268, 279, 292; and Latin America, 170, 187–88, 243, 275–76, 284, 293–94
Korry, Edward, 152
Kubisch, Jack B., 268, 276
Kuchel, Thomas, 67–68, 121 n. 16, 159
Kuchel Amendment, 91, 95, 121–22

La Brea y Pariñas, 33–34, 86, 103, 106, 115–18, 128–29, 131, 135, 148
latifundio, 30, 52
Libya, 27
Lindbergh, Charles, 317
Linowtiz, Sol, 130
Llosa, Luis Edgardo, 133–34
Lobatón, Guillermo, 71
Lockheed Aircraft Company, 233
Lodge, George Cabot, 12
Loeb, Joseph, 13, 16–18, 22, 27; recall of, 19, 25–26
Long, Clarence D., 108, 124
López Casilla, Alberto, 161–62
López Mateos, Adolfo, 39
Loret de Mola, Carlos, 117, 119, 128, 132–36

McCarthy, Eugene, 121
McCloskey, Robert, 71 n. 30, 97, 155
McGovern, George, 254, 262
McKernan, Donald, 122
MacNamara, Robert, 271
Machu Pichu, 70, 316
Maldonado Yanez, Alberto, 148–49, 165–66, 175
Mann, Thomas, 40–41, 84; and Belaúnde, 58–61; and Mann Doctrine, 40–43, 188; and Pastor, 44–47, 50–52, 55, 64–65, 82, 313; resignation of, 92
Mao Tse-Tung, 54
Marchand, Luis, 226, 235

Marchetti, Victor, 72
Marcona Mining Corporation, 122, 148, 304–7, 310
Mariátegui, José Carlos, 228
Marks, John D., 72
Martin, Edward, 14, 16, 19, 23, 27, 31–32, 35
Mayflower, 89, 96
Meader, George, 7
Meeker, Leonard C., 174
Mercado Jarrín, Edgardo, 138–39, 152, 156–58, 233, 244, 249, 281, 297, 313; and agrarian reform, 213; background of, 156–57; and CIA, 218; and emergency relief, 233–35; and expropriation, 274, 282; and fishing rights, 173, 209, 226–27, 230, 245; and IPC dispute, 194, 222; and Irwin mission, 177–78, 182, 210–11; and Latin America, 185–86, 230, 237; as moderate, 161, 223, 250; as prime minister, 259–60; as provisional president, 266–67; retirement of, 300; and Soviet Union, 165, 171–72, 263–64; in Washington, 242–45
Mesa Pelada, 73–74, 77
Mexico, 20, 32, 39
Meyer, Charles: appointment of, 176; and fishing rights, 226–27; and IPC dispute, 228; and Mercado, 187, 213, 226, 233, 242–43; resignation of, 268
military coups, 16–21, 137–39
Mirage fighter jets, 101–2, 104–11, 115, 119–20, 124–26, 134
Miro Quesada, Francisco, 56
Mitchell, George C., 54
Mobil, 148
Mongrut, Octavio, 77
Montagne Sánchez, Ernesto, 148, 161, 166–67, 178, 194, 211, 259
Moose, Richard, 187–88
Morales Bermúdez, Francisco, 126, 175, 216, 229, 255, 267, 281, 289; as president, 279, 307–9; as prime minister, 300–301; and relations with United States, 310; and Velasco, 289–90, 303
Morse, Wayne, 159
Moscoso, Teodoro, 32–34, 49
Movimiento de Izquierda Revolucionaria (MIR), 53–54, 69–72, 75
Muñoz Marín, Luis, 24
Murphy, C. Gordon, 275, 282

National Agrarian University (La Molina), 48, 100
National Telecommunications Board, 57
National University of Huamanga, 54
Naval Intelligence Service, 298

Navarro, Alfonso, 161
Neira, Hugo, 289
Newmann, Guillermo, 297
Nixon, Patricia, 224, 231–34, 240, 313, 317
Nixon, Richard M.: and expropriation, 174, 271, 277–78, 282–83; and fishing rights, 260–61; and Latin America, 169–70, 189, 211, 227, 236, 240, 247–48, 262, 309; policies of, 168–69, 251, 254, 309; resignation of, 279, 292; and special emissary to Peru, 176–79; and Velasco, 240; visits of, to Peru, 7–8, 100–101, 317
Northern Peru Copper Company, 217
North Korea, 250

Occidental Petroleum Company, 241
Odría, Manuel, 7, 16–18, 28–30, 58, 316
Oliver, Covey T., 110, 116, 118–19, 124–25, 136, 160; and military coup, 146, 151–53
Organization of American States (OAS), 14, 20, 53, 233, 250–53, 269, 277, 293–94
Ortiz, Frank, 218, 295, 301

Partners of the Alliance, 49
Pastor de la Torre, Celso, 3, 29, 48–52, 64, 81–83, 120–21, 316; background of, 44; and fishing rights, 67–68, 94–95, 119–20, 133; and IPC dispute, 81–82; and Mann, 44–47, 50, 55, 64–65, 92–93, 313; and *Mirage* controversy, 108, 119–20; resignation of, 158; and U.S. aid, 124–26; and U.S. involvement in Latin America, 66, 77, 91–93
Peace Corps, 20, 22, 24, 49, 59, 90, 125, 302, 316; criticism of, 54, 294–95; expulsion of, 294–97
Pelly, Thomas, 95–96, 190, 194, 225–26, 246
Pelly Amendment, 133, 173, 186–87, 195, 220, 223, 247, 262–63, 314
Pérez de Cuellar, Javier, 53, 153 n. 32, 234–35
Pérez Godoy, Ricardo, 22, 28
Perón, Juan, 41, 280
Peru: agrarian reform, 31–32, 47, 52, 59, 82–83, 88, 193–94, 206, 308–9; attitudes in, toward United States, 21–22, 25, 190, 194–95, 315–16; counterguerrilla campaigns in, 1, 70–78; and Cuba, 9, 13–14, 69, 82, 165, 205–6, 232, 242, 247, 250, 252–54, 309; earthquake in, 230–35, 313; economy in, 93–94, 141, 217, 238, 280, 283, 290, 319; and foreign investment, 215–16, 220, 230, 238, 241–42, 283, 310, 319; guerrillas in, 68–72; indigenous population in, 88, 124, 317; left in, 18, 300–301; military in, 31, 70–78, 92, 102, 109–10, 142, 216; military coups in, 1, 16–18, 137–39, 142, 163; nationalism in, 314; protests in, 300–301; road building in, 59, 76; and Soviet Union, 165, 171–72, 222–23, 263–64, 286–87
Peruvian Telephone Company (PERUTELCO), 57, 105
Petroperú, 230, 241
Pinochet, Augusto, 280
Plaza, Galo, 170
Poole, Richard, 15, 44, 47
Prado y Ugarteche, Manuel, 4, 7, 9, 13–14, 18–19
Public Law 480, 15, 24
Puente, Pedro, 57
Puerto Rico, 24, 64
Punta del Este summit, 98–100, 125

Radbill, José de la Puente, 310–11
Raymont, Henry, 74, 77
Richardson, Elliot, 270
Richter Prada, Pedro, 294–95
Robinson, C. W., 122–23
Roca Zela, Manuel A., 253, 255, 266, 273, 275–77, 301–2
Rockefeller, David, 85
Rockefeller, Nelson, 26, 159, 190, 194, 255, 282, 293
Rodríguez Razzetto, José, 124
Rogers, William D., 293, 298–99, 304–5
Rogers, William P., 243, 255, 262; appointment of, 160; and arms sales, 270–71; and Belcher, 208; and Cuba, 252–54; and fishing rights, 173; and IPC dispute, 213; and Latin America, 170, 269, 271–73; and military government, 272; and sanctions, 182, 208, 225
Rostow, Eugene V., 95
Rostow, Walt, 49, 87–89, 92, 100–101, 107, 109–10, 115, 132, 153–54, 313
Rotalde Romana, Miguel, 57
Ruiz Eldridge, Alberto, 175, 214
Rumsfeld, Donald, 169
Rush, Kenneth, 262
Rusk, Dean, 11–12, 17–18, 28, 32, 64, 67–68, 89, 94, 101–2, 129, 160; and military coup, 147, 154–55

Sánchez Salazar, Alejandro, 139
Saylor, John P., 19–20
Sayre, Robert, 68, 73, 108
Schlaudeman, Harry, 276
Schlesinger, Arthur, Jr., 22
School of the Americas, 36, 76
Schwalb, Fernando, 11, 32, 48, 55
Sendero Luminoso (Shining Path), 54, 311
Sears Roebuck, 176, 232, 298
Seoane, Edgardo, 128, 137

Shultz, George, 254, 262
Shumate, John, 122–23
Siracusa, Ernest V., 53, 59, 127, 129, 164, 173, 192–93, 207, 218, 295, 301
Sistema Nacional de Apoyo a la Movilización Social (*Sinamos*), 245–46, 303
Sociedad Nacional Agraria (SNA), 7
Southern Peru Copper Company, 148–49, 216–17, 223, 232, 273, 286, 301
Soviet Union, 1, 25–26, 82, 91, 169, 234–35, 264; and arms sales, 263–64, 286–87; and Latin America, 98–99, 235–36, 239; and military government in Peru, 162, 171–72, 305, 309
Special Police Emergency Unit (SPEU), 75–77
Spence, Floyd, 287
Standard Oil, 27, 56, 116, 150, 299; of California, 148; of New Jersey, 149, 153
Star-Kist, 281–82
Stedman, William P., 177
sugar, 14–15, 24, 83; quotas for, 24, 50–51, 117, 159, 173, 242; and Sugar Act, 116, 119, 130–31
Summer Institute of Linguistics, 316
Symington, Stuart, 120

Talara, Act of, 132–33, 135, 137–38, 145, 150
Tantaleán Vianini, Javier, 261, 264, 297–98
Toledo, Alejandro, 312
Townsend, William Cameron, 316

Ulloa, Manuel, 127, 133, 137
Unión Nacional Odriista (UNO), 16, 30–31, 52, 90; and IPC dispute, 102–3; as opposition, 52, 56, 59, 71, 140
United Fruit Company, 176
United Nations, 242, 244, 281
United Nations Economic Commission for Latin America (CEPAL), 186
United States: aid of, to Peru, 47, 88, 93, 100–109, 124–26, 140, 173; counterinsurgency programs of, 35–36, 38, 72–78; embassy of, 2, 4, 28; intervention of, in Latin America, 42, 65–66; investment of, in Peru, 62, 141, 183, 215, 319; Latin American studies in, 318; military of, in Peru, 17; military aid of, 190, 256, 272, 274, 286–87; and military government, 160, 178–81, 272; Peruvians in, 318–19; recognition of Peruvian government, 19–20, 23–25, 144–46, 151, 156, 158; and sanctions, 173–74, 187–88, 190, 194

University of San Agustín, 54
University of San Marcos, 7
Uruguay, 147, 280

Vaky, Viron P., 174
Valdés, Gabriel, 147, 186, 194, 220, 237
Valdivia Morriberon, Angel, 165–66, 175
Vance, Sheldon, 294
Van Deerlin, Lionel, 95–96
Vargas Caballero, Luis E., 288, 290
Vargas Llosa, Mario, 311
Vásquez Salas, Jorge, 99–100
Vaughn, Jack Hood, 65, 68, 81–84, 89–90, 92
Velasco Alvarado, Juan: and agrarian reform, 206, 308–9; and Cerro de Pasco, 274–75, 279–80; and Greene mission, 282–83; illness of, 265–67, 287–88; and IPC dispute, 172–73, 181–82, 192–93, 206, 209, 239; and fishing rights, 192, 244, 263; and military coup, 3, 124, 126, 137, 163; and Peace Corps, 294–97; policies of, 164, 228–29, 241–42, 245–54; popular perceptions of, 214, 259, 264–65, 283; and press, 288–89; and relations with Soviet Union, 162, 165, 179, 222–23; and relations with United States, 175, 178–79, 182–83, 185, 191–92, 208, 211–13, 251–52, 275–58, 303, 308, 313; removal of, 279, 307–9; United States views of, 144, 161, 170–71, 195–96, 238–39, 258–59, 290–91, 299; wife of, 212, 232, 240, 313
Venezuela, 19–20, 24, 29, 280
Vietnam, 67, 78, 88, 91, 101, 120–21, 168–69, 221, 231, 233
Villaran Rivera, Mario, 57

Walter Reed Hospital, 212, 264, 269–70, 298, 313
Warren, Earl, 317
Wells Fargo, 265
White, John, 153–54
Wilgus, A. Curtis, 8–9
Woodward, Robert, 14–16
World Bank, 271, 274, 283
W. R. Grace and Company, 15, 27, 193, 209, 242; compensation for, 214, 260, 281–82

Yarborough, Ralph, 145
Yugoslavia, 165, 244